This work is priceless to nations and co
tiple social injustices. Basilius Kasera i
social injustices are guided and guarde
how vestiges of apartheid continue to
levels in post-apartheid Namibia despite implementations of........, t
programmes. He writes clearly and passionately to discourage theologians and
critical thinkers in the areas of public planning and policies from adopting alien
frameworks for social reforms. Rather, he invites the formulation of theories and
concepts that can innovatively, creatively, and directly dismantle structures that
perpetrate injustices in each context. This work employs the hermeneutics of
doctrinal and ethical theology to promote access to resources, education, health
care, employment, political representation, equity, participation, diversity, and
human rights. It is also a theological, philosophical, scholarly, and missional
remedy against the spread of ignorant social reforms.

Solomon Amao, PhD
Academic Dean,
ECWA Theological Seminary, Jos, Nigeria

Riveting, captivating, a tour de force, and a must-read research work for anyone
searching for authentic justice in post-apartheid Namibia and beyond.

Ndumba J. Kamwanyah, PhD
Lecturer of Sociology,
University of Namibia

Over thirty years ago, after a long and painful struggle for liberation, the people
of Namibia shook off the shackles of colonialism. Since gaining independence
in 1990, the country has successfully completed the transition from a white
minority apartheid rule to a modern, multicultural, democratic society in which
citizens elect their leaders. However, the socio-economic effects of the apartheid system, as Basilius Kasera points out, are still tangible today. What should
social justice for post-apartheid Namibia look like? How can the Christian
faith and theology contribute to the search for a contextual concept of social
justice? These are the two questions which Kasera seeks to answer. I commend
this book to anyone who wants to have a deeper understanding of justice in a
post-apartheid context from a Christian perspective.

Thorsten Prill, PhD
Synod Minister, Rhenish Church in Namibia

Dr. Basilius Kasera argues that biblically informed practice of social justice takes as its model the incarnation of Jesus in a particular situation to address the needs of sinful humans and especially of poor people. He shows the inadequacy of theories which do not produce concrete actions to enable the human flourishing that God wills. The argument is rooted in the context of Southern Africa and apartheid but develops an approach to social justice that can be drawn on for all social action that claims to be Christian.

Christopher Sugden, PhD
PhD Programme Leader,
Oxford Centre for Religion and Public Life, UK

Towards A Contextualized Conceptualization of Social Justice for Post-Apartheid Namibia

Basilius M. Kasera

Langham

ACADEMIC

© 2024 Basilius M. Kasera

Published 2024 by Langham Academic
An imprint of Langham Publishing
www.langhampublishing.org

Langham Publishing and its imprints are a ministry of Langham Partnership

Langham Partnership
PO Box 296, Carlisle, Cumbria, CA3 9WZ, UK
www.langham.org

ISBNs:
978-1-83973-879-1 Print
978-1-78641-010-8 ePub
978-1-78641-011-5 PDF

Basilius M. Kasera has asserted his right under the Copyright, Designs and Patents Act, 1988 to be identified as the Author of this work.

All rights reserved. No part of this publication may be reproduced, stored in a retrieval system or transmitted, in any form or by any means, electronic, mechanical, photocopying, recording or otherwise, without the prior written permission of the publisher or the Copyright Licensing Agency.

Requests to reuse content from Langham Publishing are processed through PLSclear. Please visit www.plsclear.com to complete your request.

Scriptures taken from the New Revised Standard Version Bible, copyright © 1989 National Council oxf the Churches of Christ in the United States of America. Used by permission. All rights reserved.

British Library Cataloguing-in-Publication Data
A catalogue record for this book is available from the British Library

ISBN: 978-1-83973-879-1

Cover & Book Design: projectluz.com

Langham Partnership actively supports theological dialogue and an author's right to publish but does not necessarily endorse the views and opinions set forth here or in works referenced within this publication, nor can we guarantee technical and grammatical correctness. Langham Partnership does not accept any responsibility or liability to persons or property as a consequence of the reading, use or interpretation of its published content.

For my children, Abigail and Austin, and their generation in the pursuit of a more just world.

Contents

List of Figures

Abstract

This study explores the question of universalized justice conceptions, applied to address post-apartheid contexts without adequate contextual analysis. Its central argument is that without intentional contextualization of social justice for the post-apartheid Namibian context, society will not be able to create meaningful, effective, and transformative policies, programmes, practices, systems, and justice institutions – no matter how advantageous and well-intentioned. Therefore, there is a need to reevaluate political dialogues, social theories, and theological views advocating for social justice in Namibia. This research enters into dialogue with Allan Boesak's theological notions of justice to extract what could be helpful or may require further reflection in the search to formulate particular Namibian contextual theologies of social justice. Post-apartheid communities long for healing and reconciliation, and they must do so in order to ensure meaningful coexistence with one another. However, they need to confront honestly the lingering socioeconomic effects of the apartheid system. Reconciliation needs to be more far reaching than mere sociality; instead, there must be a recognition that grave injustice was perpetrated. Both perpetrators and beneficiaries of the previous unjust system need to engage social and economic realities with a critical regard for a more just society. Achieving this level of understanding requires an authentic search for justice that is rooted in experiences, epistemologies, and expectations of Namibians, and the resources of the Christian faith. Otherwise, injustice will continue to be prolonged if the underlying conceptual presuppositions do not sufficiently capture and readdress the effects of the apartheid system from the understanding of those it disadvantaged. Apartheid did not only affect economic aspects of the lives of Black Namibians; it also intended to deprive them of their right to self-determination. This desire for contextualized conceptualizations to transform social justice notions reinforces the continued presence and effects of injustice for disadvantaged individuals and communities. The search for justice, beyond the political understandings, is profoundly theological and ethical. It seeks to discover a relevant theological language that will engage where the dialogues of justice are taking place to ensure that God's image-bearers experience a sense of God's *shalom*. As such, it is argued that the concept of social justice would have to consider all possible notions, even those that appear to be disagreeable because of how they have been abused for political and corrupt gain. While this is theological research, it takes cognisance that to be truly conversant, theology needs to identify and embrace systems and structures that would be its allies in the pursuit of social justice. In the search to identify what God is doing in the world and how we can be part of it, secular structures are not excluded in the search. This makes the task of theology missional (that is, a participation in the work of God), as it seeks to make use of all available structures to ensure that the post-apartheid society transforms towards being more just and more human. Finally, the concluding chapter weighs the effects of theological participation in social justice for post-apartheid Namibia, not as a mere observer, but as a key component in advocating for justice and a more just society.

Acknowledgements

I would like to thank the Oxford Centre for Religion and Public Life and Barnabas Fund for the financial and technical support; particularly Dr. Christopher Sugden who has been instrumental in shaping my research, right from our first phone conversation in June 2017; the cohort with whom I was able to experience learning in a community and gained understanding in various contexts of public theology; Rev. Jacobus Schoemann and the unknown team of persons who sponsored my first participation in the programme, when I was unemployed and penniless; moreover, to Stellenbosch University for allowing me the opportunity to research on a subject I am passionate about and for assigning me excellent supervisors, Prof. Dion Forster and Prof. Nicholas Sagovsky. Finally, I thank my wife Justene for her support and enduring days and nights of my absence and allowing me to carry out this project. *Soli Deo gloria.*

List of Abbreviations

AIC	African Initiated Churches
ANC	African National Congress
AR	Affirmative Repositioning
BEE	Black Economic Empowerment
BWS	Breaking the Wall of Silence
CBO	Community Based Organisation
CBS	Catholic Bishops Synod
CSM	Civil Society Movement
CCN	Council of Churches in Namibia
COPE	Congress of the People
CRLR	Commission on Restitution of Land Rights
CSO	Civil Society Organisation
DRCSA	Dutch Reformed Church of South Africa
ELCIN	Evangelical Lutheran Church in Namibia
FBO	Faith Based Organisation
FFF	Forum for the Future
GELC	German Evangelical Lutheran Church
GRN	Government of the Republic of Namibia
HPP	Harambee Prosperity Plan
ICRC	International Committee of the Red Cross
IPPR	Institute for Public Policy Research
KAYEC	Katutura Youth Enterprise Centre
LAC	Legal Assistance Centre
LPM	Landless People's Movement
NDP	National Development Plan

NEEEF	New Equitable Economic Empowerment Framework
NGO	Nongovernmental Organisation
NID	Namibia Institute for Democracy
NP	National Party
NSHR	Namibia's National Society for Human Rights
NWV	Namibia Women's Voice
NYSDP	National Youth Sports Development Platform
ORN	Out-Right Namibia
PLAN	People's Liberation Army of Namibia
RCC	Roman Catholic Church
RMC	Rhenish Mission Church
SACC	South African Council of Churches
SACHI	Southern African Christian Initiative
SDG	Sustainable Development Goals
SWANU	South West African Union
SWAPO	South West African People's Organisation
TRC	Truth and Reconciliation Commission
UDF	United Democratic Front
UPC	Unity Protestant Church
URC	Uniting Reformed Church
UWC	University of Western Cape
WARC	World Alliance of Reformed Churches

CHAPTER 1

Introduction

1.1 Introduction

Post-apartheid conceptions of social justice, if we are serious with creating a more just society,[1] need to be reevaluated. That is, the language and concepts that define "the right distribution of the benefits and burdens of society" which "include rights, liberties, opportunities (for example, in education and employment), wealth and income, including publicly provided services" need contextual conceptions of appropriate distribution, especially of economic benefits and burdens.[2] They need revision, Johnston argues, "if they are to make a constructive contribution to the thoughts and actions that will shape our future" as post-conflict societies.[3] We engage a theological framework searching for locally crafted conceptions of social justice for post-apartheid Namibia with this background. We explore the question of social justice from the conviction that is evidenced in many texts in the Bible that being God's image-bearers comes with social implications, even revolt against conceptions, systems, and structures that do not allow the full expression of their dignity and humanity. This means that although we are making use of

---

1. We take cognisance of the complexity of the concept of society and its foreignness to the African context. In this research, the concept is used to signify any structured system that allows for a large-scale community of persons which is identifiable by certain laws that are meant to protect everyone and are self-propagating to ensure its continuity and promote a common identity, for example, Namibian. This understanding poses the challenge of contextualization; we use it here in an inhibited anthropological and sociological sense.

2. Smith, *Moral and Political Philosophy*, 115.

3. Johnston, *Brief History of Justice*, 5.

contributions from social theories of justice, we seek to make a theological contribution to social justice dialogue. This contribution is the kind of contribution that is not simply in search of contextualization for its own sake but one that uses a theological framework to call for social justice that reflects the experiences, metaphors, language, culture and "the traditions, the limits and the life of the community" as God intended.[4]

We deliberately employ Christian theological terms speaking of social justice as intentionally engaging and witnessing towards God's created order and kingdom in relation to the dignity and lives of persons. "Focusing on the freedom to truly bear the image of God as intended directs our attention to looking for evidence of justice in social processes and opportunities instead of in results given by the imperfections of a disordered world."[5] Searching for these social processes and opportunities is what we may refer to as "*kairos searching*" for opportunities where we can be witnesses to God's truth, even disruptively. In dialogue with the Black Liberation theologian, anti-apartheid icon and activist Allan A. Boesak, we seek to explore the primary question: "What can a contextualized engagement with his theologies of social justice provide for a theology of social justice in the post-apartheid Namibian context?" That is, engaging a process of disruptive theological revision inviting us to consider the possibility that many current concepts of social justice are not expressing or catering for the realization of social justice in the post-apartheid Namibian context.

This research invites us to consider not only advocating for socioeconomic justice and empowerment of previously and presently disadvantaged persons. A contextualized conceptualization of social justice recognises the agency of affected communities that they need to be part of the policies and programmes of recasting notions of social justice. We employ theological methods to advocate for this search of justice and recognize the systems and structures of our allies (for example, democratic systems and governments) to express this agency. In so doing, we engage theology to be part of minimising and even removal of hindrances (social, economic, political, and religious) embedded in notions of social justice that deprive God's image-bearers of the

---

4. Sagovsky, *Christian Tradition*, xi.
5. Bradley, *Political Economy of Liberation*, 112.

full potential to exercize their agency and obtain justice.[6] This current project comprises a theological task of attempting to imitate God by participating in activities, as Stanley Hauerwas and Samuel Wells write, of reforming "the descriptions they use to name the outcast, the sinner, and the unclean, and reshape the ways people are received, nurtured, respected, and empowered. Together they reflect on the patterns of life that build up the body."[7]

With this background, the current chapter provides the project's general framework (research problem, motivation, research questions, objective, and methodology) and the key concepts to be explored in the subsequent chapters. Thus, it serves as the primary outline of the project.

1.2 Background

1.2.1 Outlining of the Context

The context of this research is limited to Namibia. The name is derived from the Nama/Damara word !namib which can be translated as a surround or edge, in reference to the desert on the western side of the country's coastline. The name implies that the country is edged by the desert, known as the Namib Desert. This is the name that was reassigned to a country previously known as *Deutsch-Südwestafrika*, (German South West Africa) a German colony whose borders were delineated by the 1886 Berlin Conference. After Germany lost the colony, it was named South West Africa and placed under the guardianship of South Africa. The latter turned from this mandate assigned by the League of Nations and annexed the country with the intention of making it its fifth province. Regardless of the history of artificial borders, this corrupt delineation has been accepted widely to constitute a state called Namibia – one which is considered sovereign, with its own laws, political systems and citizens who identify as Namibians.

The circumstances that formed the socioeconomic and sociopolitical circumstances within a particular geopolitical environment affecting a specific demographic setting is what we refer to as the Namibian context. This country

---

6. Boesak, *Children*, 1218 of 6766; Deneulin, Nebel, and Sagovsky, "Introduction," 9; De Gruchy, *Christianity and Democracy*, 221–24.

7. Hauerwas and Wells, "Gift of the Church," 25.

now free from the apartheid rule faces different challenges. Friedman puts it this way:

> Today, the Namibian State and its inhabitants continue to nego-
> tiate their newfound democracy. This process of on-going state
> making is contested at numerous levels. At the national level,
> political parties and their leading actors guide the State through
> a programme of post-apartheid reform. Among other issues, the
> crafting of Namibian unity and the transcending of the rural-
> urban divide remain high on the list of national priorities; all the
> while, we see neoliberal versions of the democratic state model
> intersecting with the SWAPO party's attempts to retain control
> over what has become a dominant-party democracy. At the local
> level, however, we see quite a different set of parameters in the
> contestations surrounding the institutionalisation of the newly
> democratic State.[8]

The issue of social justice in this research, among other things, is deeply linked to identity. This has profound sociological implications in a country where nationhood is a political and colonial construct – both as a historical fact and post-apartheid phenomenon. There is an ongoing struggle between the *de jure* organization which does not always correspond to the *de facto* social situations. It is in this kind of a turbulent context that the research locates an opportunity for theological participation. It presupposes that amidst the po-litical turmoil is an expressed reality of a God who is gracious and loving and is concerned for the socioeconomic conditions of persons living in Namibia.

Does the context necessarily demand a motivation for social justice? Modern Namibia with reference to the Berlin Conference of 1886, resembles an injustice which has been normalized. The role of colonialism which was passed on to South Africa was that of deliberating, legislating, administering, promoting, and advocating injustice. Both colonialism and apartheid oper-ated on a particular race, political, religious, philosophical and economic theories that advantaged the White people and disadvantaged Black people. Set within this context, this research acknowledges that the complex nature

---

8. Friedman, *Imagining Post-Apartheid State*, 3–4.

of injustice we now witness, complete with structures set to discriminate against persons based on their social locale, did not start a short while ago.

The theoretical frameworks of the past have been helpful in starting somewhere rather than nowhere. Today, the task is to challenge and raise new questions regarding the background of social justice measures, programmes and policies that are currently at work. The shift in social, political, and cultural circumstances provides for both a shift and disruption in the background and presents a unique opportunity for theological participation regarding the rectification of injustice in this context. With this context, we take into consideration that we are in an environment of multiperspectives influenced by belief and unbelief. Thus, believers in God and unbelievers see the world differently. Therefore, this is not a promissory note through which theology would transform society but an attempt to bear witness to the values of God's kingdom in such a mixed context. The task becomes theological but also with overwhelming political overtones which cannot be avoided, as the kingdom of God comprises of a particular political notion and social ethics. This project is an attempt to witness to these theological beliefs and seeks to express God's kingdom in the context described above as part of Christian witness.

1.2.2 Contextual Theology

This research uses contextual theology as its hermeneutical framework. By highlighting the context and locality we seek to navigate how we can draw lessons from universal dialogues on social justice while portraying what is unique about the Namibian context. Understanding and outlining the context is important to provide a vision for constructing a particular type of social justice theology and praxis. However,

> The entire reason for doing theology contextually is so that the gospel, transmitted in scripture and tradition, can be understood as clearly as possible, both by those hearing the gospel for the first time and those believers who constantly need to grow in their faith and be more and more evangelized by it. The goal of contextual theology, in other words, is prophecy. That doing theology contextually is an exercise of prophetic dialogue is evidenced in the mutually critically *(sic)* dialogue that the contextual theologizing process entails. Dialogue is the

way that the prophetic message of the gospel is developed and communicated.[9]

The desire to be God's witnesses in our various environments, while it should be informed by Scripture, can only be made more effective or through explicit theological reflection on the context. The dialogue with Boesak is an attempt to indicate this explicit nature of theological reflection and engagement that is immersed in the immediate context but fully aware of other interplaying factors. This means "that specific situations, concerns, cultures, socioeconomic situations and political experiences are explicitly and purposefully incorporated"[10] and a shift is proposed in the way Christian theology is understood and applied in Namibia.

Contextual theology in this study comes as a radical revolt against: (1) prescriptive notions of social justice which claim unquestionable universal validity but do not generate effective praxis (see § 5.5.); (2) theological lethargy that is locked up in conformity of knowledge and concepts that fail to bear God's witness regarding social justice and God's *shalom*; (3) universalized and prescriptive approaches that fail to produce a theological understanding and praxis that bears witness to the reality of a God who understands human socioeconomic conditions and disapproves of injustice; and 4) the notion that the Christian faith is more about the *hereafter* and is little concerned with the *here-and-now*.

Reflecting and speaking to the experiences of the Namibian context, in this research, is an act of saying that Namibian Christians know their own context and can bear witness of God's rule in the creation of a just social order. Bevans refers to it as "prophetic dialogue" which he describes as follows:

> Prophetic dialogue, in the first place, is more of an attitude, a *habitus* or spiritual discipline, than anything else. It requires developing, on the one hand, "a heart so open that the wind blows through it." Such a heart has to cultivate the skills and attitudes of deep listening, "docility" or the ability to learn from those among whom we work, respect, and vulnerability. On the other hand – and only within the context of such dialogue as the

---

9. Bevans, *Essays in Contextual Theology*, 90–91.

10. Pears, *Doing Contextual Theology*, 8.

condition for the possibility – the *habitus* of prophetic dialogue demands the cultivation of clarity of speech and thought, the courage to confront evil and injustice, and the dogged conviction of hope in what might seem like hopeless situations.[11]

This engagement takes an integrated approach to explore the various notions of social justice in order to identify as to what kinds of needs need to be met to have a just society. As an act of discernment, Liberation Theology has been at the forefront of these kinds of dialogues. This is where the engagement with Boesak becomes crucial for our study, to glean the needed lessons that can be applied to construct a contextual theology of social justice that seeks to redress the effects of apartheid's injustice. In fact, the mere task of venturing into such a complex dialogue that confronts injustice "is already a prophetic act."[12]

1.2.3 Conceptualization

All social justice notions are influenced by specific contexts and influenced by diverse factors and experiences. These conceptions inform our understanding and practices regarding the conferring, distributing, and achieving embodiment of the values of social justice, for example, "income and wealth, duties and rights, powers and opportunities, offices, and honours."[13] Thus, humans construe these notions of social justice to establish principles and normative conditions that would minimize injustice (especially structurally and systematically enforced). Oppressed societies often function on pre-existent or ready-made templates, which are believed to consist of "fundamental standards underpinning judgments about fairness,"[14] but these have often not taken the humanity (their stories, understanding, and experience) of these communities into account. MacIntyre points out two things for our consideration: First, these universalized notions fall short of addressing gross inequality in life-enhancing goods and are "devoid of compensatory action to remedy inequalities which are the result of past injustice."[15] Second, these inherited

---

11. Bevans, *Essays in Contextual Theology*, 90.
12. Bevans, 90.
13. Sandel, *Justice*, 19.
14. Johnston, *Brief History of Justice*, 12.
15. MacIntyre, *Whose Justice?*, 1.

templates often do not translate into resolving the effects of injustice resulting from the unjust political and legal systems that created the socioeconomic inequality "disguised under the rhetoric of consensus."[16]

This critique implies that conceptions of social justice that are presented to offer answers to the quest for justice are sometimes at odds with the lived realities of persons and are slow to take the shape of the everyday experiences of affected communities. As far as deconstructing these concepts is concerned, we consider our task to be to engage in conceptual decolonization and liberation. We are searching for trajectories of the concept of social justice to be more meaningful, applicable, and intelligible to effect change in Namibia (considering its unique histories and experiences). For example, the apartheid system separated people into racial categories, which became the basis for constituting socioeconomic detachments. These categories ensured that White African minorities enjoyed greater privileges and better socioeconomic benefits than their Black counterparts. Within this structure, Black Africans had to live on substandard land, low wages, and poorly funded healthcare, housing, and education. Disappointingly, the effects of this history of injustice continue to impact hundreds of thousands in the post-apartheid context. Post-independence notions of social justice will be unachievable unless they find their understanding within the parameters of deliberate and systematic contextual conceptions to effect systematic and structural transformation.

As our conversation partner, we engage the person and work of Allan Aubrey Boesak (b. 23 February 1946) to draw lessons for rethinking how to address the realities that present theological conceptions of social justice in Namibia are not addressing. This study will not embrace everything he says, but adopt an analytical approach in dialogue; specifically, as to which of his theological notions of social justice provide us with a valuable framework to construct and contribute towards a Namibian theology of social justice for public dialogue. Of course, there will be some instances in which we may need to draw on the insights and perspectives of others, given Boesak's own historical, geographical, and theological context which differs from some historical and contemporary concerns in Namibia.

The intention is to provide a novel contribution for thinking theologically about social justice for the Namibian context. Philosophers, social theorists,

---

16. MacIntyre, 2.

and theologians have long been engaging in the contextualization and conceptualization of social justice. For example, Socrates conceived of justice in *The Republic*, as "the money-making, auxiliary, and guardian classes doing what is appropriate, each of them minding its own business in a city – [this] would be justice and would make the city just."[17] Under the benevolent rule of a philosopher-king, such an understanding would create unity, harmony, virtue, and happiness in society – *eudaimonia*. Plato's conception of justice emerged from the context of the then Greek *polis*. Such conceptualization – despite its practical challenges and embedded culturally approved discrimination, abuses, inequities, and dehumanization – highlights every society's need to have a concept of social justice.

John Rawls, in *A Theory of Justice*, asserts that "justice is the first virtue of social institutions, as truth is of systems of thought."[18] Thus, no other virtue can be achieved in their most real sense by forfeiting justice. For example, while efficiency is a virtue necessary for an institution's functioning, it cannot override justice if we were to make a choice. Nevertheless, to articulate and bring it into effect, social justice requires systematic contextual reflection. It is practically problematic to conceive that Rawls's attempted universal theory of justice is borne out of purely abstract motivation. Indeed, it factors in the rise of liberal democracies, increased religious liberties, and increased secularization of government, which influenced his thinking of a theory of justice. While justice is a principle, it is administered in the context of a society. One cannot think of justice resulting when such has not been contextualized to respond to the immediate needs of each society. Rawls is not exploring the metaphysical nature of justice but the nature of "right" rather than "good" or metaethics.[19] Alasdair MacIntyre argues that "in order to reason well we shall have had to learn how systematically to accord merit where it is due, that is, we shall have had, in the context of that particular specific [*sic*] form of activity, to acquire the virtue of justice, conceived in terms of desert."[20]

---

17. Plato, *Republic of Plato*, IV.434c, 113.
18. Rawls, *Theory of Justice*, 3.
19. Rawls, 21.
20. MacIntyre, *Whose Justice?*, 44.

Similarly, Rawls argues that "intuitive conviction of the primacy of justice"[21] is realized in a context-appropriate conception if it is to lead to effective and transformative social institutions and structures. This quest implies searching for a concept of social justice through which a group's interest, no matter how elite or proximate to power, cannot override the allocation of justice for the affected communities. At a practical level, it would require revisiting the "laws and institutions no matter how efficient and well-arranged [which] must be reformed or abolished"[22] if they do not serve "the appropriate distribution of the benefits and burdens"[23] that would enable conducive and human living standards. Rawls argues that simply having institutions, laws, policies, and programmes is not adequate. Neither do these things represent a well-ordered society. According to him,

> a society is well-ordered when it is not only designed to advance the good of its members but when it is also effectively regulated by a public conception of justice. That is, a society in which (1) everyone accepts and knows that the others accept the same principles of justice, and (2) the basic social institutions generally satisfy and are generally known to satisfy these principles.[24]

To have a just society, MacIntyre argues that a society needs a "particular conception and a practical rationality" that will affect "closely related aspects of some larger, more or less well-articulated, overall view of human life and of its place in nature."[25] To enforce pre-defined universal views and concepts of social justice without contextual exploration is "to insist that we cannot adequately identify either our own commitments or those of others in the argumentative conflicts of the present except by situating them within those histories which made them what they have now become."[26] Hence, this research engages Allan Boesak's theological work to explore the concept of social justice required for the post-apartheid Namibian context. We need to

---

21. Rawls, *Theory of Justice*, 3.
22. Rawls, 3.
23. Rawls, 4.
24. Rawls, 4.
25. MacIntyre, *Whose Justice?*, 139.
26. MacIntyre, 139.

assess what helpful lessons and insights his work[27] can provide in our search for social justice for a new society where the whole of human reality and flourishing can be realized. This search for a theologically sound and contextually relevant notion of social justice is part of the ongoing work of expressing God's kingdom in the world, in which the poor, oppressed, and downtrodden have a special place. We seek to reclaim this specialness by re-examining the narratives, structures, systems, and ideas which sustain injustice.

By nature, the theological concept of social justice seeks to extend beyond mere contextually reflected moral philosophy or political ambition. It integrates lessons from the social sciences and humanities and Christians' concern with social justice matters, motivated by their vision of a just God and God's creation.[28] It depicts the greatest commands of love for God and neighbour,[29] in which Christians with the rest of society seek social justice. Gadner says this love for God and neighbour motivates us to intentionally participate in the "creating, ordering, and renewing activity of God in history"[30] to ensure an environment for opportunities to promote the quality of life that would facilitate others to reflect their being God's image-bearers. The pre-eminence of God in human affairs and history, in this study, serves as the theological pretext upon which we are to engage the subject of social justice. Any philosophical language and method engaged, in this case, serve as supporting tools for enhanced critical engagement. They help to understand God's self-revelation and activity in human communities and how this revelation creates a genuine concern for participating in what God is doing in the world.

Thus, the development of a concept of justice needs to stem from an understanding of the long and widely considered theological tradition related to God's justice and notions of God's concern for justice.[31] "Central to the

---

27. See preliminary literature review (see 1.6).

28. See for example, how it is stated in Hosea 4:1–2, "Hear the word of the Lord, O children of Israel, for the Lord has a controversy with the inhabitants of the land. There is no faithfulness or steadfast love, and no knowledge of God in the land; there is swearing, lying, murder, stealing, and committing adultery; they break all bounds, and bloodshed follows bloodshed" (cf. Jer. 22:13–16). All Bible texts are taken from the New Revised Standard Version (NRSV), unless otherwise indicated.

29. Gadner, *Justice and Christian Ethics*, 29.

30. Gadner, 29.

31. Sagovsky, *Christian Tradition*, 28–31.

Old Testament's teaching about justice is the claim that YHWH[32] is the God of justice and will enforce it . . . Wherever the prophets denounce injustice, the purpose of doing so is to announce in the name of YHWH."[33] Christian reflection on contemporary issues ought to be "different" by looking at the world from the perspective of the triune God's relationship with creation, serving us with a vision in a world confronted by various forms of suffering (inequality, poverty, unemployment, diseases, violence, abuse, corruption, homelessness, and hunger). This view of God requires pointing out justice perceptions that cannot account for the ethical and practical implications. Pears writes in this vein that,

> Christianity is a religion in transition. As part of a constantly changing world that progresses, develops, renews, and reinvents itself, Christianity is subject to the changes of human cultural and social existence. In the last half of the twentieth century and into the twenty-first century, Christianity has been influenced by several cultural shifts. One of these is the shift from a perspective which views truths and human knowledge as universal to a perspective which views them as shaped, determined and even validated by specific cultural, social, and political contexts.[34]

This evaluation originates from the understanding that all theology develops in a social context. That is, it is informed by contextually unique issues, questions, and problems. But this should be with the awareness that Christian engagement, although bound to the human context, has profound epistemological roots in the transcendent. Thus, the context of God's self-revelation needs to inform our participation in society.

1.2.4 Relationship of Conceptualization and Social Justice

As the research unfolds and from the presupposition it sets forth, justice is a complex issue, not to mention bringing theology into dialogue with

---

32. Boesak refers to this concept of justice as liberation in chapter 1 of *Farewell to Innocence* in which he sees liberating the oppressed and downtrodden as Yahweh's central mission. He sees it as God engaged in evening uneven power structures in society through Black Liberation Theology.

33. Houston, *Contending for Justice*, 204; Boesak, *Farewell to Innocence* (1976), 14–40; Sagovsky, *Christian Tradition*, 28–54.

34. Pears, *Doing Contextual Theology*, 1.

secular theories and systems. It is also easy to assume that we could find an ultimate theory to create practices of justice that would undo all injustices. This research does not claim to be the ultimate dialogue. Instead, it is drawing on what has been a long-standing academic tradition of inquiry, and as a public exercize of faith it seeks to locate itself in the lived experiences of those who are victims of injustice. The above section has presupposed that conceptualization is necessary for justice. However, we still need to ask, how do conceptualization and justice relate?

Apartheid was based on a certain conception of what is good and just. It purported itself as a system that would ultimately address differences between racial groups. This dream was a conceptual error with devastating effects. Conceptual critique seeks to rectify erroneous and imposing notions that hinder the full realization of justice in the post-apartheid context. This calls for humility. We must admit that we know surprisingly little about justice. This research is merely part of this search to correct injustice. Eckstein and Wickham-Crowley hint at a relatedness of conceptualization and social justice:

> Conceptions of justice, efforts to reduce or eliminate perceived injustices, and the success of such efforts vary over time and among groups. They also vary among persons differently located within social structures and among persons embracing different values, which themselves are not free-floating but embedded in local, national, and international structures of everyday life and practice.[35]

MacIntyre, in *Whose Justice? Which Rationality?*,[36] makes a strong argument from the perspective of virtue. He argues that for persons or a society to apply measures for rectifying injustice can only come from them exercising the virtue of justice they possess. However, the rationality that informs this virtue can only be accounted for if it emanates from the context that takes into consideration the agency of those affected by injustice. Injustice is brought into effect through conceptions that are executed, either as experiments or deep convictions – the apartheid system was both an experimental

---

35. Eckstein and Wickham-Crowley, *What Justice?*, xi.
36. MacIntyre, *Whose Justice?*

process and also driven by certain sociologically, theologically, political, and philosophical convictions.

The relationship between conceptualization and social justice is not taken as a given. This research interrogates this as a possible alternative approach to addressing injustice. It seeks to be more than mere analogy; it seeks to promote community for human flourishing. It is also not a mere imbuing of the intellectual and abstract thoughts but a search for the way of thinking that prompts us to identify practices of justice. The contributors to the book *What Justice? Whose Justice?*,[37] emphasize the relation between concepts and practices of social justice. Thus, alternative practices need conceptual frameworks that can examine the effects of the systems, policies, and practices currently in place. Chapter 5 is an attempt to expand this relationship between conceptualization and social justice. It calls for an epistemological break to (re)understand the current practices, systems, policies, and structures; not by separating ourselves into a world of theory and divorced from community and practice but by exploring how we can best generate notions to witness effectively to the post-apartheid context.

1.2.5 Understanding the History and Impact of Apartheid

Apartheid systematically orchestrated disregard for fellow humans, driven by false conceptions of human differences and greed for economic and political power. Namibia is free from the apartheid legislation, but the adverse effects of the apartheid systems have continued to operate in Namibian society. Some believe the post-apartheid structures and systems exist to reinforce the apartheid legacy. Geoffrey Schneider describes this continued reinforcement of apartheid when he writes that the country's political environment has improved, but "the economic division[s] along racial lines created by apartheid are still in place today."[38]

In the context of this continued socioeconomic inequality, we should ask whether the meaning of social justice in post-apartheid Namibia provides an adequate, theologically robust enough conceptualization to allow for the freeing of the Namibian society as God's image-bearers (i.e. those who bear God's image)? Consequently, we need to interrogate the conceptual and

---

37. Eckstein and Wickham-Crowley, *What Justice?*
38. Schneider, "Neoliberalism and Economic Justice," 23.

practical appropriateness of social justice in the post-apartheid context and "help create a more inclusive public sphere in which the public anger of the silenced and excluded voices . . . can be heard and addressed by policymakers and practitioners."[39]

This search for understanding social justice is an immense and complex occupation for theology that seeks to find an appropriate language to address the effects of a systematically orchestrated racial, economic, and political system. It is a system that subjected Black Africans to severe restrictions while granting White Africans privileges to prosper.[40] Amid these structural forces, we need to construct an honest, deliberate, and collective reassessment of our theological and social values. Without addressing these issues, racial enmity and gaps in income, resources, productivity, opportunities, and capabilities will continue to grow. This does not deny that we have taken significant steps towards political equality, which continues to strengthen beyond the former oppressors' expectations. Nevertheless, the economic negotiations made by the leadership of the South West African People's Organisation (SWAPO), in Sonneborn's view,[41] adopted an economic system that creates or reinforces socioeconomic structures that continue to advance and shield the cause of the previous oppressors, their descendants, and beneficiaries, at the expense of the economically disenfranchised persons. Henning Melber is of the view that instead of dealing with the social injustices created by the apartheid era, the new government's pursuit of political construction and political themes such as "national reconciliation became the programmatic slogan for a co-option strategy based on the structural legacy of settler colonial minority rule and its corresponding property relations."[42]

Considering the depth of conceptual reflection and efforts that went into establishing the apartheid system, a lethargic philosophical-theological commitment will not be enough to abrogate its effects. As Desmond Tutu says, "apartheid [was] firmly entrenched for a long half-century and carried out with a ruthless efficiency . . . [it] is going to take a long time for the pernicious

---

39. Storrar, "Naming of Parts," 27.
40. Schneider, "Neoliberalism and Economic Justice," 24.
41. Sonneborn, *End of Apartheid*, 95–107.
42. Melber, *Understanding Namibia*, 144.

effects of apartheid's egregiousness to be eradicated."[43] Therefore, post-apartheid discussions of social justice need to commit analytically to construct critical and viable accounts of various socioeconomic, sociopolitical, sociocultural, sociopsychological, and sociotheological conditions. They must do so by questioning the epistemic underlining of views that pronounce themselves as pro-justice but could be captive to the status quo. Such discussions would move beyond the mere promotion of virtues, political dialogue, and equality, to engage social justice issues affecting people. As we see the lives of those who have been wronged and are being wronged, we need a contextually rooted understanding of social justice and a theological reflection to effect change.[44] If we are "to develop notions about the social arrangements which are needed to establish a just society,"[45] we need to confront the universal aspects of social justice in order to "redress the structural and cultural biases"[46] resulting from notions that do not consider the contexts of the wronged. The researcher aims that this study will generate a renewed moral consciousness in the theologically informed justice dialogue for post-apartheid Namibia.

1.3 An Overview of Injustice in Namibia

1.3.1 History, Politics, and Social Conditions

This section provides a brief background of the Namibian context (expanded in greater detail and depth in chapter 2). Namibia has a unique history of colonialism, first by Germany and later by South Africa. In both cases, the Namibian people resisted foreign rule but were eventually subdued by deceit and the advanced military strength of the colonisers.[47] From various historical narratives available, Namibia has been engaged in resistance to oppression throughout its history.[48]

---

43. Tutu, *No Future without Forgiveness*, 18.

44. Wolterstorff, *Journey towards Justice*, 5–9.

45. Sabbagh and Schmitt, "Past, Present, and Future," 1.

46. Sabbagh and Schmitt, 2.

47. Silvester and Gewald, *Words Cannot Be Found*.

48. Enquist, *Namibia: Land of Tears*; Herbstein and Evenson, *Devils Are among Us*; Katjavivi, *History of Resistance*; Ya-Otto, Gjerstad, and Mercer, *Battlefront Namibia*.

This history of resistance remains "concentrated mainly on the political culture and ideology cultivated since . . . independence."[49] On the other hand, this political culture fails to restructure or transform itself to redress the effects. Melber argues that the political liberators are fixated with establishing a new "hegemonic public discourse to reinvent themselves within the heroic narrative that was already being constructed during the anticolonial struggle."[50] This politicking creates a stagnant political rhetoric in the transition of political power from a minority group to the majority. Thus, there has been no effective addressing of injustice perpetrated by policies and programmes of apartheid government which sustained patterns that "reflected a number of socioeconomic distortions."[51] There is a general deterioration as far as achieving genuine social and economic emancipation is concerned.

1.3.2 Urgent Areas of Focus for the Social Justice Discourse

Namibian discussions of social justice focus on the access to and distribution of certain socioeconomic goods. These goods are: (1) *Decent housing:* In 2018, there were "308 informal settlements in Namibia with a staggering 228,000 shacks accommodating about 995,000 people in urban areas"[52] – meaning 40 percent of the Namibian population lives in shacks in urban areas.[53] (2) *Unemployment and lack of decent employment:* While employment decreases, unemployment keeps increasing – in 2016, it was estimated to increase to 37.3 percent in 2017. (3) *The increasing disparity of income:* Although there has been a slight decrease in income difference, this gap is still too broad. On the Gini index, Namibia stood at 0.572 in 2016 and estimated that it would drop to 0.500 in 2022, still making it one of the world's most unequal countries.[54] (4) *Administrative corruption:* Government administrative corruption has become a significant form of crime, surpassing all other forms of organized crime in the country. In 2011, Namibia was ranked 57th out of 183 economies, though previously ranked among the top thirty least

---

49. Melber, "Transition in Namibia," 7.

50. Melber, 5.

51. Kaapama, "Commercial Land Reforms," 29.

52. Nakale, "40% of Namibians Live in Shacks."

53. This lack of housing gives banks and real estate agents license to overprice rent and purchasing of houses (governed by the apartheid Rent Ordinance 13 of 1977).

54. National Planning Commission, "Status of Namibian Economy."

corrupt countries between 1998–2001. Financial resources that would have been used to contribute to the economic upliftment of many are being used to benefit a few politically connected persons.[55] This undermines the provision of quality education, healthcare, and all other services to improve the quality of life and quality of living. 5) *Discriminatory laws:* There remain about one hundred and forty-four apartheid laws to repeal.[56] Other than apartheid laws, new laws such as the Agriculture Land Reform Act 6 of 1995, although commendable, have only resulted in a slow process of land acquisition and distribution. Today, many Namibians cannot afford to own land because of laws that protect White Namibians who benefitted from the apartheid laws.

The post-apartheid Namibian context is characterized by rampant public administrative corruption and increasing policy translation failure. Significant changes can be observed, though these are often reversed by a plethora of new policies which reset the country in different directions with each change in government.[57] Addressing the above goods calls for structural change (pre- and post-independence), collective public participation, a political vision for social justice, and effective systems. Added to this list would be doing away with a political elitism that widens the gap of inequality. However, it also calls for theological participation in the public square, for a country whose population boasts of being dominantly Christian (80–90%).

1.4 The Motivation for the Study

In 2013, the researcher was approached to be part of a small Christian advocacy group, the Southern African Christian Initiative (SACHI).[58] Through interactions with the community and religious leaders, he became much more aware of the lingering effects of apartheid on communities. In particular, socioeconomic issues remain inadequately addressed in the post-apartheid

---

55. Duddy, "Corruption Bigger than Crime."

56. Iikela, "144 Apartheid Laws."

57. The national policies have changed under the different presidents, Vision 2030 under President Sam Nuujoma, National Development Plans (NDP) under President Hifikepunye Pohamba and now the Harambee Prosperity Plan (HPP) under President Hage Geingob. Each government resets the direction we are to go, thus, delaying the processes of implementing changes.

58. See website http://sachi-sadc.org

structures, despite the growing legal and political systems in place to create political equality.

As the theological advisor to SACHI, the researcher noticed the absence of well-conceived theological discussions about social justice in the post-apartheid Namibian context. Although the Council of Churches in Namibia (CCN) has made efforts, it struggles to be effective because of its leaders' close political links to the government. Besides the institutions, the three theological seminaries are practically absent from the public square. They do not adequately engage issues of social justice that are affecting most of the nation. This theological absence has motivated the researcher to address the subject of social justice in post-apartheid Namibia, to provide a theological contribution that can engage the complexity of what is facing Namibian society at present.

The researcher is aware that this is an academic project and is cognisant of Max Weber's thesis of not using the academic platform for advocating for another cause (partisan political or personal agenda).[59] Hence, this contribution is both critical and self-critical. That being said, the African context is not a pure esoteric pursuit; the African academic cannot avoid being an advocate. A pure esoteric pursuit of theological research is devoid of public usefulness. Therefore, Weber's warning is heeded, but also challenged; Namibia requires a more participatory and engaging academic dialogue, which should include the perspectives of theologians. The context requires that "we cannot avoid speaking up [and taking part through activism],"[60] but we need an awareness that we live on an integrated margin as academics and citizens.

1.5 Statement of the Problem

The researcher argues that a tension exists between generalized, universal notions of social justice, and contextual notions of social justice that can best serve post-apartheid Namibia.[61] This tension carries the potential to hinder,

---

59. Gerth and Mills, *From Max Weber*, 129–58.

60. Wolterstorff, *Journey towards Justice*, 20.

61. The discussions of justice which have been taking place are often based on intellectual, theological, political, philosophical, and social frameworks that cannot coordinate with the lived and material experiences of the Namibian population. For example, ideas such as national reconciliation, national unity, and national economic prosperity, although appealing, do not deal

among other things, developing a self-propagating vision and creating proactive responses, systems and structures of social justice that accommodate the society's social, historical, and political experiences. It includes theological perspectives that profess themselves as pro-justice or liberationist but commence from a social (mainly socialist-Marxist class analysis) rather than a theological analysis of social justice. These concepts and understandings of social justice, institutionalized and transported indiscriminately to Namibia, should be carefully framed not to reinforce unjust structures. This quest requires a critical dialogue that seeks to generate and incorporate contextual insights, which are inclusive of but not limited to cultural, intellectual methods and practices, and understandings of the particular that would provide a more objective framework for reflecting on social justice issues. Hence, the process of contextualization is profoundly conscious of human sociocultural evolutions, conceptual-traditions, ontological locales, epistemological pedigrees, and is intentional about God's involvement in Namibia. This contextualization does not mean that the universal or the foreign is of no value, but that its assessment is to be contextually appraised, extracted, and applied, within the confines, needs, and anticipations of the particular. This dialogue (the holding together of difference between the universal and the particular), in discussion with Allan Boesak's theology of social justice, is the subject of this research.

It is contended that a society cannot achieve genuine social justice through vague universal terms – an engaging tension is necessary between the universal and the particular. This engagement calls for what Althaus-Reid refers to as "a continuing process of re-contextualisation"[62] not necessarily as an exercize of doubting in theology but more of a permanent engagement of profound revisioning in theology. Thus, we need: (1) a conscious process of finding a language and application that adequately address the context of post-apartheid Namibia; (2) an intentional process that seeks to provide a conceptual framework of reflection to locally relevant solutions to address

---

with the essence of justice (More, 2004; Wiredu, 2004). The privation of contextual situatedness has thus created alienation and a general sense of dissonance, subjugating justice to these elaborate political concepts (Diener, 2001; MacIntyre, 1988).

62. Althaus-Reid, *Indecent Theology*, 5.

the continued presence of injustice; and (3) a process of careful examination for solutions by learning from similar contexts.

The dialogues and analyses concerning the processes and contents of what social justice is, are being imported and applied without a critical reflection on the Namibian context. This research assumes that systems, programmes, and processes, regardless of how well-intentioned they may be or the positive impact they have had, cannot produce lasting and sustainable measures in the current conceptual captivity. Contextualized conceptualization within the framework of self-propagation rejects all views and practices that may bolster injustice's continued presence. The proposition is that by God's design, all humans are endowed with self-propagating capabilities, contextualization can express these capabilities rather than merely imitate and duplicate other views and practices.

We further contend that a theology of social justice needs to be grounded in Christian anthropology from which it would advocate for the creation of social, economic, and political structures and systems in which people can freely and creatively thrive. This calls for an epistemological break from prescriptive universalized notions of justice, if Namibia is to formulate adequate measures to address the effects of apartheid and overcome the prevailing vicious cycle of socioeconomic injustice. As far as the researcher is aware, no one in Namibia has engaged in a systematic theological study questioning the impact of conceptualization in the public construction of post-apartheid social justice. Thus, there is need for theological participation in outlining explanations, clarifying distortions, showing up pseudoproblems, solutions, and incompatible theories to address the Namibian situation, after political apartheid. Conceptualising meanings of justice within a given context should not be simply because we seek to be "different" from Western (or other) concepts. On the contrary, it must be motivated by the theological conviction that there is need for justice and that the human society in Namibia is endowed by God with the capability to express the uniqueness of reflecting upon their challenges.

Moreover, it should be accompanied by acknowledging that the Namibian society has been deeply damaged by the history of the apartheid system and requires just measures to address the lingering effect of this gruesome system. The heart of this research, and the core of contemporary theology, recognises that human understanding of truth claims has changed. In the later modern or postmodern era, we have come to realize that universalized claims of meanings should not be accepted without scrutinising their relevance within a given context.[63] Therefore, the understanding of justice which has been universalized and imposed on many societies today needs to be reexamined to affect the practical processes and effect desirable changes. Or as David Johnston argues, "These conceptions must be revised if they are to make a constructive contribution to the thoughts and actions that will shape our futures."[64] However, to construct a concept of justice that addresses the post-apartheid context of Namibia, "we must first recover some of the intellectual materials out of which earlier conceptions were fashioned, scrutinising their strengths and weaknesses in the hope that we will be able to fashion ideas about justice that will serve us well."[65]

This research, interacting with Allan Boesak's notions and framing of social justice, seeks to draw lessons and conclusions to help rethink the Namibian context and the role of theological participation in the public discourse for social justice. This is done as part of a proactive Christian response that aims to inhabit our society with the values of social justice that are characteristic of the kingdom of God. It is a search for God's kingdom and how to be part of what God is doing in the world – the new reality God has begun through Jesus Christ.

1.6 Preliminary Literature Survey on Allan Boesak

1.6.1 A Biography of Allan Boesak

Allan Aubrey Boesak was born on 23 February 1946 in Kakamas, Northern Cape, South Africa. He grew up under challenging socioeconomic conditions, mainly because of the apartheid system and having lost his father at an early age which made his mother the only breadwinner. His local community was but one manifestation of the effects of continued social injustice (see further discussion in § 3.2.1.). After the 1976 Soweto uprisings, he increased his political activities through the church. Since then, he became known as a liberation theologian, demonstrated through his doctoral work *Farewell to*

---

63. Pears, *Doing Contextual Theology*, 6; Sharifian, *Cultural Conceptualisations*.
64. Johnston, *Brief History of Justice*, 3.
65. Johnston, 3.

Innocence.[66] He was then elected President of the World Alliance of Reformed Churches (WARC) 1982–91.

He became prominent in the 1980s for speaking out, writing against, and opposing the National Party's (NP) policies which promoted racial segregation and injustice. In that same period, he became more political with shifting political loyalties over the years, as patron of the United Democratic Front (UDF), then with the African National Congress (ANC) and in recent years with the Congress of the People (COPE). After quitting politics, he authored a book, *Running with Horses: Reflections of an Accidental Politician,*[67] narrating his thirty years as an activist. *Pharaohs on Both Side of the Blood-Red-Waters*[68] directly addresses what our theology, spirituality, and praxis can offer in the post-apartheid context wherever there is injustice. Detailed reflections on Boesak's life, theology, philosophy, and ministry are discussed in the *Festschrift in Honour of Allan Boesak*[69] and *Prophet from the South.*[70]

His work reflects an overall South African Black Liberation Theology which sought "for the restoration and redistribution of political and economic power as a concrete expression of love and justice."[71] Through his writing and activism, Boesak finds himself among prominent African figures who have heeded Kwame Nkrumah's[72] call and Frantz Fanon's[73] decolonization agenda, pursuing an alternative way of thinking to challenge oppression. He has done so from a theological perspective. This dissertation engages, analyses, and considers Boesak's conceptual framework for social justice. As a conceptual study, it interacts with his theology which he defines as "the attempt of Black Christians to understand and interpret their situation in the light of the gospel of Jesus Christ . . . It believes that Christianity is not a 'white man's religion,' an instrument merely for the effective oppression of black people."[74]

---

66. Boesak, *Farewell to Innocence* (1977).
67. Boesak, *Running with Horses.*
68. Boesak, *Pharaohs on Both Sides.*
69. Flaendorp, Philander, and Plaatjies-Van Huffel, *Festschrift.*
70. Dibeela, Lenka-Bula, and Vellem, *Prophet from South.*
71. Copeland, "Black Political Theologies," 275.
72. Nkrumah, *Consciencism.*
73. Fanon, *Wretched of the Earth.*
74. Boesak, *Farewell to Innocence* (1977), 14.

He sees God as fair, liberating, and siding with those oppressed by unjust structures and systems. He calls for an awakening based on the philosophy of Black Consciousness (influenced by Steve Biko) and to fight all forms of injustice. Boesak follows James Cone's Black Liberation Theology searching for Black Power, which is the "complete emancipation of black people from white oppression by whatever means black people deem necessary."[75] "Black power means black freedom, black self-determination, wherein black people no longer view themselves as without human dignity but as men [sic], human beings with the ability to carve out their own destiny."[76] It is noteworthy that Boesak does not espouse Cone's call to violent revolution.

1.6.2 A Brief Survey of Relevant Work

For this introduction, we will only give a brief survey of four of Boesak's works (chapter 3 provides a more detailed survey of his work), analysing his theologies of social justice that integrate theology, politics, and social activism. These four summarize Boesak's views of social justice from his early days to recent times:

First, *Farewell to Innocence* advocates for Black Liberation Theology, Black Consciousness, and Black Power. Although a large portion of the book comprises particular quotations, it is a vital primary source of understanding Boesak's early theological, political, philosophical development of his notion of social justice. In it, he demonstrates the influences of Black Theology and power ideologies. He seeks to hold them in balance with his Reformed theological convictions, especially with the understanding of God as a liberator.[77] The book was specifically written to create an awareness of "the Black situation" and making the will of God known.[78] He says the book intended to

> help black and white people in South Africa to understand what
> it meant to live in a world forged by our "pseudo-innocence,"
> a childishness that distorts our reality and closes our eyes to
> matters we find too horrendous to contemplate, causing us to
> make a virtue out of powerlessness, weakness, and helplessness.

---

75. Cone, *Black Theology*, 73.

76. Cone, 6.

77. Boesak, *Farewell to Innocence* (1976), 20–22.

78. Boesak, 14–17.

It is an innocence that leads to a helpless utopianism – either an idealisation of the present bad situation or escapism into a "better" world than the present one. This pseudo-innocence cannot come to terms with the destructiveness in oneself or in others and hence it becomes self-destructive. It is this innocence that uses the "ideal" to blind people so that they do not see the atrocities of the present. It blinds, paralyses, and cunningly uses all means at its disposal to cover up and rationalise guilt and sin. It is an innocence that, for its own justification, does not include evil.[79]

This book is important for this research as it is perhaps Boesak's most scholarly work grappling with ideals of freedom, epistemologies of selfhood, and notions of social justice. Although he agrees with the Black Consciousness movement's philosophical framework, his primary motives for this integration are theological. He believes that this theology should strive for a fuller understanding of social realities in the light of God's revelation through Scripture.[80] He has lived to combine these two realities with the Belhar Confession principles.

Given the nature of apartheid as a political system that claimed theological legitimacy, Boesak seeks to represent resistance combining the political and theological – borrowing from both for his pursuit of social justice. This is also the nature of Black Theology as a framework – a political one.[81] In Boesak's view, theology ought to refuse any view that seeks to impose dehumanising and oppressive structures as standard, and we should resist any form of bondage and injustice, with an indiscriminate resistance towards any form of injustice regardless of persons' race or any other social identity.[82]

Boesak contends that for liberation and social justice to be realised, it needs to begin at a conceptual and relational level. First, the oppressors must acknowledge the humanity of those they oppress. Second, the oppressed need to free themselves from mental slavery and regain their personhood. This relational change should be followed by intentional removing of social,

---

79. Boesak, "Theological Reflections on Empire," 647–48.

80. Boesak, *Farewell to Innocence* (1976), 12.

81. Copeland, "Black Political Theologies," 27.

82. Boesak, *Running with Horses*, 31.

political, religious, and economic structures, systems, and institutions that helped create injustice and inequality. Advocating for the undoing of unjust structures and systems goes beyond a political analysis, and Boesak reminds us that this is fundamentally theological and moral.[83] For such structures and systems prevent the human persons, created in the image of God, from experiencing the freedom "that God originally designed the human person to manifest."[84]

Second, the book *Radical Reconciliation: Beyond Political Pietism and Christian Quietism*, co-authored with Curtiss DeYoung, takes a less academic approach but has a strong leaning towards practical participation. It is personalized, reflecting the view of an activist. It represents an unrealized moral struggle in which the formerly oppressed have continued to be devalued by the current structures, which have failed to address reconciliation at a root level. In this book, Boesak seeks a vision of "reconciliation in society that is radical, that goes to the roots"[85] and that intends to see the removal of harmful social and political structures. He engages theology and practical demands of social justice resulting from the concept of reconciliation as the beginning to ensure lasting distribution of power. Thus, he believes in creating policies and programmes that can restore human dignity.[86] He argues that "power differentials need to be reversed and then transformed into egalitarian structures,"[87] as evidence of a reconciled community.

For Boesak, in *Radical Reconciliation*, the fight against apartheid remains incomplete without active restitution to allow victims to live fully. He summarises this restitution in ten points, using Zacchaeus as an example, a story he alludes to in an early article, *And Zacchaeus Remained in the Tree: Reconciliation and Justice and the Truth and Reconciliation Commission*.[88] He believes restitution should be exhibited through the restoration of integrity, human dignity, and human contentment.[89] The Truth and Reconciliation

---

83. Boesak, *Farewell to Innocence* (1976), 9–13.

84. Bradley, *Political Economy of Liberation*, 116.

85. Boesak and DeYoung, *Radical Reconciliation*, 1.

86. Boesak and DeYoung, 8, 43, 129.

87. Boesak and DeYoung, 76–77.

88. Boesak, "And Zaccheus Remained."

89. Boesak, 640–43.

Commission (TRC), in Boesak's view, failed to attain this because it focused only on political arrangements.[90]

Third, in his book, *Kairos, Crisis and Global Apartheid*,[91] Boesak calls for alertness to discern moments of opportunity for theologians to engage in interdisciplinary theological inquiry into contemporary public issues. In this case, the focus is on a theological reflection that would affect our praxis in matters of blatant injustice. Boesak places enormous responsibility upon Christian thinkers and their role in the global context to be God's servants who proclaim what is right with biblical prophets' panache. In this book, he calls us to seize the various moments before us to reveal "the falsehoods without which an unjust status quo cannot exist"[92] – calling Christians to greater participation as agents of social change and social justice. The book is based on influences from the *Kairos Document* of 1985. It explains a need for a global "*kairos* consciousness" or what Boesak calls "an abiding awareness . . . a prophetic alertness, a readiness for [social change and justice] when such a moment might arrive."[93] It is a continuation in dealing with what Boesak refers to as *global apartheid*, or the continued presence of injustice globally. Our theological mission is not complete but is to be on the outlook for opportunities that call for our attention (which this research seeks to do).

Fourth, Boesak explores Black Liberation Theology by revisiting its relationship in representing the questions women have and are raising. His latest book, *Children of the Waters of Meribah*, seeks to reevaluate the question "What lessons has Black theology not learned as times have changed?" In this new work, he argues that Black Theology of Liberation would have offered better answers and solutions for communities and persons affected by injustice. This book discusses an array of liberation and feminist thought for positive lessons, and issues critique and suggestions or tentative answers. It expands on his earlier book, *Vlug van Gods Verbeelding*, but with a specific rereading of the Exodus narrative in a post-colonial and post-apartheid context. Boesak engages the perspective of the Miriamic prophetic tradition (including the Hebrew midwives) to represent how women are not adequately

90. Boesak, 642.
91. Boesak, *Kairos, Crisis and Global.*
92. Boesak, 10.
93. Boesak, 10.

listened to and continue to be victimized and marginalized. And he laments, in particular, Black Theology's failure in this respect as he argues that "not hearing and following the wisdom of the women, Black Theology has missed what should have been at the heart of it all for us from the very beginning. We have failed to cross the river and we have not yet fulfilled the promise of wholeness that awaits on the other side."[94] This book offers Boesak's reflection of years "of learning and un-learning, of rereading, reinterpreting, and exploring new possibilities of understanding"[95] the application of Black Liberation Theology "to real life situations of oppressed, marginalized, and exploited people."[96] He believes that ignoring feminist voices – regardless of ongoing integration programmes for women – makes these alliances artificial, like the post-apartheid reconciliation process devoid of justice. Drawing women into talks, policies, projects, and programmes does not change the continuation of their imperilment by patriarchal cultural, political, economic, and religious institutions that hinder authentic freedom, participation, integration, and social justice.[97] That is, Black Liberation Theology and the liberation struggle have not taken women's challenges as seriously as they deserve.

1.6.3 Boesak's Notions of Social Justice

Boesak's theology which uses a redemptive model of the Exodus account, seeks to be a theology relevant to real-life experiences. He links Christ's redemptive activity to those who are connected (historically) to oppression. In Boesak's view, theology's role is to address both the spiritual and the material aspects in the here and now. Using presuppositions located within a Black Theology framework, he argues that God is biased towards the poor, weak, marginalized, and oppressed. This understanding of God as just and liberating comes with consequences. Boesak's life project may be defined as searching to practice what God's redemptive work should look like. It is a practical pursuit of God's *shalom* or the good life as God intended. It is an active and dynamic project in which the church ought to participate as God's agents of redemption. He strives for a far-reaching notion of social justice, and throughout the

---

94. Boesak, *Children*, ix.
95. Boesak, 11.
96. Boesak, 11.
97. Boesak, 12, 16.

research, these will be recurring aspects. First, he agrees with those calling for the replacing of "[social, political, economic] structures of oppression with ones that are just, and [to] remove from power those who persist in defying God's laws, installing in their place leaders who will govern with justice and mercy."[98] This replacement, in Boesak's view, is without discrimination ranging from racial discrimination to LGBTQI+[99] persons. Second, he calls for a systemic "undoing of injustice and the equally systemic doing of justice, of personal and political repentance, restitution, and the restoration of human dignity."[100] He rejects all notions of reconciliation that do not carry practical implications and holds that such an approach is not sustainable overall.

Third, he advocates for creating conditions to restore hope, dignity, and wholeness in the here and now. He refers to this as "stand[ing] up for the things of the earth" which are among others "justice, hope, dignity, redemption, wholeness."[101] For Boesak, political activism is essential and critical to bringing about the above notions of justice. It hinges on pursuing tangible outcomes of equitable material, economic, political, social and relational reforms, as captured in his *The Tenderness of Conscience*. Although Boesak's advocacy for social justice is overwhelming, his theological notions of justice need to be explored to locate what could be helpful in the search for a theology of social justice in post-apartheid Namibia. Chapters 3 and 4 offer an outline, exposition, analysis, and application of Boesak's selected works and notions (identifying gaps and how his work could be helpful or not helpful in rethinking the concept of social justice for post-apartheid Namibia).

We shall discuss these aspects in greater detail in chapters 3 and 4. This overview has served to show why Boesak's theological contribution could have great value for a theological discussion on social justice for the post-apartheid Namibian context.

---

98. Boesak, *When Prayer Makes News*, 26.

99. A cluster abbreviation that stands for Lesbian, Gay, Bisexual, Transgender and Intersex.

100. Boesak, "And Zaccheus Remained," 643–53; Boesak and DeYoung, *Radical Reconciliation*, 55–61.

101. Boesak, *Dare We Speak?*, 28.

1.7 Research Questions

1.7.1 Primary Question

What can a contextualized engagement with Allan Boesak's theologies of justice provide for a theology of social justice in the post-apartheid Namibian context?

1.7.2 Secondary Questions

We will explore the primary question by considering the following secondary questions:

1. How just or unjust is the Namibian society in its current post-apartheid state?
2. How does Allan Boesak engage notions of social justice in his theological work?
3. What are the notions of social justice being employed to address the Namibian context? In what ways are they helpful, and in what ways are they inadequate?
4. In what ways could Allan Boesak's theologies of justice be built upon to serve theologies of social justice more effectively for the Namibian context?

1.8 Significance of the Study

This research is significant because: First, despite the increase in theological scholarship about social justice issues in the post-apartheid contexts, the studies that engage the complexities of the Namibian construction of social justice in the Namibian experience are limited in number. Added to that challenge is the relative withdrawal of theology from the public arena since Namibian independence. For example, there have been no significant theological works seeking social justice in Namibia with the language and vigour of the *Open Letter to His Honour the Prime Minister of South Africa* of 30 June 1971. This research foregrounds the importance of a contextualized conceptualization of the notion of social justice from a theological perspective. It explores this line of thought by dialoguing with Allan Boesak's Black Theology of Liberation, and in particular, his understanding of justice – to lay part of the groundwork for developing post-apartheid Namibian theologies of social justice. The search for justice is not a new subject, but we seek to offer a new way of thinking regarding social justice issues from a theological perspective for Namibia.

Second, this research is unique in its conversation with Allan Boesak for the Namibian context. His work has not been adequately considered or explored for academic dialogue (in Namibia) to provoke our approach to the ongoing public discourse of social justice. It takes theology out of the private domain where it is currently largely confined, to become engaged in public concerns. This engagement with Boesak and the question we seek to answer is part of the overall understanding of a search to witness to God's kingdom as we interrogate the theological and ethical basis of present social structures and systems that affect the lives of God's image-bearers.

1.9 Objective

The research aims to discover how a contextualized conceptualization of the understanding of social justice, in conversation with Allan Boesak's theologies of justice, could establish a thicker and more contextual theological approach to addressing post-apartheid injustice in Namibia.

1.10 Research Methodology

This project is one of conceptual research within the broader field of systematic theology and Christian ethics, influenced by public theological perspectives. According to Kothari, a "conceptual research is that related to some abstract idea(s) or theory. It is generally used by philosophers and thinkers to develop new concepts or to reinterpret existing ones."[102] Thus, a conceptual research facilitates a comprehensive examination and analysis of abstract concepts, such as social justice, by exploring its understanding, framing, and application contexts. It is particularly advantageous for developing a more nuanced and informed perspective. Each chapter of this research outlines, critiques, or emphasises the historical, political, and social context necessary for creating an authentic Namibian discourse. This reemphasis provides a means of engaging with social justice epistemologies and also how

---

102. Kothari, *Research Methodology*, 4.

to construct a theology of justice, as well as the answers that need to guide the recommended praxis.

The research uses literature analysis to examine the value of contextualization of concepts to develop theological notions of social justice for post-apartheid Namibia. We choose this approach, as Dalferth maintains, to clarify conceptual problems "by exploring possibilities, elucidating conceptual options, and testing the coherence of views and positions in the area under discussion by . . . analysis and argumentation . . . and it tackles them against the background of the sciences and the culture of the day."[103] The research seeks to clarify how the concept of justice needs to acquire meaning, in the context of post-apartheid, to allow for social, legal, and political structures to respond accurately to the needs of society.

This integrated critical analytical method engages Boesak's work with intentionality, objectivity, and careful attendance to his main thoughts, arguments, and proposals. Although there will be extensive interaction with the writings of Allan Boesak, it is not an exhaustive study of every publication, rather it presents a specific engagement with his theological notions of social justice. The focus is theological, to help us establish our limits regarding the complex nature of social justice and to remain theological even while interacting with nontheological conceptions. In chapters 4 and 5, we draw upon other theologians for their theological, philosophical, and political notions and as theological voices demonstrating various perspectives of engaging the subject of social justice.

As a conceptual research, it provides an attentive enquiry of interaction between faith and public life and how theologians and the Christian community can take part in God's redemptive work in the world, through careful listening, discerning, advocating, and acting (within a context). It scrutinises the public language and how theology can become part of these dialogues to participate in the transformation of the social order. Here, we seek to know God's truth in post-apartheid Namibia to establish a meaningful discussion concerning social justice. It is an enquiry of faith in social justice matters, a strenuous activity but part of witnessing to God's truth amidst persistent injustice. It understands that the "Christian faith prompts inquiry, searches

---

103. Dalferth, "Philosophical Theology," 305.

for deeper understanding, dares to raise questions."[104] In this case, it should do so by meticulously exploring and taking part in the theories of knowledge that inform society, especially when these theories have lasting effects on the dignity of both humans and nonhuman creation. This research perceives honest questions and examines concepts as integral components of theology to participate as God's witness in public matters of social justice. It asks questions aimed at providing answers, even if they are tentative, which are motivated by authentic faith. Migliore explains such faith as follows,

> Authentic faith is no sedative for world-weary souls, no satchel full of ready answers to the deepest questions of life. Instead, faith in God revealed in Jesus Christ sets an inquiry in motion, fights the inclination to accept things as they are, and continually calls into question unexamined assumptions about God, our world, and ourselves. Consequently, Christian faith has nothing in common with indifference to the search for truth, or fear of it, or the arrogant claim to possess it fully. True faith must be distinguished from fideism. Fideism says there comes a point where we must stop asking questions and must simply believe; faith keeps on seeking and asking.[105]

We will dialogue with many other Namibian voices who are also concerned with the question of social justice.[106] These dialogues spread across the spectrum of Black liberationist, Black Liberation Theology, distributivist, reparationist, feminist, affirmative action, and the nationalist-socialist paradigms. Boesak's work extends across these perspectives and should be evaluated within a cluster of ideas that many local thinkers engage. As part of witnessing to the truth of God, we do not dismiss other avenues where this truth may be present to assist us in developing a more nuanced understanding of what we seek to achieve through this project.

---

104. Migliore, *Faith Seeking Understanding*, 25.

105. Migliore, 26.

106. Akawa, *Gender Politics*; Diescho, "Concepts of Rights"; Horn, "Churches and Political Reconciliation"; Kaapama, "Commercial Land Reforms" ; Kameeta, *Towards Liberation*; Katjavivi, *History of Resistance*; Lombard, "Detainee Issue"; Melber, *Understanding Namibia*; Silvester and Gewald, *Words Cannot Be Found*.

The dialogue seeks to add value to life in the Namibian context by providing theological insights. We will use the analytical method[107] to explore the theories, structures, and systems adopted to address social injustice. The end goal is to provide a critical reflection on various constituents of analysis and develop theological means to present an authentic alternative perspective for addressing post-apartheid social injustice. There is no standalone methodology chapter; instead, the methodology is demonstrated throughout the research as the researcher interacts with the various materials, concepts, and views of social justice to reach the recommendations and conclusion. This approach is intentional and integrates the methodology into the structure of the thesis, with each chapter showing how the integration is carried out. It is not an uncommon approach in the field of systematic theology, as long as there is a focus on drawing out multifarious implications and the researcher is able to navigate the dialogue to reach plausible conclusions.

1.11 Outline of the Research

Chapter 1: This chapter serves as a general introduction of the subject, outlining the problem, essential questions, objective, and methodology. It also gives a brief background about the critical conversation partner and some of his significant works. It sets out the dissertation's core and how the rest of the chapters are structured to answer the questions raised here through critical analysis and provide an overall synthesis.

Chapter 2: This chapter serves as a literary analysis of the various conceptual, rational, and theological assessments of social justice. It also explores how just or unjust the Namibian society is in the post-apartheid state. The chapter provides the content of previous Namibian discussions that have dealt with notions of social justice – through careful engagement with selected works. Through these discussions, we locate the research gap to provide a theological motivation for public engagement in Namibia's search for social justice.

Chapter 3: This chapter provides: (1) a survey of Allan Boesak's work, notions, and meaning of social justice; and (2) an engagement with a subset of his ideas and concepts, for example, Black Theology and Black Power

---

107. Kothari, *Research Methodology*, 3.

paradigms, and whether, from the perspective of the researcher, these views could create a meaningful discourse of recovering a society's self-understanding, aspirations, selfhood, and construct a relevant and adequate narrative to deal with injustice. The aim is to locate Boesak's views within the historical, practical, social, political context, and highlight their validity in addressing the post-apartheid South African context of social justice.

Chapter 4: This chapter facilitates a critical contextual dialogue with Allan Boesak's theological notions of social justice. It explores how Boesak's views could be helpful or may need to be developed or reconsidered in the search to construct Namibian theologies of social justice for public dialogue. The chapter follows an exposition, analysis, and application methods of selected key themes (Black Theology of Liberation, Black Power and Consciousness, reconciliation, and restitution) in Boesak's work. It also provides material to explore the Namibian notions of social justice for chapter 5.

Chapter 5: This chapter explores the discourse of social justice in the Namibian context. It touches on reconciliation, systems of justice, theological participation in the public square, and contextualization. It argues that while universal theories and frameworks of social justice have many helpful elements, we should not assimilate them without a careful contextual analysis. This chapter also explores how a contextually relevant understanding of social justice restores dignity, selfhood, and sociocultural progress.

Chapter 6: This chapter revisits the primary problem, draws conclusions, maps the way forward and suggests the future discourse beyond this research.

1.12 Summary

The present chapter introduced the theoretical framework, problem statement, motivation, research questions, and the methodology of the research. It also provided a preliminary overview of Allan Boesak's work and the key concepts, setting the expectation of what will be discussed in the subsequent chapters (3, 4 and 5). The next chapter presents a literature analysis of social justice and injustice in Namibia in its post-apartheid state and locates the research gap for the study.

CHAPTER 2

Literature Analysis of Contextualization, Epistemology, and Conceptualization of Social Justice in the Namibian Context

2.1 Introduction

This chapter provides a critical analysis of various conceptual assessments of social justice by looking at the available documentary data. It answers the question: *How just or unjust is the Namibian society in its current post-apartheid state?* We engage with scholarly works and public policy documents and programmes to outline how just or unjust the post-independence Namibian society is. Through this, we would like to locate the research gap that would provide the raw material to construct a contextual assessment valid for Namibia. The chapter also provides the needed conceptual framework for the subsequent chapters. It is the source for creating an informed critical discourse in line with Namibian history and experiences.[1]

The chapter engages the critical-dialogical method to engage various views informing our modern understandings of social justice. Although justice is an

---

1. Important to this section of the study is the task to uncover Namibian resources which are often not readily available to the public and create awareness of their existence. Finding resources in Namibia is difficult, due to an extremely low writing culture, yet it is possible if one looks in the right places and asks the right persons.

ancient and widely discussed subject, it remains dynamic in its manifestations. It needs to find a distinctive shape(s) as it pertains to Namibian experiences. In the search to formulate theologies of social justice, we need to question the existing notions of justice. This research does not make claims to invent a new theological method. It is a contextual theological critical engagement with the conceptual structures that inform post-apartheid Namibian understandings of social justice. The aim is not to attain a single-dimension or an ultra-vision of social justice. Instead, (1) we seek to generate an authentic and more free-ing conceptualization and contextualization of the social justice processes; (2) we seek the full realization of independence to have positive effects on God's image-bearers to attain social justice and restoration of dignity, and (3) we call for a theological engagement in public regarding structures and systems to develop a moral voice for reconciliation and social justice.

Rawls, in *A Theory of Justice*, assumes universal justice as the first virtue of social institutions. It could suggest that societies that lack a self-generated conception of social justice may not advance to have an efficient sociopolitical life. Societies are dynamic, and so is the concept of social justice. Globally, post-colonial societies are engaged in the search for self-definition; this in-cludes redefining social justice so that its processes are reflective of their historical, social, and political experiences. There is a growing refusal to view social truth as universally unvaried but as something "shaped, determined and even validated by specific cultural, social and political contexts."[2] This global movement occurs under various ideological themes (for example, affirmative action, decoloniality, indigenization, nationalism, and Black Consciousness movements), aligned to poststructuralist interpretations of social justice. Where does Namibia find itself as a young post-conflict society to address the effects of injustice?

2.1.1 Mapping and Describing the Concept of Justice

The plethora of academic writings on the concept and conceptions of social justice[3] show the human desire to define just acts or situations and just soci-

---

2. Rawls, *Theory of Justice*, 1.

3. Boesak, *Farewell to Innocence* (1976); Burke, *Concept of Justice*; Deneulin, Nebel, and Sagovsky, *Transforming Unjust Structures*; Fleischacker, *Short History of Distributive Justice*; Gready, *Era of Transitional Justice*; Johnston, *Brief History of Justice*; MacIntyre, *Whose Justice?*; Maluleke, "Justice in Post-Apartheid"; Sagovsky, *Christian Tradition*; Sen, *Idea of Justice*.

eties, institutions, laws or penalties. This agreement in the universal principle of justice creates occasion and opportunity for Namibians to explore and grapple with their context, in this case, with the context of post-independence and the lingering effects of apartheid.

Before the popular rise of Greek philosophy, the land of the Fertile Crescent already spoke of justice, even social justice. Their records show the ancients' preoccupation with justice. It centred, as in the Code of Hammurabi or the Babylonian Law, on "retribution, and in some cases unbridled vengeance."[4] They "uniformly embrace stark hierarchies of power, status, and wealth as embodiments of a just political and social order."[5] This hierarchical approach to justice is also seen in the works of the Greek philosophers, for example, in Plato's *Republic* and Aristotle's *Ethics* and *Politics*.

Most, if not all, of our modern understandings of justice, derive from Greek philosophy.[6] Records show that it started in Homer (in the *Iliad*, although in shadowy form) and became more substantiated in Plato.[7] These views served as the raw materials in constructing conceptions of justice, which were later conveyed across the world through colonialism. The apartheid system was a residue subsystem of colonialism that extended into the post-colonial era. Justice under apartheid meant the protection and advancement of the White African interest (including legal status, property rights, and economic conditions) at the expense of disadvantaging Black Africans. Justice meant a systematic distribution of society's goods to the advantage of the White African, trickling intentional structures of disadvantage to all who did not belong to the "acceptable" racial classification. This racial discrimination also embraced a reinterpreted ethical framework – to justify brutal authoritarianism, economic corruption, and racial violence to deter anyone from interposing and unsettling the established convention structure.

---

4. Johnston, *Brief History of Justice*, 15.

5. Johnston, 15.

6. Since the beginning of recorded history, most Greek thinkers who have written about justice have applied the concept only to relations among persons who share a common political or cultural identity. This understanding of justice dehumanised all who did not fit the category of desirable equals and gave birth to political sanctions, policies, laws, and programmes which created structures and systems of injustice; apartheid develops from this kind of theoretical framework, combined with a theological justification.

7. De Gruchy, *Christianity and Democracy*, 15–39; MacIntyre, *Whose Justice?*, 12–87; Macintyre et al., *Greek Concept of Justice*; Sagovsky, *Christian Tradition*, 1–27.

Thus, perpetuating an injustice to bring about the good of one's people was construed as justice. It was devising unjust laws[8] as the basis for law, justice, and social order.

With this background, the post-apartheid Namibian context grapples with establishing just means to rectify the harm inherited from the unjust practices of the apartheid era. To that end, the Namibian government, academics, theologians, and activists continue to explore different systems and approaches to process these concepts to their advantage. This chapter seeks to present these various views within the broader arrangement of the post-apartheid context.

2.2 Public Conceptions of Social Justice

These are not the only popular views but are among the most appealed to as measures to bring about social justice in a post-apartheid context. It is also not the aim of the research to examine and engage every conception of social justice. The views selected are based on their discussion in the Namibian post-apartheid context. These conceptions or approaches of social justice seek to provide a normative point of departure to construct just processes and means for Namibia. Altogether they focus on rights-based and egalitarian terms, lessen social burdens to improve privileges and attempt to effect distributive values by creating or establishing just "compensation criteria and the design and transformation of social structures and institutions."[9]

2.2.1 (Re)distribution and Restoration as Justice

2.2.1.1 (Re)distribution

Distributive justice is perhaps the most popular of all conceptions of justice adopted to address the effects of apartheid. This view is concerned with a collectively just apportionment of various commodities in society. The underlying principle is to ensure an apparent reduction of incidental inequalities, focusing on (re)allocation of economic goods and their distribution

---

8. This is in reference to Thomas Aquinas's view that any law that "deviates from reason . . . and has not the nature of law but violence" (I–II. Q. 93, Art. 3) and is "for the most part, contrary to the natural light" (II–II, Q. 60, Art. 5).

9. Pereira, *Elements of Critical Theory*, 81.

to society's members. Determining the kinds of goods and processes to be covered and who benefit from their distribution remains a daunting task.

The post-apartheid Namibian state has embarked on designing and implementing policies that would bring about a fairer reallocation of wealth, income, and resources to lessen economic inequality. In this case, social justice principally focuses on socioeconomic reformation, focusing on addressing poverty levels, unemployment, and general social protection. The Government of the Republic of Namibia (GRN) aims to realise this through affirmative action, here defined as "a set of measures designed to ensure that persons[10] in designated groups enjoy equal . . . opportunities at all levels . . . and are equitably represented."[11] The concept has been extended to admission to higher education, employment, awarding of government tenders, and application for state grants as a way of facilitating the envisaged (re)distribution of opportunities to persons and groups who were previously disadvantaged. Thus, the concept of distribution encompasses giving preferential treatment, in education and employment, as a means of just redress for the past conditions of oppression.

The Namibian concept of affirmative action is rooted in the Civil Rights Movement of the 1950s and 1960s in the United States of America. This movement opposed racial inequality through mass action in demonstrations, civil disobedience, and boycotts. The decision to have programmes aimed at "giving [certain] members . . . preferential treatment in employment and education" came from the authorities – referred to as affirmative action. Van Rooyen assumes that the concept of affirmative action is no longer foreign to the Namibian context because "we stand at the threshold of the implementation of a comprehensive statutory affirmative action programme throughout the country."[12] However, he cites the potential pitfalls of affirmative action, especially the political and psychological impact on people's relationships.

The argument put forward for the Namibian version of affirmative action is that this would reverse the effects of the apartheid system, which violated

---

10. Referring specifically to "racially disadvantaged persons, women and persons with disabilities," Government of the Republic of Namibia, "Affirmative Action (Employment) Act of 1998," 13.

11. Government of the Republic of Namibia, 18.

12. Van Rooyen, *Implementing Affirmative Action*.

"the principles of natural justice and fairness."[13] Although the Affirmative Action Act of 1998 hardly refers to justice, we assume it focuses on the historical context of apartheid and colonialism. This act does not delineate its basis for this approach toward social justice, except that it seeks to ensure equitable and inclusive consideration for all citizens. To achieve this policy's said objectives, the GRN organized several consultations with unions and employers before presenting it as a national operational guideline.

In 2016, the GRN embarked on having a more robust nationwide policy intentionally to correct the targeted socioeconomic effects of apartheid and colonialism. Thus, the early Affirmative Action Act of 1998 needs a far-reaching framework to ensure "an equitable and socially just society in which the distribution of income becomes far more equitable than it is at present."[14] This redesigned policy framework is to implement the GRN's plan to ensure security, economic prosperity, and "a life of human dignity for all Namibians."[15] This framework is called the New Equitable Economic Empowerment Framework (NEEEF).

With the assumption that the effects of apartheid continue to affect those who were previously systematically disadvantaged, NEEEF would serve as a driving force calculated to address unemployment, poverty, and inequality. NEEEF is technically a replica of the South African Black Economic Empowerment (BEE) founded in 2003, initially designed to motivate the private business sector "to become more equitable and to make a greater contribution towards national economic empowerment and transformation."[16] The programme faced a huge public outcry, accusing it of coercing White business owners to sell shares to Black Namibians. The Institute for Public Policy Research (IPPR) criticized the policy as one with the potential to transfer wealth to already well-off individuals.[17] It also suggests that NEEEF will further corruption, peddling, and the economic elevation of a politically connected elite.

---

13. Government of the Republic of Namibia, "Affirmative Action (Employment) Act of 1998," 24.

14. Government of the Republic of Namibia, "The New Equitable Economic Empowerment Framework (NEEEF)," 5.

15. Government of the Republic of Namibia, 5.

16. Government of the Republic of Namibia, 6.

17. Institute for Public Policy Research, "Comment on National Equitable," 4.

In response to fighting increasing poverty levels, which have remained virtually unchanged for many Black Namibians, President Hage G. Geingob established the Ministry of Poverty Eradication and Social Welfare (now defunct). In 2016, under Zephaniah Kameeta (former Bishop of the Evangelical Lutheran Church in the Republic of Namibia, ELCRIN), the ministry framed what it called the *Blue Print on Wealth Redistribution and Poverty Eradication.* The document contains a brief paragraph that links social justice to the lingering effects of colonialism and apartheid. It describes the situation as one in which "poverty and inequality have been deep-rooted and structured in such a way that the division between poor and nonpoor or disadvantaged and advantaged is evident in all social and economic spheres . . . Unless these are addressed and resolved, people will have no hope for a better future."[18]

The above analysis serves as a description of the unequal distribution of resources, resulting in rampant poverty levels. In response to this inequality, *Blue Print* provides measures to address the socioeconomic situation as analysed in Section III.[19] The focus is on creating social safety nets through wealth and resource (re)distribution. It is not clear how the *Blue Print on Wealth Redistribution and Poverty Eradication, National Development Plan* (NDP, in its divergent phases), *Vision 2030, Poverty Reduction Strategy for Namibia, Harambee Prosperity Plan* (HPP),[20] and *UN Sustainable Development Goals* (SDGs) differ from each other. All these documents repeat the same ideas, concepts, and strategies as far as policy formation is concerned. It needs to be questioned whether they are replicas or multiperspectival approaches to addressing the socioeconomic conditions.

In summation, (re)distribution is envisioned as what will bring inclusive economic growth, improve social conditions, right the historical wrongs,

---

18. Ministry of Poverty Eradication and Social Welfare, "Blue Print on Wealth Redistribution," 12.

19. Ministry of Poverty Eradication and Social Welfare, 27–45.

20. Immanuel and Iikela, "Harambee Fails Economy." A second version of this programme was launched in 2021, named HPP II. This is despite the early version being declared a failure by public critics and the president admitting that it was over ambitious. The programme has not attained most of its goals in the first five years of Hage Geingob's presidential term, except that it became a political *mantra* or concept for accessing government funding and tenders. Shinovene and Iikela's report indicate how out of 92 targets, 54 (58.69%) were not attained, mostly the economic ones. Regardless of this failure, the GRN invested resources costing millions of dollars to relaunch the same programme, the only difference being in the wording.

and achieve sustainable social justice. The concept of (re)distribution comes with immense complexities in implementation and questions. Part of these complexities include whether the state's ability in directing the administration of social justice through affirmative action can influence new perceptions of the environment of the current social order. Furthermore, it also involves whether the (re)distributive paradigm can effectively redress the condition in which the advantaged group exploits prospects that are supposed to cater to the disadvantaged.

2.2.1.2 Restoration

The transition from a racist system with profound effects on society – even after it has been abrogated – is a process ridden with daunting choices in deciding just measures. This difficulty is evident in the emphasis on the (re) distribution of public goods (see above) as a just means for a more equitable share of resources, as not everyone agrees with that notion. To complement, or even search to replace redistributive justice, some advocate for restorative justice.[21] Albeit there is no uniform description or definition of restorative justice, its underlying conception is to heal the wrongs of the past. It seeks offenders to take responsibility through restitution, making amends and restoring the offended or broken community's dignity. This understanding has been the basis for forming the South African TRC. The process is also accused of being deeply based on Christian principles,[22] while Schoeman argues that restorative justice is deeply entrenched in African cultural conceptions of justice found in the notion of *ubuntu*.[23] The Namibian conception of restorative justice seems to centre around material restitution, although some views emphasise relational restoration. Below are various expressions of restorative justice in Namibia.

First, Joseph Diescho sees restorative justice as the best form of justice that the entire African continent must adopt to address "her unjust experiences before and after colonialism."[24] Being an anti-apartheid icon and an advocate for social justice, he applies the same thinking to address the effects of

---

21. Kößler, "Public Memory, Reconciliation"; Niitenge, "Evangelical Lutheran Church."
22. Verdoolaege, *Reconciliation Discourse*, 28.
23. Schoeman, "African Concept of Ubuntu," 291–92.
24. Diescho, "Concepts of Rights," 28.

apartheid. He sees this as a form of justice that needs "cooperative processes that include all stakeholders" to effect the desired outcomes.[25] Thus, he recommends vigorous and deliberately coordinated policies and processes to restore justice towards people previously dispossessed of their fundamental rights by an oppressive system. His concept of restoration appears to be the same as that of the South African TRC. He hopes that as communities heal and recognize each other's humanity, they would devise their power and economic distribution processes.

According to Tötemeyer in *Church and State in Namibia: Politics of Reconciliation*, this approach is also known for removing state interference and grounding the process of social justice in the communities' hands. An offence, in this case, extends beyond law breaking to something that affects and harms people, their communities, and relationships. Such harm would require radical measures to redress. He also argues that it is the kind of redress that seeks to address the needs of victims, perpetrators, and communities to meet and refashion their solutions.[26] Thus, Johnstone and Van Ness argue that "the people most affected by the problem," not the state, should "decide among themselves how it should be dealt with"[27] and Diescho argues for constitutional reform.[28] He holds that for social justice to have a meaningful and sustainable effect requires functional constitutions. Not that constitutions would accomplish any change, but African states need guidance for political, moral, and cultural realignment to protect their citizens' rights. He concludes that it is the role of the state to "grapple with making life more meaningful and better for all, to the extent that every person expects to be treated with dignity and respect – as s/he is expected to treat others, in a milieu that is transparent and equitable."[29]

Some sections of the *Blue Print on Wealth Redistribution and Poverty Eradication* refer four times to this as a way of restoration. It frames restoration in the language of the South African TRC Act 3, which reads to "restore the human and civil dignity of such victims by granting them an opportunity

---

25. Diescho, 29.
26. Tötemeyer, *Church and State*, 36–38.
27. Johnstone and Van Ness, *Handbook of Restorative Justice*, xxi.
28. Diescho, "Concepts of Rights," 28.
29. Johnston, *Brief History of Justice*, 32.

to relate their own accounts of the violations of which they are the victims."[30] It is challenging to derive what it means since it speaks of restoration in vague and undefined terms. In this case, the Namibian conception links it to wealth (re)distribution. While this understanding of restorative justice seems to be commonly accepted, it seems only for pragmatic political reasons. The South African TRC engaged this method and has been criticized for ignoring "political and economic realities for the sake of political acceptance in the international community."[31] Thus, it has failed to realize that apartheid aimed to ensure that society remained unjust – structurally enforced. Focusing on individual perpetrators and victims denies ensuring "systematic reform of society as a whole."[32] This criticism leads to the restitutive view of restorative justice.

The second conception of restorative justice in Namibia concentrates on material restitution, especially of land.[33] It broadly borrows from Marxist dialectical materialism. Thus, material restitution would eventually give birth to the immaterial values of reconciliation, unity, and healing (ideal virtues). Given the division of society along structures caused by socioeconomic inequality, justice would imply undoing or significantly reducing these structures' effects. With this view of restoration in mind, neorevolutionary groups such as the Landless People's Movement (LPM) and the Affirmative Repositioning (AR) movement (ideological equivalents of the South African Economic Freedom Fighters (EFF) political party) are calling for restitution in the form of land and business shares for those who were previously deprived of them by an unjust system. Advocates of this perspective still "hold to the idea that Namibia would do better to . . . adopt socialist policies."[34] Conversely, Saunders, in response to those who claim to be socialists, says that they appeal to selective, opportunistic, and pragmatic tactics with no evidence of commitment to socialist principles unless it is convenient for their agenda.[35]

---

30. Ministry of Poverty Eradication and Social Welfare, "Blue Print on Wealth Redistribution," 11, 14, 14, 30.

31. Boesak, "And Zaccheus Remained," 641.

32. Boesak, 641.

33. Melber, "Colonialism, Land, Ethnicity," 80–81.

34. Melber, *Re-Examining Liberation in Namibia*, 197.

35. Saunders, "Liberation and Democracy," 97.

Neorevolutionaries think the constitution protects the interests of the wealthy class (consisting of perpetrators and beneficiaries of the apartheid system). For example, chapter 3 of the Namibian constitution speaks of various human rights and freedoms, including the right to private property ownership (Article 16). Lamentably, it does not address property rights in the historical context. It is silent on forceful and illegal expropriation of land and livestock or violent and fraudulent measures under colonialism and apartheid. Land continues to serve as a constant reminder of injustice; addressing it is extremely slow, and the politically connected stand to benefit the most. It means the state must use forceful expropriation without compensation, as various restorationists suggest. Expropriation of property without compensation is illegal and a constitutional violation.[36] Expropriation could also have profound local and international implications such as a breakdown in social relations, political instability, sanctions, and breaking ties with more significant donor and trade partners. The constitution advocates (indiscriminately) for a Lockean conception of property protection, but this right does not protect victims of apartheid and colonial violence.

Moreover, the restorationists think of the current arrangement of expropriation with compensation, willing-buyer-willing-seller, and government resettlements as expensive and time-consuming. They also believe that these procedures prolong the effects of injustice, which continue to disadvantage people, creating a vulnerable situation due to legislative shortcomings. This scepticism stems from the view that the government processes to deal with the social-economic inequities have been abandoned for a post-apartheid narrative of legitimising its stay in power.[37] With this new elitism, the former liberation movement abandoned its ideals favouring structures and strategies that favour the new elite. Thus, to keep in line with these liberation movement concepts, much more radical and swift measures are thought to be needed to guarantee that social justice is done to redress the wrongs of apartheid.[38]

Restorative justice implies dealing with both the victims and offenders' hurts and needs. Restitution is an outward and material manifestation of restoration. That is, those who have been victims of the apartheid system's unjust

---

36. Fuller, "Namibian Path for Land," 83.
37. Du Pisani, "State and Society," 1–6.
38. Vries, "SWAPO Pays Lip Service."

practices cannot merely accept social restoration. Apology and reconciliation ought to include specific measures of restitution. In a country with abysmal wedges of economic disparities caused by a history of injustice, Dickey argues that we cannot overlook the importance of restitution as a critical aspect of restoration.[39] It must note that pursuing restitution requires careful rethinking and systems to safeguard it against elitist exploitation. Without public trust in our public institutions, whatever alternatives to redress injustice will not trickle down to those who need it the most. This violence would have us ask, as Boesak does regarding the Black majority governments as to whether they "sufficiently understood the nature of power, and sufficiently engaged the possibilities of creating a power dynamic entirely different than the kind of power they were struggling against, a use of power that would be geared toward a humanizing struggle and as a result, a humanizing future."[40]

Namibia continues to be one of the most socioeconomically unequal societies, with no prospect that the poor and vulnerable among us would experience social justice. Melber, in "Namibia's Long-standing Land Issue Remains Unresolved," argues that without a wilful demand for restoration through restitution, both capital and production will continue to be in the hands of the previously advantaged White Africans and their descendants.[41] Kößler also argues that although this is a growing and critical demand, we should not be naive to think it to be a "straightforward affair." He appeals for a careful examination as "issues of restitution and material reparation clearly go beyond a general recognition of past wrong and suffering. They highlight the vital question of the subjects of memory as well as of claims based on the past."[42]

Thus, if restitution must be fundamental to socioeconomic transformation, it needs systematic safeguarding against using political and public office to cash in on the nation's resources. It should extend beyond mere material demands to compensation for the nonmaterial values (culture, identity) destroyed through the crime of apartheid, which means that restitution should

---

39. Dickey, "Forgiveness and Crime," 107.

40. Boesak, *Pharaohs on Both Sides*, 2–3.

41. Henning Melber, "Namibia's Long Standing Land Issue Remains," *The Conversation*, https://theconversation.com/namibias-long-standing-land-issue-remains-unresolved-105301.

42. Kößler, "Public Memory, Reconciliation," 103.

ask the human question and not just the economic quest. Kaapama contends that a mere focus on material restitution would only entrench the present post-liberationist entitlement culture. He believes that social and material restoration is the way towards a holistic redressing of past injustice.[43]

2.2.2 Political Power and Social Justice

The liberation struggle[44] was to get independence from the illegal South African White minority rule over Namibia. As ideas of Marxist-socialism and nationalism emerged from African nationalism of the 1950s and 1960s, Namibia was not spared.[45] The aim was liberation from an oppressive rule with the intention of self-governance.

Katjavivi narrates that after failed negotiations of 1962 for a political process, SWAPO formed a military wing, the People's Liberation Army of Namibia (PLAN).[46] This decision was for an armed struggle for self-rule, independence, and social liberation – with an understanding of justice based on a profoundly communist-socialist philosophy. Under the leadership of Andimba Toivo Ya Toivo, SWAPO resolved to take up arms as a last resort to force the apartheid regime to relinquish its illegal occupation and rule.[47] After twenty-three years of war and a negotiated settlement, Namibia gained independence from South Africa in 1990. Paving the way for a majority rule system, "SWAPO (was) reconstituted as a political party composing the government."[48] This reconstitution was a fundamental sociopolitical change; Melber echoes that,

> the spectre of prolonged civil war and the need to keep the econ-
> omies running prompted policies of compromise. This came

---

43. Kaapama, "Commercial Land Reforms," 140, 143.

44. The researcher would like to make it clear that this study does not promote the idea of liberation-centred history as presently propagated by many contemporary Namibian historians. The history of Namibia as a country is much deeper and richer than the armed struggle that began in the 1960s against the South African illegal occupation. However, since the research is focused on a particular perspective of history (apartheid and post-apartheid), the reference to the liberation struggle is limited to only this rather than as an indiscriminate descriptor of Namibian history.

45. Katjavivi, *History of Resistance*, 41.

46. Katjavivi, 59.

47. Katjavivi, 58–60.

48. Melber, "From Controlled Change," 134.

also as a result of pressure exercised by international actors on both the colonial powers and the liberation movements. Hence the transition to independence negotiated and implemented for Namibia under the initiative of the United Nations was a process of controlled change, which finally resulted in changed control.[49]

These changes created new control of the state structures. But it did not affect much of the structural and psychological effects of the apartheid system. For example, the settlements resulted in the drafting of a new constitution that grants various liberties and promotes a political ideal of equality for all citizens. Thus, the formation of a consolidated democracy granted liberties previously denied to Black people under the apartheid rule. This political equality granted through the constitution seems to be taken as justice, especially that it is under the guardianship of the Black majority.

While there is a constitutional guarantee of liberty and equality, SWAPO's compromize and agreement with the apartheid government needs rigorous interrogation. The evidence of the change in power needs reciprocal measures to create structures to transform society's socioeconomic milieu. Unfortunately, SWAPO's project to ensure the social transformation is rigged with neoliberal economics. Thus, the political structure now caters for an elite-driven environment, and under the banner of national reconciliation, it treads around social justice cautiously. Bond argues that Namibia inherited structures that were difficult to manage and complex to understand (because of their historical developments).[50] It is especially proven when it came to transforming economic imbalances and creating functional systems for equitable socioeconomic justice. In Bond's view, regardless of these conceptual impediments, Namibian policymakers have settled for replacement politics of embracing policies and practices that potentially worsen rather than rectify apartheid's socioeconomic effects.

Political equality is not congruent to justice, given the cap of silence on socioeconomic issues, sealed by the Bill of Fundamental Human Rights of the constitution. The gap between political equality granted by political instruments is yet to translate into affecting avenues that would cause social justice. Like its counterpart, South Africa, Namibia had to settle for a deal for

---

49. Melber, 134.
50. Bond, *Elite Transition*, 15.

independence that has not defined social justice or its measures in line with the context of its history and experiences. Eventually, this raises questions regarding the sustainability of such a political achievement.

The overwhelming political outlook favours socialist structures to deal with the socioeconomic imbalances, notwithstanding having opted for a neoliberal economy (referred to as a mixed economy) at independence. Thus, the desire to see socioeconomic transformation seems to conflict with the context of a democratic state that favours free-market enterprise. Amukugo critiques this arrangement, primarily liberal democracy's "incapacity to seriously consider and tackle the issue of social equity. In essence, this thought gives the concept [of] democracy a social dimension and stresses both the need and possibility of finding an alternative to liberal democracy."[51]

Politicians continue to battle for the creation, expansion, and strengthening of structures for formal justice. The extent to which these structures exist to ensure access to resources to effect socioeconomic changes inspires little public confidence. Melber notes that although the Namibian government has been eager to devise policies and programmes for social justice, "little has been recorded in terms of monitoring achievement."[52] Thus, the paperwork, policies, assessments, planning, and strategising fail to translate into measurable outcomes. He thinks that this failure is compounded by "a lack of any coherent development strategy" and of a conceptual framework to translate these concepts into action.[53] Thus, the government's policies and blueprints do not seem to reflect adequate understandings of the principles of social justice or effective planning and execution. To create effective systems and structures of social justice would then require a renewed approach to public administration, beginning at the conceptual level, extending to moral renewal and to governance to create measures of sustainable social cohesion.[54] At this rate, social injustice remains hidden through systems and structures, and the vulnerable of society continue to feel the brunt of socioeconomic violence.

---

51. Amukugo, "Liberal Democracy, Education," 146.
52. Melber, "Transition in Namibia," 114.
53. Melber, 114.
54. Melber, 115.

2.2.3 Civil Society and Social Justice

Conflict, as witnessed during the apartheid and post-apartheid eras, often creates new opportunities, structures and rules of engagements, and participation in public life. These responses are aimed at challenging the imprints of injustice, and this was the case with the rise of civil society in response to apartheid and post-apartheid socioeconomic and sociopolitical structures. The church, during the liberation struggle became the lifeblood of the civil society movement (CSM). In fact, the church pioneered the way for civil society organizations (CSOs), as many such movements were restricted under the apartheid laws. Samson Ndekwila's book narrates the various levels in which the church and church-based organizations (CBOs) were instrumental in the formation of the CSM.[55]

Especially with the banning of civil liberties, the church's role during the apartheid era and post-independence years was vital. CSOs provided the needed insight in addressing and redressing various social, political, and economic issues. These organizations are influenced by a myriad of political, development, economic, religious and sociological ideologies but many are born out of the liberation movement. Tapscott observes that "the structure of civil society in particular may be seen to have been shaped not only by imperatives of colonial rule, but also by practices of the national liberation movement."[56] He acknowledges the importance of civil society in the construction of a post-apartheid society that would promote social justice and equality. Tapscott, however, also shows the danger of civil society formed around political partisan ideology.

A good example of this is the now-defunct Namibia Women's Voice (NWV) formed under the CCN as part of meeting the donors' gender-inclusive demands. NWV was in practice a SWAPO women's wing. It focused on bread-and-butter issues, which received little attention in the official structures which were fixated on removing the White minority's oppressive government. Price and Britton narrate that "despite the popularity of NWV, the group disbanded in 1989, shortly before Namibia officially gained its independence. SWAPO believed that NWV had lessened the SWC's [SWAPO Women's Council] influence and prioritized the improvement of women's

---

55. Ndekwila, *Agony of Truth*.

56. Tapscott, "Class Formation and Civil Society," 308.

status over Namibia's independence."[57] This close relation, according to Tapscott, has been the precedence of a weak civil society.[58]

In section 2.2.2. we discussed the role of politics, especially of SWAPO, which have inhibited civil society from creating active participation outside the formal political structures. Tapscott attests to this problem when he writes,

> The influence of autocratic tradition authority structures, follow-ing their co-option by the colonial government, further mitigat-ed against the establishment of community-based organisations. For many chiefs and headmen, autonomous and democratically elected community structures posed a threat to their power and influence over local communities. Likewise, despite the impor-tance of their roles in mobilising communities, rural churches were not broadly participatory in structure. Finally, the dictates of the struggle for independence and SWAPO's own penchant for authoritarianism implied that the dominant political force in large sections of the north was both military and hierarchical in orientation for much of the past two decades. Under these circumstances it was not possible for a tradition of mass-based organisation to develop in the rural areas.[59]

This historical basis would have a profound impact on the general con-struction of civil society's participation even in urban areas. The political influence of both colonialism and homegrown understanding of power, con-tinue to influence civil society and its presence. With few exceptions, many nongovernmental organizations (NGOs), community-based organizations (CBOs), and faith-based organizations (FBO) are embattled with this politi-cal reality.

But we need to point out that the Namibia Tapscott is writing for has changed significantly. Even though the political ideologies have barely changed, the role of civil society has increased and has become more vo-cal. While NGOs, CBOs, and FBOs have increased, their lifespan has not inspired much confidence. According to the *2019 Civil Society Organisation*

---

57. Price and Britton, "'If Good Food,'" 301.

58. Tapscott, "Class Formation and Civil Society," 322.

59. Tapscott, 322.

Sustainability Index, there is also inadequate supply of data "on the size of the civil society sector in Namibia."[60] According to the same report,[61] regardless of a large presence of civil society organizations they continue to be hampered by an unconducive legal environment, inhibited organization capacity, growing financial constraints, and lack of resources for sectoral capacity building. But a good amount of service delivery and media coverage has contributed to a positive public image.[62]

CSOs are involved in various activities of social justice and community engagement. This is helpful in strengthening measures and activities of intervention. At present, CSOs are involved in advocacy for minority sexual groups (Namibia Equal Rights Movement (Equal Namibia) and Out-Right Namibia (ORN)), HIV/AID awareness creation, and in mobilising against sexual and gender-based violence (Ombetja Yehinga Organisation Trust, Catholic AIDS Action Trust). Youth empowerment programmes like Katutura

---

60. United States Agency for International Development, Bureau for Democracy, and Center of Excellence on Democracy, "2019 Civil Society Organization," 2.

61. United States Agency for International Development, Bureau for Democracy, and Center of Excellence on Democracy, 2–8.

62. "There are signs that Namibians feel comfortable engaging with and expressing themselves through CSOs. The Afrobarometer survey conducted in mid-2019 showed that some 69 percent of those surveyed felt that Namibians should be able to join any organization, whether or not the government approves of it, while 31 percent said that the government should be able to ban any organization that goes against its policies. The protests over the FishRot scandal were a positive sign that CSOs and individual activists can work together to galvanize public concern about national issues.

In 2019, unlike in previous years, President Geingob did not launch verbal broadsides against civil society representatives as "failed politicians." Despite the reduction in criticism from the president, public officials overall remained skeptical about the role and purpose of civil society. For example, at a press conference, the Ministry of Information and Communication Technology criticized a report by IPPR on surveillance by the state. Officials often seem to be under the impression that civil society is overly critical of government efforts and policies, holds vested interests pushed by donors, and is itself not accountable to an electorate. As a result, the government seldom engages openly with CSOs. For example, the government excluded civil society representatives from the multistakeholder National Governing Council for the African Peer Review Mechanism, which was appointed at the end of year.

The business community has mixed perceptions of CSOs and prefers to work with and support only certain subsectors of civil society, such as environmental organizations. The private sector would like to see more evidence of well-organized and transparent CSOs.

In 2019, Namibian CSOs continued to underestimate the importance of engaging on social media to announce events and broadcast them live. There were, however, some notable exceptions." United States Agency for International Development, Bureau for Democracy, and Center of Excellence on Democracy, 2019 Civil Society Organization, 7.

Youth Enterprise Centre (KAYEC)[63] and National Youth Sports Development Platform (NYSDP) feature among organizations that seek socioeconomic interventions. Others play more academic roles that are engaging the social and political ideas that inform systems, structures, and governance (Namibia Institute for Democracy (NID) and Institute for Public Policy Research (IPPR)).[64]

Many CSOs have become defunct for reasons stated by Tapscott but also for lack of relevance, mismanagement, and lack of clear separation from direct-political engagement. While CSOs have been accused by the SWAPO government of being instruments of failed political parties, they also serve as valuable entry levels for the kind of dialogue needed for post-apartheid Namibia. However, while many CSOs are doing a wonderful job at running programmes, they are not effectively engaged at the conceptual level needed to reimagine issues of social justice. It is also the case that CSOs operate on borrowed financial life, with an extreme high dependence on donor funds, who also dictate terms and conditions of engagement. As such, the need to survive and avoid flight of capital plays a huge role – making CSOs, especially those operating on project funding (which are the majority), weak in engaging with conceptual issues that would affect policy makers and donors (now called development partners).

The Council of Churches in Namibia (CCN) has played an important role as a CSO during the liberation struggle. This has been a commanding organization that reshaped the understanding of Christian participation. Not only did CCN lack ethical integrity to apply critical solidarity, but it also failed to exercize critical participation as it became a spiritual-political wing of the liberation movement – unashamedly pro-SWAPO. Trade unions are guilty of this same affiliation which have rendered them ineffective to engage post-apartheid structures. Tapscott argues that even "the emergence of a strongly independent union movement has been constrained by the fact that some of its most prominent leaders are still linked to SWAPO . . .

---

63. An initiative of the Anglican and Lutheran churches, it still actively offers grants and vocational training to underprivileged youths.

64. A detailed but not complete database of CSOs can be found on https://www.civic264.org.na/cso-namibia (accessed on 16 August 2021).

In general . . . the trade union movement is in disarray and has yet to find a strongly independent voice within the civil society."[65]

CSOs played positive activities and roles. Whether they have truly taken conceptual shapes that are reflective of addressing social injustice becomes difficult to tell, especially in the face of many donor interests exerted on them. This positive outlook of the role of CSOs is emphasized by Job Amupanda in *The Fight against Corruption in Namibia: An Appraisal of Institutional Environment and a Consideration of a Model for Civil Society Participation.*[66] His critique of the state-owned parastatals and their failure to address corruption effectively, proposes that civil society could play a significant role to hold government more accountable. The paper is more of a promotion of his own activist group called the AR, which has now moved on to be part of the local government as of 2021. While Amupanda strongly points out the structural and administrative issues underlying the government's efforts to fight corruption, the role of civil society is totalising. Tapscott's critique is a glaring rebuke which neither Amupanda nor the *2019 Civil Society Organization Sustainability Index* are taking into consideration.

We also cannot ignore that there are significant attempts for contextualization. But the level of contextual relevance is constantly hampered by powerful donor agendas, who carry the power of capital. On the other hand, the need to clarify the role of CSOs as to whether direct political engagement is a viable option and to adopt a redefinition of critical engagement, remains a challenge. Moreover, while CSOs play a vital social role, the government has often viewed them as being anti-government or anti-SWAPO. This narrative, besides poor publicity, has placed CSOs in a negative light with the public and received limited local support. It is especially true for CSOs with strong political overtones like the Forum for the Future (FFF)[67] or those that provide critical analysis of the government activities like IPPR and NID.

---

65. Tapscott, "Class Formation and Civil Society," 323.

66. Amupanda, "Fight against Corruption."

67. "The organisation's primary concerns are to further consolidate Namibian's democratic system, educate on economic justice, and actively advocate for civil society to participate in the democratic network. The Organisation is committed to the vision of working together with like-minded organizations and individuals, to advance a new wave of democratization countrywide." Keulder and Hishoono, "Guide to Civil Society," 28.

The call for CSOs to reorganize themselves into a competent force that can challenge structures, systems, policies, and programmes, is yet to be answered effectively. The ongoing interventions these organizations serve in communities should be seen as commendable entry levels. Have CSOs truly taken up intentional measures to engage issues of social justice with long-term goals to bring about transformation? That many of these are short-term intervention programmes driven by the availability of donor funds hinders the creation of presence and influence. For example, many of the organizations listed in the *Guide to Civil Society in Namibia* of 2009, within just a span of ten years, have become defunct. Sadly, the reasons include mismanagement of donor funds, lack of funds, and unsustainable structures.

These challenges are realized by the main donor communities, especially that the CSOs cannot be effective without developing their "capacity and skills." In response, programmes like "Action for Becoming a Credible CSO in Namibian Communities has helped build the capacity of organizations in five regions but came to end in August 2019."[68] But the problem remains that the survival of CSOs is highly dependent on the intervention of international communities. Regardless of the efforts by the international community, the post-apartheid CSOs need to address their own internal challenges and formulate themselves to truly be contextual in their policies and programmes.

A silver lining in this challenging context of CSOs is that more established CSOs are challenging public policies and programmes. Notably, we have the Legal Assistance Centre (LAC)[69] which serves to challenge public policies on issues of social justice, in particular, human rights-related issues. While their vision is not necessarily aimed at apartheid as a system, many of the legal issues they address are historically linked to the apartheid era. It is the NID and IPPR that are providing the intellectual muscles to question the viability of public structures that are designed to address social injustice. Through their publications, they seek to interrogate the common large questions facing

---

68. United States Agency for International Development, Bureau for Democracy, and Center of Excellence on Democracy, "2019 Civil Society Organization."

69. Its motto reads, "We, the Legal Assistance Centre, being a public interest law centre, collectively strive to make the law accessible to those with the least access, through education, law reform, research, litigation, legal advice, representation and lobbying, with the ultimate aim of creating and maintaining a human rights culture in Namibia." Keulder and Hishoono, "Guide to Civil Society."

society and what kind of collaboration may be required for the common good. What conceptual frameworks drive many CSOs is difficult to tell as we seek to find how they can become valuable conversation partners in search of social justice.

If a CSO is driven by an Aristotelian notion that individuals by themselves cannot produce happiness, then the vision of social justice would be informed by the need to promote virtue. That is, they become conduits of advocating for persons to embrace society as where they learn to live a morally good life. Social justice then is an expression of seeking to promote the common happiness. On the other hand, if CSOs are to be conceived in a Hegelian sense, they become entities with separate interests outside of the state. Like the market, their services are responding to the needs created by change of social circumstances. The existence of CSOs then is to satisfy the needs of society by hiring experts to provide the specialized skills. With this outlook, CSOs become a separate society, if not a class. Not only are we to conceptualize the notions of social justice but also the framework through which CSOs receive their understanding of social participation.

While CSOs have and continue to contribute immensely to the progress of Namibian society, repurposing them to reflect the sociocultural realities could make them more viable in search for social justice. This would imply taking into consideration what it means to be a civil society in Namibia that can present itself with authentic autonomy in its relation to the state, and institutionally different from the state. Added to this search for a unique identity is the need to become institutionalized to meet the demands of society and confront the various elements that threaten CSOs from making deeper footprints in the search for social transformation.[70]

2.2.4 Feminism and Social Justice

Women happen to be part of those who feel the brunt of failing structures and systems. They also experienced discrimination under apartheid on various levels. First, within their cultural communities, women were made subservient to their male counterparts, which resulted in social deprivation. Second, they also suffered from the political system of racism, which restricted them to specific activities by being women and Black, impeding their developmental

---

70. Keulder, *State, Society and Democracy*, 5–8.

process. Third, they were economically disadvantaged. For example, under the then labour system, women were not employable. They were economically dependent on their male relatives sending financial aid. This discriminatory labour system created an economic power vacuum between men and women. Thus, Black women under apartheid experienced multiple facets of discrimination (socially, politically, and economically) and injustice which require redressing. Little attention has been paid to women's place in the history of apartheid, making the Namibian narrative male-centred. Ellen Namhila's[71] *Mukwahepo: Woman, Soldier, Mother*, Martha Akawa's[72] *The Gender Politics of the Namibian Liberation Struggle*, and Libertina Amathila's[73] *Making a Difference (Namibia)* are works written from feminist perspectives to influence the historical narrative. They also remind us of women's efforts in pursuing social justice and the ongoing struggles that the post-independence structures have continuously overlooked.

The recognition of social injustice against women is not ignored or overlooked. It is the adequacy and effectiveness of these efforts that are under question. For example, as a response, the post-apartheid government caters for the protection of women through various state-initiated policies and legislations. The general understanding is that women are part of vulnerable groups who need to receive preferential treatment through policies and legislations such as the Affirmative Action (Employment) Act (Section 18).[74] The constitution also guarantees the equality of persons and protection from discrimination based on sex or gender roles. Inclusion and recognition were previously not granted under the apartheid structures.[75] These legal measures are helpful starting points, but they are not adequate in addressing and delivering social justice for women and girls. There are also deeper underlying issues of identity, dignity, and personhood, which these legislations often do not capture because they are prejudiced and insensitive towards women – making the entire exercize questionable.

---

71. Namhila, *Mukwahepo*.

72. Akawa, *Gender Politics*.

73. Amathila, *Making a Difference*.

74. Government of the Republic of Namibia, "Affirmative Action (Employment) Act of 1998."

75. The establishment of the *Ministry of Gender Equality and Child Welfare* is an offshoot of the pursuit to create a visible public representation of women.

Feminists seek to ensure that these rights are defended and executed for the liberation, protection, and upliftment of women. Martha Akawa, in *The Gender Politics of the Namibian Liberation Struggle,* argues for the deconstruction of the liberation narrative that tells of women only in men's shadows. This historical misrepresentation, she believes, contributes to ineffective policies and institutions and cannot, in the new structures, shield women from both historical and new gender structural imbalances. She argues that "having a constitution and a government that advocates equality for women is one thing, but having this commitment translated into tangible results requires result-oriented policies, effective institutions and an enabling environment."[76] She advocates for recognising women in society as equal contributors, which can only change through collectively deconstructing history that narrates male-centred perspectives. Added to this writing of history from a female perspective, Akawa advocates for the disbanding of "the unequal relationship between men and women . . . related to the social, economic and political structures that have not yet been sufficiently transformed to effect changes."[77]

Akawa belongs to the generation of feminists of the post-liberation struggle era, sharing their experiences and reflecting on women's place in a post-apartheid era. One must point out that this seems to be a fresh approach to gender issues, but with a strong leaning towards structural reforms. It seeks the place of women as complete human participants and makers of history. As such, it seeks the emancipation of male-dominated structures that only pay lip service to women's empowerment and gender equality. She calls for ensuring that public policies translate into the meaningful creation of a society where men and women are equal. Although there is evidence that women's empowerment is happening in various public sectors, Akawa believes that this can be improved by being intentional about women's empowerment. Alluding to the promises made during the liberation struggle and independence, she calls for structural reforms that will give women genuine power to transform their lives and communities.

The second form (of feminism) advocates for the recognition of women's liberties. It seeks to address how cultural and legal-political systems have side-lined women or even forced them to live by a male-oriented society's

---

76. Akawa, *Gender Politics,* 178.
77. Akawa, 79.

standards and expectations. The apartheid-era exercised a stronghold and control over women (both Black and White). It controlled both professional and domestic choices, which decided the economics of women. For example, it used their gender rather than skills, abilities, qualifications, or quality of work as the basis for financial compensations.[78] The system also socially disempowered women, for example, by taking away the power to negotiate.

Post-liberation feminism seeks to ensure a sociocultural revolution to grant women the liberty to free themselves from patriarchal social control. Sister Namibia[79] is among the pioneering Namibian feminist organizations, which started publishing in 1989, shortly before the independence elections. It stands as a group who speak up against "the oppression of and discrimination against women on all levels and wherever it may occur" including but not limited to "political, social, economic, cultural and legal situations."[80] It sums itself up under the motto "There can be no free men until there are free women"[81] to create awareness regarding women's place in society and deconstruct harmful sociocultural constructions of women. It has been calling women to rise and organize themselves as active participants in politics, policymaking, and demand for equal employment benefits. Thus, it is a feminism that seeks to assert women's essentialness in advancing the post-independence society.

Originally founded in Germany, Sister Namibia promotes a liberal idea of feminism with a conceptual framework and a profoundly Western liberal theory. As such, it poses a new contextual challenge to existing and deeply held cultural beliefs, norms, and even legal statuses. The magazine discussions continue to cover several topics such as the sexual rights of women, employment conditions, social security benefits, baby dumping, and inheritance rights. It has since advanced to advocate for sexual reproduction rights and the protection of sexual minorities.[82]

---

78. Akawa, 172–73.

79. "Our vision is a society that recognises, protects and celebrates the full personhood of all women and girls including respect for our dignity, diversity, sexual choices and bodily integrity. We aim to inspire and equip women to make free choices and act as agents of change in our relationships, our communities and ourselves. We are dedicated to developing a new feminist politics and consciousness. We work for transformation through education, information, collective action, and celebration." Keulder and Hishoono, "Guide to Civil Society."

80. Sister Namibia, July 1989.

81. Sister Namibia, 1990, 9.

82. Sister Namibia, July 2019.

Finally, feminists believe that women have and continue to experience injustice. It is an injustice that requires radical structural change, political will, legal measures, and pressure that can convey change. Although the country is independent, women continue to be marginalized. Feminism, so far, sees social justice as the emancipation of women to become full participants in the construction of the post-apartheid society. They see these hindrances as rooted in history, politics, and culture whose narratives and foci are male, which results in the systematic sidelining of women.

2.3 Theological Perspectives on Social Justice

2.3.1 Historical Background

By the twentieth century, theologians from the Global South raised fundamental questions regarding social justice, especially in response to colonialism, coloniality, neocolonialism, imperialism, and apartheid.[83] These questions aimed to tackle specific contextual issues that Western theology failed to address or to which it has been inadequate to provide answers. The rejection of apartheid was part of rejecting Western hermeneutics, which enforced racial biases against Black people.[84]

During apartheid, churches in Namibia, like many others across southern Africa, "actively identified themselves with the national liberation movements."[85] This time also called for newer theological reflections and approaches to South African rule's violent and repressive presence. The escalation of the South African presence and apartheid ideology was taking place at a time of history when Europe was recovering from the effects of Nazism. It was preceded by the German genocide of the Namas, Damaras, and Hereros.[86] This historical memory also created new fears that the South African presence would repeat that history for the Namibian society if left to continue. The most prominent and first direct engagement with the apartheid government was the *Open Letter to His Honour the Prime Minister of the Republic of South Africa* addressed to John Vorster on 30 June 1971. He was

---

83. Grugel et al., *Demanding Justice*; Hanlon, Barrientos, and Hulme, *Just Give Money*.
84. Parratt, "Introduction," 7–9.
85. Wallerstein and De Bragança, *African Liberation Reader*, 180.
86. Olusoga and Erichsen, *Kaiser's Holocaust*, 4830–31 of 8894.

an overt supporter of German Nazism, something for which he and other future apartheid leaders were imprisoned.[87] This letter helped to declare the "Black" church's position on apartheid, the first of its kind in which the church engaged the South African administration.

Other documents were also being circulated by the church for creating awareness regarding the sociopolitical conditions in Namibia, both national and internationally.[88] Liberation Theology was the leading theoretical framework for the leading Black church leaders engaging the apartheid regime. However, the German Evangelical Lutheran Church (GELC) refused to support the Black churches seeking to engage in politics directly and propose a change in the social system and change of government. While they (GELC) opposed the inhumane treatment, they distanced themselves from the position of the Evangelical Lutheran Church in Namibia (ELCIN), primarily expressed in the *Open Letter*. Frostin writes how John Vorster, who was a member of the Dutch Reformed Church of South Africa (DRCSA), would later use similar lines of reasoning as that of the GELC, arguing that his cooperation was guaranteed if the church stayed out of political issues and focused on spiritual matters.[89]

The position of the GELC would today raise theological and ethical questions. How did they afford to keep such silence in an era that witnessed the first massacre of the twentieth century in Namibia, followed by Adolph Hitler's Nazi Germany, responsible for millions of people's deaths? How did the GELC overlook a model like Dietrich Bonhoeffer in resisting oppressive governments and political structures? While apartheid was a system that advocated Afrikaner supremacist ideologies, the GELC found this kind of government suitable to advance its racist attitude. It also explains why the GELC distanced itself from the *Open Letter* issued by Black church leaders. The incident between the Black and German Lutherans was not just a result of their history of division. It reveals a new layer of the complex and subtle nature of apartheid and the support it received at different levels by both Black and White Namibians.[90]

---

87. Wielder, *Praise for Ruth First*, 44–45.

88. Frostin, "Theological Debate on Liberation," 133–206.

89. Frostin, 55.

90. Botha, "Church in Namibia"; Clark and Worger, *South Africa*; Miller, *African Volk*.

The theology of social justice during apartheid and even afterwards became polarized[91] between Liberation theology and dualistic, anticommunist theology.[92] Liberation theology eventually took the leading role among Black theologians, and the separation of state and church view dominated among White theologians. In contrast, both groups advocated for justice; how that justice should come about created tension. Influenced by socialist-liberation ideologies, Black theologians identified Namibia's plight as one that required a revolutionary intervention. Several prominent church leaders and theologians were also senior SWAPO leaders,[93] who then linked their theological and political convictions into one system.[94] The CCN became the spiritual-political wing of SWAPO in Namibia, using its structures to generate funding for SWAPO.

Katjavivi, a Marxist-socialist academic, politician, and historian, describes the theology that permeated the church as of African origin. In his view, the church created a new self-awareness among ordinary persons and matured when it embraced Black Theology. He also points out that besides cultural and sociological motivations, the church stood against oppressive governance based on biblical and Christian concepts of love and compassion for one's neighbour. Nevertheless, his intentions for endorsing the church's political participation only apply as far as it opposed the apartheid government and supported SWAPO "after independence in the process of reconstruction of a new society."[95] Otherwise, he foresees a political end in which the church would move to a nonpolitical role,[96] pre-empting a church that would be a political handmaiden.[97]

---

91. Frostin, "Theological Debate on Liberation," 52.

92. It is important to note that the "dualistic, anticommunist theology" is not a generally accepted term, neither was it the common position of those who opposed Liberation Theology. Frostin writes as someone who is pro-communistic or socialist ideologies, thus, his own bias towards those who took a different stand is manifesting through this broad-brush label, a categorical misrepresentation.

93. Katjavivi, Frostin, and Mbuende, *Church and Liberation in Namibia*, 3.

94. Trewhela, "Swapo and Churches."

95. Katjavivi, Frostin, and Mbuende, *Church and Liberation in Namibia*, 3, 11, 24.

96. Did Katjavivi anticipate that the church would cease to be a force for justice? It may be noted that Katjavivi is a politician, with an interest to gain the support of the church for SWAPO to remain in power. His work only serves as a historical voice (although it is one-sided).

97. Botha, "Church in Namibia."

2.3.2 Theological Framework of Social Justice

Many church leaders who led the resistance against apartheid embraced Liberation theology as their underlying theological approach. They thought it to be a better theology to confront the degree of "human suffering, anguish, death and humiliation" and that it possessed the necessary tools to create a consciousness for the oppressed to rise and defend "their God-given lives."[98] Thus, a response to "traditional" Christian theology was deemed to have failed to capture the intensity of the Black situation of injustice, pain, frustration, and desire for freedom, which Liberation theology addresses.[99]

Although social justice is not precisely defined, it seems to imply resisting unjust systems that cause harm. These unjust systems need replacing with more just and humane systems and structures. Thus, the redemptive work of Christ serves as a justification to resist oppression and injustice. This salvific understanding also provided a political framework and ground upon which Namibian theologians deemed apartheid as both a crime and a heresy that oppressed and denied the image of God reaffirmed through the death and resurrection of Christ. Mujoro and Mujoro see the social injustice perpetrated by apartheid as both a legal and spiritual issue or as "a crime against the Namibian people, but it is also a threat to the gospel of Jesus Christ."[100] This realization motivated a call to action stated as: "We can no longer remain silent. We feel that if we, as the Church, remain silent any longer, we will become liable for the life and future of our country and its people."[101]

Based on the realization that silence in the presence and effects of the oppressive apartheid system would only give birth to a greater evil, the church needed to act. This created an urgency for meaningful action (not by lulling the poor and "oppressed" into complying with suffering or the hope of a heavenly reversal) with the view of redemption attainable in the here and now. The church engaged in a political battle to ensure that the oppressor relinquished the illegal shackles of cruelty, violence, and humiliation so that the people may enjoy their liberty in their land. The context was all the

---

98. Mujoro and Mujoro, "Namibian Liberation Theology," 97.

99. Fortein, "Allan Boesak," 103.

100. Mujoro and Mujoro, "Namibian Liberation Theology," 97.

101. *Epistle to the Namibians*, 30 June 1971, Windhoek. Sent to the ELCIN leaders and their congregations on the same day the Open Letter was sent to Prime Minister John Vorster. Katjavivi, Frostin, and Mbuende, *Church and Liberation in Namibia*, 137–38.

oppressed Namibians regardless of their religious affiliation. It is unclear whether the ELCIN and other churches worked with people from other political parties than SWAPO. Shekutaamba Nambala's article "From Colonialism to Nationalism in Namibia,"[102] published in the *Lutheran Quarterly*, shows the pro-SWAPO stance, practically campaigning for it to become the government upon independence.

Social justice has been understood as the liberation of the oppressed, violated, and humiliated Namibians from the illegal administration of South Africa. The church leaders saw themselves as having a divine duty to pronounce themselves against the apartheid regime and serve as a voice of the voiceless. How does this theology present itself in addressing the present context of prolonged effects of apartheid perpetrated by the corruption, maladministration, and mismanagement of the government with which the church sided during apartheid? What is the meaning of social justice today, and what is the theological position of the same church that stood up to address injustice?

The overwhelming theological framework among many Black theologians leans towards Liberation theology. This approach to social injustice has become conceptually superficial to the public and individualized. For example, Kameeta's book *Towards Liberation: Crossing Boundaries between Church and Politics*[103] is based on a Liberation theology framework. He sees the liberation framework as one that would warrant the establishment of a functional post-apartheid society. While the book deals with the relationship between the church and state or politics, it offers a historical summary of the church's role during apartheid. The author derives, extensively, his understanding of social justice and contextualization from Gustavo Gutierrez's *A Theology of Liberation: History, Politics, and Salvation* and Stephan Bevans's work, *Models of Contextual Theology*.[104] Kameeta deems social engagement as a fundamental missiological[105] phenomenon: therefore, the gospel is an instrument

---

102. Nambala, "From Colonialism to Nationalism."

103. Kameeta, *Towards Liberation*.

104. Gutiérrez, *Theology of Liberation*.

105. Kameeta considers social engagement as missiological and part of the reason Jesus came into the world, and that the message of the gospel is centred on liberating humanity from all forms of oppression.

for liberating humanity from all forms of oppression.[106] He does not provide enough space to elaborate on the concept and meaning of social justice, except that we assume that it is based on Gutierrez's work. His social justice concept focuses on poverty reduction in a section titled *After Independence of Namibia*, although it is only four brief paragraphs in the entire book.[107] In this book, Kameeta seems to assume that the Namibian public is a Christian public, and without qualification, calls for a renewed worship of God, reconciliation, unity, hope and peace. This assumption may be understood as advocating for Christendom that seeks its establishment through political alliances. It somehow illuminates church leaders' apathy towards SWAPO's reported abuse of detainees in several camps.[108] This response and relationship would initially taint the role and place of the Christian voice in the present public life and discourse of social justice.[109]

Kameeta criticises the church (ELCIN, ELCRIN, GELC) for losing its vision, although he does not elaborate.[110] It may imply its spiritual vision or its missiological mandate in a post-apartheid context. While he calls for unity, forgiveness and reconciliation in the church and nation, he uses nuances to blame colonialism or what he calls "Western Christian civilisation" nearly for everything wrong with the Namibian public. This view infantilises Namibian people and deny them of their agency. However, his criticism of the church's failure does not extend to the political players in the *Political Lectures/Speeches/Addresses* section, perhaps because of his political loyalty to the ruling party. In 2015, Kameeta became the first minister of a newly created Ministry for Poverty Eradication and Social Welfare[111] to lead the government's war on poverty based on a philosophy of redistribution. It is

---

106. Kameeta, *Towards Liberation*, 81–126.

107. The book seems to make more sense if dealt with in sections rather than the individual chapters in it.

108. Trewhela, "Swapo and Churches," 85–88.

109. Botha, "Church in Namibia"; Horn, "Churches and Political Reconciliation"; Lombard, "Detainee Issue."

110. Kameeta, *Towards Liberation*, 186.

111. This ministry was disbanded in 2020. It was also one of the most criticized ministries as a waste of public resources and a duplication of already existing governing departments. Many of my weekly articles on poverty in Namibia, published in *The Patriot*, criticized the administrative failure of this ministry. Three years in a row, this ministry was voted as irrelevant by the board of panelists of *The Patriot*, citing that it will not be missed even if it closed for business in 24 hours.

also to serve as an instrument to collaborate strategies addressing the effects of both apartheid and colonialism. The following year (2016), the ministry developed and launched the *Blue Print on Wealth Distribution and Poverty Eradication*. The document has socialist connotations, although the government has adopted a mixed-economy system that is strongly procapitalist in practice.

Following the theological framework of Liberation theology, Niitenge researched the ELCIN and poverty, in *The Evangelical Lutheran Church in Namibia (ELCIN) and Poverty, with Specific Reference to Semi-Urban Communities in Northern Namibia – A Practical Theological Evaluation*. His research claims that "the Church's role is to work for a just society by struggling (fighting) against social, economic and political structures and systems that generate and perpetuate injustice and which dehumanize people."[112] He further places the burden of social transformation on the church, distinguished by the phrase "the church's role," although it is unclear whether this is a primary, secondary, or integrated role. Niitenge believes that the church ought to be the messenger of God's liberating message both from spiritual and socioeconomic poverty, and the latter is the key focus of his research. While his research focuses on poverty among a specific people group of Namibia (Aawambo), he intends to see the principles of his findings and recommendations modelled across the country.

Niitenge attributes the present effects and manifestations of poverty to the apartheid structures, mostly how it systematically disenfranchised those in rural areas.[113] Unlike Kameeta, he critiques the present government structures that continue to contribute to poverty levels among the rural people, who are the target of his research. He specifically focuses on administrative levels of corruption as a key in undermining socioeconomic transformation. Niitenge also points out that the entire country is affected by corruption levels either as perpetrators or victims. The definition of corruption seems to be limited to the abuse of power and financial resources by the government. While he is correct in outlining how corruption affects the country's development, his definition of corruption might be much more accurate if we termed it "white-collar theft."

---

112. Niitenge, "Evangelical Lutheran Church," 15.
113. Niitenge, 13.

As a way of mitigating the incidence and prevalence of social injustice both inherited and self-caused, Niitenge calls for "social rebellion" in which the church should actively take part if it is to see a change in society. He assumes that without such a rebellious stand against "poverty, humiliation, injustice, corruption, and degradation,"[114] society will continue to fall deeper into fear and abuse by those with political, social, and economic power. While Niitenge does not present a theology of social justice or a conceptualization of what it is, he bases his practical theological framework on works of Gutierrez, Bosch, and Cone.[115] His approach to fighting social justice is through a socialist-missiological framework coupled with Black Liberation Theology. Although he seeks to establish a "biblical" vision of justice,[116] his understanding of addressing social justice borrows heavily from the Western framework of theological socialism. These theories or views of social justice are in many places applied to the Namibian context verbatim, as seen from the application of a liberation conception by Niitenge and Kameeta.

Niitenge also assumes that the ELCIN participation during the liberation struggle against apartheid was a resounding success.[117] His assumption is shared by other theologians, historians, and political scientists.[118] But this view seems to ignore Paul Trewhela's[119] critical work that reports on the ELCIN and ELCRIN ineptitude to hold SWAPO accountable for its violation of human rights during exile. He selectively uses these historical events to motivate engaging present socioeconomic challenges. The ELCIN resisted the apartheid system but with uncritical solidarity, if not biased towards SWAPO. Many of its key leaders became beneficiaries of the post-independence government structures. Niitenge ignores this significant component when he critiques the

---

114. Niitenge, 70.

115. We note that Kameeta refers to Gutierrez only once in his entire work (although he has two bibliographic entries), and the provided page numbers (33 and 140) do not deal with what he is referring to, they are both end bits of chapters. It is possible that he may be referring to another work of Gutierrez and mixed up the pages. However, we need to give him the benefit of doubt that he interacted with the Liberation Theology ideas of Gutierrez.

116. Niitenge, "Evangelical Lutheran Church," 40.

117. Niitenge, 96–105.

118. Kameeta, *Towards Liberation*; Katjavivi, Frostin, and Mbuende, *Church and Liberation in Namibia*; Katjavivi, *History of Resistance*.

119. Trewhela, "Swapo and Churches"; Trewhela, *Inside Quatro*.

government's post-independence failure, sparing some of his contemporaries and colleagues from it.

These theological works aim at being contextual applications for Namibia. They are all offshoots of liberation ideologies advocating, like many South African theologians, that the liberation struggle continues in a distinct form today. While many South African theologians continue to express Liberation theology by qualifying it as "Black Liberation,"[120] those in Namibia seem to have intentionally avoided the colour-based identity of their theology (except for Kameeta), perhaps because of the various underlying claims of striving towards national reconciliation. In contrast, this covert label is overtly pro-Black in its foundations and is advocated by Black theologians and church leaders. For example, Kameeta's prior work, Why, Oh Lord?, is written as a pro-Black liberation work, and his present work as a politician is focusing on Black people as the marginalized and previously disadvantaged. Thus, a search for a language about God and God's working in human affairs (social, political, economic, ethical, and spiritual) is to contextualize the language of theology and give a response to the needs that arise.[121]

As far as social justice issues are concerned, a few White theologians have provided viewpoints. Christo Lombard[122] writes extensively on religion's role in a secular context and addresses the detainee issue that has remained unaddressed since independence. For Lombard, Namibian history needs an honest analysis if there would be any meaningful national progress. While he calls the ruling party to own up to its involvement in dehumanising and violent acts against Namibians, he mostly calls the church to cease being a partial prophetic voice. Lombard argues that the church, which has been vocal and active against the apartheid regime, has failed to exercize the same rigour of prophetic criticism.[123] He holds that justice is required not only from the perpetrators/aggressors of apartheid but also from the oppressed (especially the

---

120. Makheta, "Doing Liberation Theology"; Tshaka and Makofane, "Continued Relevance."

121. Leonard, Moment of Truth, 105; Pears, Doing Contextual Theology, 19–20, 68.

122. Christo Lombard left the DRCSA and joined the URC; this was both a theological and political statement of his rejection of the apartheid theology. The researcher had an in-person discussion with Prof. Lombard to familiarise with the background of theological engagement during and after apartheid. The meeting was not an interview, therefore, the information discussed is not incorporated into the text.

123. Lombard, "Detainee Issue," 66–67.

SWAPO's military wing) who committed crimes against their fellow citizens.[124] He firmly holds that without addressing the injustice perpetrated by SWAPO against Namibians, the course of justice will continue to be lopsided. Lombard uses a reconciliatory framework to address injustice, with a deeply Reformed epistemological perspective. This silence or detachment by White theologians on social justice justifies many Black theologians who have adopted colour-lined Liberation Theology. It could also imply the inoculation of many White theologians from the day-to-day realities of social injustice witnessed by Black theologians in Black communities.

Besides White theologians, Roman Catholic Church (RCC) theologians have stayed out of dealing with the political dimension. There is also a general absence of theological material that focuses on the concept of social justice for the post-apartheid context. The Catholic Bishops' Synod (CBS) serves as the ideological governing body, which seeks to implement a general RCC theology of social justice as seen around the world. Thus, the institutional structures do not allow for social justice engagement in a theological format that is specifically Namibian. This theological contribution of the RCC is regardless of its involvement in the liberation struggle against the apartheid system. It is important to note that the prior engagement of the RCC in the liberation struggle alongside many other denominations does not imply a change of positions. The liberation struggle's engagement was based on so-cial justice belief as stipulated in the church's general social teachings. For example, the Catechism says:

> The Church's Social Teaching comprises a body of doctrine, which is articulated as the Church interprets events in the course of history, with the assistance of the Holy Spirit, in the light of the whole of what has been revealed by Jesus Christ ... The Church's social teaching proposes principles for reflection; it provides criteria for judgement; it gives guidelines for action.[125]

The latter part of the above quotation is a powerful motivation for the RCC, which has shown various social justice activities and programmes, such as education, healthcare, food programmes, and HIV/AIDS community-based

---

124. Kornes, "Negotiating 'Silent Reconciliation.'"
125. Paul II, *Catechism*, 586.

programmes. Could this imply that a well thought-out conceptual framework in addressing social injustice issues seems crucial in developing valuable courses of action? While the RCC may not be in the public forefront of developing academic dialogue for the Namibian context, it is guided by a specific conceptual framework absent among many Protestant denominations and even the government. It is also worth noting that there is no clear Namibian RCC voice that seeks to incorporate this kind of conceptualization.

Added to the theological contribution, or the absence thereof, are many independent churches. At the time of this research, there is no scholarly or even pastoral work regarding social justice from Baptists, charismatics/Pentecostals, or African Initiated Churches (AICs). Baptist churches have not taken a public stand on social justice issues. Buys and Nambala's narrative of the Baptist history in Namibia does not recall any links of their participation *against* apartheid.[126] They indicate the Baptist church's role in supporting apartheid, especially its theological education that displayed the apartheid structures by having separate seminary training for Black and White persons. Most charismatic and Pentecostal churches have adopted prosperity theology to address social injustice in society.[127] Historically, early Pentecostal missions were established along racial lines of the apartheid structure. Few within the Apostolic Faith Mission adopted Liberation Theology's views and resisted the racial divide of missions and the apartheid system,[128] besides the *Oruuano*[129] Church (Unity Protestant Church – UPC), which was initially involved in the liberation struggle. Unfortunately, its effects have not extended to meaningful and engaging post-independence public theology. Like most AICs, it is absent in public on social justice matters and is now more of a Christian cultural representation of the Herero people.[130] Buys and Nambala see AICs as "the forerunners of the liberation struggle in Southern Africa"[131] because they were part of the first groups to advocate for African independence from

---

126. Buys and Nambala, *History of Church*, 125–30.

127. Kasera, "Biblical and Theological Examination," 23–71.

128. Buys and Nambala, *History of Church*; Horn, "Churches and Political Reconciliation."

129. *Oruuano* is a term in otjiHerero (a Namibian language) which means unity, oneness or coming together (Unity Protestant Church, UPC). The *Oruuano* Church became an independent church after breaking away from the Rhenish Mission Church (RMC).

130. Kgatla and Park, "Healing in Herero Culture."

131. Buys and Nambala, *History of Church*, 172.

missionary oriented Christianity. These groups' focus has been profoundly on spiritual aspects, although some are engaged in community work but have scarcely contributed to any theological work. Thus, there is a general absence of theological conceptualization or academic engagement that would propel a discourse of engaging the public.

The above absence of other theological perspectives other than ELCIN and ELCRIN creates a material poverty of resources needed to engage the theology of social justice and public participation. Nevertheless, it provides an opportunity for theological participation in the ongoing public dialogues of social justice. This shortage serves as an opportunity for this research project, as there is a gap that needs addressing.

2.4 Research Gap

On the basis of the preceding summaries of the concepts of social justice, this research asserts that the understanding of social justice we have today requires intentional conceptualization to make it contextually applicable. Thus, addressing the present effects of injustice requires robust measures, developed from a better understanding of the Namibian context. While Namibians are aware of the need for social justice,[132] they need to step out of borrowed conceptions and systems to legitimize the meaning of social justice for their context. Namibian search for social justice emanates from Western contexts, such that the systems of social justice today remain replicas of foreign theological, contextual, and philosophical architecture. While by nature, all humans are "aware" of the concept of justice, and we can borrow from each other, wholesale replication of ideas creates contextual incapacity to deal with issues affecting the replicating context. While these concepts have been widely accepted, they have not been interrogated for their relevance or resemblance to a Namibian context of social injustice caused by close to a century's oppressive racial structures.

It will be naive to assume that Namibian scholars have absorbed these borrowed concepts with no attempt to adapt them to their context. Even borrowed concepts can be contextualized to serve as immediate responses

---

132. Akawa, *Gender Politics*; Kameeta, *Towards Liberation*; Katjavivi, Frostin, and Mbuende, *Church and Liberation in Namibia*; Tötemeyer, *Church and State*.

to the moment's needs and aspirations. These would require to be revisited and reexamined to challenge the epistemological contexts underlying these concepts of social justice. Thus, both the theological and intellectual frameworks that shape the discussion on social justice have not examined the need to contextualize conceptualization. Mainly the theological discussion is stagnant in the history of liberation.[133] This stagnation and lack of reimagining the concept of social justice undermines the creative experience of allowing God's truth to be expressed in a way that speaks to a post-apartheid context. It cannot dialogue with the public because Namibian theology seems ill-prepared to understand or know the secular public's context and language.

If Christianity is a questioning, thinking, and engaging faith, then the present complacent and estranged nature of theology from the Namibian public is not being a faithful witness. Matters of socioeconomic inequality are intricately theological and cannot be decided by the secular state alone. What is God like? How is God present in the post-apartheid public space riddled with immense structural injustice? What does it mean to bear responsible witness in a context with a dehumanising presence? How does our own experience of God's grace through Jesus Christ motivate us to be present in the world, in every aspect of life, to ensure the improvement of human living conditions? These are the questions that call for theology in Namibia to take a more public presence. The absence of theology from the public space to bear witness to God's concern for people and the need for more just, contextual, effective, humane social justice policies and programmes raise questions about its use or relevance. This research seeks to serve as foundational work to provoke this theological dialogue in the post-apartheid understanding of social justice.

2.4.1 Conceptual Framework for Social Justice

Although the government has embarked on various programmes to ensure social protection to deal with a painful history that left many in inhumane socioeconomic conditions, these concepts of social justice are undefined. As stated in the discussion above, concepts such as restoration, restitution, and distribution are vague. Their vagueness could be the reason many

---

133. Buys and Nambala, *History of Church*; Kameeta, *Towards Liberation*; Mujoro and Mujoro, "Namibian Liberation Theology"; Niitenge, "Evangelical Lutheran Church."

programmes have failed to materialise. These concepts are also foreign and do not speak to the Namibian context, which includes the effects of apartheid. Most times, the government has hired external development experts to design its social policies and programmes, resulting in policies being drafted without understanding of the local contexts and their implications. The government's approach is a general top-down approach to social injustice: these policies' theoretical frameworks are borrowed and forced onto the Namibian context.

An analysis of the *Blue Print* and the HPP, which ought to be a framework for combating poverty and social injustice, shows that it nowhere defines, explains, or clarifies the concept of social justice. It ought to be a practical framework of the HPP and Vision 2030, the former being President Hage Geingob's 2014–15 campaign slogan and promise. It was envisioned as the programme that would lead to the materialization of "the Namibian narrative[134] . . . to usher Namibia into the epoch of Prosperity."[135] Inversely, this document does not represent a clear conceptual framework that is contextually relevant to the Namibian experiences; mostly, it duplicates both the language and ideas found in many international conventions. For example, the section *War on Poverty and Sustainable Development Goals*[136] is taken straight out of the *Universal Declaration of Human Rights* (Article 25) and *Sustainable Development Goals* (1–2).

These documents are significant for general guidance in keeping with international agreements. Unfortunately, indiscriminate replication cannot provide a critical assessment or contextualized conceptualization of the meaning of social justice. This absence or lack of an applied agreement on the conception and meaning of social justice raises questions regarding the construction of means and processes to address injustice. The lack of an agreed conception of social justice may undermine the efforts and expense of millions of dollars to develop policies and programmes that cannot be implemented. Such absence of conceptualization – as previously stated – impedes pursuing meaningful social justice because the various national documents do so without (1) a conception of social justice which can be accounted for (in

---

134. This narrative is not defined or explained. It sounds like it is assumed that there is a Namibian narrative, but it is that which is defined by the politicians in power.

135. Government of the Republic of Namibia, "Harambee Prosperity Plan," i.

136. Ministry of Poverty Eradication and Social Welfare, "Blue Print on Wealth Redistribution," 12.

terms of assessment); and (2) tested procedures to engage critical questions emanating from the Namibian context. The motivation is driven by political pragmatism rather than careful conceptual analysis, often short-lived or with no far-reaching influence. These are often put forward in the vaguest terms. This vagueness may be confirming Aristotle's[137] assumption that without a clear conception and conceptualization, a society would lack the ability to formulate itself into a vibrant and functional political community. Thus, a vague or unexamined public life would affect the methods used by those in the seats of power to design policies and programmes meant to effect social justice.[138]

Examining the several national documents (policies and programmes) shows that the present assumptions of social justice in the Namibian context have not adopted a contextually relevant conceptual framework. This conceptual absence creates an unstructured approach to addressing social justice, inadvertently questioning both the ability and capability to address the effects of injustice that extend from the days of apartheid. Ogunmokun,[139] critiquing feminist approaches to social justice, writes that the conceptual framework used to deal with gender imbalances, especially women's rights, is borrowed from and influenced by Western liberal theory. This criticism applies not only to a feminist outlook on social justice. It is something that affects the entire nation's way of thinking regarding social justice. For Namibian scholars, adopting social justice so far has been confined to issues of empowerment through employment, business funding, and study grants. The key concept is "empowerment" – expressed in different concepts as access to power, decent payment, recognition, respect, and deconstruction of male-centred historical

---

137. Aristotle, *Complete Works of Aristotle*, 3931–3933.

138. This research does not seek to distinguish between *shalom* and *eudaimonia*, that is, it sees them as related themes divided by culture and context. However, our concept of conceptualization does not start from Athens but from Jerusalem, grounded in Yahweh's self-revelation through the nation and prophets of Israel. It derives its reason for participation in the search for meaningful concepts, policies, and programmes of justice in the Bible's creation account – human beings are God's image-bearers. Thus, injustice is not because of social definitions but because it violates this Genesis account and is an affront to God. It is not Black Namibians versus White Namibians, but a collective societal and communal participation in God's work by ensuring that the human systems function to fulfil God's *shalom* for all.

139. Ogunmokun, "Analytical Exposition," 5.

narrative.[140] Given feminism's conceptual variability, pursuing social justice needs to be thoughtfully engaged to affect thousands of women's quality of life.

2.4.2 Theological and Contextual Framework

The above discussions indicate that there is no lack of theological engagement, however it is inhibited by an epistemological approach based on generalized theories and universal ideas. This habit of unfiltered adoption of theological methods and practices of engaging the post-apartheid context not only becomes a mere academic exercise but also less convincing in its usefulness to affect public thinking. Such theological exercise creates a constant borrowing and importation of concepts and practices that have little meaning for Namibia. The current thinking is deeply stuck in history, buried in the nostalgia of a narrative that has not earned its unique place in the place of ideas that have changed our society.

If pursuing social justice is something to be learned from God, as also confirmed by Liberation Theology, applying the mind to discern God's will for the Namibian context becomes crucial. The present theological frameworks lack thicker imagination which hinders appropriate social imagination that can affect social injustice. It has created a theological praxis locked up in populist semantics, offering an insufficient challenge to the existential situation resulting from oppressive socioeconomic structures.

While this lack of contextualized conceptualization may lead to significant social changes in each community, it is not sustainable – eventually. Without considering that the Namibian context has its history, interpreting it through universal histories would not create a genuinely Namibian critical tradition. Instead, such extensive duplication of ideas only creates ideological stagnation upon a society. The theology that should respond to the present needs of social injustice needs to be authentic. While borrowed concepts might have helped Namibia's initial stages, the theology should have evolved by now.

For example, Niitenge provides an excellent summary and analysis of the socioeconomic conditions (poverty, unemployment, corruption, crime, and exploitation) in Namibia.[141] However, he does so by reiterating the same theoretical framework of the independence struggle that focuses on the

---

140. Akawa, *Gender Politics*, 177, 182–183, 193, 196.
141. Niitenge, "Evangelical Lutheran Church," 274–87.

practical side of addressing social, economic, and political structures but does not question the underlying conceptual approaches of his assumed praxis. How do the concepts of liberation and holistic transformation apply to Namibia? As an academic work, it ought to be interrogating these concepts and their validity and relevance in addressing social injustice.

What is a theology of social justice for Namibia? How does this theology engage both past and present structures that have contributed to injustice and its continuation? How do the affected perceive social justice? Social justice is assumed on behalf of the poor, marginalized, and exploited, but with borrowed views. This patronising approach emanates from taking the meaning and concept of social justice for granted. Both state policies and theological writings mention social justice without unpacking its nature and meaning, making the discourse of social justice both vague and ineffective.

The approach to dealing with social injustice in Namibia has remained stagnant. Failure to develop conceptually and epistemologically has many theologians, politicians, and social scientists rotating in an impasse for addressing social injustice. This absence of an explicit construction of a theological conception of social justice can only create a voice of ignorance among those that would-be prophets. The present theological framework disappoints as it fails to "demonstrate a biblical and theological profile," and the language of justice is superficial "religious window-dressing."[142] Borrowed concepts of social justice or even the theology of justice cannot challenge underlying conceptions and practices that hinder meaningful policies and programmes.

This does not imply that the work, although rudimentary, serves no purpose; they provide a wealth of history of the Namibian struggle against unjust systems and structures. They also provide us with a broad background of social, economic, and political conditions; but the deficiency of high order engagement with the concepts and ideas that inform public decision does not offer theology both a credible and desirable voice in public. While the aim of theology should not be to entertain mere esoteric pursuits, it should be presented in a way that offers credible academic rigour, and has a logical structure and robust theological credibility to gain public attention.

---

142. Smit, "Does It Matter?", 71.

2.4.3 Contextual Articulation

As stated in chapter 1, this research seeks to provide an academic enquiry of the concept of social justice for theologians to rethink their dialogue and practices of social justice. Therefore, it requires considering the context and thinking carefully through the various underlying conceptual challenges that impede social justice. It is not adequate to be prophets, often hiding behind religious language, without carefully rethinking the theoretical foundations that inform us.

Contextualization should move from the mere adaptation of terms, concepts, and ideas to owning and making them relevant. Given the nature of theology as a public discourse, it needs to engage the underlying concepts of social justice that may contribute to socioeconomic injustice. While being prophets requires making the will of God known and proclaiming it, it also requires discernment. Thus, prophetic participation is not just about the spiritual nature of things but engaging the ideas, as Christian academics, that drive inadequate and even ineffective policies, programmes, and structures. While many theologians in Namibia have opted to engage the practical aspect of theology, they have not created a culture that interrogates the concepts that inform their praxis: especially, their viability, meaning, usefulness, relevance, and translatability into formidable academic ideas that would challenge the conceptual status quo and hegemony.

The need to interrogate these adopted concepts' validity should be crucial for establishing just systems to redress the lingering effects of past and present injustices. If public theology is the search to pronounce God's will in all matters of life, then the search to identify meaningful concepts that seek to influence the public perspective and understanding of social justice in Namibia should matter. How individual societies conceptualize their concepts of social justice is profoundly connected to their identity because unjust systems affect economics and how people view themselves. Thus, engaging in the (re)contextualization and (re)conceptualization of social justice would also mean reimagining Namibians' social identity. The impact of this reimagination of identity cannot be overemphasized. The proliferation of the adoption of universal concepts and notions of social justice should be examined for both their effect on the creation of a more just society and the social identity it creates. Thus, it requires a robust theological reflection that extends beyond mere religious window-dressing.

Contextualization should go beyond the mere attempt to indigenize the meaning of foreign concepts of social justice. It should address the meaning of social justice in a country with a history and presence of gross perpetrations of injustice that continue to afflict hundreds of thousands of people. The work of contextual studies should not be the search for a means to conform to or compel the acceptance of pre-existent views. Instead, it should seek a proper understanding of the concepts and their implications on society. In a departure from mere appeal to uniformity to ideas borrowed from somewhere, it seeks to abolish false notions of conceptual uniformity. If all theology is contextual, then contextual theology should critique the epistemologies informing our approach to social justice. Writings in Namibia rarely offer critiques of the underlying concepts of social justice in redressing historical effects of injustice; Akawa's work focuses on analysing these underlying concepts of social justice in addressing inequality issues for women. She attempts to interrogate the meaning of social justice for women from a feminist perspective. Nevertheless, her concept of feminism also needs interrogation, whether its theoretic and conceptual framework do address injustice perpetrated against women is valid. It may suggest that we do not understand what we mean by the concepts we use since we do not unpack their rationality – because the narratives and rationality of social justice cannot be recognized to address post-apartheid challenges of social injustice. Such unclarity creates further dislocation in terms of the way forward and hostile alienation in the present structures and systems. This research assumes that understanding our epistemic condition and our relationship to God in our context would trigger a new or renewed approach to address social justice in Namibia.

This research seeks to find a theological basis that could engage and trigger a discourse of relooking at the meaning, models, applications, and concepts of social justice and taking into consideration, primarily, God's self-expression throughout human societies. While realized through the coming of Christ and God dwelling with humanity, this self-revelation continues to be an unfinished task. God's self-expression extends not only to salvific ends but is also deeply concerned with human dignity, liberty, and social justice – calling Christians to be part of humanising the future. We cannot deny the philosophical, theological, and political nature of these concepts. Social justice and the just systems we seek cannot solely be left to secularist inventions.

While we allow politicians to play their role as assigned by the state, Christian academics represent both the human and divine.

Part of this research is to interrogate any conception of social justice that "fails to accord due recognition to the fact that human beings [by God's design] legitimately hold a plurality of conceptions"[143] of justice. It calls for (re)conceptualising social justice's basic principles to create a basic structure that is somehow coherent and speaks to the Namibian context. Thus, it differs from merely modifying and adapting existing social justice views that seem to function on borrowed presuppositions. We should also be cautious that this does not become a tool of imposing Christian ethos onto a society that rejects its basic premises of faith and conduct. Therefore, this research is on social justice conducted with a Christian worldview, but academic and from a specific context (Namibia).

This search for contextually relevant concepts of social justice should not pursue contextualization for its own sake. We intend to uncover the meaning of social justice and the ontological realities obscured by the apartheid system and post-independence structures. Among these are identity, selfhood, independence, self-determination, dignity, and *shalom*. To design a functional and practical system, we need to reconstruct the fundamental (in the Rawlsian conception of justice) aspects that have been damaged. It is impossible to think of affecting a people's economic and political systems without first leading them to discover a new social reimagination that would grant them the power to structure a just society following their own experiences, hopes, and aspirations. Such reconstruction and reimagination cannot be achieved by indiscriminately transmitting concepts from other contexts.[144]

2.5 Summary

This chapter points to the various discussions of justice or social justice in Namibia. The issues they refer to are pressing and urgent, for example, land distribution, income gap, gender power imbalances, poverty, and unemployment. However, only by understanding the characteristics of their concept(s) of social justice can they attain a systematic approach to social justice in a

---

143. Johnston, *Brief History of Justice*, 204.
144. Cabral, *Return to Source*, 39–56; Hull, "Black Consciousness"; Nkrumah, *Consciencism*.

post-apartheid context. While many Namibians recognize injustice and have spoken regarding its symptoms or manifestations, their engagement stems from conceptual frameworks that do not recognize the Namibian context (see § 2.2). The contextual theological approach seeks to engage the meaning of social justice for the Namibian situation and not borrow concepts, policies, and programmes to apply. Thus, concepts need a rigorous examination to discover meaning, reducing conceptual obscurity, and distinguishing social justice to create a good life – *shalom* for the Namibian context. Thinking and limiting local contexts to universalized terms removes alternatives, reinforces conceptual hegemony, and hinders meaningful socioeconomic transition. While these universal terms suit the general genre of social justice terminologies, they inappropriately reduce the affected communities to passive observers rather than active participants in the social reimagining and transformation of their context. Amid scholarly attempts to address social justice issues, the challenge remains: how do we address the practice of social justice in a post-apartheid context without a homegrown conceptual framework? How can the present theology provide a credible academic engagement with the public in expressing God's self-communication regarding social justice in society and self-determination following principles found in Scripture? (see § 2.3). The research gap (see § 2.4) which this research seeks to cover is the general absence of contextualized conceptualization of the meaning of social justice, but particularly the absence of theology to engage these public discourses. It will be pretentious to assume that this research seeks to settle this quest and question in one attempt. This seminal research engages theology to take a public role in the discourse of social justice. Therefore, the next chapter examines Allan Boesak's work and his theological, political, and philosophical reflections on social justice.

CHAPTER 3

Allan Boesak's Theology, Epistemology, Praxis, and Framing of Social Justice

3.1 Introduction

This chapter will provide: (1) a survey of some of Allan Boesak's work that is relevant to this study, it will also focus on how he conceptualises notions of social justice and their possible meanings; and (2) an analysis of a subset of his ideas and subsidiary concepts, for example, Black Theology and Black Power paradigms, and will ask whether these views could create a meaningful discourse of recovering a society's self-understanding, aspirations, selfhood, and construct a relevant and adequate narrative to deal with injustice (with the contemporary Namibian context in mind). The aim is to locate Boesak's views within the historical, practical, social, political context, and their legitimacy in addressing the post-apartheid southern African context of social justice.

The works of Boesak cited in this chapter are chosen because of their specific focus on his theological views, philosophical framework, and political understandings. He is an extremely prolific author. It is not possible to focus on all his work within the limited scope of a single doctoral study. As such, the researcher, after having done extensive survey research of Boesak's work, chose certain key texts for engagement in this study. They were chosen since they address the following themes that are important for the purposes of this research project:

1. History of his personal experience (Running with Horses);[1]
2. Background of his theological roots (Black and Reformed);[2]
3. Concept of social justice concerning apartheid (Radical Reconciliation;[3] Comfort and Protest,[4] and all his books);
4. Philosophical and political analysis (The Tenderness of Conscience;[5] If this is Treason, I Am Guilty,[6] Farewell to Innocence);[7]
5. Cultural critique of post-independence structures (Pharaohs on Both Sides of the Blood-Red River);[8] and
6. Revisiting of Black Theology of Liberation regarding social justice for women and all the oppressed and marginalized people (Children of the Waters of Meribah).[9]

Boesak's post-apartheid works sometimes repeat important concepts and arguments, as a way of reminding his new readers of where he is coming from, even when exploring newer concepts. These conversation texts provide a diverse genre (theological, political, popular, academic, devotional, sermons, speeches) of Boesak's views on justice regarding post-apartheid. This chapter serves as a curated outline rather than a critical analysis; chapter 4 attends to this latter aspect.

3.2 Boesak's Conceptual Roots

3.2.1 Personal Circumstances

Chapter 1 (see § 1.6.1) provided a short biographic introduction to Allan Boesak. It is helpful to reiterate that information here in order to inform our understanding of the role that his life circumstances played in shaping his theological perspectives. This information will also be kept in mind in

---

1. Boesak, *Running with Horses*.
2. Boesak, *Black and Reformed*.
3. Boesak and DeYoung, *Radical Reconciliation*.
4. Boesak, *Comfort and Protest*.
5. Boesak, *Tenderness of Conscience*.
6. Boesak, *If This Is Treason*.
7. Boesak, *Farewell to Innocence* (1976).
8. Boesak, *Pharaohs on Both Sides*.
9. Boesak, *Children*.

chapter 4, since Boesak's personal experiences shaped his perspective and understanding of notions of justice.

Boesak grew up under apartheid, and its laws, which contributed to his early life's extreme socioeconomic difficulties – for his family and Black people in general. To add to the social troubles was his father's passing, which left the family vulnerable as his mother had to take up various roles, all by herself with eight children. His family is reported to have been so poor that they could not even have birthday parties; their only gift was the Scripture reading that his mother would share on such a day. In the book *Running with Horses,* he describes how his mother's life (spiritual devotion) influenced his knowledge of God and faith.

Boesak grew up with deep concerns about the way that society was structured. He was concerned with how God would respond to the inhumane conditions of Black people. Kakamas, his place of birth, was a physical embodiment of the effects of both slavery and apartheid. It was evident in the shacks in which Black people lived, the schooling system, and his own family's lives. Witnessing such great suffering all around him, which was caused by an unjust sociopolitical system, raised serious questions in his mind regarding social justice.

After completing his theological training, as a young minister among needy church members, he continued to witness his people's wretched conditions. Added to that poverty came the forced removals. For example, he recounts the story of Meraai Arendse, an older woman who asked questions about God's seeming silence in the face of the evil and injustice of apartheid.[10] Boesak recalls how his theological training did not prepare him for his congregants and community's existential questions. He was critical of his primary theological training, considering it as a disembodied qualification which did not prepare him for ministry in his context.[11]

Boesak's awareness was not initially politically motivated; in fact, it was based on wanting to make sense of his faith amid the realities of the apartheid system. For him, he sought to see all his life, including politics from the perspective of faith. He has not discarded this view regardless of the raging presence of poverty and evil perpetrated in the name of God by the apartheid

---

10. Boesak, *Running with Horses*, 8.
11. Boesak, 34.

government. The circumstances of his life should not be divorced from how they shaped him into the person he became, advocating for social justice. His theology and actions in public should be understood within the context of his personal experience. Thus, his is not a disembodied theology but one born and formed from personal experiences of suffering. Inasmuch as it can be critiqued, we cannot escape the fact that Boesak was a child of his times and had to make use of what he had at his disposal. These times include personally painful experiences. While this research is not a biographical study of Allan Boesak, we cannot ignore his personal struggles and how they might have had an impact on his outlook on justice.

Boesak has had his own share of personal struggles, especially in relation to his divorce (in 1991), as well as the 1999 charges of fraud, which he experienced as a personal betrayal from political allies. The latter resulted in his imprisonment, but he received a presidential pardon in January 2005. It is reasonable to consider that such experiences would have shaped his life and informed his theology. His admission to the charges of an extramarital affair was followed by him willingly stepping down from his preaching role, and as president of the WARC. He would also decline taking a post in the United Nations. Boesak does not say much about these experiences in his works. One must infer the influence that they have had on him.

Pharaohs on Both Sides of the Blood-Red River expresses his view of politics and justice from the perspective of an outsider (he had left active politics by the time of its writing). Without adjudicating his guilt or innocence, his views in this book provide interesting dialogue regarding liberation politics in the post-apartheid context. He was charged with fraud (he maintained his innocence and was ultimately pardoned by President Thabo Mbeki). Was he a victim of criminal injustice or some political agenda? Was he betrayed by his comrades of the struggle? How did this experience shape his thinking regarding justice generally? He addresses some of these questions in his memoir *Running with Horses* and the above-mentioned book. He does not categorically define notions of justice, but he narrates new perspectives on issues of social justice, the role of politics, and Christian participation in public life.

The role of women in his life, particularly in his personal relationships, is another matter that clearly shaped his thinking. We are yet to see an open dialogue with Boesak on this chapter of his life and the challenges in his marriage. *Children of the Waters of Meribah* could be seen as a work that expresses some form of self-redemption. However, it avoids a direct engagement with his past and how being a male in a position of power might relate to the identity and roles of women. Nevertheless, it is an excellent contribution that could stimulate future work in which Boesak engages his maleness to redress issues of social justice in relation to women.

The subsections below provide a fuller background of Boesak's theological foundation because it is the primary framework that informs his interpretation of the world and actions. Maluleke summarises Boesak's theological roots that serve as the basis for his thinking.[12] This chapter also discusses how his how his theology and understanding of God (or the revelation thereof) informs his understanding of life, including his notion of justice. Below, we have divided his theological understanding into three key components that inform his notions of social justice, they are: (1) Reformed Theology: Calvinism and Social Justice; (2) Black Theology; Identity Politics and Social Justice; and (3) The God Concept. These are outlines of the conceptual roots of his theology, justice, politics, and identity. The chapter also discusses his public participation informed by his faith, his personal experiences, and those of his community.

3.2.2 Reformed Theology: Calvinism and Social Justice

To understand Allan Boesak, one needs to understand his theology or its roots. It will be careless and an injustice to ignore the conceptual framework that informs his view of social justice – his political theology. Although he gained popularity in the South African political arena, he insists that he is primarily a theologian and a politician *ab accidente*.[13] However, the concept of being an accidental politician is somehow paradoxical. It also conflicts with his roots in Reformed theology that holds firmly to the concept of a sovereign God and that all human activities unfold without catching God by surprise. Therefore, the concept of *accidental* in his book could imply several things:

1. An Aristotelian metaphysical conception regarding the property of a thing but not necessarily a part of its essence. In this regard, being a politician was just an added characteristic which did not define his existence.

---

12. Maluleke, "Boyhood Lost Too Soon."
13. Boesak, *Running with Horses.*

2. An Epicurean perspective that events are unpredictable; thus, getting involved in politics was never pre-planned but instead happened with the turn of events.
3. Being a theologian, he could be employing a theological framework around the concept of an accident to imply God's actions manifested through him – leading him into the forefront of politics unintentionally.
4. An entrance into politics without having gone through the traditional steps of rising through the party ranks (although he went through processes of being elected to the Western Cape ANC leadership). Or,
5. An expression of being caught off guard about where his first public address of 1976 with a political overtone would lead.[14]

The above interpretations of Boesak's meaning of being an accidental politician indicate the difficulty of separating him from politics. He does not provide a clear argument of the differences he seeks to paint to his readers.[15] Boesak grew up in a time of political upheaval in South Africa; the kind influenced both by theology (for and against apartheid) and political theory (for and against apartheid).[16] Boesak's political and theological views are intertwine in such a complex way inthat any attempt to set them apart risks creating a dualistic and false framework. For example, Maluleke writes that Boesak grew up in a context of faith and made sense of the world around him through that lens.[17] He gives a background of how Boesak's life has always intersected between theology and politics, church, and society. Maluleke describes Boesak as one of the "new crop of leaders" that emerged "from the unlikeliest of sections of society."[18]

Two of his early writings *Farewell to Innocence* and *Black and Reformed* depict the formation of his theological and political thoughts. He integrates Black Theology and the philosophy of Black Consciousness to formulate a

---

14. Boesak, 1–3.
15. Boesak, 8; Maluleke, "Boyhood Lost Too Soon," 11–12; Maluleke, "Making of Allan Aubrey."
16. Boesak, *Farewell to Innocence* (1976), 29–32.
17. Maluleke, "Making of Allan Aubrey," 62–63.
18. Maluleke, 62.

theological, moral, and political basis to resist the injustice of apartheid.[19] It is from this integrated view that he says "apartheid is not just a political ideology. Its very existence as [a] political policy has depended and still depends on the theological justification."[20] Thus, there is no seemingly obvious time that Boesak did not think on political issues of his time.

Most importantly, he wanted to make sense of his theological tradition – which was at its heart propagating and benefiting from racially divisive theology. Thus, being Black and belonging to a Dutch Reformed tradition raised both ethical and political questions. Unfortunately, his primary theological training, he claims, "was totally inadequate to deal with the crises of faith that grew out of poverty, socioeconomic injustices and political oppression."[21] His theology found its shape in a profoundly political context, and he seeks to make sense of how to apply that theology, in response to the issues he felt his primary theological training was not addressing.

Moreover, being Black and Reformed, in a sense, was conflicting. How could one legitimately claim that a theological tradition at the core of so much pain and injustice to Black people was still worth advocating in public? Boesak circumvents this challenge by redefining the concept of being Reformed by adding a phenotypical qualifier. Thus, his blackness was a gift of God rather than a curse and he uses a Reformed framework to argue that true reformed theology dismisses the apartheid theology. He is doing what Tshaka calls "engaging his Africanity within the Reformed tradition."[22] Rather than rejecting the Reformed doctrine and tradition altogether, he rejects the notion of Reformed theology that does not embrace a comprehensive vision of the humanity of Black persons. While he embraces aspects of Reformed theology, he rejects its White anthropology which offers nothing positive to the existential realities of Black people. Therefore, he adopts a theology or tradition that he believes took into full consideration Black persons' humanity.[23] In most

---

19. De Gruchy, *Struggle in South Africa*, 149–84. John De Gruchy in *The Struggle in South Africa* provides one of the earliest historical but scholarly summaries of the development of Black Consciousness in South Africa and how it also involved churches and theologians. He was one of the blacklisted White Christian academics under the apartheid system, for being outspoken against the system.

20. Boesak, *If This Is Treason*, 9.

21. Boesak, *Running with Horses*, 34.

22. Tshaka, "African, You Are!," 1–2.

23. Boesak, *Black and Reformed*, 90–107; Tshaka, "On Being African?"

of his writings, he points out that the DRCSA's theology of apartheid was not in conformity with the teaching of John Calvin, the Scriptures, or Christian tradition. As a result, he describes it as a theology that misconstrues God's word to enslave, oppress, persecute, terrorise, and kill Black people.[24] These dehumanising conditions influenced by Reformed theology led Boesak to ask, "What does it mean to be Black and Reformed in South Africa today?"[25]

3.2.3 Black Theology: Identity Politics and Social Justice

Boesak, in the context of racial oppression, needed to make sense of his identity and experiences. Could his theology provide answers to his quest? He argues that "within the Christian message itself lies the indestructible seed of rebellion against inhumanity, injustice and oppression."[26] Thus, he searches for theology or a theological framework that would resonate with the oppressed people's lived experiences, a framework that embraces a theological and political language and shape of the situation. His theological framework indicates significant influences by James Cone that theology is "a rational study of the being of God in the world in light of the existential situation of an oppressed community, relating the forces of liberation to the essence of the gospel, which is Jesus Christ"[27] – with a special concern for the experiences of the oppressed Black people. It also indicates Gustavo Gutiérrez's utilitarian or functionalist view of the incarnated word.[28] He describes the progression of this theological, social, and political integration as a merging that allowed the unlocking and creation of future hope for "oppressed people," thus reclaiming the gospel and restating the prophetic vision for social justice (following Habakkuk 2: 2–3). For him, this is a spiritual renewal that would weaken the social, political, and theological claims of apartheid and restore the humanity of Black persons.[29]

The "Black condition" required a theoretical framework that would also translate into action. Boesak's Black Theology is a practical, theoretical

---

24. Boesak, *Black and Reformed*, 97
25. Boesak, *Walking on Thorns*, 91; Fortein, "Allan Boesak, Black Theology"; Tshaka and Makofane, "Continued Relevance."
26. Boesak, *Tenderness of Conscience*, 10.
27. Cone, *Black Theology of Liberation*, 17.
28. Boesak, *When Prayer Makes News*, 7–12.
29. Boesak, *Tenderness of Conscience*, 10.

framework meant to evoke Christian activism or radical social praxis. The framework is applied in *Black and Reformed*, a collection of addresses to various affected and sympathising groups of people calling, indeed advocating for, radical community action against social and political injustice. He expresses a radical approach to preaching that deals with injustice and provides a framework to redress or address the suppressed consciousness of Black people. It also serves as a tool to help him legitimize his moral-political resistance to the apartheid theology and system. It argues that the premise of God as a liberator of the oppressed implies that blackness needs to feature in God's grand narrative – previously dominated by whiteness. Thus, the demand for liberation in the here and now, was coupled with access to life-enhancing goods and opportunities. By so doing, it stands opposed to a futuristic eschatological utopia that accepts the suffering of Black persons in the here and now as ordained by God, as advocated by apartheid theology. Thus, he sees it as a theological framework that articulates the reality, the meaning of faith, understands the struggles, and can restore the dignity of Black people.[30]

Boesak is opposed to racism. His understanding or interpretation of blackness makes Black Theology a broad-brush discipline. First, he explains blackness as a symbol of oppression rather than a physical feature of skin colour.[31] Blackness, according to Douglas Murray,[32] becomes a political ideology which people can take up to follow. Thus, the abuse of political structures creates a condition of being deprived of privileges and rights, which can only be corrected by an equivalent political resistance. For Boesak, Black Theology is a political theology against all forms of oppression, not only of Black persons. Thus, he uses it as a catholic framework to delegitimize "oppression." He uses this rearrangement of Black Theology and Reformed theology to advocate for social justice in other areas. This advocacy ranges from the Israeli occupation, violence and apartheid towards Palestinians, the ANC's corruption, and the dehumanization of LGBTQI+ persons.[33] Thus, he sees and uses Black Theology as a framework that would enable making sense of faith in an era of growing doubt because of social injustice. In

---

30. Boesak, *Black and Reformed*, 28–33.
31. Boesak, *Farewell to Innocence* (1976), 19, 26–29.
32. Murray, *Madness of Crowds*, ch. 3.
33. Boesak, "Restless Presence."

this sense, Black Theology is a theology of the oppressed taking after Paulo Freire's *Pedagogy of the Oppressed*.[34] It serves as a tool to help the oppressed rediscover their humanity and pursue the various platforms and structures to find social justice and liberation from oppression.[35] This view of blackness is mutative. Thus, White persons can also join in the condition by repenting of their sins of oppression and, furthermore, take collective responsibility for the evil perpetrated on Black persons and commit "themselves to the struggle for liberation."[36]

Second, Boesak relates to James Cone's and Steve Biko's concepts of blackness. His commodious understanding of blackness places so-called Coloureds, Indians, and Black people under one category. This fusion stems from Boesak's anthropological understanding based on the New Testament that God has created new humanity through the reconciling work of Christ.[37] He argues against Nelson Mandela's idea of racial identity.[38] Thus, he defines blackness as a universalisable concept for all persons affected by apartheid. This concept of Black Theology calls for Black persons to reclaim dignity and not accept their oppression as a normal condition. In dealing with existential issues, the answers must come from Black Theology.[39] It is not clear whether this means that only "Black" persons can provide answers to "Black" conditions. This understanding also raises suspicions of the relevance of "non-Black" persons to the experiences of Black persons. The latter notion should be dismissed as it does not accurately reflect Boesak's association with the likes of Beyers Naudé, Nicholas Wolterstorff, and Dietrich Bonhoeffer. Still, it does not exempt the fact that he speaks of Black questions and Black answers or Black ownership of their situation and destiny. He is clear with blackness based on colour, places it within the Messianic narrative, and portrays a Black-led soteriology from oppression. Although Boesak argues that God is the liberator,[40] Black people

34. Freire, *Pedagogy of the Oppressed*.

35. Boesak, *Black and Reformed*, 24.

36. Boesak, 24.

37. It is worth noting that in this one human race concept, Boesak is using Christian symbolism, meant for the believers in Christ, and applies it indiscriminately regardless of religious beliefs or any other social identity.

38. Boesak, *Tenderness of Conscience*, 12–13.

39. Boesak, *Farewell to Innocence* (1976), 14–15.

40. Boesak, 20–22.

are not to be passive in this process. This perspective of blackness has a sense of being a movement that opposes whiteness altogether. Boesak strives to clarify how embracing blackness does not negate whiteness, except if whiteness represents a system of oppression, unjust privilege, and dehumanization but never as a race or colour of skin.[41]

Third, although Boesak insists that Black Theology is not political, he still speaks of its inevitable relationship to politics. Whether this is intentional or simply a consequence is part of his latter debate as he narrates his political journey in *Running with Horses: Reflection of an Accidental Politician*. Black Theology of Liberation by its admission, or at least the definitions given by its proponents, is political. For example, Boesak adopts it as a theological framework during apartheid, and Cone during the Civil Rights movement. That is, it is a theology formed in a profoundly political context with influences from social analysis. Boesak's affinity for Gustavo Gutiérrez's work, which he cites generously in his early work, is evidence of its political nature. While Boesak does not wish to primarily emphasize the political nature of Black Theology, his speeches and addresses (as in *Black and Reformed*) are political responses, using a theological framework. This political nature of Black Liberation Theology explains why the apartheid National Party (NP) responded to it in the *Schlebusch/Le Grange Report*. In response, the South African Council of Churches (SACC) in *A Statement*, led by Manas Buthelezi, combined both political and theological language as a Christian response to the apartheid government. This theological framework, undeniably, was essential in sparking the civil resistance and a grassroots civil rights movement, particularly the UDF. Copeland alludes to the political nature of Black Theology which also made it a political movement with a profoundly Christian bent. He tells of various Christian leaders (including Boesak), engaging with various measures to confront the apartheid system. These leaders focused on how the theological error of apartheid affected the interpretation of human nature and relationships. By bringing Black Theology into public discourse, it demanded "the restoration and redistribution of political and economic power as a concrete expression of love and justice."[42]

---

41. Boesak, 27–28.

42. Copeland, "Black Political Theologies," 275.

Fourth, Black Theology demonstrates another characteristic – it is revolutionary. Quite like Freire's *Pedagogy of the Oppressed*, Boesak engages similar lines of thinking in *Farewell to Innocence*. With this, he calls for a mental reorientation of "oppressed minds" to be liberated from the slavish mentality that glorifies oppression and the oppressor, and normalises weakness. Black Theology, in Boesak's view, is opposed to any Christian theology that is indifferent to human suffering and is "the only authentic way for Blacks to pursue their Christian faith."[43] It calls for confrontation with the powers that be to ensure that just political, economic, and social structures are in place. This resistance can only happen when Black persons stop seeing themselves as perpetual victims and reclaim their place in the world. For Boesak, there is a need to liberate the mind of the "oppressed" as the starting point to wholeness, which he terms reconciliation.[44] He appeals to a liberation didactic theory to assist with the reeducation of the oppressed. He believes only such reeducation would make them realize their humanity. This education includes casting off all symbols of "oppression" that keep them captive (mentally, spiritually, politically, and socially).

The above are some early views that grounded and shaped Boesak's theological path. Over the years, he has reconsidered aspects of the concept of Black Theology but has maintained it as his theological framework. The concept of Black Theology of Liberation is less overtly prominent in Boesak's later writings. *Children of the Waters of Meribah* may be referred to as a Boesak comeback to advocate for Black Theology of Liberation. In this book, he revisits the role of Black Liberation Theology regarding social justice towards women and all the suffering, marginalized, and oppressed persons. It has morphed into a representative blackness referred to in the first characteristic of Black Theology (an analysis of this will be provided in the next chapter). Unlike Cone, Boesak is tactful about his view of blackness but also different because of his christological analysis as the starting point of social identity. He is careful not to come across as advocating for Black domination over White Africans. Thus, his use of blackness represents suffering and all who are living under unjust structures and not blackness as an ontological perspective. This understanding of blackness may explain why Boesak advocates for

---

43. Boesak, *Black and Reformed*, 2.
44. Boesak, *Farewell to Innocence* (1976), 27.

reconciliation, rather than seeking a separate Black society. His understanding of reconciliation, even in the face of injustice, represents his theological understanding that humanity can achieve more by being reconciled. But on a deeper level, while his approach does carry a political label, it reflects a profound commitment to being faithful to the work of God and the call of the gospel.

3.2.4 God Concept

Theology can be narrowly defined as the study of God. We have stated Boesak's theological tradition (Reformed) and theological framework (Black Liberation Theology) but not what he believes about God in the struggle for social justice. Although we can draw hints from his Black Theology, it will be a disservice not to interact with his concept of God and its impact on social justice in society. Boesak makes clear in *Black and Reformed* that he comes from a Calvinistic background. As such, the concept of God is not absent from his activism and pursuit of social justice. It is impossible to find any work of Boesak in which he does not mention or refer to God. Therefore, it is crucial to explore this God concept and its bearing on Boesak's framing of social justice.

Boesak does not argue to establish his view of God. The Christian conception of God is assumed across all his works. He often writes with the assumption that the Christian understanding of God is the default South African position or that his audience is Christian. His work is a radical revision of seeking to integrate Reformed theology with Liberation Theology. While both Reformed Theology and Liberation Theology do speak of God and derive this from the Bible, each is an outcome of different theological assumptions and hermeneutical frameworks.

The primary premise of Boesak is derived from the salvation narrative. *Farewell to Innocence* starts with this salvation narrative, in which he sees liberation as not something "part of" or "consistent with" with the gospel but its very "content and framework."[45] While it speaks of the gospel and liberation, the interpretative framework is that of Black Liberation Theology that is grounded in the Black experience and situation. His language of decolonization philosophy has been given a theological framework, as that which finds

---

45. Boesak, 14.

its origin in God, as he narrates Israel's exodus account.[46] Boesak does not give a specific theological discussion about God (for example, a discussion of the doctrine of God) as the basic foundational framework of his theology.

The concept of liberation is central in all Boesak's work. He is described as a "liberation theologian" in *Radical Reconciliation*, and "liberation" is a reoccurring concept in *Prophet from the South* and the *Festschrift in Honour of Allan Boesak*. This theme (of liberation), in many ways, reflects his understanding of God. It is not clear as to whether Boesak sees God as the theoretical framework for liberation or sees liberation as the theoretical framework for understanding God. This emphasis on liberation seeks an integrated theological epistemology regarding God – using a thematic (liberation) approach. He translates the entire history of Israel as that of social justice, when he writes, "Nothing is more central to the Old Testament proclamation than the message of liberation [from oppression]. God's history with Israel is a history of liberation [and] forms the content of the life and faith, the history and confession of Israel."[47]

Many Reformed theologians understand liberation from the redemptive narrative. Boesak does not dispute that interpretation. He opposes its disengagement and indifference to the lived experiences of those who experience injustice. Therefore, in his understanding, liberation ought to address present-day oppression. Whether Boesak provides God's perspective of social justice or the Black person's understanding of social justice is difficult to distinguish. Nevertheless, it establishes his argument, in his early theology, that the Black Liberation view is "a new way of theologizing, and a new way of believing."[48] In his view, this liberating God is different from the one White people have been advocating. Not that the nature of God has changed but that there is more to God than the view that was espoused by some theologians who supported apartheid. Except that he grounds its genesis in the book of the Exodus, focusing on God's liberating act and uses this as a defining difference

46. Boesak, 20–22.

47. Boesak, 20–22.

48. Boesak, 15.

of who God is. He refers to God as "the God of the exodus"[49] and to Jesus as having a liberating revolutionary vision.[50]

This pedagogic method seeks to present new epistemologies of God and God's action. Boesak does so by pointing out that God needs to be recontextualized, reincarnated, decolonized and represented for a "Black" context. He believes this can only be achieved through a Black Liberation Theology framework. The title of his first chapter "The Coming of the Black Messiah" in *Farewell to Innocence* is intentionally written to reorient our perspective and understanding of God. This Messianic concept is a fluid contextual and epistemological approach as he uses "blackness" to interpret the person and activity of God. To what extent does this view of God help redress a racially divided context? Boesak simply assumes "Black" Theology, Messiah, and God to help redress "Black" self-identity. He does not provide room for self-critical analysis suited for a context divided by racial theologies, philosophies, politics, and social structures.

Boesak also sees God as the creator of a just and equitable world, in the here and now, for the Black persons. In opposition to a spiritualized interpretation of Luke 4 (cf. Isa 61: 1–2), he proposes a material and this-worldly fulfilment of liberation. He holds to a similar understanding as Gutiérrez that "the elimination of misery and exploitation is a sign of the coming of the Kingdom."[51] That is, the concept of liberation is for the here and now.[52] Any other view of liberation, according to Boesak, compartmentalises life and makes light of the suffering of the oppressed who need to be liberated.[53] This liberating view of God is central to Boesak's theological work.[54] As stated in § 3.4, it serves as the basic framework. This liberation framework sets the theological standard he applies in his search to contextualize Christian participation in the search for social justice and the effects of injustice (post-apartheid). His view of God is clearly stated as that of one whose entire focus is to liberate, in *Die Vlug Van Gods Verbeelding*, he writes that God sides with

---

49. Boesak, *Walking on Thorns*, 77.

50. Boesak, *Black and Reformed*, 79–83.

51. Gutiérrez, *Theology of Liberation*, 97.

52. Boesak, *Farewell to Innocence* (1976), 23–26.

53. Boesak, 24–25.

54. Boesak, *Walking on Thorns*; Boesak, *If This Is Treason*; Boesak, "And Zaccheus Remained"; Boesak, *Running with Horses*; Boesak, *Dare We Speak?*

the weak. He argues that *"dit is die swakke wat die gang van die geskiedenis bepaal, omdat God die kant van die swakke kies en hulle stryd vir hulle stry. Waar die stem van die magtelose stilgemaak word, word die stem van God die duidelikste gehoor."*[55]

For Boesak, God is involved in human power relations. He refers to the Exodus account as God's active presence and manifestation, of interfering in ungodly power relations. Many of his examples are derived from the deliverance of Israelites from slavery, and the later prophets who speak out against unjust conditions aimed at the poor, widows, orphans, and foreigners. It is God who looks to grant power to all the marginalized and powerless. This understanding of God explains how he integrates Black Consciousness and Black Power into his theological framework. In his attempt to deconstruct "White" history, he adopts concepts that he believes would aid in the ousting. Thus, his theological framework required a philosophical framework to counter the sociohistorical and power structures of apartheid and create a new imagination of power for Black people under apartheid. The next section discusses this philosophical framework and how Boesak applies it in a theological context.

3.3 Black Consciousness and Power

Dirk Smit opens his exposition of the life of Boesak as one fascinated by power,

> by questions of power, real power, political power, social and economic power; by the power of language, the power of the word, the power of rhetoric and persuasion; by the relationship between morality and power, the questions of ethics and power, the relationships between justice and power, peace and power, violence, non-violence and power, human interests and power; by the nature of power, the power of the powerless, black power, the power of the poor, the power of the marginalised; by power struggles, the struggle against powers and the powerful, by

---

55. Boesak, *Die vlug van Gods*, iv. Translation: "It is the weak that determine the course of history, because God chooses the side of the weak and fights their battles. Where the voice of the powerless is made silent, there God's voice is clearly heard."

naming power, unmasking power, challenging power, resisting power; by theological, particularly Christological claims about power; by prayer and power, and by spirituality and power.[56]

This occupation with the theology of power stood out quite early in his work, as proven in *Coming in Out of the Wilderness: A Comparative Interpretation of the Ethics of Martin Luther King, Jr., and Malcolm X.* In this work, he considered King's theology as centrally aimed at balancing the distribution of power, particularly that the oppressed need to obtain power if they are to be free.[57] Boesak's work falls under the umbrella of contextual theology, a label he willingly endorses or accepts in many of his writings. He holds that every generation must work within its context, and the critical task of theology is to be meaningful and relevant in present circumstances. Power issues are central in his work which is power talk with the search to contextualize power relations. He gives at least two meanings or views of contextualization: first, as an analytical theological method that can help come to terms with a given situation through a critical application. It advocates the need for newer but locally cultivated epistemologies that would reorient the Black person's consciousness as entry levels for effecting change. Thus, the need is to restructure the views adopted from colonial epistemologies to discover one's identity and humanity. It could be argued that it sounds like a quest for Black knowledge to counter White knowledge or intellectual and cultural liberation like the decolonization views shared in *Decolonial Voices.*[58] How he intends to separate his view from falling within the same category of racial categorization of people is not entirely clear to the researcher.

Second, he sees contextualization as a "prophetic" expression, that is, it borrows what is complementary from the past to evaluate the present contexts to open future perspectives.[59] It is a view that looks to separate itself from mere indigenization to be much more dynamic to engage the issues that characterize the moments facing us. He explains the prophetic nature in the words of Shoki Coe and deduces that Black Theology of Liberation coupled with Black Power and Consciousness, is the appropriate medium of action.

---

56. Smit, "Resisting 'Lordless Powers'?", 11.

57. Boesak, *Coming in Out*, 10–11.

58. Aldama and Quiñonez, "Introduction," 1–10.

59. Boesak, *Farewell to Innocence* (1976), 17–18.

This approach would then provide the grounds for the rejection of Western theologies and epistemologies which failed to address the historical, political, socioeconomic, and religious context experienced by those under apartheid.

For Boesak, as with many of his contemporary Black men and women who stood against apartheid, liberation as a theological concept extended to ideological struggles. Gerhart provides a narrative of this development of intellectual striving amongst Africans to counter colonial and oppressive ideologies.[60] He records that ideologies were propagated to create psychological dominance which decided on behalf of Black people without their permission or input. The Black Consciousness and power movement provided the theoretical framework of countering the apartheid philosophy and psychology. Boesak opted for this theology because he believed that apartheid was a multilayered system, consisting of power structures that defined and predetermined "the reality of the black life."[61] Thus, Black Consciousness provides the philosophical foundation for Boesak's theology, even though he claims that it is his theology that justifies his philosophy., There seems to be a connection between a theology that believes that it starts from below and adopting a philosophy from below that would provide the intellectual backing to confront White hegemonic power structures. Power imbalances, according to Boesak, are principal causes of exploitation, oppression, dehumanization, and injustice. This power question brings us to his understanding and notions of Black Power, which integrated with Black Theology and consciousness.

Boesak holds that injustice is because of unequal power structures, in favour of White persons and to the disadvantage of Black persons. This can only change by a conscious decision to cut off "that innocence which refuses to face reality, which clings to empty promises and makes blacks apathetic."[62] The idea of Black Power and Consciousness is also linked to that of Black self-love that calls for the hate of White oppression and enslavement rather than the hate of White persons.[63] He uses the concept as one of the entry points to diminish Black powerlessness created by apartheid theology, philosophy, and politics. He firmly believes that without striving to empower Black people,

---

60. Gerhart, Black Power, 1–11.

61. Boesak, Farewell to Innocence (1976), 48.

62. Boesak, 48.

63. Boesak, Black and Reformed, 14–20.

the instruments of power would remain in the hands of the minority White Africans. This powerlessness, he believes, would continue to affect the access and distribution of life-enhancing goods – education, housing, safety, decent employment, land, and legal representation.[64]

When it comes to understanding Black Power or appealing to it as a means of intervention, Boesak resorts to philosophical, sociological, and political arguments and gives them theological justifications.[65] Thus, he expresses a contextualization which espouses theology for the social sciences.[66] In a similar vein to Steve Biko, he argues that, unless the mind of the oppressed is liberated to think, the oppressor will continue to exercize power over them. Boesak believes that most oppression is because the oppressed have tolerated the oppressors and credited them with mystical and divine powers. Interestingly, he limits this concept of oppression to White persons towards Black persons and somehow claims that history has always been between White oppression and Black resistance.[67] However, he does not say much regarding Black submission to White control.[68] He says Black people have resisted oppression since the colonialists began to explore Africa, and Black Consciousness has always done so;[69] when did they lose their consciousness? He uses William Du Bois, Malcolm X, James Cone, and Martin Luther King's views, to infer that Black Africans under apartheid faced mental suppression.

---

64. Boesak, *Farewell to Innocence* (1976), 48–49.

65. Boesak, 49–54; Boesak, *Black and Reformed*, 17–21; Boesak, *Tenderness of Conscience*, 5–38.

66. Parratt, "Introduction," 8.

67. Boesak, *Farewell to Innocence* (1976), 52–53; Boesak, *Black and Reformed*, 16–17.

68. Pesch and Murray, *Omaruru*. There is a complex relationship between oppressed persons and their oppressors. For example, in the small town where I grew up – Omaruru (historically the first town in Namibia), the first German settlers were all merchants. The then OvaHerero chief resolved that settlers could buy land if they wanted to live and trade in Omaruru, but land on the northern part of the river was not for sale. It was reserved for the locals. This was the practice for decades until the chief died. His son who took over the leadership realized that more money could be made from selling land. He started selling land, even the land reserved for Black people, and in less than 100 years (apart from any forceful removals) the entire groups of Hereros and Damaras living in that area became landless. To date, there is not a single farm in Omaruru that is owned by a Black person born in Omaruru. I argue that it is important to note that Black people have had a complex and at times compromised role in colonialism and apartheid. There is some moral blame on corrupt greedy individuals. *Pharaohs on Both Sides of the Blood-Red River* addresses this issue but not as a pre-colonial, pre-apartheid phenomenon.

69. Boesak, *Farewell to Innocence* (1976), 53–54.

Boesak's espousal of Black Consciousness and power indicates the influences of the dominant resistance movements of his time, and where he found theological justifications for it. In his writings are notions that identify with three strands of resistance movement: (1) African liberation movement (nationalists, decolonialists, socialists, and humanists); (2) Latin American liberation and; (3) the United States Black Liberation movement (Black Power, Black Consciousness, and civil rights). All these ideas are present in Boesak's work, although layered in theological and biblical language. They are formative for the multilayered nature of Boesak's political theology in the wake of African nationalism and liberation ideologies which dominated the political scene from the 1950s to the 1970s. Thus, these were the dominating ideologies of the time, and Boesak sought to integrate them into a theological framework to address the apartheid conditions.

Boesak uses the Black Power and Consciousness ideologies as a means for the oppressed to stand up against the oppressors. In a sense, it is a psychological, philosophical, and political framework that seeks for Black people to see themselves as fully human and equal to the oppressor.[70] However, they need to take power to be able to determine their destiny and reinvent themselves as free men and women. Oppression is because the oppressors think of themselves as more human and entitled to all the life-enhancing goods based on the colour of their skin, political advantage, or economic power. This oppression, he argues, should be countered through a new consciousness – the kind that "does not primarily designate [the] color of [the] skin' but 'enables black people to form new alliances on a basis completely foreign to the oppressor's way of thinking and thereby effectively deposes [or deprives] him of the ideological power over blacks."[71]

Appealing to Black Power and Consciousness is based somehow on the belief that only an equal ideological force can confound apartheid as an ideology. Since apartheid affirmed White humanity and identity, and affirmed blackness, using the political and legal structures was a suitable way of countering it. Whether this adoption of Black Power and Consciousness is the logical outcome of his Black Liberation Theology or driven by the need to contextualize is challenging to distinguish. It can be argued that his desire to create

---

70. Boesak, *Die vlug van Gods*, 15.

71. Boesak, *Farewell to Innocence* (1976), 55.

a "holistic" framework to deal with injustice blurs and creates multiple contours. It also indicates the complex nature of redressing the injustice created by the apartheid system. However, Boesak is convinced that the psychological orientation which used Christianity as the conduit for oppression, can only be overcome through a counteraction by Christianity when he argues that "within the Christian message itself lies the indestructible seed of rebellion against inhumanity, injustice and oppression, and within it is the undeniable surge toward freedom ... despite its misuse for the subjugation of people, it became . . . the ideal religion for the liberation of the same people."[72]

In his defence of Black Power, consciousness, and theology, Boesak believes that this merging "unlocked the door to the future for the oppressed people . . . at a time when most . . . thought that all was lost. It rekindled the almost decayed hope in the hearts of the downtrodden . . . It reclaimed the gospel for the poor and the oppressed."[73] In his view, Black Power, Black Consciousness, and Black Theology were catalysts in resisting various forms of oppression and shaping the courage to be Black.[74] He narrates in *The Tenderness of Conscience* that

> it was an undaunted pride in blackness which was necessary to overcome the psychological ostracism and alienation that white domination brought and on which it thrived, and an unshakable faith that this battle for freedom would be won. Within the context of apartheid . . . it was absolutely wrong to continue to internalise the apartheid mentality by categorising ourselves in terms of the self-defeating definitions created by the oppressor.[75]

Today, Boesak is engaged in promoting political democracy and human rights using the same ideologies, to redress the social and economic effects of apartheid. The political understanding is embedded in a social analysis of the divide between the powerful and powerless, oppressor and oppressed dialectics. It believes that the fight for the decolonization of the Black mind is far from over, without the creation of authentic Black epistemologies. Thus, we need to confront present social, political, and cultural structures that are (re)

---

72. Boesak, *Tenderness of Conscience*, 10.
73. Boesak, 10.
74. Boesak, *Farewell to Innocence* (1976), 48–50; Boesak, *Tenderness of Conscience*, 8–17.
75. Boesak, *Tenderness of Conscience*, 20.

customized to continue structurally enhanced oppression and injustice. Thus, for Boesak, Black Liberation Theology, Black Power, and Black Consciousness are contextual attempts to address injustice and lay the foundation to enable living in dignity.

Political apartheid as a legalized system has been abrogated. However, its effects remain. Boesak continues to use the same theological and political lines of thought to address the post-apartheid context. The remaining sections of this chapter will interact with how he now speaks within a post-apartheid context of social justice that combines his theology, philosophy, and politics. We must acknowledge that Boesak's early work to integrate various ideologies and theologies to address social injustice is complex and daunting. This work is still finding its place and is far from being fulfilled – especially given the post-apartheid conditions which replicate the very oppressive system it fought to eliminate in the first place.

3.4 Theology of Power and Consciousness

Boesak's theology begins and ends in the notion of the God who liberates. Without liberation, his entire theological structure would disintegrate. God is concerned with delivering people from oppression and enabling them to free themselves from those that perpetuate such systems and structures. It is impossible to come across Boesak's work that speaks of theology that does not touch on matters of social justice or a concept of God that is lethargic to issues of social justice. There can be no Boesakan theology without the concept of liberation – he dismisses any view that does not agree with a liberative theological motif. To understand Boesak's theology of justice, we need to mention some important theological documents that continue to inform his theology.

3.4.1 Kairos Consciousness

Boesak's theology was developed within a tense political context of apartheid. This political context has influenced his thinking. Besides having adopted Black Liberation Theology perspectives, theological confessions ground his theological pursuits (influenced by the *Kairos Document* of 1985 and the *Belhar Confession* of 1986). Thus, Boesak sought to construct a view of Liberation Theology based on Reformed confession. However, he takes it a step further by introducing a liberationist ecclesiology which sees the church as the agent of, and for, social justice. He insists that the church is endowed with the duty to discern its different moments and respond accordingly. That is, to have a *kairos* consciousness.

Consciousness, discussed above, represents the gospel and missional activity, and the church is called to resist "the powers of evil, for the sake of the wronged and powerless, and for the sake of the Gospel."[76] While the appeal in *Kairos, Crisis, and Global Apartheid* is to the Reformed Church tradition, it is by extension to the whole church. Boesak's view is that the gospel should concern itself with the here and now, and material reality.[77] He believes that "the gospel proclaims that God is at work with us now, actively fighting the forces that would make man [sic] captive."[78] This understanding makes the gospel revolutionary in nature, and the church becomes the agent of the revolution. Social justice would then only come by revolution.[79] Revolutions are God-ordained means to rewrite history or the human course, especially in favour of the oppressed.[80] Boesak further argues that God is at work both through the church and the world at large to bring liberation for all.[81] The Holy Spirit achieves these activities through different conduits since God is at the centre of all human history through revolutions. This helps us to understand why Boesak is both a theologian and a political activist. This view of revolution and participation in the formation of human political history to bring about a just society could help to explain his role in the UDF.[82]

3.4.2 Radical Social Imaginary

Boesak's theology introduces a social imagination that sees the political as an act of the Christian community, which should be part of the social and political revolution.[83] In line with Emmanuel Katongole's question, "Does

---

76. Boesak, *Kairos, Crisis and Global*, 17.

77. Boesak, 22.

78. Cone, *Black Theology*, 38.

79. Boesak, *Farewell to Innocence* (1977), 95–98.

80. Boesak, 90.

81. Boesak, *Kairos, Crisis and Global*, 21–22.

82. Boesak, *Running with Horses*.

83. Boesak, *Kairos, Crisis and Global*.

Christianity have the power to save Africa?,"[84] Boesak believes that to over-come the pervasive and persistent oppressive structure, Christians need to occupy and participate in the political to influence policies and power structures. This is clearer in *The Tenderness of Conscience* as he advocates an African Renaissance, in support of Thabo Mbeki's call for the rebirth and rediscovery of a united Africa that would free itself from the shackles of history's oppression and present global manipulations. Boesak believes that religion, especially Christianity, holds the answer and can save Africa from the present evil, by injecting moral consciousness into the present body politics.[85] In so doing, they are taking steps of faith to fulfil the promises of Christ, of liberation. Given that there is no dichotomized narrative of history (secular and salvation history), Christians are to participate in its unfolding to effect, especially, "the new discovery of selfhood, freedom, dignity, new forms of society, and the search for the meaning of life."[86] He interprets this as the meaning and practical exercise of discipleship, in the order of Bonhoeffer. Thus, in Boesak's view, we need a theology that stands by God, that is, stand-ing actively with "those who suffer in the world," for all God's actions are aimed at redeeming the oppressed.[87] This standing with God cuts across the contours of religious beliefs, social classifications, political affiliations, philosophical associations, moral convictions, and nationalities. He puts it in a rhetorical question:

> Why should we see this in Martin Luther King Jr., but not in Malcolm X; in South Africa but not in Palestine; in Nelson Mandela's work for reconciliation but not in the women's fight for dignity and the protection and assertion of their rights; in the brave men and women fighting for eco-justice but not in the equally brave women and men who are claiming their God-given humanity as LGBTI persons; in the masses following Gandhi but not in the masses of the Arab Spring uprisings?[88]

---

84. Katongole, *Sacrifice of Africa*, 20.

85. Katongole, *Future for Africa*; Katongole, *Born from Lament*.

86. Boesak, *Tenderness of Conscience*, 22–23.

87. Boesak, 22–23.

88. Boesak, 23.

Theology, from this interpretation, is an exercise of living in the moment, always on the lookout for the suffering, oppressed, and marginalized. In a sense, the Christian community becomes the practical and earthly instrument of realising the liberation of God's creation. For Boesak, this active anticipation and search for opportunities to take part in social justice is gospel work and evidence of obedience to Christ's mission. The Christian community then becomes a unified body of social reformers. That is, they are to put in practice the theology of resistance with radical dynamism as a public witness and display of gospel transformation in the social sphere.[89] This participation, in Boesak's view, resembles "the inverted order" of God's kingdom "with its saving grace, its radical demands for justice, peace and the liberation of God's people; with its good news for the poor . . . and the fulfilment of their human potential."[90]

The spirit of this theological reflection and application is what Boesak and DeYoung refer to as "radical,"[91] both in attitude and practice. The centrality of social justice in Boesak's work while it rejects violent takeover, is willing to take up any means to effect justice. Here, Boesak's concept of God's sovereignty assumes that any tool that would bring about the desired results of social justice should be considered as God-ordained.[92] He argues this from the view that the lordship of Jesus Christ is over all creation and human institutions. We may assume that any actions that can lead to inclusiveness and social justice "fall under the sovereignty of Christ."[93]

Boesak speaks of Black Theology, Black Power, Black Consciousness, and liberation. His reconciliation perspective serves as the turning point of what he seeks to achieve, a just society for all persons, regardless of sexual orientation, religion, race, or tribe. It is worth noting that Boesak, at least in his own words, does not advocate for antiwhiteness. He stands for Black solidarity which weighs the oppression of Black people as primarily caused by racism and colonialism.[94] This perspective grounds or blames the Black situation

---

89. Boesak, 1–13.

90. Boesak, 91.

91. Boesak and DeYoung, *Radical Reconciliation*.

92. Boesak, *Farewell to Innocence* (1977), 91.

93. Boesak, *Tenderness of Conscience*, 166.

94. Boesak, *Farewell to Innocence* (1976), 109–12; Phiri, "African Women's Theologies," 148.

on colonialism or oppression and thus seeks to overthrow White power. This overthrow, particularly of oppressive structures, for a more racially, culturally, spiritually, socially, and politically inclusive society is in Boesak's view the entry-level to a just society. In this case, theologians are to play a prophetic role, like that of the prophets of the Old Testament.

3.4.3 Prophetic Witnessing

Boesak has also been called a "prophet" by some scholars,[95] for speaking out against structures and systems of racially motivated injustice. The concept of the prophetic is linked and described in radical terms and language. Boesak uses the text of Amos as an example. The prophetic witness became more than an ideology; it had substantial life-altering effects on him. The prophetic resistance became a way of life which placed him in a position of disadvantage with the government[96] and laws of apartheid.[97] He describes it as follows, "Half my ministry has become a confrontation with the South African government and its forces, in the pulpit and, because of that, in the streets. Arrested, threatened, imprisoned in solitary confinement, walking into rifles and machine guns, tear-gassed in churches, faced with horrors."[98]

His friend Nicholas Wolterstorff narrates in *Journey towards Justice*[99] how Boesak's convictions frequently placed him in conflict with the government.[100] Boesak publicly defied injustice at any time he had the opportunity to do so. In his own words, he acknowledges this defiance: he "said publicly that apartheid is evil . . . a blasphemy, . . . a heresy . . . [its] government is unjust . . . undemocratic . . . unrepresentative, it does not have the love or the support of the people, it has no right to exist, it is illegitimate, it should not be there."[101] Because the then South African government was morally wanting, he

---

95. Dibeela, Lenka-Bula, and Vellem, *Prophet from South*; Flaendorp, Philander, and Plaatjies-Van Huffel, *Festschrift*.

96. Boesak, *If This Is Treason*, 74–83.

97. *If This is Treason, I Am Guilty*, is a speech Boesak delivered at a gathering of the UDF in Durban, 27 February 1985, which became the title of his collected speeches published in 1987.

98. Boesak, *If This Is Treason*, 13–14.

99. Wolterstorff, *Journey towards Justice*, 129–39.

100. Olivier, "Withdrawal of a Passport."

101. Boesak, *If This Is Treason*, 83.

called on religious communities to . . . "pray that God should give . . . another government"[102] and concluded that based on these convictions,

> if this is treason, then I am guilty of treason, and . . . if I am guilty of treason, then charge me with treason and put me in jail. I say this . . . not out of a sense of bravado. I have no desire to be a martyr – God knows my life for the last month or two has been hell enough. I say this not out of defiance, because I know that the minister to whom I am speaking now is a very powerful man, a man without a conscience who can do whatever he likes and get away with it. But I say this because in a perverted, unjust, and cruel society such as ours, where those who fight for freedom and peace and human dignity are banned, detained, and charged with treason while criminals sit in Parliament and receive accolades from those who share in their power and privilege, this is the only decent thing to do.[103]

This ensuing personal suffering, according to Boesak, is the radical nature of the prophetic. He borrows much from Dietrich Bonhoeffer's resistance to Adolph Hitler's fascist Nazi government. He opposed not only the philosophical and political nature of apartheid but also its theology, which he saw as heresy and blasphemy. This public resistance of the apartheid government was the beginning of branching out of academic and pastoral work that was a move from speech to action (activism). Boesak saw his actions as part of what God requires us to do where there is injustice. For, injustice does not represent God's nature and order of creation. Using Wolterstorff's conception, this could be referred to as an application of "prophetic social imagination."[104]

In his conception, Boesak had come to believe that the Christian's role is to stand up for social justice in an unjust society. Religion (inclusively) ought to advocate for social justice and be the voice of the oppressed and silenced. Advocacy, in Boesak's view, integrates proclamation, (using the pulpit, lectern, street, stadium), and political involvement. Thus, prophetic action results in activism. For Boesak, this activism had commenced since his initial address as

---

102. Boesak, 83.
103. Boesak, 83.
104. Wolterstorff, *Journey towards Justice*, 173.

chaplain at the University of Western Cape (UWC), as he narrates in *Running with Horses*. However, it is only in 2015 that he pens this idea of activism for a post-apartheid context in *A Restless Presence,* calling for the church's active occupation with social justice. Central to his proclamation and denunciation of apartheid, he proposes overthrowing it through the ballot for a democratically elected and gender and racially inclusive government.

Beckoning support from the Old Testament prophets, he advocates for a more just system. He combines the prophets' call for justice with the philosophy of political liberation, to forge a theology of resistance against unjust structures. Throughout his early struggles, Boesak concerned himself with the relevance of Scripture to his context, especially the South African one. He tried to address issues with this background in mind. To an extent, he saw everything in the Bible with the question in mind, "how does it speak to the South African context?" To him, the prophetic implies speaking into the situation of injustice and proclaiming God's justice and righteousness, in other words, contextual proclamation in the given moment and time.

It is therefore not unbecoming that Boesak reevaluated the message of the book of Revelation and applies it to the South African context. His collections of addresses equate the sufferings of South Africa as a nation to those of the suffering church. Boesak does not seek to explain a theology of the church. He intends to use the church's suffering (in Revelation) as the suffering of the nation, and how God would deliver it from the oppressor. Whether this is a matter of applying principles from the biblical text to speak into the current situation of his country or that he is creating a new hermeneutical approach is not clarified. However, he is clear that he seeks to find a new understanding and application of the apocalyptic text to speak to the South African context, rather than the symbolism it represents.[105] The prophetic resistance that Boesak promotes opposes oppressive structures and powers that exploit the weak, powerless, and defenceless. He compares the then Roman systematic oppression and cruelty towards all who held to divergent religious, political, social, and cultural views to that of the apartheid government.

When he was placed in solitary confinement for defying the apartheid government, he likened his experience to that of John on the island of Patmos. He feels comforted that he is not the first to be incarcerated for taking a stand

---

105. Boesak, *Comfort and Protest,* 13–14.

against oppressive powers but was one among many brothers and sisters. Like John's message of God who is sovereign and powerful over evil, Boesak foresees the end of apartheid, marked with new hope for the oppressed people of South Africa. He likens the South African government to the dragon with hellish and destructive power that seeks to dominate and oppress;[106] to the beast from sea and earth exercising power without mercy upon the weak;[107] and to Babylon the apostate state drunk with greed, exploitation, and violence.[108] He ends by saying that judging from history, even the apartheid government would end, like the then oppressive Roman state.

As the title of the book *Comfort and Protest* shows, Boesak places hope in the power of God to bring about a miracle to overthrow injustice. However, he encourages human political participation. The comfort Boesak provides is that injustice would eventually end and there shall be universal peace and justice. The message of this commentary is deeply buried in Christian theology, rightly so, because they were theological lectures and sermons. This book is Boesak's work that is most specifically addressed to a Christian audience,[109] although deeply laced with political nuances. This commentary seeks to sensitize Christians to the realities of their political environment, a subject Boesak is quite passionate about and which stands out in these lectures and addresses.

In Boesakan conception, the prophetic is radically active in resisting exploitative systems. These power structures that exploit, oppress, and dehumanize need to be destroyed for more just structures. This resistance is advocated in Boesak's various writings, challenging power relations as in *Walking on Thorns*; mental reorientation as in *The Tenderness of Conscience*; resistance as in *If This Is Treason Then I am Guilty* and mobilising the oppressed to a new consciousness as in *Farewell to Innocence*. Could these concepts of power (its (re)distribution, sharing and removal) be Boesak's way of referring to justice? A society whose structures and institutions of power remain unchallenged would continue to reinforce deficient and precarious approaches to social justice. However, this requires developing an adequate conception of social justice that consists of a rational and orderly manner

---

106. Boesak, 79–92.
107. Boesak, 93–107.
108. Boesak, 108–24.
109. Boesak, 15–19.

that captures the essence of the meaning of social justice within the given context and reflects a proper understanding of a thing's essence. It leads to interacting with Boesak's notions or his conception of justice derived from his theology, philosophy, and political conviction. They are notions because social justice, in general, is discussed in a cluster of family concepts – all aimed at seeking to achieve a satisfactory expression of what could be judged as just. One can never understand Boesak's view of social justice by only assuming one perspective because he uses multiple views, symbols, metaphors, and narratives to describe it.

3.5 Towards an Understanding of Boesak's Notions of Justice

Boesak's concepts of justice are deeply linked to his theological and political roots. This section outlines a cluster of themes and concepts (power, liberation, revolution, restitution, and reconciliation) used in his work to describe or define some of the dominant aspects of the concept of justice. These concepts do not constitute a definition but are arrangements building up to what he thinks would represent social justice or a just post-apartheid society. His concept of social justice is written in the form of action rather than theory, best described in Nicholas Wolterstorff's *Journey towards Justice*. They are attempts to provide a Christian voice in the public sphere for processes contributing to the view that stands out in Boesak's work as components of social justice or even as justice.

3.5.1 Power and Social Justice

Power is a recurring theme in Boesak's works. Dirkie Smit considers this to be his central framework – referring to it as a fascination with power and its relationship to various issues.[110] This fascination with power could be rooted in his experience of powerlessness which encumbered his early life. The apartheid system was among other things centrally a play of power, the powerful exploiting the powerless. This power was displayed in the forceful removal of Africans from prime areas, confining them to townships, and shooting and killing school-going children; conferring disproportionate access

---

110. Smit, "Resisting 'Lordless Powers'?" 11.

to life-enhancing goods to White Africans while denying Black Africans, forging for them a substandard education system and inadequate healthcare services. These were some of the practices used by the apartheid system to dehumanize Black people.

According to Boesak, the apartheid system created a colossal chasm of power, whose effects can only be reversed if the scales of power are balanced or readjusted. He believes that excessive and unequal power denies people of the power *to be*. It also denies living with dignity; therefore, the post-apartheid context requires relegislation to give (political, economic, and social) power back to those who were disempowered by force. For Boesak, power is the primary entry point to attaining lives of dignity. Social justice ought then to include giving power to those who were disempowered. He is not speaking of power to dominate others but to enable individuals and communities to reclaim their dignity and personhoods which were defiled by the apartheid system.

To some measure, this explains why the Black Power movement resonates well with Boesak because power enables reclaiming and establishing one's dignity and confidence. Whereas apartheid has painted the image that persons have no value and are subhuman, empowerment through adequate education can enhance a new consciousness to counter falsehood. Whereas apartheid has normalized economic deprivation for millions, only adequate skill enhancement can bring employment and wages, which would eventually trigger better living conditions. Whereas apartheid created structures that prohibited access to resources, new and enabling structures are needed that will make resources available and grant access that would allow the balancing of the scales of use. Boesak argues for a restorative approach to address past injustices inflicted by the apartheid system.[111] That is, reconciliation ought to evidence itself in a system that leads to the realization of socioeconomic justice and fundamental structural transformation that would enhance it.

Although Boesak does not say "power is social justice," it is implied to some extent. Thus, social justice begins in the ending of certain forms of power – oppressive power. However, the ending of an oppressive power relation should be replaced or substituted for a substantial one that grants power to the previously oppressed. Boesak is calling for an affirmative response of

---

111. Boesak, *Tenderness of Conscience*, 202.

empowerment, particularly socioeconomic empowerment that would create new structures.[112] This newness, he believes, should be able to deracialize capital or economic power which is still concentrated among White Africans. Thus, affirmative action creates equitable access to economic power, to remove what he believes is the primary level of powerlessness.

He disagrees with what he calls the myth of a Christian view of reconciliation that denies social justice, particularly in response to the TRC's way of handling the reconciliation process. The business sector, which has benefitted from illicit power structures that favoured it at the expense of Black Africans under apartheid, has remained virtually unchanged in the promotion of hegemonic racial economics. This lack of economic power in Boesak's view is a continuous onslaught of social injustice towards those who were disadvantaged by a systematically orchestrated arrangement. Without a transformative impact on the economic structures, Boesak argues, we become but prophets of secular hyper-capitalist markets. If reconciliation is having any bearing on the post-apartheid structure, it ought to have begun by insisting on equal distribution and access to goods that grant economic power.

Like many liberation theologians and politicians, Boesak places high emphasis on economic issues. Poverty or its elimination has been central in the anti-apartheid movement both in Namibia and South Africa, besides the political situation. Boesak believes that something so endemic to the existence and progress of apartheid has been left untouched.[113] Merely focusing on relational restoration deprived millions of Africans of attaining the social justice they deserved. As a result, although the socioeconomic conditions of Africans have improved, they continue to be hampered by the effects of the past structures, unequal distribution of and access to resources which still exists today. In his argument for this, he holds that reconciliation, which was a national project that left out material aspects of restoration, cannot be authentically referred to as reconciliation – in the biblical sense.

However, he narrates how the newly empowered Black elite have become perpetrators of socioeconomic injustice.[114] Thus, even where resources have been made available, a few would steal these for purposes of self-enrichment.

---

112. Boesak, 202–3.
113. Boesak, 202–4.
114. Boesak, 30, 50, 62.

This siphoning of state resources, he believes, is due to the lack of account-ability structures. In Boesak's view, we need a new revolution to replace un-just governments that damage the livelihoods of people. Thus, he calls for continuous activism and political engagement to address issues of economic disempowerment in the new structures. Boesak, however, is still convinced that although enormous wealth has been transferred to many Black Africans, capital in general needs to be deracialized. It is not deracialized if those who actively benefit from it are the politically connected elites. He argues that "all it means is that the tight circle of the new, empowered black elite have joined the white rich and the rich are still getting richer."[115]

He ties this form of economic power-sharing to the idea of love for one's neighbour – a recognition of the humanity of another. Thus, the wealthy and powerful ought to be held accountable to share their resources to redress these historical effects of poverty. This view assumes that all creation falls under God's control, regardless of one's religious or lack of religious beliefs. Boesak uses a social hermeneutical approach which he believes should be applied to a secular society, even those who reject the Christian ethos. He uses Christian concepts and text, for example, to affirm that humanity is one body united by God. This unity then implies that the wealthy are to be held accountable for their extreme wealth, especially the kind given to them under an unjust structure.

The hermeneutical applications borrowed from John Calvin in Boesak's view speak to the post-apartheid context today. Whether this is an intentional selective application of Calvin will be examined in the next chapter. Boesak firmly believes the rich should share their wealth with the poor: first, as a way of obeying God, and second, as an act of human solidarity in narrowing the economic power gap created by both past and present structures of unequal distribution and access.[116] However, to date, Boesak has not yet engaged the complexity of distribution of wealth taken from the wealthy in a practical economic sense. His contribution, up to now, is based on what is good and right, not yet on how this could be achieved. He proposes that the wealthy are mostly wealthy because of unjust structures created by a previously op-pressive system or currently corrupt one. While he assumes that it is a good

---

115. Boesak, 203.
116. Boesak, 203–5.

thing to distribute the wealth accumulated by the wealthy, it is not clear how it would be done on a mass scale. He, however, assumes an affirmative action approach for economic transformation, and the need for redistribution of the ownership of land from minority White ownership to a more just and equitable distribution.

Power, as a concept, cannot stand on its own. It is a concept that relates to other different concepts, to find concrete expression. In the previous section, we discussed how Boesak links socioeconomic emancipation, particularly the distribution of and access to capital, to power. Nevertheless, in most, if not all his works, Boesak refers to liberty as a form of power and as an expression of social justice. Borrowing from John Calvin, he argues that oppression is denigration and violation of human dignity, but more so an insult to God.[117] Without liberty, humans cannot be fully human and are robbed of the power to live as they ought to.

His view of liberty, while rooted in the history and experiences of apartheid and colonialism, incorporates the challenges of social justice within a post-apartheid context. In his view, the post-apartheid political system did not do much to abolish injustice and create structures that would enable human flourishing. In *Dare We Speak of Hope? Searching for a Language of Life and Faith in Politics*, he points out how the ANC's failures are similar to those cited in Namibian post-apartheid literature.[118] He takes the concept of liberation much further than mere political liberty to a search for and promotion of human dignity. Giving the political language a spiritual form is indicated in *Tenderness of Conscience: African Renaissance and the Spirituality of Politics*.

Liberation takes a new form – one that appeals to the awakening of the conscience of those in positions of economic, social, cultural, and political power. Boesak is not advocating taking away power from the powerful but for sharing this power through established or transformed democratic structures. He incorporates Parker Palmer's views that seek to use democratic structures to transform society.[119] It is not clear whether this is a turn from the previous position of an external revolution by now replacing or even integrating it with an internal revolution. The latter is a search for spiritual transformation

---

117. Boesak, 203.

118. Hishoono et al., *Constitution in 21st Century*; Melber, "Namibia."

119. Boesak, *Dare We Speak?*

within the structures of power or what Palmer refers to as the creation of "a politics worthy of the human spirit."[120]

Power, according to Boesak, is at the centre of advancing injustice. In that case, it needs to be redistributed by creating structures that offer real freedom to the powerless, to level out the imbalances. Boesak advocates for this redistribution of power through a politics of the conscience. Christian advocates for social justice have a duty to take up public platforms of sensitising the hearts and minds of those with power (economic, social, cultural, religious, and political) to transform structures. He argues that real power is not demonstrated in hoarding but by carrying out acts of social justice towards the vulnerable in society. If the distribution of both economic and political power remains limited only to a selected few, the post-apartheid context has become a shrewd imitation of oppression and enslavement. This unequal distribution of power, in Boesak's view, only accentuates and immortalises an endless cycle of a permanent, unmentioned, and unremembered underclass.[121]

Thus, in terms of a consistent intervention, regarding the future of post-apartheid states and social justice, the power question needs serious attention. Power structures need to be deconstructed to create sustainable quality standards of living which the apartheid system had destroyed. However, "political will" alone will not suffice to address the rampant gap of power, which is causing the doom of many in the post-apartheid setting. Power to produce a just environment in which hope and human wholeness thrive requires a firm theological stand that can challenge and resist the status quo that fails to embrace change but relentlessly promotes cycles of oppression under new governments. This kind of decision (which Boesak refers to as acts of faith and obedience to Jesus Christ) and stance against unjust and inhumane power structures "is indispensable for the understanding and nurturing of hope."[122]

Boesak argues that if the structures of power remain to reinforce socio-economic hegemony, social justice and transformation will linger as distant imaginations. This power imbalance needs to be tilted if we are to have an equitable distribution of goods and benefits. The primary role of the church is to enforce liberty and justice. When those in power refuse to address the

---

120. Palmer, *Healing the Heart*, 16, 18, 26.
121. Boesak, *Dare We Speak?*, 22–23.
122. Boesak, 15.

plight of the disadvantaged, such systems, Boesak believes, should be confronted with a revolution that confronts the post-apartheid conditions to ensure that power is distributed equitably across the racial, social, and gender spectrums of society. Boesak's idea of revolution is nonviolent and falls within the broader category of civil disobedience. By it, he implies: to disrupt the system until it is adjusted and adapted to benefit everyone rather than a selected few or elites. While the resistance to power imbalances has political connotations and implications, Boesak thinks this to be an outcome of prophetic resistance or a theology opposed to adaptation to existing conditions of oppression and injustice.

Thus, Christians do not have to look far to see what inspired "slave revolts and resistance against colonial oppression."[123] Their theology, he argues, was their source for devising resistance to power imbalances in the post-apartheid context. The disenfranchised and disempowered cannot live a life of dignity unless they are accorded and have the power to do so – which will not happen without radical intervention. To be liberated, in Boesak's view, is to have the power freely to make decisions about where to live, what to eat, where to raise children, to which schools to send them, and to negotiate your wages. That is, socioeconomic issues are at the centre of social justice. However, this can only be achieved through a determination "that is unprepared to accept the [post-apartheid] world as it is and the powerful [or powers would be] have made."[124]

Restructuring and redistributing power, for Boesak, is an entry-level for social justice as all social injustice is a result of power imbalances. He cannot seem to foresee the possibility of an authentic and sustainable national reconciliation after apartheid without challenging and balancing the power relations between apartheid beneficiaries and survivors. Therefore, Boesak has remained critical towards the reconciliation narrative of post-apartheid South Africa, which he criticises as a manoeuvre for political accommodation. It does not have social justice as its aim. It has failed to demand a radical change in socioeconomic conditions. According to him, it implies a poor understanding and application of the biblical meaning of reconciliation. He argues right at the introduction to the book *Radical Reconciliation* that the

---

123. Boesak, "Restless Presence," 26.
124. Boesak, "Hope Unprepared," 1055.

prevailing understanding of reconciliation favours the interests of the wealthy and powerful and promotes powerlessness. According to him, referring to the TRC model, what is happening is "not reconciliation" but a system designed "for reasons of self-protection, fear, or a desire for acceptance by the powers that govern our world [to] seek to accommodate this situation, justify it, refuse to run the risk of challenge and prophetic truth telling, we become complicit in deceitful reconciliation."[125]

He deduces that the concept of reconciliation is inadequate if it fails to address the power relations in the post-apartheid context. Nevertheless, he applauds the *ubuntu* idea of reconciliation as employed by Desmond Tutu in the establishment of the TRC. He says *ubuntu* is a unique gift of South Africa to the world but finds its extent to be inadequate.[126] Boesak does not think apartheid to have simply been an offence to be forgiven and that the different camps should reconcile and move on with life from a blank slate. He believes such an approach to the history of oppression only widens the gaps of power, as it fails to address how to redress the inequalities that came about because of the apartheid system. He writes regarding this failure to address power relations that,

> in not being nearly as insistent with the perpetrators and benefi-
> ciaries of Apartheid as with the victims on this point, the TRC
> perpetuated the powerlessness of the victims because it exploited
> both their faith and their powerlessness to exact remorse. The
> same was not done with the powerful. They were both too pow-
> erful and too protected by the institutions of power: Parliament,
> the courts, the media, government. The same is true for the
> powerful institutions themselves. The TRC chose to make the
> radical (Christian) interpretation of reconciliation the litmus
> test for the victims, especially those who are Christians.[127]

Boesak centres his view of radical reconciliation on both the philosophy and theology of power. First, he argues that social justice can only be realised if perpetrators and beneficiaries of apartheid system are in shared positions

---

125. Boesak and DeYoung, *Radical Reconciliation*, Introduction.

126. Boesak, *Tenderness of Conscience*, 51, 63, 197–98.

127. Boesak, "And Zaccheus Remained," 648.

of power. Beneficiaries must confront and take accountability for the advantages and privileges accorded to them by an unjust system.[128] Second, power should be distributed in such a way that it results in the restoration of human dignity – especially for the survivors and their posterity. These power relations, in Boesak's view, should have been addressed during the TRC hearings. It should have allowed the survivors to have their voices heard, rather than coaching and training them on what they should and should not say during the trials.[129] Third, failure to address the power relations caused by apartheid has social, political, and economic ramifications, particularly, the lack of contentment. The survivors and their posterity continue to be lagging in the processes of development as they have no means, or are extremely limited in their efforts, to flourish. Besides the effects of apartheid are neoliberal economic structures that fail to recognise, honour, and uphold the rights of the previously disadvantaged. This economic disempowerment is aggravated by BEE policies and programmes that distribute (corruptly) large portions of wealth to a few well-connected "tenderpreneurs."[130]

While Boesak upholds a strong theological basis for arguing against power imbalances and its deification that results in perpetual dispossession of many, he suggests a political intervention. He argues for a political culture and systems of the conscience that recognize African culture, Christian principles, and a social distributive framework.[131]

3.5.2 Reconciliation, Restitution, and Social Justice

3.5.2.1 Reconciliation

Distribution of power creates an equal footing of access to resources. However, power itself is not an adequate instrument of social justice. While such (re) distribution is fundamental to forge the creation of policies, programmes, and institutions for social justice, they do not necessarily result in material gain. The material cannot be excluded from the discourse of social justice in a post-apartheid context. Boesak insists that material restitution, and all talk of social justice, forgiveness, and reconciliation carry no meaning without

---

128. Boesak, 643–46.

129. Boesak, 646–49.

130. Boesak, 649–51.

131. Boesak, *Farewell to Innocence* (1976); Boesak, *Tenderness of Conscience*; Boesak, "And Zaccheus Remained"; Boesak, *Running with Horses*.

restitution from the perpetrators and beneficiaries.[132] Boesak has been a keen advocate for reconciliation. This concept of reconciliation, like forgiveness, remains hugely contested among South Africans from different theological convictions. Dion Forster highlights key aspects of what is causing the tension, primarily that the concept has been abused to take advantage of victims of apartheid, especially the process of the TRC.[133] He also highlights that a majority of youth think that liberation ideas and convictions are no longer relevant to their context and that they have been let down by the liberation icons.[134] Boesak's version of reconciliation incorporates social justice into its process, which DeYoung explains should, "be understood as exchanging places with 'the other,' overcoming alienation through identification, solidarity, restoring relationships, positive change, new frameworks, and a rich togetherness that is both spiritual and political."[135]

It turns on the Habermasian approach used in the TRC, which focused on the truth process by making reconciliation the process. Boesak seeks to redeem reconciliation from the captivity of what he terms pietism and quietism which fail to make radical demands on perpetrators and beneficiaries of apartheid. He refuses to promote a hope of a reconciled South Africa which ignores the status quo of socioeconomic incquities (defended and protected by public institutions). While he recognises the task of the TRC and the liberation efforts of the ANC, he criticises them for their failure to call institutions and persons (who were perpetrators and beneficiaries of the injustice) to account. Anneliese Verdoolaege writes about the political division in South Africa regarding the reconciliation discourse that

> in the years following the Mandela era a subtle kind of competition was going on between two components of political reconciliation discourse, namely reconciliation itself and *ubuntu*. Under Mandela, especially after 1995, reconciliation seemed to be the most outspoken way to characterise the ideal relationship between South Africans. It appears that under the presidency of Mbeki the concept of *ubuntu* gained in popularity. We could

---

132. Boesak and DeYoung, *Radical Reconciliation*, 49.
133. Forster, "Politics of Forgiveness?," 82.
134. Forster, 82–84.
135. Boesak and DeYoung, *Radical Reconciliation*, 4.

say that under Mbeki, political rhetoric became slightly more Africanist-oriented, stressing the fact that South Africans should feel proud to be Africans in the first place. As a result of this ideological move, political discourse felt more comfortable to embrace the term *ubuntu* than reconciliation. Reconciliation was strongly associated with the TRC and with the person of Nelson Mandela. *Ubuntu,* on the other hand, also embodied this reconciliatory dimension, but in addition it had a very strong traditional African connotation. Since it was perceived as typically South African, *ubuntu* also had a strong nationalist relevance, which suited the post-Mandela political rhetoric. Moreover, it seemed as if the term reconciliation necessarily referred to the apartheid past, while *ubuntu* rather had implications for the present and the future.[136]

Without dismissing the benefit of the African concept of *ubuntu* and the reconciliation roadmap set in the 1990s, Boesak believes that reconciliation requires an angle of social justice. As with Wolterstorff, he holds that justice comes with a social dethroning of the status quo.[137] This inversion should be expressed and established through reciprocal acts on the parts of beneficiaries. These include but are not limited to cultural restoration, land, access to economic power, and doing away with neocapitalist structures that reinforce inequalities and exploitation. He equates the coming of justice directly with the socioeconomic inversion of apartheid, state capture, corruption and post-apartheid neocapitalism beneficiaries because the "rectification of injustice requires not only lifting up the low ones but casting down the high ones."[138]

Boesak strongly believes that Christians have a moral obligation not to settle for a cosmetic version of reconciliation which does not make demands for what is right. While reconciliation is the end goal, it can only be achieved when the issues that hinder its achievement are effectively addressed and redressed. That means this long-term goal of reconciliation needs to be accompanied by radical acts of reciprocity to restore the dignity of the survivors and their posterity. Boesak does not attempt to engage any philosophical

---

136. Verdoolaege, *Reconciliation Discourse,* 161.

137. Wolterstorff, *Justice: Rights and Wrongs,* 124.

138. Wolterstorff, 123.

ideas that may be opposed to this view. He is convinced that this is the biblical route, citing the stories of Rizpah,[139] Zacchaeus,[140] and interpretation and application of Pauline texts.[141] He assumes his interpretation of reconciliation without a critical theological analysis of other views.

Because the TRC (see its model below) was headed by Desmond Tutu, it can be argued that Boesak assumes that the concept of reconciliation has religious connotations (specifically Christian). Because apartheid politics were deeply religious, it is then fair to engage the spiritual nature of these politics to stand up to face the outcomes of its spiritual implications of reconciliation.[142] This insistence carries merit if the religious nature of South African politics cannot be ignored and exchanged for a secular narrative. However, theological application in political dialogues (that are avowedly secular), needs to be critically analysed. Boesak assumes a "Christian" interpretation on behalf of everyone. Thus, if society is to achieve authentic, action-based, sustainable, and durable reconciliation, it needs to consider the radical framework he proposes. His concept of reconciliation stands starkly opposed to the TRC's approach (see Figure 1 below) which was employed to spearhead the national process of healing and reconciliation.

The TRC emphasized truth-telling of perpetrators to the victims to reach a shared understanding of what had transpired. In Boesak's view, this approach and process were compromised. Truth-telling was used to substitute "for the radical, systemic distributive justice the people deserve and without which reconciliation would never be complete, sustainable, and durable."[143] He believes perpetrators had an advantage, protected by the system, and did not allow the victims to present competing versions of truth claims to reach a fair consensus. The theory of truth (Habermasian) as a process,[144] according to Boesak, is not adequate, because it is not thorough in engaging the perspective of the victims who are not part of the shaping of the objectives of reconciliation. Thus, victims continue to be at the receiving end of an unfair arrangement. They play cosmetic roles because the process and

---

139. Boesak and DeYoung, *Radical Reconciliation*, 21–29.

140. Boesak and DeYoung, 50–61.

141. Boesak and DeYoung, 66–73.

142. Boesak, "And Zaccheus Remained," 652.

143. Boesak, *Pharaohs on Both Sides*, 15.

144. Isaac, "Critical-Theoretical Study," 3, 11, 65–68.

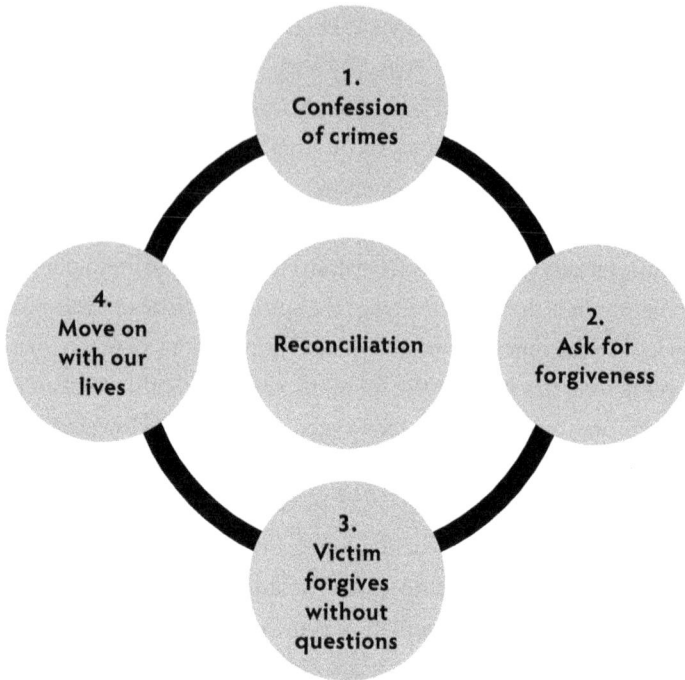

Figure 1. The TRC's Model of Reconciliation

the outcomes are already decided – and victims should accept the outcome. Boesak believes that, if anything, at least the truth-telling process should have come with some substantial restoration – social justice for the victims. He argues that this was an exercise of the powerful speaking over the needs and expectations of the powerless.[145]

While Boesak uses a theological lens to interpret and champion the concept of radical reconciliation, he seeks to do so within an African contextual framework. In *The Tenderness of Conscience* and *Pharaohs on Both Sides of the Blood-Red River*, he engages *ubuntu* as an African theoretical framework with a restorative approach towards justice. *Ubuntu* in Boesak's view is not only a cultural framework but something with deep roots in African spirituality. While he admires this spiritual nature of *ubuntu* in the process of forgiveness, healing, and reconciliation, he criticises it for making Africans complicit. That is, they fail to demand social justice because of their cultural

---

145. Boesak, *Tenderness of Conscience*, 198.

orientation.[146] Thus, he thinks *ubuntu* is a helpful primary framework for establishing forgiveness of the perpetrators; but it should also demand social justice, not in a vengeful way but as a way of undoing (partly) the damages and effects caused by apartheid.

Ubuntu has been used by advocates of forgiveness to call for reconciliation. Boesak thinks that such an appeal without challenging the social arrangement of perpetrators and beneficiaries is artificial. That the TRC called for perpetrators to confess and tell the truth of their crimes was a good starting point; because, "apartheid . . . led to separation, to estrangement, to alienation, to a deep lack of mutual understanding and acceptance, resulting in mistrust and suspicion, fear and hurt, even bitterness and hatred, in short, an urgent need for reconciliation, for acceptance and forgiveness, for building bridges over the deep divides separating people."[147] However, that alone does not settle the social and material losses incurred by the victims/survivors. He argues that "the process of reconciliation in our politics and socioeconomic life and the justification of ongoing injustice afterwards, this too constitutes a situation where ubuntu has taken flight."[148] For ignoring or rushing over the "deeply painful areas" in exchange for a hastened need to move on betrayed the discussion of reconciliation from dealing with the vital details.[149] As such, this has reduced the discussion of reconciliation to a simplified and relaxed attitude of "'let bygones be bygones,'" "'live and let live,'" "'leave the past behind,'" and "'forgive and forget.'"[150]

This kind of approach to reconciliation in Boesak's view fails to bring about the genuine liberation that is required to live in dignity. It is a talk of reconciliation that lacks the meaning of "togetherness" and "the solidarity of humanbeingness." It fuels self-centred individualism leaving the affected with no social justice except with slogans and media addresses by politicians for appearances.[151] This attitude towards reconciliation without social justice, Boesak believes, created a new platform for the new government to continue trumping the same people who have been victims of apartheid.

---

146. Boesak, 66, 186–87, 198–200.

147. Smit, "On Belonging," 153.

148. Boesak, *Pharaohs on Both Sides*, 119.

149. Boesak, *Tenderness of Conscience*, 199; Verdoolaege, *Reconciliation Discourse*, 19–21.

150. Boesak, 199.

151. Boesak, 226.

The socioeconomic field has remained uneven because the rules are being made by the very people who created the unequal system (except for a few well-connected Black Africans).

3.5.2.2 Restitution

Reconciliation, in Boesak's view, ought to combine with material acts of restitution. He argues that the TRC was somehow fearful to demand for social justice. They did not want to come across as being extreme and wanted to find the quickest possible means of compromise. This failed to deliver social justice. Boesak has always advocated for reconciliation. He never foresaw a cheapened or watered-down approach as the way of achieving it.[152] For him, reconciliation needed to happen between equals: first as equal human beings, second, as political equals, third, as material equals. One cannot speak of reconciliation without creating or forging an enabling environment in which there will be equitable means of developing and enjoying life. Thus, speaking of reconciliation, forgiveness and love without social justice betrays the acts of oppression and injustice committed against the survivors who live with the effects of such injustices. He argues that pursuing the doing of social justice even amid reconciliation, is a way of liberating the perpetrators and beneficiaries – "for their freedom, against their fear; for their human authenticity against their terrible estrangement."[153]

In this order of thinking about reconciliation, Boesak sees it as a radical view rather than one that only speaks to the political context without demands on the lives of the perpetrating systems, institutions, individuals, and beneficiaries. The task of reconciliation according to Boesak needs to start from the basis that,

> there are some whites who perpetrated the system of apartheid, but all of them benefited from it. And this is how we should address the question of guilt, repentance, reparations, and restitution. It is galling that this truth is so vehemently denied when it is so devastatingly self-evident. All whites did benefit from apartheid: in schools and education, economic opportunities, salaries and job reservation, health care and homes, the chance

---

152. Boesak, *Farewell to Innocence* (1976), 102–9.
153. Boesak, 115.

to build a wealth platform from which successive generations could be launched; the self-confidence that comes from the easy access to the world of power, nationally and internationally, and in the myriad subtle ways which constitute the self-esteem of human beings.[154]

Confession of the perpetrators, according to Boesak, is not adequate without the truth-telling of the beneficiaries. Since the oppression and exploitation happened in compulsive and systematic measures, reconciliation should be able to follow a similar path of systematically restoring the dignity of the victims. If the central doctrine and philosophy of *ubuntu* are "humanbeingness"[155] and dignity, then reconciliation should be able to foster such an environment that allows for full human flourishing. This discomforting situation that demands social justice for the victims, in Boesak's view, is equal to a revolution, unsettling the status quo. He writes that, "this transformation of society can be called a revolution and this revolution need not necessarily be violent. We understand such a revolution to be a fundamental social change. It is a transformation, a movement from what is to what ought to be. For a Christian can never acquisce (sic) with the status quo, but . . . continually challenges the structures of society where they fall short of the fullness revealed in Christ."[156]

In his book *Radical Reconciliation*, co-authored with DeYoung, he appeals to Zacchaeus's conversion story[157] as the model of genuine, reliable, and sustainable reconciliation. A model, he believes, which can bring desirable social change for the post-apartheid context. He adopts this model on the basis that reconciliation, at least in the South African context, is deeply influenced by a spiritual and religious context, Christian thinking. On that basis, he designs this model, which he thinks conforms with the claimed Christian ethos of reconciliation. That is, if the framework of the TRC hearings is to materialize and wield meaningful outcomes, it must demand social justice from the perpetrators and beneficiaries. Below is a graphic illustration of his ten steps, components, or levels of radical reconciliation. The graphic (below) only

154. Boesak, *Tenderness of Conscience*, 190.

155. Boesak, *Tenderness of Conscience*, 26. Boesak uses the term as a synonym of what the African concept of *ubuntu* means. Thus, the word means more than just humanness but also infers to interdependent existence of humans i.e. we are humans together.

156. Boesak, *Farewell to Innocence* (1976), 114–15.

157. Boesak and DeYoung, *Radical Reconciliation*, 50–61.

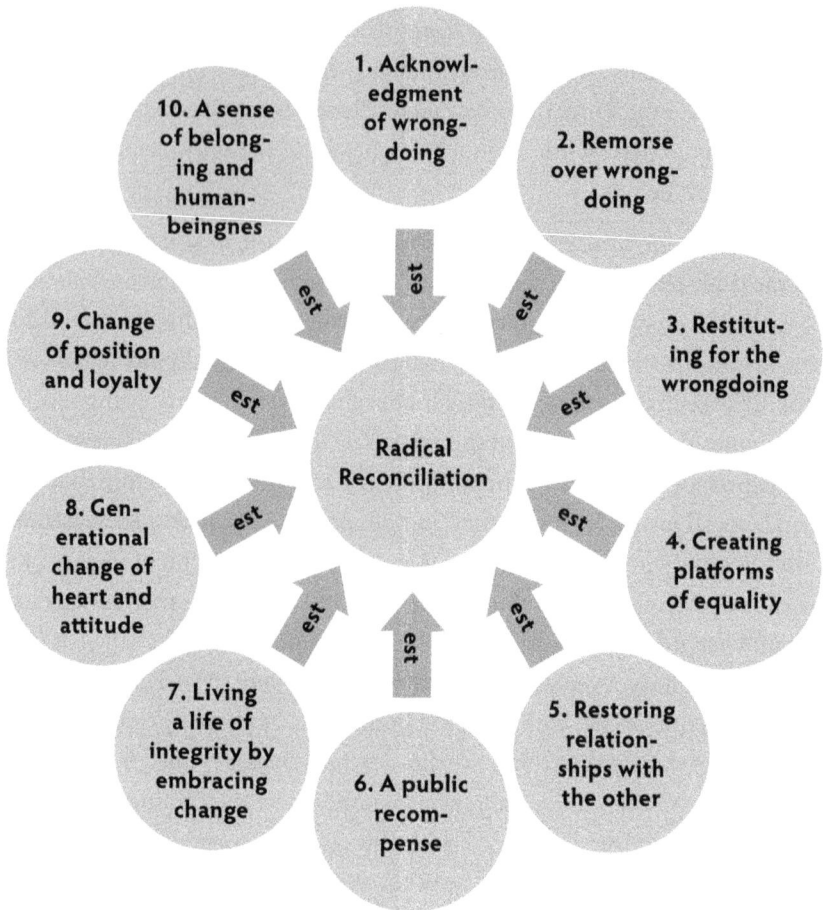

Figure 2. Boesak's Model of Radical Reconciliation

demonstrates the components he thinks should be included in the process of reconciliation for it to be meaningful and lasting.

Due to "an incomplete and nonjustice pursuing reconciliation model,"[158] reconciliation, in its real sense, has not taken place. This model of reconciliation, Boesak argues, focused on: "'the fractured elite' (perpetrators and victims) instead of on society, on individuals instead of on the systems of injustice that apartheid essentially was, so that justice never became a demand for systemic reform of society. We did not seem to get beyond the

---

158. Boesak, "And Zaccheus Remained," 641.

single perpetrator or the single victim."[159] The TRC model then, according to Boesak, while it was a step in the right direction, treated the question of social justice with disproportionate courteousness that compromized the betterment of lives of affected communities. It failed to obtain social justice for those who became vulnerable, poor, and weak because of the apartheid system that contributed to their current state through discriminatory laws. Instead, it adopted "the concept of reconciliation as a political subterfuge without understanding, and honouring the biblical demands that inevitably come with it. So now everywhere there are signs that our efforts towards reconciliation are floundering."[160] He dedicates an entire chapter to analyse the crucial role of reconciliation in the process of nation-building. Towards the end of the chapter, he emphasises identity. That reconciliation ought to bring about a new identity is demonstrated in the actions of Zacchaeus. Interestingly, when it comes to the subject of identity, Boesak emphasises the Christians, not society. He writes that,

> reconciliation, in order for it to be genuine, demands that we give up our identity as shaped by our past and accept a new identity which can embody our hopes for the future. Giving up that identity as conditioned by our past in order to accept a new one embodying the future can only be done if we, as Christians, do not find our identity within ourselves as shaped by our experiences, but in Christ, as shaped by his love.[161]

This conclusion poses new challenges of placing particularly Christian demands on a non-Christian society. How can non-Christians practice Christian ethos when they cannot identify with the faith demands placed upon them? Or, does this imply that there is a general category of a "society-demand" on people, even if they are not Christians, because it is what is morally acceptable, although using a Christian interpretation to arrive at it? Or, should we assume that the way the whole reconciliation programme was set up implied that a Christian theological response of the meaning of reconciliation and social justice was to be pursued?

---

159. Boesak, 641.
160. Boesak, 642.
161. Boesak, *Tenderness of Conscience*, 211.

3.6 Social Justice

The Zacchaeus model of reconciliation, according to Boesak, provides adequate means and processes of meting out social justice. If all ten steps are
in place, according to Boesak, we will witness structural inversion, cultural
revolution, power balances, a growing sense of humanbeingness, and eventually the rolling of social justice for the victims. Social justice, in Boesak's
view, does not wait to happen in the afterlife, but restoration (although not
entirely) should happen in the here and now. As such, he rejects any version or
understanding of social justice that does not address the material restitution
for victims and sufferers. Therefore, he criticises the outcomes of the TRC
for not placing demands that would affect the socioeconomic conditions of
the perpetrators, beneficiaries, and victims. He believes that the victims have
just joined the long lines of the forgotten, which is manifesting itself in the
levels of poverty, unemployment, illiteracy, powerlessness, lack of economically beneficial skills, poor housing conditions and homelessness, and lack
of access to sanitation and quality healthcare. These things (socioeconomic
goods) should have been a reasonable minimum, had the TRC demanded
for social justice.

True reconciliation ought to bring liberation from socioeconomic oppression. Without socioeconomic liberation, apartheid continues, in a brutally
protected style. As such, human suffering becomes normal through post-
apartheid neoliberal and hyper neocapitalist economic structures. Lephakga,
writes in agreement with Boesak,

> (1) that reconciliation needs to be affected with the community
> in order for it to be genuine; (2) that reconciliation has to be
> transformational if it is to mean anything (transformational of
> the life of both the beneficiary and/or perpetrator and victim,
> the lifestyle of both the beneficiary/perpetrator and victim, the
> relationship between the beneficiary/perpetrator and the com-
> munity, especially those that were wronged); and (3) that rec-
> onciliation means the restoration of justice.[162]

Boesak advocates a restorative approach to compensate for the
wrongs committed in the past against the majority of South Africans. The

---

162. Lephakga, "Radical Reconciliation," 6.

reconciliation process headed by the TRC sparked new hope, and so raised lofty expectations but failed to provide a lasting foundation for a new course of justice.[163] The terms and conditions were politically motivated and did not allow for the victims/survivors to express what they understood. Neither were they accorded what they sought as measures of social justice if they were ever to move on from the painful realities of the apartheid history. These are the questions that Lephakga raises in *Radical Reconciliation: The TRC Should Have Allowed Zacchaeus to Testify?*, regarding the process of inquiry regarding reconciliation, in the same line of thinking as that of Boesak.

Boesak's theological background in Liberation Theology cannot come to terms with the idea of reconciliation that falls short of meeting the basic requirements of social justice. Although he is concerned with the subject of social justice as the chief end of all processes of reconciliation, the researcher did not find a great deal of reflection on the conceptualization of social justice in the context of the victims/survivors. While his advocacy sparks new questions and ways of how to approach the matter of historical injustice, "whose justice, whose rationality?" does not seem to feature a great deal in his approach. Appealing to the text of the Bible, Boesak advocates for a Christian understanding of justice as the basis for any search for social justice to be meaningful. However, he does not provide a comprehensive conceptualization (or systematic explanation) of social justice, although he suggests practical measures for what needs to be done to reverse the effects of the apartheid system.

Moreover, he is determined that *radical reconciliation*, as he has proposed, would be the only means of addressing injustice. Only this approach, he argues, "questions the assumption that justice can be served, social contracts honored, and solidarity enacted through politics and policies grounded in a neoliberal capitalism whose very survival depends on the exclusion of the powerless, the exploitation of the poor, and the nurturing of inequality."[164] He pushes to the "full" spiritual demands of the concepts used in reconciliation, to have outward implications on governments and societies at large. Only then can we be assured that reconciliation has been followed to its logical conclusion. Without this full application of the spiritual language of reconciliation

---

163. Smit, *Essays in Public Theology*, 113–14.

164. Boesak and DeYoung, *Radical Reconciliation*, 136.

and forgiveness, political reconciliation alone cannot bring about the desired results of social justice.

Boesak ardently believes that only a notion that takes reconciliation (as stated above) to its logical conclusion (demands for social justice) can create a new humanity and society of equals. This material restitution would liberate the oppressed mind from the false innocence it acquired through ignorance which it mistook for piety. Furthermore, it is the only way to deliver the oppressor from his/her imprisonment and restore him/her to full humanness. It is a process of shedding false identities regarding the self and the other, and beginning on a clean slate to create new memories of interdependent and interconnected humanity. Only within such a framework can *ubuntu* be meaningful, by the evidence of the fruits it bears on the quality of human life, not the political rhetoric without tangible measures. This approach embraces the spirituality of the struggle for social justice to heal the heart of politics as we know it, to construct a vision of social justice to advance human good.[165] Alternatively, he argues that "not to respond at the deepest spiritual level, is not to understand the African soul at all. If this is denied, then all talk of ubuntu is either total nonsense or unbearably cynical."[166]

We must point out that the reconciliation model of Boesak stretches beyond the effects of apartheid's socioeconomic consequences. As mentioned earlier, he uses the same argument to argue for a wide range of social issues as they arise in society. He applies it including, but not limited to, the liberation of Palestine from Israeli occupation, the granting of rights and protection to LGBTQI+ persons, the liberation of women from patriarchal social structures, calling corrupt political leaders to account for their actions, and striving for world peace. He holds that the reconciliation view advocated in the New Testament is of a Christ who can create universal peace and social justice. So, the world can become a place for all to live, as one humanity united under God. This universal oneness defines the work of the liberating Messiah – bringing everyone under the lordship of Jesus Christ as his subjects. The imperial theology and philosophy of human kingdoms are then all subdued under the reign of Christ. Jesus the Christ is the only one capable, just ,and omnipotent to hold *all* power and use it for just purposes. By so

---

165. Palmer, *Healing the Heart*.

166. Boesak, *Tenderness of Conscience*, 186.

doing, all the human kingdoms would become kingdoms of the Lord ruled in true justice, peace, and righteousness.

3.7 Summary

This chapter surveyed Boesak's work with the intention of understanding how he conceptualises and articulates notions of social justice. It analyses his critical theological, political, and philosophical views and how they influence his understanding of social justice for the post-apartheid context. The chapter sought to establish Boesak's theoretical framework upon which he pursues a theological basis for social justice in the public square for the apartheid victims/survivors. The chapter also outlines that while Boesak does not have a working definition of justice (that is, a single systematized view of the concept), he uses a cluster of concepts to describe social justice (see § 3.5). However, central to his argument is the idea of power (see § 3.3, 3.4 and 3.5.2) which he believes can be restored through appropriate measures and steps that he believes would lead to radical reconciliation (see § 3.5.2.2). While Boesak supports the work of the TRC, he rejects its practical outplay for not embracing and pursuing social justice as part of its fundamental purposes.

Furthermore, he interrogates the concept of *ubuntu*. He suggests that it can only be effective if it embraces humanbeingness with demands for social justice. Although Boesak does not have a single definition for justice, he does advocate for restitution, based on his interpretation and application of the story of Zacchaeus (see § 3.5.2). These views will be critically analysed in chapter 4, examining their validity in search of a theology of social justice that speaks to the Namibian post-apartheid context.

A Critical Dialogue with Allan Boesak's Theological Notions of Justice

4.1 Introduction

The post-apartheid Namibian context continues to display enormous socioeconomic gaps and multidimensional poverty. The political rhetoric of a better future by liberation movements has turned out to be nothing more than empty promises. Ending apartheid as a legal system was just the beginning of the long struggle for social justice. Allan Boesak is an apartheid liberation hero but also a theologian who questions the outcome of the liberation promises. This chapter follows the steps of exposition, analysis, and application. We focus on the themes of Black Liberation (§ 4.2), Black Power and Consciousness (§ 4.3), reconciliation (§ 4.4), and restitution (§ 4.5). We will examine these key themes which were outlined in chapter 3 to extract lessons for post-apartheid Namibia. Boesak, like many other Black liberation theologians, "remains of incomparable value and importance when evaluating this subject matter."[1] But, "seeing beyond the predecessors means introducing new categories and rejects the tendency by some to simply recycle the same concepts without significant development."[2] Hence, this chapter engages other conversation partners (Bradley, Sagovsky, and De Gruchy) to provide theological insights on the issues of social justice, reconciliation, and

---

1. Bradley, *Political Economy of Liberation*, xiii.
2. Bradley, xiii.

restitution that may help to texture and nuance aspects of Boesak's theological views on social justice.

4.2 Black Liberation Theology for a Post-Apartheid Context

4.2.1 Exposition and Analysis

The previous chapter outlines Boesak's work and his main theological framework – Liberation Theology – resulting from his life's experience of apartheid and search for a contextual reading of Scripture in relation to pain, suffering, oppression, marginalization, discrimination, dehumanization, and humiliation. Itumeleng Mosala narrates this theological development as follows:

> Black theology in South Africa first emerged in the context of the Black Consciousness movement during the late 1960s and early 1970s. It came into being as a cultural tool of struggle propounded by young black South Africans who were influenced by the philosophy of the new Black Consciousness. The immediate target of black theology was the Christian church and especially Christian theology. The point of contention was the perceived acquiescence of the Christian church and its theology in the oppression and exploitation of black people. Black theologians argued, justifiably, that not only was the church relatively silent on the question of oppression but that the thoroughly Western and white outlook of its theology helped to reproduce the basic inequalities of an apartheid society. Consequently, black Christian activists emphasized the need for a black theology of liberation.[3]

Farewell to Innocence reevaluates the theological framework of Black Theology and offers an evolving Black ethic that arises from the oppressed community, a Black Consciousness that Boesak believes should apply to recapture Black humanity and dignity, not as a construct against whiteness. It is also a search to counter what Achille Mbembe calls "the West's obsession with, and circular discourse about, the facts of 'absence,' 'lack,' and 'nonbeing,' of

---

3. Mosala, *Biblical Hermeneutics*, 1.

identity and difference, of negativeness – in short, of nothingness."[4] Boesak compactly defines this theological position as follows:

> Black Theology is a theology of liberation . . . Black Theology believes that liberation is not only "part of" the gospel, or "consistent with" the gospel; it is the content and framework of the gospel of Jesus Christ. Born in the community of the black oppressed, it takes seriously the black experience, the black situation. Black Theology grapples with suffering and oppression; it is a cry unto God for the sake of the people. It believes that in Jesus Christ the total liberation of all people has come.[5]

This paragraph stipulates Boesak's framework for resisting oppression and injustice; it questions the ability of the systems and structures that define society to evolve into becoming more equitable and just. He advocates for something more significant, that is, a society defined by the virtues of "solidarity, respect for life, humanity, [and] community."[6] The above quote also refers to the (re)formulation, (re)understanding, and (re)contextualization of the gospel, as a device for undoing the philosophy of apartheid. Today, while apartheid as a legal system has ended, the question of the validity of Liberation Theology remains an open debate among theologians but one defended mostly by Black theologians.[7] Some Black scholars believe that Black Liberation Theology is still needed to inform theologians and motivate theological participation in contemporary dialogues.[8] Tshaka and Makofane are of the view that the new post-apartheid context shows the need for Black Liberation Theology's relevance.[9] They also argue that,

> Black Theology (and for that matter Black Consciousness) must be credited for helping to instil a sense of self-worth into black people. We cannot deny the economic discrepancies that still

---

4. Mbembé, *On the Postcolony*, 4.

5. Boesak, *Farewell to Innocence* (1977), 9–10.

6. Boesak, 152.

7. Fortein, "Allan Boesak, Black Theology"; Kameeta, *Towards Liberation*; Makheta, "Doing Liberation Theology"; Niitenge, "Evangelical Lutheran Church"; Rowland, *Cambridge Companion*; Tshaka and Makofane, "Continued Relevance."

8. Kobe, "Black Theology of Liberation?"; Tenai, "The Poor and the Public"; Tshaka and Makofane, "Continued Relevance."

9. Tshaka and Makofane, 532–33.

exist between black and white, however a Black Consciousness which is aimed at developing a positive sense of the black self without seriously considering the economic element which bends blacks to the will of their white masters proves to be impotent to the most vulnerable. There can be no doubt that the issue of the economy of the country has not enjoyed much attention in much of the black theological reflections of the past. It remains as significant today particularly in the wake of the growing black middle class.[10]

They acknowledge that Black Liberation Theology's contribution to economic transformation has been scanty but maintain that this does not negate its role as a questioning theology. Among other issues, they cite post-apartheid's democratic capitalism and a "growing black bourgeoisie"[11] for Liberation Theology's continued validity. The Black bourgeoisie concept is not associated with socialist-Marxist analysis, narrative, and trajectory of class struggle. Their focus is on the post-apartheid structural continuation of social and economic racism and classism fuelled by a violent neoliberal economic philosophy. A combination of these factors fosters inequality of power and privilege in terms of access to various life-enhancing goods at the expense of others, for the Black population. Boesak follows a similar line of reasoning to advocate for social justice through a Black liberation theological framework, which he sees as an active expression of faith. For Boesak, according to Fortein, "Theology is passionately involved in the actual struggles and suffering within a given situation and community. Thus for black people this means that theology must engage itself in the black experience."[12] Fortein concludes that,

> Boesak's exposure to Black Theology opens an entire new theological point of reference and handed him the "language" to engage within (sic) oppressive context of apartheid. That enabled Boesak to answer the call and challenge of Steve Biko. This "language" is still being used today and will be for a long

---

10. Tshaka and Makofane, 541.

11. Tshaka and Makofane, 533.

12. Fortein, "Allan Boesak, Black Theology," 509.

time to come. Allan Boesak still helps us today in addressing the crucial issues of global apartheid and oppression.[13]

It is these many lessons of courage, presence, and witness we would like to test in the search for theologies of social justice for the Namibian context. Deane Ferm profiles Boesak among the world's top thirty-six liberation theologians.[14] The essays and chapters in the *Festschrift in Honour of Allan Boesak* and *Prophet from the South* affirm the extent of his theological work and influence. Boesak demonstrates his theological convictions through active personal involvement. We see this involvement in his: (1) protest speech as a young chaplain; (2) request to the WARC to declare apartheid as a sin and heresy; (3) confrontations on the streets with the apartheid police forces; (4) and delivering speeches such as those found in *Black and Reformed* or *Comfort and Protest*. In their appraisal, Dibeela, Lenka-Bhula, and Vellem are of the view that Boesak's contribution to the Black Theology of Liberation remains unsurpassed and will continue to influence social justice's theological discourse for a long time in southern Africa.[15] This makes him an important conversation partner in our search to understand and develop Namibian theologies of social justice. Boesak employs the liberation framework to address a myriad of issues that are also of concern to the Namibian society and the globe. These include but are not limited to the continued social and economic discrimination;[16] social, political, and economic discrimination of women in relation to patriarchy;[17] theology, the state and democracy;[18] and advocating for social justice for all persons regardless of race, religion, and sexual orientation.[19]

Boesak's understanding of Liberation Theology seeks to address every aspect of human life where people experience injustice. As he puts it, in his latest work *Children of the Waters of Meribah*, Liberation Theology is a theological search to help "in the people's continuing struggle against damnation

---

13. Fortein, 519.

14. Ferm, *Profiles in Liberation.*

15. Dibeela, Lenka-Bula, and Vellem, *Prophet from South*, 2.

16. Boesak, *Tenderness of Conscience*, 57.

17. Boesak, 1, 52; Boesak, *Dare We Speak?*, 48, 128; Boesak, *Pharaohs on Both Sides*, 1–15; Boesak, *Children*, 566 of 6766.

18. Boesak, *Tenderness of Conscience*, 19–20.

19. Boesak, *Children*, 141 of 6766.

and oppression, and for freedom, justice, peace, and dignity."[20] This latest work focuses on addressing patriarchy and injustice against women and girls and what Liberation Theology needs to do to be meaningful and valuable in the struggle to liberate all oppressed people. He questions his Calvinist Reformed tradition and calls it from its Eurocentrism to be repurposed towards a rethought and renewed project and development of Black Liberation. It is a development towards a comprehensive approach in relation to what the liberation question means for oppressed people. In it, he admits that Black Liberation Theology has missed something significant and would remain incomplete unless it begins to pay careful attention to questions women are raising. He admits to this failure, saying that "women have tried to teach us, but we have not always listened well enough."[21] Would the present struggle for social justice have taken a different turn had "the men" listened? Or, to put it in Boesak's words,

> if Black Liberation Theology had taken the issues mentioned here much more seriously, struggled with them much more intensely, thoroughly, and honestly, would it have been in a better position to help oppressed black people in South Africa and the United States, in fact in Africa as a whole, and oppressed communities everywhere face the challenges of the last twenty-five years? I think we would have.[22]

Boesak's latest work calls for renewal of Black Liberation Theology's project by revisiting women's social struggles for the twenty-first century and beyond. Albeit tentative, it offers captivating discernments for all who consider issues related to social justice. However, we still must ask why Black Liberation Theology missed an opportunity to address women's questions for nearly a century. While Boesak speaks of some male Black liberation theologians' repentance, the movement remains mostly tethered to male-centred conceptions of liberty and social justice. Countering the patriarchal tendencies within Black Liberation Theology, which placed women's issues as appendices (for decades) in the dialogues of women's call for social justice, requires

---

20. Boesak, 137 of 6766.
21. Boesak, 114 of 6766.
22. Boesak, 233 of 6766.

an epistemic reorientation. We also need to ask whether Black Liberation Theology has not lost a great opportunity (and current dialogues may be raising suspicion of Black Liberation Theology trying hard to make a comeback). I do not doubt that Boesak is genuine in his concern for women. Black Liberation Theology's provenance of male-dominated structures needs liberation from this stain. Nevertheless, raising these questions indicates the wide extent of Liberation Theology.

Boesak argues that liberation is God's main activity in human history or that "nothing is more central to the Old Testament proclamation than the message of liberation."[23] In his view, this centrality culminates in the coming of Christ – the universal liberator.[24] Christ is not some out-of-touch liberator but one who shared in the experiences of the marginalized of society. He identifies with them through his incarnation into full humanity, living in the context of injustice and dying an unjust death.[25] This position means that Christ has come to ensure all people's liberation and create a new order that does not conform to the rich and powerful status quo. He cites the Exodus account as the preamble to Christ's liberating work. It is a dynamic liberation in which the oppressed, disenfranchised, and marginalized persons move "with God – away from meaninglessness and alienation, away from uncertainty and misery, from pain and humiliation toward service of the living God."[26]

He explains his definition of theology as (1) a critical reflection on historical praxis, and (2) faith manifesting in action within history.[27] Thus, it analyses history from a Reformed perspective, using a benchmark that seeks to liberate the oppressed by applying hermeneutics to deconstruct notions of social justice that disadvantage a large portion of our society. This theological framework that views God as all-good, just, and liberating, for Boesak, needs to translate into tangible measures. A theology that does not and would not insist on the realization of liberation is not taking the gospel's message seriously and dishonours God. Theological participation in this liberating activity is a fulfilment of God's will for creation. In Boesak's view, the absence

---

23. Boesak, *Farewell to Innocence* (1976), 20.
24. Boesak, 14.
25. Boesak, 15–17.
26. Boesak, 20.
27. Boesak, 14–17.

of this life-enhancing and dignity-restoring liberation is a sin against God.[28] He believes that society needs to consist of equals. That is, people who recognize one another's humanness as equally valuable as their own. Therefore, we become morally bound to stand with those who suffer injustice and fight for their liberation. Doing this is being on the side of God. The recognition of a fellow person's dignity is not in the state's power or persons in control of power structures. Instead, it is God-given. When he calls for Christian participation, it is not for political reasons but theological presence and witness; he refers to it as "a restless presence" which is an activity of:

> the prophetic church – an alternative to the Christianity of the established church, a church in tension with and in resistance to both society with its systematic injustices, and the dominant church with its embedded, privileged complacency. This alternative Christian approach is the difference between those who always seek ways to negotiate with the hegemonic powers that rule society and those drawn to and gathered around Jesus of Nazareth, the defender of the poor and powerless, the revolutionary teacher who exposed and resisted the established powers of the palace and the temple, who was rejected and crucified by those powers on the cross of an occupying power. Like him, they live in resistance on the margins of the institutional church and of society, representing a radical rather than an accommodationist Christianity.[29]

He takes this idea from that of Charles Villa-Vicencio, which begins in the quest for human dignity because humans are God's image-bearers. He writes of:

> a restlessness located within the essence of what it means to be human . . . it is articulated in relation to the need to transcend the real or imaginary limits imposed on the individual or the community as a whole. The Christian tradition is primarily concerned with the interpretation of this restlessness, the quest for wholeness and the cry for emancipation from captivity (both at a

---

28. Boesak, *Kairos, Crisis and Global*, 25–26.
29. Boesak, 25–26.

communal and an individual level), in terms of what it identifies as a liberatory reality located within history and attributable to the presence of God.[30]

Restlessness is not necessarily calling for mere political activism but one of Christian presence in structures, systems, activities, and places as ways of bearing witness to God's truth and justice. The concept of restlessness may be considered as a call to discipleship in God's kingdom, and a witness to God's kingdom. It could also refer to the outward consequences of embodying Christian truth and faith. In that case, restlessness is a call to a faithful presence. Borrowing David Fitch's words, it is the church's search to witness faithfully and concretely to the reality of God's presence in the world. Through this restless presence or faithful presence, Fitch argues, "God's kingdom becomes visible, and the world is invited to join with God. Faithful presence is not only essential for our lives as Christians, it is how God has chosen to change the world."[31] As a word of caution, we should not stray too far from Boesak's notion, which not only calls for theological articulation, his idea of restlessness also calls for action. He has an activist church in mind that should discern society's social, economic, and political conditions and act accordingly.[32] This kind of church should make Christ (the liberator) heard in every sphere of life through involvement in sociopolitical action.

If any challenge stands out from Boesak's work, it is that theology needs to abandon the notion of disembodiment (conceptual problem) and disengagement (practical problem). The notions of participation in the search for social justice need to be a communal reality for the church. This is countercultural to the marketplace of ideas of social justice in search of an "understanding of the nature and action of God that associates it inalienably with the highest personal qualities: of mercy, covenant love, creativity, trustworthiness and inclusiveness."[33] The church is part of society, not a separate entity with a mission that is divorced from everyday life's realities. It also needs to become a way of life that reflects what it means to be transformed humanity. This transformation is an act of tangibly witnessing the kingdom of God. The

30. Villa-Vicencio, *Theology of Reconstruction*, 24.

31. Fitch, *Faithful Presence*, 6 of 312.

32. Boesak, "Restless Presence," 31–32.

33. Sagovsky, *Christian Tradition*, 41.

question is whether post-apartheid theology has the required set of disciplines to influence both the church and society. We also must ask about the authenticity of theological participation. What difference does theological dialogue bring to the table?

Injustice, as experienced under apartheid, had its origins in both theological and political visions. This indicates that theology has connections to social analysis but has its roots in different kinds of presuppositions. Thus, this research does not dismiss the truthfulness in the social analysis as it helps us name the social conditions of the community in which we seek to bear witness to God's truth. It is the very social analysis that would engage the world with Christian convictions and provide alternatives in social justice dialogues. Boesak's work (for example, *The Tenderness of Conscience*, and *Dare We Speak of Hope?*) contains political language because the political arena informed the social policies and structures that discriminated against Black persons. Still, he maintains a theological approach to it while conversing with the political notions of the time. *Black and Reformed* is a compilation of various speeches that address the political nature of apartheid's injustice. Boesak is not necessarily heralding a political programme couched in theological language; he seeks a theology that addresses the unjust political systems and structures. Leonard Sweetman, who wrote the introduction to the book, portrays Boesak in a profoundly political manner by referring to him as the voice of suffering Black people.[34] While Boesakspeaks for Black people, he speaks for the suffering people all around the world, inclusive but not limited to Western warmongering, corruption of post-independence African states, the global desecration of women, and global economic exploitation by powerful nations and their allies.[35] The victims of these various forms of injustice and God's preferential treatment towards them are the subject of Black Liberation Theology. It (Black Liberation Theology) refers to suffering, poor, oppressed and unjustly treated persons; he is the voice for all suffering persons or all God's image-bearers. For their political content, these addresses, like those of *Comfort and Protest*, offer a political view that promises liberation based on an eschatological vision that is future orientated, yet presently unfolding. It calls Christians to participate in resisting systems, structures, and powers

---

34. Boesak, *Black and Reformed*, xi.

35. Boesak, *Children*, 225, 885–86, 1502 of 6766.

that dehumanize God's image-bearers.[36] In this interpretative framework, Liberation Theology is a new way of theologising and engaging or resisting pretentious theologies, laws, powers, and politics that promote injustice as God's will or a natural consequence of it.

Black Liberation Theology also has a pedagogical component and much more. In Boesak's case, it is a Black Theology of Liberation with Black Consciousness as its central component. The need to acquire the proper knowledge is essential for the oppressed to reclaim their dignity. Part of the reason oppression continues, without blaming the victims for their condition, is the potential ignorance of the victims who deify their oppressors. Those who experience victimization need to realise the destructive habit that makes a virtue out of their captivity and its perpetrators.[37] Such conscientization bestows power to be free from self-imposed misconception towards the oppressor and oppression. Black Liberation Theology, according to Boesak, can play a significant role in helping people substitute false notions of self and their humanity "with identification with oneself, with self-respect and self-affirmation, it can no longer be taken for granted that the ideas of others are superior to one's own, nor that the disparity between the *is* and the *ought* with regard to one's life is "natural" or satisfactory"[38] (Italics in original).

Boesak's theological work emanates from a specific understanding of God which carries existential consequences. He contends that, "The God of the Bible is the God of liberation rather than oppression . . . of justice rather than injustice . . . of freedom and humanity rather than enslavement and subservience . . . of love, righteousness, and community rather than hatred, self-interest, and exploitation."[39] If this is our understanding of God, how are we to live to ensure that these attributes of God are real in the lives of God's image-bearers? Does our God concept reach so deep that it creates "a restless presence" not to settle for anything other than social justice? What is the sociopolitical consequence of our understanding of God in the context of socioeconomic injustice?

---

36. Boesak, *Comfort and Protest*, 19–20.
37. Boesak, *Farewell to Innocence* (1976), 2.
38. Boesak, *Comfort and Protest*, 43.
39. Boesak, 15.

With this perspective of liberation (God's active presence in human affairs), the church's mission is to extend beyond itself and adopt a much larger role in society and history. This view is an inversive approach compared to the pietistic attitude towards social issues. The church community is not a community unto itself but within a larger society. Boesak argues that "The life of the world, the destruction of this world, and the future of this world, are therefore the concern of the church.[40] We have a responsibility for this world, for it is God's world. If this world is threatened by the evils of militarism, materialism, greed, racism, it is very much the concern of the church."[41] Boesak further says that this participation needs to be connected to Jesus Christ, the Saviour of the world. He says, "we must humbly and without any hesitation, renew our commitment to Jesus Christ, the life of the world. And this faith, this commitment, must be the basis of our action on the issues of peace, justice and human liberation."[42]

As such, how are we to share our faith in the context of our communities? Boesak, like James H. Cone, believes a political intervention is needed to realize the hopes of those affected by injustice.[43] Political participation is a means to witness, and making God known is made evident by standing up for the wronged of society.[44] By extension, there can be no more excellent platform of witnessing about God's concern for the oppressed, to borrow Cone's words, "except through God's political activity on behalf of the weak and helpless of the land."[45] God confronts ungodly powers, as he did in Exodus 22, through political activities to bring a commitment to good order in a society.

Unlike James Cone, who integrates Marxist thoughts as part of his theological framework for political participation, Boesak accepts the socialist-Marxist analysis of society (to an extent) but rejects its atheistic framework.[46] Although living when socialist-Marxist philosophy dominated southern African politics, he rejects its basic presuppositions but learns the good from those who hold to Marxist views (Cone, Biko, and Fanon). He argues that

---

40. Boesak, *Tenderness of Conscience*, 115–17.

41. Boesak, 155.

42. Boesak, 155.

43. Cone, *Black Theology*, 59; Boesak, *Kairos, Crisis and Global*, 23–62.

44. Boesak, *Comfort and Protest*, 116.

45. Cone, *Black Theology*, 59.

46. Boesak, *Black and Reformed*, 135.

he does not resist injustice because of "political intentions" or motivated by Marx but by Jesus Christ.[47] He also refutes, in his response to Mandela, that the road to post-apartheid reconciliation was the work of Marxist persuasion for such a philosophical system whose founder "violently rejected Christian love, Christian social principles and poured scorn on the Christian concepts of love, forgiveness, and justice."[48] He disagrees with Biko's critique of the Christian faith as a mechanism for maintaining the subjugation of Black people.[49] Boesak believes that embedded within the structures of Christianity (although it can borrow from other relevant sources) is an "indestructible seed of rebellion against inhumanity, injustice, and oppression."[50] That is, Christianity has an inherent self-correcting mechanism regarding the destructive course set by the apartheid heresy and all other heresies propagated in the name of God using the Bible. This conviction about the Christian faith's usefulness in the struggle for social justice encourages confrontation with all philosophies and systems contrary to the gospel and God's nature.[51] This understanding makes advocating for justice the activity of God "against our resignation, our need to compromise with evil, and our tendency toward despair and hopelessness, against our willingness to sell the dream of God for God's people to the highest bidder in the name of 'realism.'"[52]

This understanding of God's activity in the world through human institutions, as Boesak's premise for liberation, lays a colossal challenge to post-apartheid theology's withdrawn attitude. In *The Tenderness of Conscience*, he points out that God works through political activity and rebukes the silence of many Christians in the face of injustice. He reflects on Albert Luthuli's example and argues for a Christian presence that can inculcate spirituality into the public arena. Without that spirituality of politics, he contends, in the face of "politics fuelled by greed for power . . . human-made philosophies . . . [and] dubious exigencies of nationalism . . . our democracy will stall, sputter, and die."[53] This spirituality of politics is a means of God's grace to affect

---

47. Boesak, 132.
48. Boesak, *Tenderness of Conscience*, 124.
49. Boesak, 57.
50. Boesak, 10.
51. Boesak, 95, 123, 132.
52. Boesak, *Dare We Speak?*, 143.
53. Boesak, *Tenderness of Conscience*, 111–12.

the epistemological frameworks of those who perpetrate injustice. Only the gospel can open the perpetrators' eyes to treat everyone like fellow human beings. He brings in the gospel aspect at this level of dialogue, for only the gospel has the power to reconcile people in a meaningful way.[54] This siding with the oppressed links to his early work on blackness or standing in solidarity with the oppressed groups, which he refers to as "becoming black."[55] This epistemological argument implies a social imaginary through a liberation framework in which Boesak holds that our understanding of God needs to be brought into public dialogue to demonstrate what freed society should look like. While this creates theological debates, it attempts to cut off from compromized Christian realism, which avoids seeing the Christian faith's political embodiment. In Boesak's view, Liberation Theology is grappling with this political nature of the faith expressed in Jesus's own life and his kingdom language.[56] He implies that concern with humans' spiritual realities needs to be demonstrated by participating in emancipatory activities. According to him, to create a version of a God who is only concerned with the spiritual and does not participate in socioeconomic deliverance creates a false dichotomy and "serves to sanction unjust and oppressive structures and relations."[57] This dualistic approach with deistic elements cannot offer hope in the present circumstances.

4.2.1.1 Living in the Here and Now

Theology, in Boesak's view, must address present questions and problems and not seek to escape from the *historical dimension* of life. He writes that,

> within the black situation, solidarity with the oppressed becomes active engagement for liberation, leading . . . to the transformation of oppressing and inhuman structures. Black Theology knows that the biblical message of God's liberation has historical as well as eschatological dimensions. It does not only rest upon the historical event of the Exodus, but it also points to the

---

54. Boesak, 111.

55. Boesak, *Farewell to Innocence* (1976), 14–17.

56. Boesak, 14–17.

57. Boesak, 24.

future, the future of Yahweh which he has also made the future of his people.[58]

That God is not out of touch with his creation has an immense bearing on present living conditions. Boesak believes that the needed liberation must "search for a totally new social order"[59] that incorporates African values and social norms. This order incorporates a socioeconomic vision to eliminate inequitable socioeconomic structures and replace them with more human ones. This search emanates from the notion that our conviction of God's future restoration of the world should affect how we live here and now. Christians must work towards a society that reflects this creation narrative and restoration vision. The search for a theology of social justice should seek to engage the present realities of those affected by injustice.

Engaging the present is essential to Black Liberation Theology. The present context of humiliation, poverty, and corruption needs to be corrected. The book of Exodus, an essential source of Boesak's theology, sets a challenge to rethink redemption and how we can gather fresher perspectives for a theological engagement suited for Namibia. According to Boesak, this engagement comes with "political consequences" for those who challenge the status quo.[60]

The idea of the *here* and *now* raises a new challenge of the length to which Christians are ready to go for the sake of truth and justice. This view calls for a reorientation of our priorities to participate in uplifting the socioeconomically downtrodden. True alternative consciousness informed by Scripture has profound radical implications for faith, and social and political order. He believes that,

> the power of the powerless is the power of truth – the truth about the inhumanity of the oppressor which exposes the lies, injustice, and fear which the demonic power structure parasitizes in order to survive. This truth is not just to be heard and acknowledged; it is to be believed and done. Black Power is thus the truth about white and black people, about history and the present. This truth opens perspectives for the future and

---

58. Boesak, *Farewell to Innocence* (1977), 145.

59. Boesak, 151.

60. Boesak, *Tenderness of Conscience*, 115–16.

becomes authentic reality in the action of love within history; this truth shall make us free.[61]

Boesak's call to make a difference in the *here* and *now* seems to agree with Brueggemann's argument that "the notion of human justice and compassion" is in biblical terms "a foremost factor in ordering a community."[62] In the present social realities, being God's community comes with its social imagination that gives rise to an alternative social order. The vision of the future redemption creates restlessness not to accept the present dehumanising social order.

4.2.1.2 Blackness in a Post-Apartheid Context

Blackness, both ontological and metaphorical, is a central feature of Boesak's theology. This study uses blackness in its ontological sense, referring to a group of people based on their biological features. This usage does not deny that persons who are not Black have suffered at times and do suffer. Instead, most people who are presently vulnerable in the post-apartheid context happen to be Black. The researcher does not deny the conceptual benefit of metaphoric blackness to represent various systematically marginalized persons. This benefit can be observed in his latest work, *Children of the Waters of Meribah*, as he provides a theological argument for how power structures continue to affect women.

Boesak's *Farewell to Innocence*, although it touches on metaphoric blackness, is written in the context of ontological blackness upon which the apartheid regime unleashed its wrath. However, we do not want to usurp Boesak's explanation that "Blackness does not in the first place designate color of skin. It is a discovery, a state of mind, a conversion, an affirmation of being, which is power. It is an insight which has to do with wisdom and responsibility."[63] We do not assume that the metaphor of blackness is independent of blackness as skin colour. Has the position of ontological blackness changed in the prospect of opportunity, skills, economic wealth, access to healthcare, and education? While many Black people, for example in Namibia (and South Africa by extension), have more legal rights, Bobek, Moritz, and Horvat have found that the country is plagued by "tremendous inequality conditions" which block

---

61. Boesak, *Farewell to Innocence* (1977), 56.

62. Brueggemann, *Prophetic Imagination*, 22.

63. Boesak, *Farewell to Innocence* (1977), 139.

access to economic opportunities for advancement.[64] Thus, more needs to be done to redress the socioeconomic inequality cycle created through colonialism, apartheid, and post-independence structures. The socioeconomic conditions described in chapter 2 imply that Black persons continue to be disadvantaged.

While the present context is not that of apartheid as a legal system, specific fundamental issues need to take place in order to achieve authentic post-apartheid liberation. First is *the quest for identity*. Social justice is not for political reasons or to advance certain ideologies (African or foreign). Instead, for Boesak,[65] Black Theology is a "search for true and authentic human identity and liberation."[66] Taylor argues that "behind the issue of inequality and justice lies something deeper, which touches what we would call today the 'identity' of the human beings."[67] It is about restoring God's image-bearers to live as God intended them to be and not as an oppressive system has made them believe. If so, this understanding of Black Theology challenges social justice approaches that make projects and targets out of people. If God is a God of community, as Boesak says,[68] then a faithful presence that shares life with the affected persons cannot be left out of the equation. In *Farewell to Innocence*,[69] Boesak lays a moral argument for Black Theology and power, which he believes could help create a new society if everybody cooperated in a society of equals. Thus, Black Liberation Theology serves as a social intervention from the margins to transform unjust power structures.[70] It begins in a vision in which Christ would be the ultimate sovereign to end all dehumanising powers.[71] It does away with an oppressive ideology that manifests itself in various structural privileges that disadvantage most persons. Post-independence settings of privilege extend to both Black and White Africans and even those from within the Christian faith community. We are

---

64. Bobek, Moritz, and Horvat, "Namibia's Triple Challenge," 7.

65. Boesak, *Farewell to Innocence* (1976), 36.

66. Boesak, 40.

67. Taylor, *Modern Social Imaginaries*, 54.

68. Boesak, *Farewell to Innocence* (1977), 11.

69. While working on chapter 4, I switched from the 1976 edition to the 1977 edition. The former was a library copy and I could no longer continue using it. The 1977 edition is an electronic version.

70. Boesak, *Farewell to Innocence* (1977), 14–15.

71. Boesak, *Comfort and Protest*, 126–38.

not referring to what is termed as "White privilege" but to the structural arrangements to which Goulet says,

> society is so organized that only the representatives of certain interests enjoy access to the wealth, culture, contracts, information, and influence without which decisions cannot be made. Consequently, meaningful policy changes cannot be brought about simply by "throwing the rascals out" because those who replace them may emerge from the same structures and represent identical interests.[72]

A country of about 80–90 percent Christians that does not reflect a Christian ethos in the public structures implies a severe identity crisis. Brueggemann rebukes this loss of Christian identity, which has become complacent instead of radically being countercultural. He writes that

> the internal cause of such enculturation is our loss of identity through the abandonment of the faith tradition. Our consumer culture is organized against history. There is a depreciation of memory and a ridicule of hope, which means everything must be held in the now, either an urgent now or an eternal now. Either way, a community rooted in energizing memories and summoned by radical hopes is a curiosity and a threat in such a culture. When we suffer from amnesia, every form of serious authority for faith is in question, and we live unauthorized lives of faith and practice unauthorized ministries.[73]

Boesak's quest for restoring identity primarily places a great responsibility upon the church and its role in undoing dehumanising structures.[74] Otherwise, as Brueggemann argues, "The church will not have power to act or believe until it recovers its tradition of faith and permits that tradition to be the primal way out of [false, reluctant and harmful] enculturation."[75]

Second, *doing away with deterministic and fatalistic notions* regarding Black persons' suffering calls for confronting the present pietism, classism,

---

72. Goulet, *Development Ethics*, 20.

73. Brueggemann, *Prophetic Imagination*, 12.

74. Boesak, *Tenderness of Conscience*, 13, 25.

75. Brueggemann, *Prophetic Imagination*, 2.

and racism, which continue to disempower Black people strategically. In Boesak's view, this revictimises the suffering with a false political consciousness cloaked in biblical justifications.[76] If a post-apartheid theology must speak into today's context, it needs to reclaim the biblical understanding of the nature of God – regarding social justice.

> The Bible speaks of God as a loving God, because Yahweh's love is seen in Yahweh's love for justice and Yahweh's outrage at injustice that continues to create victims. It is an outraged God who "observed" the misery of God's people, who "heard" their cry, who "know(s)" their sufferings. Yahweh knows who the victims are. "I have come down to deliver them" (Ex 3:7–8). It is an outraged God who rails against the injustices inflicted upon the poor and powerless. It is the voice of a God who knows the victims – the poor, the orphan, the widow, the stranger; demeaned, impoverished, voiceless, powerless; and who knows that they were the victims of the rich and powerful who pervert all justice and equity.[77]

Such participation that can confront the systemic classism and structural imbalances calls for a theology to speak to these structures, identifying the philosophical fallacies and ideology of power and inequality, as a prophetic witness to reclaim the marred humanity. Boesak's early decrying of apartheid injustice still applies to post-independence structures which have not proven that they are prepared to include previously disadvantaged communities to come out of the shadow of powerful elites.

Third, the *undoing of unjust power structures*. This confrontation of concepts upon which society is structured represents power relations that are sustained with justifications to keep the status quo that enhances social inequality. The understanding we derive from Boesak is that theology needs to challenge false notions that sustain unjust systems and confront the hierarchical Greek, Roman, colonial, apartheid, and post-independence corrupt and inhumane social imaginary "built on class, power, and privilege,

---

76. Boesak and DeYoung, *Radical Reconciliation*, 91.

77. Boesak and DeYoung, 93–94.

and the arrogance and entitlement."[78] This confrontation of unjust powers
is what Boesak calls a "theology of refusal,"[79] that would not relent as long
as injustice remains. This confrontation applies to any theology, philosophy,
or social and political theory that uses language synonyms for the status
quo. Melber charges post-independence structures with constructing fluid
notions of democracy and social justice, which allow those close to political power to benefit the most and use the system to shield the interests of
apartheid perpetrators and elite liberation heroes.[80] Boesak describes these
as "the pharaohs" or "the present powers of oppression and exploitation" that
"physically look like us."[81] He points to post-independence settings in which
"we are fighting people whom we have honored as liberators and entrusted
with political power for the sake of justice and dignity."[82]

Fourth, we need to engage the systems and structures of power. Boesak's
Black Theology would have us engage at the public level where the interest
of the powerful and the structures that enhance them should be scrutinized
rather than forcing the disadvantaged to accept injustice as divine fate. In
Boesak's view, Black Theology of Liberation is concerned with righting the
distorted order.[83] He contends that it is a framework that understands opposing unjust structures, motivated by the understanding that if God is a just
God, this justice ought to manifest in all of creation.[84] He intends to make
people aware that God is concerned for the wellbeing of the poor and fighting for their cause, and so should Christians everywhere. He cites Dietrich
Bonhoeffer and Beyers Naudé as examples of Christian scholarship, theology, and witness in the face of injustice. In Boesak's understanding, Black
Theology is not only about ethnicity but about taking risks for the sake of
the gospel to challenge all kinds of structures of power that would not bow
to the lordship of Christ.[85]

---

78. Boesak and DeYoung, *Radical Reconciliation*, 56–57.

79. Boesak, *Farewell to Innocence* (1977), 26.

80. Melber, "Limits of Liberation," 14.

81. Boesak, *Pharaohs on Both Sides*, 101 of 6855.

82. Boesak, 101 of 6855.

83. Boesak, *Farewell to Innocence* (1976), 26–29.

84. Boesak, 26–29.

85. Boesak and DeYoung, *Radical Reconciliation*, 72.

For the post-apartheid context, this is revolutionary. It seeks to cast a new vision of theological engagement in public, to advocate for the undoing of unjust structures that systematically disadvantage people based on their skin colour. It is a call not to leave this to the hands of secularists to drive change, but that Christianity which has been central in the liberation struggle against apartheid, needs to continue to undo post-apartheid structures of injustice.

4.2.2 Application

Injustice is painful and raises emotions, but how do we construct an authentic theology that understands the subtleness of the social situation? We started in chapter 1 on a note of suspicion towards Black Liberation Theology, but we did not dismiss it. As a theology, it has pioneered Christian participation leading up to independence, making us all indebted to its efforts against an oppressive system. This history needs to be linked to contextual models of political and economic dialogue and organization to transform unjust structures. This current project does not ask Black Liberation to abandon its belief. However, the Namibian Black Liberation Theology needs its own conceptual liberation to pursue a meaningful social justice course. For example, Kameeta,[86] Niitenge,[87] Mujoro and Mujoro,[88] and Nambala[89] provide Namibian theological works that advocate for Black Liberation Theology. They provide detailed depictions of the social issues affecting mostly Black persons. These theological views, although helpful, manifest the inadequacy of theological, political, philosophical, economic, and legal notions to engage the post-independence systems that deny social justice. The challenge from Boesak for the Namibian context is that theology needs to recover the true meaning of liberation, beyond being a mere historical project. It needs to be rooted in political, cultural, and economic reality and active participation and not just promises of socioeconomic liberation and justice. Analysis of post-liberation Black Liberation Theology by the Namibian historian Botha[90] portrays it as a struggling theology that does not know how to articulate itself

---

86. Kameeta, *Towards Liberation*.

87. Niitenge, "Evangelical Lutheran Church."

88. Mujoro and Mujoro, "Namibian Liberation Theology."

89. Nambala, "From Colonialism to Nationalism."

90. Botha, "Church in Namibia."

or lacks conceptual clarity and demonstrates "the inability to devise concrete alternatives to the current social order."[91] This struggle for social justice needs to ask contextually relevant questions and not simply adopt theological suggestions because they are being used everywhere else. This requires an honest theological, philosophical, and contextual self-analysis that would reimagine beyond historical projects and move towards actual enacting of its notions.

People's lack of power based on social structures is a central theme of Boesak's theology. Namibian theology is yet to engage actual themes of power in the post-independent public sphere. This engagement would need the creation of spaces to address unequal structures to allow the materialization of alternative communities, not necessarily as a community of the margin but a community of people living as God intended. Boesak warns against equating Christian participation with an ideology of social justice and encourages that our faith should be able to relate to social justice ideologies.[92] He argues that this ideological awareness would make the cause of theology "more human and realistic, through bringing them under the criterion and power of the New Humanity in Christ."[93] This calls for theological and social discernment. Thus, to engage the socioeconomic issues, we need to discern the present circumstances. Ours is a call to the truth that addresses the Namibian question of injustice, not to idolize social ideologies, theologies, or interpretations.

This search for an authentic Namibian understanding should be coupled with probing existing concepts. For example, the concept of "blackness" cannot be adopted without considering what it means for every context. While it is a central theme in Boesak's theology, the concept needs to find a uniquely Namibian identification. Most people at the receiving end of social injustice are Black. But framing the descriptive language regarding these unjust conditions requires careful reconsideration. "Blackness" may serve as a helpful starting point for lack of better descriptors but needs awareness of the negative connotations it may carry.

While Black Liberation Theology creates awareness of what is wrong in society, these analyses need careful examination, even where there seems to be an obvious socioeconomic divide. For example, we cannot escape the

---

91. Petrella, *Future of Liberation Theology*, ch. 1: 8.

92. Boesak, *Farewell to Innocence* (1977), 83.

93. Boesak, 83.

demands of the claim; God *par excellence* takes side with the oppressed.[94] It is not a mere sociopolitical claim; it carries profound theological implications. The claim also questions our cultural exegesis and the paradigms of our cultural praxis. In response to the poor, the political question would be geared towards institutions, policies, and programmes. But the theological question of the poor as God's image-bearers goes much deeper than social analysis. It begins in God. The idea of God siding with the poor should prompt us to ask whether our society's structures reflect God's vision of human flourishing (*shalom*). What does a good life look like in this society that needs to be extended for the good of all? What sort of a Christian community would it make us if we become complicit with our culture's way of life that has a misplaced vision of a good life and no regard for the poor? Such an approach provides a better starting place for what James Smith calls "discerning the shape of the kingdom"[95] and how we can participate in it.

The Genesis narrative of humans' creation as God's image-bearers could impact how we approach social justice. It may help reshape how we view society and the consequences of belief in God's created order. As Forster argues, our belief "has a concrete expectation for the way in which Christians live in the world, how they relate to other persons, how they form their laws, and how they work towards justice and human flourishing."[96] The consequence of such a belief is also the basis for searching for a theology that advocates for liberation. De Gruchy argues that our level of desire and motivation is influenced by what we believe about people or that our anthropology affects our perspectives and participation in social issues.[97] If humans are accidents of nature or without a *telos*, advocating for social justice carries no meaning for Christians unless they believe that humans are created in the image of a triune God. Liberation Theology then becomes truly an egalitarian theology in matters of social justice and a powerful ally.

Given that humans are created in God's image, does it matter that we understand the social circumstances? Boesak answers "yes." He argues, in *Dare We Speak of Hope?*, that we need to understand the surrounding social

---

94. Boesak and DeYoung, *Radical Reconciliation*, 41.

95. Smith, *Desiring the Kingdom*, 91.

96. Forster, "What Hope Is There?", 4.

97. De Gruchy, *Christianity and Democracy*, 240.

circumstance and warns against being naive in our search for social justice.[98] Theology will only be meaningful if it does not make excuses for apartheid and post-independence structures affecting God's image-bearers. At the heart of Christian ethics lies this spiritual reality – "to love God is to love one's neighbour and love one's neighbour to love God, demonstrated by siding with the poor, downtrodden and marginalised."[99] Based on this conviction, liberation would ensure that hearts and minds will be transformed into Christlikeness in the kingdom's reception. Thus, liberty is never for its own sake but unto God's will in the service of humanity. It is the liberty to become witnesses and advocates of God's righteousness in society. De Gruchy expands on the consequences of this creation account:

> The Christian understanding of God as self-disclosed in Jesus Christ has led Christian faith to its conviction about the triune nature of God. For this reason, the Christian understanding of the imago Dei is grounded in the doctrine of trinity. The Christian God is not "the absolute" or "ultimate" affirmed or rejected by philosophers ancient and modern, but the creator and redeemer who in Jesus Christ and through the presence and empowering of the Spirit seeks to renew the earth and establish a new order in which justice dwells.[100]

Dion Forster puts forth a similar perspective that,

> faith in the Gospel of Christ has a concrete expectation for the way in which Christians live in the world, how they relate to other persons, how they form their laws, and how they work towards justice and human flourishing. In short, the Christian faith has significant social and political consequences that reach beyond the walls of the worshipping congregation.[101]

Boesak is concerned with the practical outplay of this creation narrative. The search for justice, he believes, is a manifestation of being created in the image of God and therefore we cannot be at peace where this image is being

---

98. Boesak, *Dare We Speak?*, 26.
99. Boesak, *Farewell to Innocence* (1976), 21.
100. De Gruchy, *Christianity and Democracy*, 240.
101. Forster, "What Hope Is There?", 4.

oppressed. Boesak understands that applying the redemptive narrative (of Exodus) to every aspect of human life calls for courage not "to run away from our responsibilities, political or otherwise, and so doing run into the arms of the myth-makers in the service of the imperial logic."[102] We could do all of this and merely be advocating a social programme that uses God. An evangelical vision of social justice would be inadequate if it does not bring Jesus Christ in the centre of such dialogues.

The Messianic view of a radical Jesus needs to encapsulate the Messianic vision of salvation and not just socioeconomic redemption. Social transformation is a missional activity, making Christian participation a social activity if it does not encapsulate the gospel message. In its *Cape Town Commitment*, the Lausanne Congress for World Evangelization (2011) advocates social participation as participation in God's mission. It reads that

> the Church from all nations stands in continuity through the Messiah Jesus with God's people in the Old Testament. With them we have been called through Abraham and commissioned to be a blessing and a light to the nations. With them, we are to be shaped and taught through the law and the prophets to be a community of holiness, compassion and justice in a world of sin and suffering. We have been redeemed through the cross and resurrection of Jesus Christ, and empowered by the Holy Spirit to bear witness to what God has done in Christ. The Church exists to worship and glorify God for all eternity and to participate in the transforming mission of God within history. Our mission is wholly derived from God's mission, addresses the whole of God's creation, and is grounded at its centre in the redeeming victory of the cross. This is the people to whom we belong, whose faith we confess and whose mission we share.[103]

It will be naive to base a theological engagement purely on a social analysis of history. If the Christian understanding of justice is mere social participation in society, we are close to becoming beneficent social interventionists. Boesak does not entertain such an interpretation. But if liberation is the gospel, do

---

102. Boesak, *Dare We Speak?*, 26.

103. The Third Lausanne Congress on World Evangelization, "Cape Town Commitment," 188–89.

we then speak of the human heart's sin[104] and need for redemption as part of Christian social analysis? Jesus spoke against oppression and exploitation, not as specializations of the rich and powerful but as sins that every human heart can exercise if given the opportunity. Jewish and Roman rulers' hearts were just as corrupt as those they exploited. When Jesus brings the radical message of repentance, nobody (rich and poor, oppressor and oppressed, victimiser and victim) is excluded. We need to keep in mind that the Israelites were not made righteous because they were victims of slavery. Instead, we are told that

> they are not innocent, and that in fact blood will have to be shed if they are to be redeemed. So, God gives them instructions for slaughtering the Passover lamb (Exodus 12). Even after the exit from Egypt, it is clear that the people are not in a free and perfect relationship with God. They are still sinful people, and as a result they are to remain separated from him. So God tells Moses in Exodus 19:12–13 to set limits around Mount Sinai and forbid the people to go up it or even to touch the edge of it. If anyone does, God says, he will be killed. God may have chosen them and rescued them, but their sin remains and mankind's exile from Eden is still in effect.[105]

What is the likelihood of becoming reticent to truth and faithful witness if we only speak out against the oppressor's sins but not the heart of the oppressed or victim? Botha[106] and Horn[107] (see § 5.3 for details of their critiques) demonstrate how the church's failure to place moral demands on both the perpetrators and victims resulted in a post-independence situation in which former victims have become perpetrators. Standing up against dehumanising

---

104. Paul II, *Catechism*, 453. We use sin in this text as defined in the Roman Catholic Catechism that "Sin is an offense against reason, truth, and right conscience; it is failure in genuine love for God and neighbor caused by a perverse attachment to certain goods. It wounds the nature of man and injures human solidarity. It has been defined as 'an utterance, a deed, or a desire contrary to the eternal law.' Sin is an offense against God: 'Against you, you alone, have I sinned, and done that which is evil in your sight.' Sin sets itself against God's love for us and turns our hearts away from it. Like the first sin, it is disobedience, a revolt against God through the will to become 'like gods,' knowing and determining good and evil. Sin is thus 'love of oneself even to contempt of God.' In this proud self-exaltation, sin is diametrically opposed to the obedience of Jesus, which achieves our salvation."

105. DeYoung and Gilbert, *What Is the Mission?*, 66.

106. Botha, "Church in Namibia."

107. Horn, "Churches and Political Reconciliation."

establishments and placing them under the scrutiny of Scripture and the gospel requires courage. The source of such courage is a vision of courage based on Christ's example.

Boesak's idea of a radical Messiah calls for a review of how our faith should play out in public.[108] What makes Jesus's message radical? Is it his courage to confront the oppressors? Is it his refusal to take up power that resembles the Roman political system? Jewish nationalists who sought revolutionary power were just as corrupt at heart as those they opposed. Their position of being exploited did not exempt them from the reality of the spiritual separation from God. If we take the radical message of Boesak to its logical conclusion, then transforming a society of people whose model of power is abusive power cannot happen by merely granting them power. This means looking for something that presents us with a better model and epistemology of power to counter the misguided models of power borrowed from apartheid and colonialism and those exercised in post-independence structures. It can be an emblem that draws, through a "radical conversion,"[109] people with a misplaced understanding of power, freedom, and social justice to a community with an imagination based on the heavenly vision that would motivate a prophetic presence through which the kingdom is manifested on earth and expresses what redeemed humanity should be.

Boesak's Black Messiah image (see § 3.2.4 discussed along with Boesak's concept of God) needs to provide us with a conceptual framework to dismantle the idolatrous nature of racial identities and structures that insidiously shield injustice. This should also cause us to challenge all beliefs that could mistakenly assume that the opposite of whiteness should be blackness or White freedom should be contrasted by Black Liberation – making it to be a mirroring theology of apartheid and colonial ideologies. This contrast creates further torsion in our understanding and mending of (1) broken racial relationships, and (2) social justice measures. Boesak demonstrates in his opening chapter (The Coming of the Black Messiah) of *Farewell to Innocence* that Christology ought to be the centre of Christian motivation for social justice in the world. This blackness concept still needs careful reading for the Namibian aim to redress racism and injustice. It could be misconstrued

---

108. Boesak, *Farewell to Innocence* (1976), 22–26; Boesak, *Black and Reformed*, 37–38.
109. Boesak, *Tenderness of Conscience*, 154.

as regurgitating the racial divide that apartheid employed using theological analogies. Addressing existing realities of socioeconomic inequality that affects Black persons could also be misconstrued as reinventing apartheid. Affirming God's incarnation in Jesus Christ comes with a realization of different humanity and higher demands for social justice in society. Ziegler, citing Bonhoeffer,[110] argues that to "assert that divine promeity[111] has as its end the truing of humanity, [is an] ingredient in which is a liberation of human beings to exist for others,"[112] because the gospel and the work of Christ secure and signal "by his cross the reconciliation of the godless world with the God it has refused, and wins space for a new and"[113] authentic humanbeingness.

This understanding of liberation considers the inherent cause of oppression and structures of injustice to be the sin problem of the human heart. Boesak acknowledges that "human nature is selfish and self-centred, tends toward evil rather than good, is tainted by sin."[114] This is a vivid analysis of the reality of humanity's spiritual condition and how only change at this level would ensure the transformation we envision. Black Liberation Theology, in general, has rarely emphasised this spiritual condition and has been termed "the social gospel" because of its emphasis on the social conditions but very little on the gospel and salvation of the soul. If Black Theology of Liberation is to redeem itself from this misreading, as Anthony Bradley argues, it needs to relocate an authentic Christian identity.[115] Otherwise, it will merely be a social branch of politics submerged in theological language. He further argues that

> Black Liberation Theology is in danger of losing a distinctively Christian identity . . . In general, black liberation theologians only offer a sociocultural interpretation of the atonement . . .

---

110. Bonhoeffer, *Letters and Papers*, 262.

111. *Promeity* (from the Latin *pro me* [for me]) is a term used in Bonhoeffer's work referring to the presence of Christ and its implication for how we will live out this reality. This research refers to witnessing the truth of the incarnate and resurrected Christ in the face of injustice. Bonhoeffer in the letter to his friend Eberhard Bethge raises his concerns about the meaning of the Christian faith and "who Christ really is, *for us* today." We understand this as a quest for a contextual appropriation of the presence of Christ in various social circumstances in which we seek to articulate our faith.

112. Ziegler, "Christ's Lordship and Politics," 71.

113. Ziegler, 71.

114. Boesak, *Tenderness of Conscience*, 127.

115. Bradley, *Liberating Black Theology*, 227 of 265.

while the atonement does have social implications, Christ's work on the cross is a manifestation of power and is the source for the hope of overcoming all sins in human life, personal and social alike . . . Black theology needs a biblical anthropology. In contrast to the sociopragmatic approach of Black Liberation Theology, which defines the imago Dei in terms of race, class, gender, and sexual orientation, a distinctively biblical approach recognizes the innate equality of human ontology in terms of human dignity. It is grounded in its deepest form in Genesis 1:26–28 instead of in Marxist categories . . . Black Liberation Theology needs to recover the doctrine of salvation . . . [it] places such an overwhelming emphasis on the analysis of human oppression and the liberation of the oppressed that issues of what is required for an individual to be reconciled to God either go unanswered or are redefined in terms of social activism. Namely, either being oppressed or advocating for the oppressed seems to be all that is required, which contradicts the plain teaching of Scripture in several places.[116]

This Christian identity needs, among other things, to acknowledge that our socioeconomic conditions, to an extent, reflect humanity's spiritual condition. Spiritual liberation and the right relationship with God are the entry levels to authentic altruism. Boesak indicates that humans have, in themselves, no capability of achieving forgiveness because of their natural disposition.[117] Bonhoeffer sees the gospel's proclamation going hand in hand with active social participation.[118] He argues that

what we are concerned with here is the free communication of the Word from person to person, not by the ordained ministry which is bound to a particular office, time, and place. We are thinking of that unique situation in which one person bears witness in human words to another person, bespeaking the whole consolation of God, the admonition, the kindness, and the

---

116. Bradley, 226–28 of 265.
117. Boesak, *Tenderness of Conscience*, 127.
118. Bonhoeffer, *Life Together*.

severity of God. The speaking of that Word is beset with infinite perils. If it is not accompanied by worthy listening, how can it really be the right word for the other person? If it is contradicted by one's own lack of active helpfulness, how can it be a convincing and sincere word? If it issues, not from a spirit of bearing and forbearing, but from impatience and the desire to force its acceptance, how can it be the liberating and healing word?[119]

This holistic embrace of our task in the world is crucial. Humanity's spiritual alienation from God and its effects on social order are not separate entities of the gospel. Both Boesak and Bonhoeffer's concern is that we may fall into the trap of simply paying lip service. Evangelical theology can become divorced from social realities if it thinks evangelism is the only real task of being missional. DeYoung and Gilbert argue that the gospel of Jesus Christ is of foremost importance; but they warn "against a careless, loveless indifference to the problem and potential opportunities all around us, a dualistic disregard for the whole person."[120] On the other hand, we must be responsible and keep our social participation in perspective, especially against "overly (and exhausting) utopian dreams, a loss of God-centredness, and a diminishment of the church's urgent message of Christ."[121] Namibian theology needs to generate a theological perspective that keeps these tensions in balance in the search for social justice and more just living.

Boesak challenges us to be actively involved where our presence is needed in fighting injustice. It is a call to discern the *kairos* and active discipleship that identifies with suffering persons. Boesak believes that,

> it is not our religion that makes us believers and followers of Christ; rather it is participation in the sufferings of God. We are called to share the suffering of God at the hands of a hostile world. We are disciples of Christ when we stand by God in the hour of God's grieving. In other words, if we stand by those who suffer in the world, wherever and whoever they may be, we are

---

119. Bonhoeffer, 45.

120. DeYoung and Gilbert, *What Is the Mission?*, 23.

121. DeYoung and Gilbert, 23.

standing by God. It is for their sake that God is at work in the world, so that creation as a whole may be redeemed.[122]

He calls for a discerning attitude that is cognisant of the various interplaying elements. This may require engaging the political structures but with an overtly Christian commitment in our search for social justice. It calls for active commitment to the gospel and selfless men and women whose faith is rooted in God. While the political can be instrumental in creating social awareness, Christian motivation should be for gospel reasons that aim at transforming not just the political but also human hearts and minds. This means becoming fully aware of the spiritual realities behind the unjust structures occupied by humans who do not recognize God's sovereignty over their lives. This aspect is where theological participation in public life becomes missional.[123] Black Theology of Liberation needs to be seen as creating awareness and dialogue regarding injustice's persistence. This implies a theology that extends beyond mere social-historical analysis and looks at issues with a critical analysis that speaks to the Namibian context. Boesak's Black Liberation Theology and its political perspective, although not entirely matched to the Namibian context, could help construct a dynamic and reflective practice (holistic) and how the Christian faith can engage public issues.

4.3 Theology of Power and Consciousness

4.3.1 Exposition and Analysis

The notion of a liberating God, in Boesak's view, should result in a pedagogical outcome that creates a liberating awareness to resist both unjust conditions and structures. Combining this theological understanding with Black Power and Consciousness forms an epistemological framework for social justice. It informs the basis upon which Boesak argues that social institutions should distribute life-enhancing goods to create an equal society. It encourages the radical change of society's social structures. In this view, the understanding and knowledge of God are believed to ignite a new consciousness that demands the dismantling of structures that are part of the imposed status quo. Oppression (which is the outward manifestation of power and its abuse),

---

122. Boesak, *Kairos, Crisis and Global*, 23.
123. DeYoung and Gilbert, *What Is the Mission?*, 22–24.

according to Boesak, can only end when the oppressed come to their senses and refuse these abnormal and inhumane conditions. This theology of refusal is the beginning, without which the oppressed minds will never gain the power to claim their liberation.[124]

Boesak discusses a consciousness born out of Black solidarity, which he describes as the "discovery of, a state of mind, a conversion, and affirmation of being, which is power."[125] He interlinks consciousness with power; one cannot exist without the other or "Black Consciousness as an integral part of Black Power.[126] Consciousness then is a search for humanbeingness that can challenge the structures that disempower and dehumanize people based on their skin colour or other social classifications. For such consciousness to thrive, a system that grants equal rights for all persons to lead a life of dignity and self-respect,[127] and granting the same legal rights to Black persons as those given to White persons, making them legally equals, needs to be pursued.

Black solidarity is presented as the antithesis to White racial, ideological, political, and cultural domination, something Boesak believes is the core for ending the imbalanced power relations to usher in a nonracial consciousness. Thus, conscientising the oppressed to reclaim their place is needed to pave the way for liberation in all other areas which racist structures have normalized. Unlike James Cone, who called for exclusively Black participation in emancipation, Boesak uses a concept of inclusive Black solidarity. It is not solidarity towards assimilation nor, as Biko says, "to reform the system because so doing implies acceptance of the major points around which the [oppressive apartheid] system revolves."[128] Biko's concept of consciousness is to attain liberation through a radical transformation of the existing social structure. He argues that,

> Blacks are out to completely transform the system and to make of it what they wish. Such a major undertaking can only be re- alised in an atmosphere where people are convinced of the truth inherent in their stand. Liberation, therefore, is of paramount

---

124. Boesak, *Farewell to Innocence* (1977), 58, 93, 115.
125. Boesak, 110.
126. Boesak, 66.
127. Boesak, 110.
128. Biko, *I Write What I Like*, 46.

importance in the concept of Black Consciousness, for we cannot be conscious of ourselves and yet remain in bondage. We want to attain the envisioned self which is a free self.[129]

We should note that the conscientization Boesak is advocating is also linked to a cultural reclamation, through which he calls for the reexamination of Christianity. He questions the harm caused by a "White centred" theology that demonises everything African and Black and apotheosises all that is Western and White. This liberation from conceptual domination allows the oppressed to see themselves in a different light and "not . . . as defined by the racist ideologies of oppression, not allowing our humanity to be prescribed and proscribed by apartheid."[130] Through a reexamined Christianity, he seeks to establish a consciousness that reaffirms God's plan to create Black persons. Boesak believes that Christianity which provided the theological instruments for oppression, can also be the instrument of liberation, countering Steve Biko's anti-Christian notions. This then becomes the ground for granting power that would enable the oppressed to pursue their dreams in freedom and live in dignity or "being able to be human, sharing in God's power of creation."[131]

Boesak seems to use consciousness in abstract terms as the philosophical template, which would lead to the right course of action if appropriately understood. Besides tackling the apartheid philosophy, Black Consciousness counters Hegel's abstraction that the African has no sense of self-awareness.[132] Thus, it counters the philosophical basis that gave the apartheid system power to legitimize Black persons' dehumanization. Consciousness implies the ability to conceptualize one's situation, point out the mistaken justifications

---

129. Biko, 49.

130. Boesak, *Tenderness of Conscience*, 9.

131. Boesak, *Farewell to Innocence* (1976), 43.

132. Hegel, *Philosophy of History*, 110–11. Hegel believed that "In Negro life the characteristic point is the fact that consciousness has not yet attained to the realization of any substantial objective existence – as for example, God, or Law – in which the interest of man's volition is involved and in which he realizes his own being. This distinction between himself as an individual and the universality of his essential being, the African in the uniform, undeveloped oneness of his existence has not yet attained; so that the Knowledge of an absolute Being, an Other and a Higher than his individual self, is entirely wanting. The Negro, as already observed, exhibits the natural man in his completely wild and untamed state. We must lay aside all thought of reverence and morality – all that we call feeling – if we would rightly comprehend him; there is nothing harmonious with humanity to be found in this type of character."

of apartheid, and affirm the Black persons' humanity. It calls for reforms because "the people" can articulate what they want, social justice, freedom, and equality. This consciousness became the basis for resistance that pressured the apartheid government to surrender finally to the people's demands. According to Boesak, this consciousness is the definition of Black Power.[133] It provided power for self-propagation and allowed Black people to voice what they wanted, not as beggars to those who controlled the system, but as equals.

The pursuit of power links to the concepts of rights which Nicholas Wolterstorff calls "a normative social bond" between persons "whereby the other bears legitimate [mutual] claims on me as to how I treat her."[134] Boesak discusses this bond as one forged on a mutual understanding of social justice and not just a mere social arrangement. Social justice, in Boesak's conception, has material consequences, which is why he criticized the outcomes of the TRC, which went no further than verbal apologies (from the perpetrators and beneficiaries) and declaration of forgiveness (by the victims) (see § 3.5.1 and 3.5.2).[135] Under apartheid, only one group had claims over the other, and the oppressed group was to honour the social arrangements. Apartheid took captive the consciousness of those it subjugated and made them believe that they were less human and undeserving of better socioeconomic conditions because of their racial identity. Black Consciousness calls for recognising the appalling nature of these conditions created by the apartheid system to call for active rejection of racism and subjugation of persons and replace such a system with an inclusive one.

Boesak sees the formation and participation of the UDF as the manifestation of Black Consciousness among South Africans.[136] He refers to it as the founding of their pride and an impetus that ushered in a new phase for the liberation struggle. Boesak's concept of Black Consciousness was influenced by Steve Biko, who defines the concept that would later become central in the struggle against apartheid.

> Black Consciousness is, in essence, the realisation by the black
> man of the need to rally together with his brothers around the

---

133. Boesak, *Tenderness of Conscience*, 7–8.
134. Boesak, 6.
135. Boesak, 185–90.
136. Boesak, 9.

cause of their operation – the blackness of their skin – and to operate as a group in order to rid themselves of the shackles that bind them to perpetual servitude. It seeks to demonstrate the lie that black is an aberration from the "normal" which is white. It is a manifestation of a new realisation that by seeking to run away from themselves and to emulate the white man, blacks are insulting the intelligence of whoever created them black. Black Consciousness therefore, takes cognizance of the deliberateness of God's plan in creating black people black. It seeks to infuse the black community with a new-found pride in themselves, their efforts, their value systems, their culture, their religion and their outlook to life.[137]

Boesak adds a Christian element to the consciousness movement. Below, we engage with the theological basis of consciousness found in Boesak's work and its place in the post-apartheid dialogue of social justice. Boesak believes that Black Consciousness was a significant philosophical development in the history of liberation: an injection of a new perspective that focused on true being, "a decision toward and an act of solidarity, a black solidarity which encompasses all the different ethnic groups in the black community, sharing the solidarity of the oppressed. It is a positive, conscious determination to break down the walls erected by an Apartheid-inspired false consciousness."[138] He reflects upon this development and argues that "Black Consciousness, Black Power and Black theology merged and emerged as the key which unlocked the door to the future for the oppressed people . . . at a time when most of us thought that all was lost."[139]

4.3.2 Application

The quest of Black Consciousness should be seen as something more profound than only a political quest. It is a search to counter the hermeneutical injustice perpetrated by apartheid theology and philosophy which was a political, cultural, and philosophical system that wielded results that constantly disadvantaged Black persons and their communities. This calls for us to think

---

137. Biko, *I Write What I Like*, 49.

138. Boesak, *Farewell to Innocence* (1977), 135.

139. Boesak, *Tenderness of Conscience*, 10.

deeper about the effects of injustice that continue to affect millions (billions, if one takes the global population) of Black persons to this day. It calls for a theological consciousness that seeks God's will in the face of injustice and confronts the false narratives that justify the continuance of injustice in post-independence contexts. Boesak's theology of power and consciousness challenges us to rethink the psychological realities that have marred millions of Black persons' self-image.[140]

Black Consciousness provides a challenge at a foundational level of being. While an intellectual movement, its far-reaching quest raises the question of what it means to be human and the need to reclaim human dignity and reconfigure structures and institutions. While this may have started as a political, intellectual, and social movement, a theological contribution is essential. The apartheid system had a profound psychological effect on Black persons. Achille Mbembe describes the depth and three effects of the apartheid system from the perspective of Black Consciousness:

> First . . . is *separation from oneself.* Separation leads to a loss of familiarity with the self to the point that the subject, estranged, is relegated to an alienated, almost lifeless identity. In place of the being-connected-to-itself (another name for tradition) that might have shaped experience, one is constituted out of an alterity in which the self becomes unrecognizable to itself: this is the spectacle of separation and quartering. Second is the idea of *disappropriation.* This process refers, on the one hand, to the juridical and economic procedures that lead to material expropriation and dispossession, and, on the other, to a singular experience of subjection characterized by the falsification of oneself by the other. What flows from this is a state of maximal exteriority and ontological impoverishment. These two gestures (material expropriation and ontological impoverishment) constitute the singular elements of the Black experience and the drama that is its corollary. Finally, there is the idea of *degradation.* Not only did the servile condition plunge the Black subject into humiliation, abjection, and nameless suffering. It also incited a process

---

140. Boesak, *Farewell to Innocence* (1977), 135–39.

of "social death" characterized by the denial of dignity, dispersion, and the torment of exile.[141]

The system engaged ethically unprincipled, socially disruptive, and systematic psychopolitical tools to destabilize Black communities and normalize social injustice. In the 1980s, John Dommisse gave a psychological analysis that the apartheid policy and activities carried immense psychological effects on Black communities. He writes that "forced removals and dumping of millions of people into small, disconnected, barren, poor reserve areas, bereft of adequate medical, psychiatric and public health services (the 'final solution' of the 'native problem') causes widespread malnutrition, infectious and other diseases, and high mortality and mental-illness rates."[142] Dommisse's analysis is in agreement with Mbembe's three categories, which were carried out through extended exposure to inferior services and economic activities. In terms of consciousness, this indicated a deliberate social and psychological goal to dehumanize Black persons in social location, education, metaphor, language and religion. These repressive measures have affected how formerly oppressed communities view themselves decades after abolishing the legal apartheid system. Although they never lost their sense of self, they were deprived of freely determining their pace of progress and were made to live under conditions for which they never bargained. Thus, they were systematically disempowered so as not to function effectively even long after apartheid had ended. Deneulin, Nebel, and Sagovsky describe it as follows:

> Unjust structures, or structures of sin, were said to be rooted in personal wrongdoing: such acts of personal wrongdoing cumulatively build a structure which creates a "reality" in which it becomes difficult for human beings to amend or even see their personal wrongdoings. The structure comes to represent a reality which constrains individuals' actions in ways over which they have no control, and often no insight . . . First, unjust structures generate the experience of an impossible choice. The person is driven to undertake actions that he disapproves of, producing what can be called "alienation," Within the perverted structure,

---

141. Mbembe, *Critique of Black Reason*, 78.

142. Dommisse, "Apartheid as a Public," 510.

the person is bound to play a social role which he disapproves of but cannot escape. There is a disjunction between what the person really is and the role he plays in the social structure . . . Second, when alienation is prolonged and when the perversion of structures in all spheres is such, people may become "enslaved." The person can no longer see his own alienation. He has been blinded as much to his complicity in the unjust structure as to the contradiction between what he says and what he does. Worse still, this inability to see is intensified, so it seems, by an inability, even if he wanted – but he does not – to break free from this dynamic of unjust interaction.[143]

Boesak describes these effects in the context of apartheid:

There are, however, circumstances that work such destruction of one's self that even this fundamental drive is lacking. Persons under severe pressure can build up a devastating contempt for their own self. This was the lot of blacks. Slavery, domination of others, total dependence, lack of legal rights and the status of an alien whether in one's own land or in another land, discrimination and humiliation – all have had a devastating influence on the spiritual life of blacks. In the society dominated by whites, "white" was the acme of all that was "good"; "black" was the symbol of everything that was of little value or status.[144]

Central to Boesak's Black Consciousness theology is the desire not just to dismantle structures but to restore humanness and search for a better world, the humanness that seeks to end the false racial superiority and inferiority epistemologies, in search of new hope.[145] The theology of consciousness is a search for a new language and imagination about our social condition. The reason is that "the old language of our colonized and crippled minds, the language of fear and trepidation, of disbelief and cynicism, of ignorance

---

143. Deneulin, Nebel, and Sagovsky, "Introduction," 6–7.

144. Boesak, Black and Reformed, 16.

145. Boesak, Dare We Speak?, 24–25.

and resignation of internalized inferiorities and externalized submissiveness, cannot produce a new language."[146]

Apartheid was carried out on false, heretical, and criminal ideologies, so our response to its effects should be more than merely mirroring them. Our response must move away from defining the consciousness of the perpetrator's status, which makes the affected into perpetual victims with no end in sight. If the message of Black Consciousness is to take root, we need to counter the ontological victimology analysis.[147] The consciousness should then be based on something higher than a sociopolitical analysis or construct, transcending notions of unending inferiority, suffering, victimhood, and powerlessness.

Institutionalized structural injustice carries long-term effects, especially that it makes people believe that there is no way out, even to a degree of fatalistic acceptance of its existence. Boesak repudiates this fatalistic adoption of unjust structures and calls the oppressed to accept that they are no less deserving in contrast to the indoctrination of the apartheid philosophy and theology. Black Consciousness acknowledges this damage "whereby the Blacks are made critically aware of their situation of oppression based on their skin colour and of the need to analyse the situation and to struggle against it."[148] The systematic transformation advocated by Biko provides an interesting starting point.[149] This transformational approach may require an epistemological adjustment that does not make ontological pronouncements of victims. Victimology reading or critique should always keep the social contexts in mind. For example, Bradley's critique of Cone's victimology epistemology needs careful examination.[150] Cone and other Black Liberation theologians speak of victimhood as being ontological; we may deduce that they speak of human structurally-induced victimhood. No liberation theologian believes that Black persons' victimhood is an act of God. So, we should not dismiss the victim narratives without carefully engaging the social realities that continue to victimize Black communities today.

---

146. Boesak, 24.

147. Bradley, *Liberating Black Theology*, ch. 3: 11 of 16.

148. Ukpong, "Developments in Biblical Interpretation," 56.

149. Biko, *I Write What I Like*, pt. 46.

150. Bradley, *Liberating Black Theology*.

In *Dare We Speak of Hope?*, Boesak argues that the issue is not victimhood but having the integrity to address woundedness, recognize that injustice was committed, and that individuals and entire communities were wounded in numerous ways that cannot be repaired in a single lifetime. Some wounds continue to be manifest in the economic and social arrangements, which reinforce suffering. Speaking of victimhood is not a blame-game but recognises these sufferings and refuses to be silenced by voices of privilege or cowardice. The perspective of living on the margin rather than just visiting the margins drives the victim narrative. But finally, it is rooted in a theological understanding that holds firmly that the present conditions do not reflect God's *shalom* for his image-bearers. For Boesak, this is not a social analysis but a theological analysis of the social conditions of Black people's living circumstances.

Boesak speaks of "humanbeingness," which could be understood as a concept like the *ubuntu* philosophy, which carries a deep sense of humanness.[151] This dynamic philosophy challenges inhumane post-apartheid social structures and practices. Consciousness, then, seeks for something much more profound and lasting than a sociopolitical establishment for victims. It reaffirms their God-given humanity to pursue life by obtaining a vision of self that does not derive from the apartheid narrative. The structural ontology of victimhood understands that the dehumanising effects of apartheid are not acquiescent merely to adjusting political changes. Victims will remain perpetual victims unless the present power structures undergo systematic restructuring which is part and parcel of reaffirming Black humanity. Injustice, Boesak argues, is about power relations, and such continued protection of institutionalized structures need to be opposed[152] "with another interaction" to situate everyone "at the same level of power."[153]

Thus, Black Consciousness is to the disenfranchised a voice that allows them to resist all forms of structures of humiliation and to reclaim their humanity, not to reshape themselves into the image of the apartheid structures, but as God intended them. This would then be the basis for retelling their own stories and establishing their identities. This consciousness ought to create newer power structures and redistribute life-enhancing goods. This approach

---

151. Boesak, *Tenderness of Conscience*, 172.
152. Boesak, "Restless Presence," 14.
153. Deneulin, Nebel, and Sagovsky, "Introduction," 7.

argues that the affected speak for themselves instead of being spoken *to* and *for* and recognises the people's selfhood to be principal participants in their course and the cause of social justice.[154]

The need to confront social injustice must incorporate measures that would reverse the de-humanization advocated for decades that have robbed communities of self-worth. Amartya Sen's capability approach provides a complementary nexus to the concept of consciousness.[155] Without definite prospects to live the choices they want to make, they only become powerless self-aware people in contrast to the dehumanising system. Thus, it must take more than the rhetoric of activism to create an authentic "narrative of identity" towards a world as God intended it to be. This Christian response to human needs requires caution. It should also listen to other theologies in order to go beyond, as Stanley Hauerwas warns, presenting illusions, even of identity issues that are linked, intricately, to social justice.[156]

If the theology of Black Consciousness were to seek to recover self-worth and identity, it would give the Namibian pursuit of theologies of social justice a theology of consciousness, not for political expediency, but to attain the dignity of God's image-bearers. Therefore, a theological pursuit of social justice need not reject Black Consciousness as an aberration but see this social movement as an ally in fighting for social justice.[157] As a philosophy, it may also help gain a deeper understanding of Black communities' social construct, without which it may be difficult to advocate for them to charter the process of redressing past injustice and its effects that continue to affect them today.

An apparent connection between Christian thought and concern, and Black Consciousness, should not translate as a blanket endorsement of the latter's tenets. What Boesak defines as "a decision toward and an act of solidarity, a black solidarity which encompasses all the different ethnic groups in the black community, sharing the solidarity of the oppressed"[158] is based on a Christian understanding of humanity that should not escape us in this dialogue of consciousness. This perspective is also what makes Boesak different

---

154. Deneulin, Nebel, and Sagovsky, 8.
155. Sen, *Idea of Justice*.
156. Hauerwas, *Wilderness Wanderings*, 54.
157. MacIntyre, *Whose Justice?*, 389.
158. Boesak, *Farewell to Innocence* (1977), 134.

from Cone. Cone sees race as an ontological category, if not a system through which theology must be done, and Jesus and salvation must be understood. Whereas, Boesak starts with Jesus (as a good Reformed Christocentric theology would) and then looks for coherences with humanness.

God's liberation in Christ is for all persons, so those who need liberation are recognized for who they are and liberated as they are. However, it is not their identity that shapes their liberation but the activity of Christ. Overall, the concerns raised by the philosophy of Black Consciousness are congruous with Christian social concern. This anthropological understanding informed by the gospel motivates our resistance to all forms of injustice and provides a different social vision that confronts a permanent narrative of victimhood. Where people have experienced extended systematic victimization, we need to restore their dignity without making them feel that they belong to another confederation, but without ignoring how they see themselves as people. This approach focuses on reaffirming their humanity and that their social conditions are not their identity. We need to question the analysis of Black Consciousness, which defines the victims' consciousness by their social status and as the premise of a hermeneutic for theology.[159]

While injustice victimises people, its effects need not be dignified as historically and psychologically limiting. The post-apartheid search for social justice needs to pursue a theology of consciousness that dispels what Sen calls "a 'solitarist' approach to human identity,"[160] which continues a narrative of endless alienation. Nevertheless, addressing the marred self-worth of those previously oppressed needs to start somewhere. In this regard, Black Consciousness provides some necessary raw materials for engagement.

However, it must engage the practical rationality of the affected communities to construct "traditions of rational enquiry which are at the same time traditions embodied in particular types of social relationship."[161] Christians believe this would be near impossible to attain as long as the starting point of such consciousness and search of society is not made "in a way that promotes human dignity and the *imago Dei*."[162] Black Consciousness, therefore, even with good intentions, can go wrong if not linked with a healthy and

---

159. Bradley, *Liberating Black Theology*, ch. 3: 12 of 20.

160. Sen, *Identity and Violence*, 16.

161. MacIntyre, *Whose Justice?*, 389.

162. Bradley, *Liberating Black Theology*, ch. 4: 1 of 23.

responsible theological analysis. Our task is theological; therefore, the need to bring out this theological questioning of Black Consciousness is crucial. Theological intervention in such a divided environment comes with challenges that should neither be taken lightly nor rushed with incomplete answers.

This social intervention is part of the task of faithful action that discerns "that the crisis we are facing is not just economic, social, and political; it is at the deepest level a moral crisis."[163] A theology of consciousness is concerned with God's image-bearers' dignity but does not naively believe that secular sociopolitical interventions alone would result in the needed transformation. Part of this theological participation is to guard against ideologies and practices that pretend to be advocating for social justice while merely mirroring apartheid's discriminatory ideas.

The theology of Black Power and Consciousness provides us with the platform to raise critical questions about human dignity which need to go beyond static historical analysis that may not be true for the post-apartheid context. The political landscape of social injustice needs a theology of humanity to rearticulate a social imaginary that values humans as God's image-bearers endowed with the ability to chart the meaning of social justice for them. Part of the search for healing in the post-apartheid context must be couched in the need to explore the Christian faith's radical social nature to counter philosophies that perpetuate and ignore a sense of humanity. This calls for a theology that seeks new conceptualization that affirms the humanity of the previously disadvantaged, not as powerless people but as God's image-bearers, endowed with capabilities to own their narrative and be part of the processes used to plan and implement social justice measures.

4.4 Reconciliation and Social Justice

4.4.1 Exposition and Analysis

Chapter 3 outlined Boesak's philosophy and theology of social justice, which emanates from extensive Liberation Theology and Black Consciousness and power. This section examines his concept of radical reconciliation as a framework for social justice.

---

163. Boesak, "Restless Presence," 14.

Boesak has advocated for reconciliation from his early days. He opposes cosmetic forms of reconciliation that avoid addressing social justice. He sees the post-apartheid narrative of reconciliation as a good starting point. But he criticises it for being injudicious as it advocates "assimilation, appeasement, a passive peace, a unity without cost, and maintaining power with only cosmetic changes."[164] In *Farewell to Innocence*, he denounces the concept of reconciliation that does not challenge the status quo of oppression.[165] His understanding of reconciliation confronts the sociopolitical and religious window-dressing, which seems unwilling to go the extra mile to demand social justice. In *Radical Reconciliation*, the authors seek to employ reconciliation inclusive of social, political, and economic aspects of social justice.[166] While Boesak discusses reconciliation in the context of social justice and within a political framework, he believes that reconciliation for a divided society can only happen by God's intervention. He refers to the South African process. He argues that,

> it is not in the legacy of Marx, nor in the radically atheistic, working-class consciousness of the black proletariat that the political leadership of Black South Africa found the astonishing willingness of South Africa's people to rise above themselves and deny their most basic human instincts for revenge and bitter retribution, and gave the ANC the opportunity to move so quickly into the seats of power.[167]

Contrary to the secular and even Marxist-socialist version, he argues that the miracles of a peaceful transition and reconciliation reflect "the rich memory of the powerful acts of God, in the truth of the prophets, in the life, death and resurrection of Jesus, and the joy of discipleship."[168]

Boesak is a sharp critic of how F. W. de Klerk and his advisors usurped the programme of the Truth Commission by adding a politically calculated and deceptive concept of "reconciliation," thus diluting a process meant for

---

164. Boesak and DeYoung, *Radical Reconciliation*, 2.

165. Boesak, *Farewell to Innocence* (1977), 89.

166. Boesak and DeYoung, *Radical Reconciliation*, 2.

167. Boesak, *Tenderness of Conscience*, 124–25.

168. Boesak, 125.

coming to terms with a brutal past.[169] He has been suspicious that *reconciliation*, first, given the history of the apartheid government, was going to be used only for political window dressing and to avoid dealing with the real issues – of social justice and equity. Second, given the history of apartheid's ability to reengineer the Bible for a White nationalist agenda, the National Party's intervention had no intention to apportion social justice as part of the critical outcomes of the process. Boesak reflects on his suspicion regarding the concept of reconciliation as follows,

> I was not against the idea. In fact, in the light of my own Christian convictions . . . I welcomed it . . . The issue was not reconciliation; it was, rather, our understanding and interpretation of it . . . I did not have much faith in the National Party's declarations and I strongly suspected that we should here not just look at the political motivations of De Klerk and the National Party, we should seriously be considering the religious and theological motivations as well since in the Afrikaner mind these always go together. From experience in the church as well as in politics, we knew how the Bible was used in Afrikaner politics, and how the radical message of the Bible was made a servant to ideology, domesticated for purposes of subjection and control. I feared that this was what was at play here. The NP needed the word "reconciliation" for political purposes for which the theological cloak of reconciliation was a perfect cover. It would appeal to religious people, white and black and by far the majority in the country, and it would give the NP a weapon the ANC did not understand.[170]

He questions the motives of the NP for suggesting reconciliation, which never intended to address the injustice committed against millions of Africans, who continue to live under deplorable socioeconomic conditions resulting from the apartheid system. He thinks that this was a manipulative use of the concept of reconciliation because it appealed to the undiscerning public of most Christians. Additionally, he argues that "adding the 'soft' touch

---

169. Boesak and DeYoung, *Radical Reconciliation*, 3, 15.
170. Boesak, *Tenderness of Conscience*, 182.

of reconciliation with its gospel imperatives of forgiveness and acceptance would in turn allow the softening of that truth, should the country ever be confronted with it."[171] Thus, an approach of transitional justice that fails to serve restitutive measures to ensure a better quality of life and living, in Boesak's view, is not justice at all. The concept of reconciliation Boesak opposes is like the transitional justice process De Sousa Santos describes as one with contradictions in,

> calling for breaks with the past that may end up being continuities; in highlighting some abuses of power while hiding other, perhaps even more serious, ones; in criticizing some exercises of power while at the same time legitimating the power exercising them; and in changing the debate about the past in such a way that the causes of the injustices committed are not mentioned and hence are not eliminated.[172]

In his analysis, Boesak thinks that truth and social justice were sacrificed for reconciliation. He writes that "we know that we know more about the truth that still lies buried than the 'truth' that has been allowed to be heard. F. W. De Klerk's successful court action to block publication of specific documents and his offensive 'let-bygones-be-bygones' rhetoric . . . There is deep anger at the government's inability to bring some dignity to the process of compensation of victims and at the fact that too many 'got away with it.'"[173] Wiredu, however, thinks that the TRC's emphasis on reconciliation is a model response to dealing with violence in Africa and that "the thinking underlying it sought a mutual balancing of the imperatives of truth, justice, and reconciliation in circumstances in which a single-minded fixation on justice would predictably have generated violence of unpredictable consequences."[174]

Boesak gives a theological argument of what reconciliation ought to mean and how it should apply (detailed summary provided in § 3.5.2). In *Radical Reconciliation*, he brings his thoughts on the subject in one place – the largest of its kind on the subject. He believes that the adoption and application of reconciliation fails or is inauthentic unless it meets certain conditions and

---

171. Boesak, 186.

172. De Sousa Santos, *Epistemologies*, 158.

173. Boesak, "And Zaccheus Remained," 639.

174. Wiredu, "Introduction: African Philosophy," 20.

expectations of social justice. We put these steps in a graphic form (see §
3.5.2 Figure 2), which in Boesak's view, is the biblical and even logical order
of reconciliation derived from the story of Zacchaeus. His recommendation
seeks to improve what the TRC had omitted in the initial discussion of forgiveness, reconciliation, and social justice. However, this critique must not
be taken at face value and may need to also be seen in the light of the realities
under which the TRC had to operate.

Simcock argues, in opposition to Boesak's critique, that the TRC never
downplayed the aspect of justice. Instead, it was not given enough mandate
and power to execute its task, especially when corporations refused to cooperate when they were invited to the hearing. However, it "recommended"
several reparations, including, corporate taxation which the new administration ignored, as he writes, "at the time that the TRC issued its final report
and closed its doors in 2003, a post-Mandela presidency was well underway.
The new administration was keenly focused on reducing the country's high
unemployment rate, and on growing the nation's GDP. The new administration determined that foreign investment was critical to these efforts, and shied
away from actions which might deter first world investors."[175]

Boesak also took issue with the theology of the process and he claims that
there was a "profound lack of theological debate throughout the process of
political reconciliation" mixed with "poor quality of theological participation by Christians."[176] In *The Tenderness of Conscience*, Boesak discusses the
various theological and political challenges facing the post-apartheid society
regarding reconciliation.[177] In this book, he bemoans the process as one falling deeply short of the gospel understanding of reconciliation; "Hence the
insistence on confession, repentance and forgiveness with the likes of P. W.
Botha and F. W. De Klerk, openness, transparency and truthfulness in regard
to the National Party and the ANC on issues such as violence."[178]

Understanding reconciliation as a far-reaching concept to effect social
justice calls for examining its validity, both as Christians and citizens in constitutionally secular states. Reconciliation, like liberty, is a concept that runs

---

175. Simcock, "Unfinished Business," 253.

176. Boesak, *Dare We Speak?*

177. The term appears 254 times in *The Tenderness of Conscience* and about 500 times
in *Radical Reconciliation*.

178. Boesak, *Tenderness of Conscience*, 186.

throughout the Bible and a vital theme of the gospel. It is an essential concept to move on from the bitter and painful history of apartheid. Reconciliation in the context of social justice, as applied by Boesak and DeYoung, poses important questions of contextualization. They are writing for a different time and context; this research seeks to draw lessons that can be applied to address twenty-first century Namibia (of socioeconomic conditions addressed in chapter 2). What does reconciliation mean in the face of socioeconomic inequality? Does political reconciliation without the demand for social justice undermine the socioeconomic conditions of the affected communities? How should Namibian theologies of social justice discuss reconciliation so that it does not neglect socioeconomic realities?

If it were to learn from Boesak, the post-apartheid theology is to incorporate matters of social justice in its public expressions and not succumb to the language of the neoelites who now occupy the seats of power. This is a practical way of expecting more from our hopes of independence and not merely settle for empty social arrangements of forgiveness and reconciliation.

Reconciliation is not an end but an entry point to the kind of society we would want. Demanding social justice that would restore previously disadvantaged communities' dignity should not be retaliative but an extension and practical outcome of authentic reconciliation. Should reconciliation always go hand in hand with social justice in every dialogue? Nothing implies that they cannot be separate but interlinked concepts. Such separation should not lead to a dualistic vision, which is what Boesak critiques regarding the TRC's overseeing of the matter. There is no dichotomy between reconciliation and social justice; promoting the former without the latter reinforces disempowerment and false peace.

Boesak believes that the best possible Christian application of reconciliation is the radical view thereof,[179] which is costly and does not paper "over the cracks, knowing it is not possible but between equals. It calls for systemic justice, a radical reordering of power relationships and sustained transformation of society. That it also calls for transformation of the heart and mind is not in contradiction to the call for justice. Rather, that is how reconciliation is sustained."[180]

---

179. Boesak and DeYoung, *Radical Reconciliation*, 136–37.

180. Boesak and DeYoung, 136.

4.4.2 Application

In principle, the researcher does not object to Boesak's arguments of connect-
ing reconciliation with social justice. Years of work and thought have gone
into reaching his conclusion. What does it mean for Namibia? How are we
to bring this concept of reconciliation into dialogue with existential issues
of the Namibian society?

In *Dare We Speak of Hope?* Boesak calls for Christian political participation in public dialogue and urges that it must not be abandoned to secularists.
He believes theological presence and the witness of God's people are moral
voices needed to advocate for corrective measures. While politics does not
determine the outcome of events, Christians cannot avoid politics and its
effects on society.[181] In this case, theology serves to call society to embrace
values that can create liveable conditions for all its citizens. Reconciliation
is a term not of abstract hope. For Boesak, it is hope captive to the idea of
the possibility of achieving social justice for the downtrodden multitudes of
apartheid victims. Boesak's notion of reconciliation would have us think, as
Wolterstorff puts it, that "perhaps there is something more that we hope for,
or should hope for"[182] when we speak of reconciliation. It is not a theological engagement from some disembodied location but with the background
of writing from the margin – making reconciliation a social concept that is
expectant with hopes for social justice. This implies dreaming for a better
world and formulating our language and action towards such a world. In this
case, the terms hope, *ubuntu*, reconciliation, forgiveness, and nationhood
are not mere abstract terms. We learn from Boesak that these terms must be
in the context of human relations, the kind that always has social justice in
mind, else they carry no existential value. This pursuit for social justice is not
because the politics of our times dictate it but because of a Christian vision
that is "life-affirming" and trust in a God that is "life-giving."[183]

For Namibia, it is essential to remember the interconnectedness of our
faith. No theological concept is an orphan, or to be employed simply for
intellectual curiosity. For Boesak, our faith carries public consequences. It
should be employed to help conceptualize a new, dynamic, and far-reaching

---

181. Boesak, *Dare We Speak?*, 139.
182. Wolterstorff, *Journey towards Justice*, 212.
183. Wolterstorff, 176.

demand on issues of social justice in the post-apartheid context. In this section, the particular focus on reconciliation calls for theological reflection that challenges the status quo in which the term is employed. Does reconciliation involve the pursuit of social justice? Does it capture the anger, pain, dreams, and hopes of victims of injustice? Does it confront the political powers reinforcing the dehumanising living conditions? Wisdom could be collected from Boesak's integrated understanding of reconciliation. However, it needs to be forged in the struggles of Namibian society and not merely transplanted. (See § 5.3 of chapter 5, addressing the issue of reconciliation and social justice).

The researcher concurs that reconciliation serves as a helpful entry point to address past hurts or as a measure of restored relationships between different social groups. Boesak also provides helpful pointers for contextualising reconciliation. This implies the need to study the very Scriptures that inform our faith to construct theological notions of reconciliation suitable for Namibia. How does Boesak's contextualization of reconciliation challenge the Namibian search to adopt a more far-reaching reconciliation framework than the current social and political narrative? Boesak, like Sagovsky, holds that we need a liberated "formation of a Christian 'conscience' (a knowledge and awareness of both God and reality)"[184] to construct radical theological notions that would expect more than just an apology when speaking of reconciliation.

Reconciliation, as Boesak outlines it, should not be laicized from its theological context. We are to remain firmly grounded in the conviction that advocating for reconciliation is an act of bearing witness. This needs to be informed by the contemporary challenges and not be distracted by the empty rhetoric of reconciliation that shields the privileges of those who advance social injustice. Unless our understanding of reconciliation is far-reaching and transformative, theology may become captive to inhumane rhetoric that continues to halt changes to unjust structures. As we dialogue with Boesak, we should also be aware that "there are no easy answers to the problems created by our contemporary condition, but by changing our personal habits, recovering church practices that convey God's holiness, and rethinking how we participate in culture, we can offer a disruptive witness that will help people to see the world anew, as created by a living and sustaining God."[185]

---

184. Sagovsky, *Christian Tradition*, 205.
185. Noble, *Disruptive Witness*, 10.

Boesak is not naive regarding the political and theological vocabulary of reconciliation. While he recognises their intersection and complementary aspects, he calls for a theology that challenges the political status quo that refuses to meet primary justice. A reconciliation that seeks social justice, in Boesak's view, is deeply anchored in the Christian understanding of hope for better living conditions post-apartheid. He is aware that inasmuch as he encourages political participation, the present political "reconciliation process is stuttering, not bringing the radical justice and reconciliation that it must and that the oppressed deserve. Instead, it is playing handmaiden to the cynical processes of 'realpolitik,' which dictate the nature of our democracy."[186]

The researcher notes Boesak's depth of reflection on reconciliation. Nevertheless, we need to reexamine it for Namibia. No one needs to accept Boesak's understanding of reconciliation as final, but what we gain from it could play a significant role in our theological endeavours. De Gruchy cautions against setting ourselves on a quest for social justice on presuppositions that may not be true to our context.[187] Therefore, we need to see Boesak's work as one of many voices regarding reconciliation post-apartheid. We affirm the essentiality of social justice post-apartheid but should do so by a robust study of the text and in full consideration of our social context. Added to this is the need for a theology that emanates from a robust understanding of Christ's reconciling work.

This Christo-centric understanding of reconciliation would deploy "a formation that is responsive to God's justice that would not lead to a turning away from the realization of justice" post-apartheid.[188] Thus, we need "to envision a synthetic positive Christian vision of the common good that deploys robust theological" reasoning and context analysis to guide society to become more equitable.[189]

Moreover, the theology of reconciliation should challenge the divided Christian community. The reconciliation concept should motivate the Christian community to become a truly reconciled one that reflects the gospel's demands in a society that continues to bear the scars of racial division,

---

186. Boesak, *Dare We Speak?*, sec. Introduction.
187. De Gruchy, *Reconciliation: Restoring Justice*, 15.
188. Sagovsky, *Christian Tradition*, 205.
189. Kidwell and Doherty, "Theology and Economics," 1.

forging and becoming a new community that finds its identity in God and socially considered in Jesus Christ as new humanity rather than alongside racial or any other sociopolitical categories. This will be a Christian identity under which concepts such as Black Theology, consciousness, and power ought to dissipate as we place ourselves "within the dynamic whereby the Church [the new humanity through Christ] prays and hopes, acts and suffers for the coming of God's justice."[190]

The Christian demand to reflect the meaning of reconciliation to encompass wholeness cannot be understated. Putting the reconciliation challenge before us into practice in the community of faith and seeking to replicate it, is the accurate measure of faith in action. For, social justice is not just a concept but an embodiment of Christian values and witness through participation and modelling.

The next section explores the theological implications of reconciliation. Boesak argues for restitution as the outward expression of genuine reconciliation and repentance and as a way of reversing the socioeconomic inequities of apartheid.

4.5 Theology of Social Justice (Restitution)

4.5.1 Exposition and Analysis

Boesak argues that justice is not negotiable, and the past cannot be adequately addressed by theory and good talks alone. As such, neither independence from apartheid nor political power in the hands of majority Black government should be confused with justice. He writes that,

> shift of power into black hands is not *ipso facto* a shift toward the kind of justice that defines freedom, and that the people having the vote is not the same as the people finding their voice . . . our reconciliation process would remain incomplete, unfulfilled, unsustainable, and cheap if it is de-linked from the costly demands of the systemic *undoing* of injustice and the equally systemic *doing* of justice, of personal and political repentance, restitution, and the restoration of human dignity . . . an incomplete

---

190. Sagovsky, *Christian Tradition*, 206.

revolution is the same as a postponed revolution, and that if we could not find the courage to face the sins of our past we would not gain the integrity to face the challenges of our future[191] (italics in original).

Apartheid created a state of immense socioeconomic inequality, and we continue to witness its effects today, notwithstanding independence. This section critically analyses Boesak's theology of social justice, with an emphasis on restitution. It is part of the larger search for an epistemological transformation of the notion of social justice. Boesak speaks of justice using the language of immanence and urgency, to be done in the here and now and not be relegated to a political or spiritual future.[192] In chapters 4 to 6 of *The Tenderness of Conscience*, Boesak uses language with a particular focus on the agency of social justice, calling the church to action. The church's role in the social change of society cannot be ignored. Neither should the church relent from participating in the political arrangements of its society. Even in the face of growing political cynicism and detachment of Christians from the political, he calls for Christians to embrace a vision of hope and argues that their efforts will contribute to the politics.

Instead of fleeing from the places where political decisions are being made, Boesak calls the Christian community to "strengthen our commitment to the politics of justice, peace, and equity."[193] Injustice in the Boesakan conception is deeply linked to power relations – injustice is a deprivation of the power to achieve a life of dignity. In *Kairos, Crisis and Global Apartheid*, he appeals to various Christian confessions that call Christians worldwide to strive for social justice, emphasising the *Confession of Belhar* and the *Kairos Document*.[194] He believes that these documents entail "a defining presence" that "takes us closer to the cause of Yahweh and Jesus . . . than any other."[195] Because truth and human dignity are at stake, the discourse of social justice "calls for critical

---

191. Boesak, "Restless Presence," 31–32.
192. Boesak, *Farewell to Innocence* (1977), 26, 46.
193. Boesak, "Hope Unprepared," 21.
194. Boesak, *Kairos, Crisis and Global*, 17.
195. Boesak, 102–5.

judgment and acts of prophetic faithfulness and prophetic courage" not in an imposing and arrogant way but in "humility, truthfulness, and integrity."[196]

Boesak derives his argument for social justice from his interpretation of the Zacchaeus narrative, interlinked with his view of reconciliation.[197] Before publishing *Radical Reconciliation* (2012), Boesak published a similar document in *Verbum et Ecclesia* using the Zacchaeus narrative to indicate the inadequacies of the TRC towards the victims of apartheid. Injustice is an effect of power or its abuses.[198] Therefore, for him, social justice begins in the redistribution and restoration of power. He emphasises this in his critique that the TRC's process did not explore social justice options by restoring power relations (see § 3.5.1). In his view, the TRC process was based on unequal power settings, which favoured the powerful and left the afflicted more vulnerable in accepting the terms and conditions with no bargaining power.[199] He says that the focus on the individual victim and individual perpetrator failed to consider "the system of injustice that Apartheid essentially was, so that justice never became a demand for systemic reform of society as a whole."[200]

In Boesak's view, the reconciliation narrative has never been adequate for challenging the political system to secure the vulnerable and needy person's right. It ignored the weak persons' positions to attain a political discourse that has continued to protect the interests of perpetrators and beneficiaries. He also partly blames Christian leaders who silently watched the implementation of a reconciliation process that seemed artificial in pursuing social justice. The unequal power relation, in Boesak's view, fails at three levels: (1) absence of integrity because the key perpetrators were not made to account for their crimes, participation, and benefits; (2) human dignity was compromised as victims were placed in a position that prompted forgiveness as the only option, and (3) human contentment was ignored, and no meaningful discourse was taken to ensure a systemic transformation that will grant the affected communities better standards of living and quality of life.[201]

---

196. Boesak, 17.

197. Boesak and DeYoung, *Radical Reconciliation*, 60–61.

198. Boesak, "And Zaccheus Remained," 636–54.

199. Boesak, 646–49.

200. Boesak, 641.

201. Boesak, 643–51.

Boesak defines the three aspects mentioned above as justice components.[202] He believes another is linked to the restoration of human dignity – restitution. First, he believes that the injustice committed against the victims of apartheid had an economically material impact. Big businesses exploited Black Africans' labour and skills, sanctioned by legislation.[203] Second, this created colossal power gaps along racial lines; restitution is necessary because it restores and secures power.[204] Third, restitution is an outward manifestation of an inward change and an expression of making right one's wrong, as in the Zacchaeus narrative.[205]

Fourth, restitution is an acknowledgement of wrongdoing, "that through my actions someone was wronged, acknowledging that my victim has a right to righteous anger. My victim also has a right to restitution – it has nothing to do with my magnanimity, it is all about justice."[206] Fifth, reconciliation is an outflow of restitution. Unless people can meet as equals, there can be no real and lasting reconciliation. Thus, public and material expression of remorse is needed in the same way the victims' suffering has been public and material.[207] Sixth, restitution leads to restoration of full humanity and acceptance, and people "are released from the generational curse of guilt and shame that comes with exploitative, systemic relationships."[208]

The subject of restitution is social justice, not revenge or retaliation. It is in the context of rights violated under an unjust system and cannot be wished away without adequate reparations. In Boesak's view, restitution is the logical outflow of reconciliation, a part of doing more and the true meaning of *Wiedergutmachung* or reparation (literally means "to make good again").[209] Because apartheid has disrupted people's happiness, self-hood and dignity, there can be no real sense of *shalom* without settling the socioeconomic damages and other adverse effects. Although freedom from socioeconomic

---

202. Boesak and DeYoung, *Radical Reconciliation*, 55–59; Maluleke, "Justice in Post-Apartheid."

203. Boesak, "And Zaccheus Remained," 650.

204. Boesak and DeYoung, *Radical Reconciliation*, 22.

205. Boesak and DeYoung, 55.

206. Boesak and DeYoung, 56.

207. Boesak and DeYoung, 58.

208. Boesak and DeYoung, 59.

209. Boesak, *Tenderness of Conscience*, 173.

worries may not guarantee the absence of pain, it could be a good start to experience both healing and satisfaction of a sort.

Thus, restitution is "to make right what has gone wrong, to give back what has been unlawfully taken, to restore to the person and the community that which has been appropriated."[210] With this understanding of restitution, Boesak calls for radical systemic transformation aimed at society beyond a "romantic" version of reconciliation that avoids asking material justice questions. Boesak does not see restitution as charity but as a moral repair for the harm caused.[211] How should this restitution be executed? Boesak says that systematic exploitation of Black communities has created victims and beneficiaries down through the generations.[212] For example, the forceful removal and dispossession from the land through the Land Acts of 1913 and 1936 or legalization to steal land was a violent crime from which communities have not and cannot recover without restitution in the form of land.

Material restitution counts as the least that can be done to repair the wrongs of apartheid because the extent of its damage is irreparable by any material means. Beyond apartheid, Boesak argues, we continue to see social engineering, which made structural injustice permanent, now impoverishing many people. He disapproves of those who would not own up to their ancestors' crimes and complacency. He says, "if white youth want to disown any responsibility for apartheid and its disastrous consequences 'because they did not vote for it,' then the first thing they must do is to disown the inherited benefits of it."[213] Boesak also thinks this interpretation of justice is a prophetic commitment "to a public witness . . . before God and before the public."[214] He does not go into the details of discussing the concept of social justice; he focuses on the manifestation of social justice. In his view, the absence of material means deepens the levels of powerlessness. Therefore, it is inhumane and unjust to speak of reconciliation and forgiveness while failing to address the immediate material needs, which continue because the unjust structures inherited from apartheid remain permanent.

---

210. Boesak, 209.
211. Boesak, 172–73.
212. Boesak and DeYoung, *Radical Reconciliation*, 123.
213. Boesak and DeYoung, 123.
214. Boesak and DeYoung, 124.

The view that while not all White Africans perpetrated the apartheid system, yet all of them benefitted from it, holds that only through restitution can there be a just means to restore a prior just distribution (and correct an unjust distribution) of life-enhancing goods which the apartheid system distorted.[215] This is, for Boesak, the logical and hermeneutical outcome of radical reconciliation deriving from the account of Luke 19. Without revisiting the protracted debate regarding the practical outplay of what social justice should look like, it is contextually relative to argue whether this is right or wrong.

We can learn from Boesak the need to explore theological conditions that can facilitate social justice measures or work towards a fairer and inclusive post-apartheid society. Boesak does not promise that restitution is the perfect form of social justice or without internal theoretical challenges, political resistance, and theological disagreement. He suggests it as a minimal display of justice since nothing can be done to unwrite, delete, or undo the history of apartheid. Therefore, some form of compensation is doable to allow victims to rebuild and live their lives in conditions that accord with a life of dignity. Teresa Phelps writes that "history shows us that revenge cycles end only when victims cede what was once a sacred duty and a right to take revenge to the state *and* the state properly fulfils this duty. That is, when the state acts in their behalf, the victims are somehow satisfied that they have retrieved something that they have lost. What they get back, of course, can in no way be commensurable with what was lost by the harm. Nonetheless, it must be, in some measure, *satisfying.*"[216] However, this is not clear whether it includes restitution since she is focusing on storytelling in the process of recovering from the wounds and hurt inflicted by apartheid.

Boesak's theology of justice does raise questions and the need for a conceptual framework that is engaging to ensure a more socioeconomically just society. This would require multidimensional approaches to formulate theological methods and approaches that correspond to the contexts of the various post-apartheid communities. The restitution approach and every approach of Boesak towards social justice may sound *this-worldly*. Undoubtedly, social justice or the very idea of justice is *this-worldly* by nature, a search to glorify God by fighting for the dignity of the victims of injustice. The theology of

---

215. Boesak, *Tenderness of Conscience*, 189.

216. Phelps, "Narrative Capability," 106.

social justice reflects a future reality of *shalom*, in which God would end all present evil.[217] God's creation of humans was based on a perfect vision, in a world in which everyone would receive justice, have their needs met, and would be treated with dignity.

The idea of being God's image-bearer carries this utopian concept as De Gruchy says, "to say that every person is created in the image of God means that everyone, irrespective of race, gender, or religion, has an unconditional God-given dignity which no one can rightly deny. Human beings belong to God. This is the basis for a Christian doctrine of human rights"[218] and social justice theology. Yet, the concept of *this-worldly* needs to be embraced critically. On the one hand, it inspires participation in God's world, informed by biblical hope that God's reign is not only in the future. On the other hand, no human effort, no matter how well organized, will achieve perfection. This should not serve as the reason for being withdrawn; instead, it is the very reason to adopt a vision of social justice because this is the world of a just God.

Thus, while the critique of an over-realised eschatology should not escape our minds, this eschatological vision also motivates Christian participation in the public discourse for social justice. It is a heavenly-mindedness grounded in the things of the earth to serve God's image-bearers in the here and now. Christians should be more utopian in their thinking, considering the present order does not reflect God's: (1) initial creation (Gen 1–2); (2) future creation (Rev 20–21); 3) and present demands of "You shall love your neighbour as yourself" (Matt 12:31).[219] In this regard, the utopian vision of Liberation Theology does challenge us to rethink our task in the here and now, as far as social justice is concerned, especially post-apartheid.

The pursuit of social justice and seeking contextually relevant conceptual frameworks calls for responsible theology that can articulate intersecting concepts of justice, to find a way of living together as humans and fellow citizens and not antagonists. Restitution, in this case, is but one form of seeking justice. While Boesak outlines significant issues of present-day social injustice, we cannot ignore the need to rethink the model we need to adopt for solidarity amidst different conceptions.

---

217. Boesak, *Comfort and Protest*, 126–38.

218. De Gruchy, *Christianity and Democracy*, 242.

219. Boesak, *Comfort and Protest*, 16.

Boesak's view of restitution should be welcomed, set free in the world of theological ideas, and examined as a far-reaching thesis in social justice dialogue. How do we bring the subject of restitution and its realization into a robust dialogue for Namibia post-apartheid? Although being employed in sociopolitical terms, restitution, from Boesak's interpretation, is a moral term with a spiritual connotation that transforms human hearts to bring spirituality into politics to affect systems and laws to bring about "what human beings will need to lead fulfilled lives."[220] "Restitution," theologically, as we learn from the story of Zacchaeus, is an outflow of a right relationship with God.

While restitution is an intervention of ensuring that victims receive some material compensation, we fall short if we only end at providing an improved quality of life (which measures satisfaction) and standards of living (which measures the quantity of material good or means to access it). There should be more fundamental human questions of lasting independence and the good life. The underlying approach of restitution needs to dialogue around the human question "What is she actually capable of to do and to be?"[221] (italics added). Restitution should then be discussed within the overall context of restoring human potential, identity, and dignity to thrive. Thus, restitution does not imply an infinite distribution of compensation to victims and descendants of apartheid. This quest of restitution, in general, has no cap, probably because it lacks precision and method.

For example, Boesak identifies the restitution of land as a good required to live a dignified human life. Can land restitution serve as justice in the public square for the altered life demands of modern post-apartheid citizens? This has no simple answer. The understanding of land in Namibia and South Africa needs to go beyond economic sustainability. Research shows that the post-apartheid land question is a profoundly human question rather than an economic one.[222] Hunter writes that "the implications of commercial land reform for the socioeconomic development of Namibia as a whole are believed to be minor . . . Primarily, land reform needs to be understood as the reclamation and restitution of identity and history. It needs to be clarified whether land reform should be part of a sustainable agrarian and

---

220. Sagovsky, *Christian Tradition*, xvi.
221. Nussbaum, "Capabilities and Social Justice," 123.
222. Fuller, "Namibian Path for Land"; Ntsebeza and Hall, *Land Question*.

developmental strategy, or if it is to be regarded as an isolated procedure."[223] Ntsebeza and Hall, writing for the South African context, cite similar issues that "while there may be a demand for land as an economic asset, owner-ship of land in South Africa also represents a source of identity and a sym-bol of citizenship. Land reform is therefore also a political imperative and continuing inequality in land ownership is a highly [dynamic], emotive and controversial issue."[224] While the land is central in the political discourse and essential in its way, like all other material forms of restitution, we need to search for a theology that engages more central aspects required for living a life of dignity. These should be such that without them, human life would cease to be or be significantly diminished.[225]

The apartheid system meant to dehumanize people based on their skin colour through systematic measures to ensure a permanent state of forbid-ding them of any chance to live a life of dignity. To do justice to this violation would need a "costly commitment of human beings to the identification and the implementation of action for justice."[226] Thus, an abstract commitment to social justice will not suffice in addressing the social evils resulting from the lingering effects of apartheid. Boesak understandably does not engage with views he believes are not powerful enough to challenge the lingering impact of structural inequalities. In particular, the notion of reconciliation, that does not make demands for justice as mentioned before, which is worth repeating:

> reconciliation is not possible without confrontation of evil – both the evil from the past, the evil of on-going injustice, and the evil of acquiescing to that injustice because it is to our benefit. That reconciliation is not possible without equality, which means profound and fundamental shifts in power relations. Neither is reconciliation possible without the restoration of justice, human

---

223. Hunter, "Who Should Own Land?," 4.

224. Ntsebeza and Hall, "Introduction," 8.

225. The demand for social justice although material, needs to be separated from materialism and envious ideology that often see White persons as thieves of Black wealth. It thinks of justice as the ransacking of White Africans. Moreover, the land restitution carries specific identity arguments which cannot be ignored, inasmuch as the restitution debate seems in adequate.

226. Sagovsky, *Christian Tradition*, xvi.

dignity, and hope. We forgot to remind the nation that reconciliation is not possible without restitution.[227]

Boesak provides us with an account of the good and the goods required
to live a dignified human life, drawing his analysis from the philosophy,
theology, and hermeneutics of liberation. This understanding of the good is
subject to the modern post-apartheid public as the construction of multiple
publics. The plurality of publics signifies the multidimensionality of meanings
and expectations of social justice that cannot be understood if we place them
all under a general theory of justice. Even restitution needs to be discussed
within the context of these mutative social dynamics.

Therefore, rather than suggesting populist ideas of land restitution as social
justice, a theological discourse is needed that wrestles with these conceptions.
Failure to consider, as mentioned before, the various communities' social
imaginaries, epistemologies, and interpretations of social justice would make
all talk of restitution lofty but empty. An intentional and reflective theology
(contextualized) is not a disembodied exercise but one grounded in a human society.

Boesak suggests what he deems to be social justice, in retrospect of apartheid, out of many options (even though he does not interact with them all at
the same level). While he advocates that such a framework of social justice
is an expression of working towards society's healing, he also argues that it
reorders the African value system of *ubuntu* to be more forward and asser-
tive towards right action.[228]

Thus, the interrelational aspect that the reconciliation policy promises
and that requires tangibility or measurability should not be considered as
vengeance or retaliation but an authentic expression of togetherness and
solidarity of humanbeingness or mutual humanity.[229] Further reconciliation
and forgiveness become meaningless terms if former perpetrators and beneficiaries under apartheid continue to "live lives of self-centred individualism" that "exude the spirit of postmodern cynicism" when it comes to their
material resources.[230]

---

227. Boesak, "Hope Unprepared," 1069.
228. Boesak, *Tenderness of Conscience*, 172, 186–87.
229. Boesak, 172.
230. Boesak, 226.

Boesak sets a challenge regarding the nature of post-apartheid socioeconomic justice. He argues that this is beyond charity and requires significant rectification of the socioeconomic conditions. It is a search for "sustainable, systemic social justice."[231] Thus, social justice takes to task the underlying conceptions that reinforce the present structural injustice. This restitutive outlook provides a challenge to embrace the material aspect of justice. But it requires a robust theological language to speak to the various post-apartheid publics regarding the materiality of social justice. This language comes with ethical recommendations to transform our social foundations to respond to human needs.[232]

4.5.2 Application

Boesak's theology of social justice is not disembodied. It is a view of social justice that needs to be seen as the coming together of specific experiences and social imaginary.[233] De Gruchy captures this intersection clearly by stating that "there is no such thing as a disembodied mind, theological or otherwise. Our minds are shaped by the context in which we are nurtured during our formative years, and by those years that soon follow as we pursue our careers and callings."[234] Thus, Boesak's theological and philosophical outlooks are interconnected with his own experiences of harsh socioeconomic and political conditions.

Injustice in its various manifestations is a moral issue that cannot be treated with gentility until better living conditions and standards become the norm for the average post-apartheid citizen. The current socioeconomic order does not reflect humane standards and must be transformed. How this socioeconomic justice should be implemented calls for a theological approach that is interdisciplinary, intercontextual, and multiconversant to contribute

---

231. Boesak and DeYoung, *Radical Reconciliation*, 121.

232. Forster, "Social Imagination of Forgiveness."

233. Dion Forster, in his article *A Social Imagination of Forgiveness* argues that there is supporting data for the logic underlying the complex, and even conflicting, views of forgiveness among Black and White South Africans. For each group of persons, the hermeneutic informants of their understandings of forgiveness are to a large extent related to their cultural and social imagination. This notion of forgiveness and reconciliation extends to the understanding of justice

234. De Gruchy, "Constructing South African," 35.

relevantly to affect dialogues and implementation processes.[235] However, Boesak does not provide us with a clear vision of how restoration should be done, besides the brisk mentioning of land issues.

A contextualized conceptualization of social justice challenges the accepted common purpose approach, which is indiscriminate towards how injustice's multiple-layered nature affects different communities. Social justice, to be secured, needs a clear distinction of the causes of injustice. That is, every cause of injustice must be addressed uniquely and not grouped indiscriminately under broad categories. In question here is the capability to create a Namibian narrative of social justice without plunging into punitive ideologies that seek to reimpose the sins of the past upon White citizens. This search for social justice would require a systematic shift from a congruent generalization of expectations.

For example, the land question and restitution[236] need to consider both the supporting and counterarguments. This is an essential aspect of the debate

---

235. Forster, "Nature of Public Theology," 19–23.

236. Van Leynseele and Hebinck, narrate the South African land restitution as follows: "Land restitution in South Africa was designed as a means to redraw the apartheid map of racially and unequally distributed land after the first democratic elections of 1994. But the miscellaneous legislation that supports restitution encodes divergent goals . . . On the one hand, the objective of 'just and equitable redress' refers to the undoing of a painful past when racially motivated acts of dispossession confined black landholding to 13 per cent of the land. It involves the compensation by government of a group defined as 'historically disadvantaged' for past grievances and the loss of land rights. On the other hand, concerns are expressed by the state and the international donor community over sustainability, productivity, and farm efficiency. The prospects of environmental degradation and the collapse of the capitalized and commoditized commercial farming sector have proved potent counter-arguments to a populist wide-scale land redistribution programme." Van Leynseele and Hebinck, "Through the Prism," 164.

They go on to point out the various narratives of the restitution of land and the post-apartheid conceptions that need to be taken into account. They write, "Reflecting its legalistic nature, restitution was 'designed as a stand-alone, legally driven programme without linkages to other planning or development processes' . . . The limited scope of restitution policies led the Commission on Restitution of Land Rights (CRLR), more commonly known as the Land Claims Commission, to view land restitution primarily as a legal process with the core responsibility of fulfilling the constitutional requirements of 'just and equitable redress.' Its remit has thus been restricted to the formal resolution of land rights. The lack of strategic advance planning has meant that much of the subsequent activity has been outsourced, with contract consultants, financing institutions, local farmers' associations, and local municipalities assuming a prominent role in post-settlement stages of land restitution. Accompanying the role of these actors and development agencies, there is a shifting articulation, from land seen as a means of reconciliation towards land as an economic asset to be commoditized or safeguarded from exhaustive usage." Van Leynseele and Hebinck, "Through the Prism," 164–65.

for social justice and an attempt to make sense of the ethical imperative regarding unjust conditions. The land question is one aspect of restitution and not an absolute end. The question incorporates complex spatial issues, temporal aspects, and social processes to redress the history of injustice by colonialism and apartheid. For Namibia, we need a theological "processual framework which will allow us to situate the accounts that follow in terms of where they fit in the restitution story."[237]

Restitution is being discussed within the broader spectrum of justice. What should inform discussion of this concept? Throughout various texts in the Bible, Sagovsky suggests, we learn of God's justice as a central aspect of God's nature for "God makes justice the very foundation upon which there is a world at all."[238] *Farewell to Innocence* opens with this conviction of a just God who would go to any extent to liberate the oppressed. Developing a nuanced theology regarding God's presence becomes a a great necessity for developing the view of justice.[239] Therefore, the task of theology in a public space, we learn from Boesak, should not be taken lightly.[240] Theology must equip itself to wade through complex sociopolitical and contextual issues for the post-apartheid dialogue. The absence of Christian input in the public discourse would only result in constant moral erosion evidenced by social injustice's continued presence.[241]

This call to participate in public needs careful rethinking and taking into consideration the Namibian social context and the systems in which we can operate. Boesak's calling upon the church to be radical in its demands in the public sphere is encouraging; however, this is not a political pursuit. Theological studies and research should place greater demands on the church to be fully present in the world and not become irrelevant to society through false escapism. A programme to transform a society that is affected by social injustice, at every level of its social structures should address the root of the problem – the human heart. It should also address the sinful structures that continue to keep people in positions of disadvantage. This is a discipleship

---

237. Fay and James, "Restoring What Was Ours," 6.

238. Sagovsky, *Christian Tradition*, 32.

239. Boesak, *Farewell to Innocence* (1977), 16–17.

240. Boesak, *Kairos, Crisis and Global*, 102–6.

241. De Gruchy, "Kairos Moments," 2.

task that should encourage Christians to participate in the community's politics and practice their Christian ethos within those settings.

Through this participation, we bring spirituality into our body politics "that should shape the soul of the nation."[242] It affects the liturgies of selfish politics, markets, and social structures managed by persons who do not acknowledge the lordship of Christ. As we witness it post-apartheid, social injustice is instead a branch of a deeply seated human problem (root) – sin.[243] It manifests the absence of God's knowledge that would inform the ethics and understanding of doing what is good and right. That means the pursuit of social justice is an act of worship, recalling people to turn to the standards of God. This approach makes the search for contextual notions of justice a missional activity. As the church participates in socioeconomic redemption, it does so by first calling people back to God. These transformed persons then continue to live in their communities – using their various gifts, skills, and resources to create a culture of resistance against dehumanising practices in society.

In *The Ongoing Challenge of Restorative Justice in South Africa*, Bowers du Toit and Nkomo say that "If we believe that the church has a key role to play in terms of modelling Christ's example and possesses the moral, financial and social resources to do so, then we are compelled to do just that – try."[244] Thus, while we do not neglect the political and encourage many Christians to participate in the political transformation, the post-apartheid church should manifest what it means to experience the gospel's transforming power. The search for social justice informed by a transformed social imaginary creates a new community altogether: a community that seeks the collective good in the form of security, education, employment, decent housing, economic security, access to opportunity or the assumed prosperity needed to live a life of dignity as part of a humane and transformed society.

Such imagination of an ideal society is something we derive from the nature of God. Our utopian vision is based on a radical transformation of the human heart, which becomes the basis for ushering in God's kingdom among fellow humans, through the various instruments we think will assist in

242. Boesak, *Tenderness of Conscience*, 25.

243. Sagovsky, *Christian Tradition*, 83–85.

244. Bowers du Toit and Nkomo, "Ongoing Challenge," 8.

creating a social order "in which our purposes mesh, and each in furthering himself helps others."[245] This means that while seeking to remain relevant and present in society, the Christian community holds to standards and reasons that make sense only to its members. These cannot be enforced on a society that does not accept them. Similarly, our approach to social justice should not be driven by instruments, approaches, and methods that force us to adopt foreign programmes of action and participation in the world.

The dialogues of restitution, from a theological perspective, need to consider various elements. Although one may agree with it in principle, it is controversial. We need adequate data for evidence that the concept of restitution is itself a just pursuit, for example, to establish as valid notions that restitution could result in socioeconomic conditions that would have been had apartheid not taken place. It should also include robust criteria that would warrant someone worthy of restitution or be absolved from restitution. It should create a watertight procedure to avoid restitution from becoming a post-apartheid revictimization process.

All the above puzzling concerns remain to be answered, especially on the nature of consciousness, power, reconciliation, and justice that would affect the Namibian context. Developing a theology of justice needs to grapple with many questions. While Boesak's views and insights provide invaluable information for developing a theology of justice for post-apartheid Namibia, this development is an uphill struggle. Boesak is not writing for Namibia and is informed by different social imaginaries. Therefore, everything he suggests needs to be examined through the lens of Namibian society.

We would not like to lose focus of the missional role of our search for a contextualized conceptualization of social justice, in which we must courageously and prophetically confront attitudes that deny God through denying justice to God's image-bearers. It is a complex role to conscientize the public to social, political, cultural, and economic realities, yet without departing from the gospel mission. It is not a conscientization for hatred, partisanship, and revenge but for reconciliation which sees "the prime location of justice is in personal relationships."[246] Boesak's view is that reconciliation demands justice; it is not abstract but as it were in the case of Israel "mediated by a

---

245. Taylor, *Modern Social Imaginaries*, 14.
246. Sagovsky, *Christian Tradition*, 38.

right use of the land [life-enhancing goods] or . . . a right sharing of the land."[247] Such transformational experience of extending sharing of resources is a miracle (an initiative of God) born out of primarily, "a right relationship between God and human beings."[248] "However, in taking the initiative, God looks for a right human response, the response of a people which is faithful to the covenant relationship with him."[249]

We need to be reminded of: (1) the complex nature of these issues and that we need a robust theological engagement "capable of making a constructive theological contribution in situations"[250] where the debate is heated and fierce; (2) our need for a robust vision inspired by a heavenly vision of a God who is good and just, but also fully aware that not all our efforts may be realized in the here and now; (3) our need to strive for a contextually more precise and adequate notion of justice worthy of challenging the prevailing public notions that undermine the role of the Christian faith in the public dialogue; (4) our need to learn from theologians like Boesak to engage the meaning of justice actively and intentionally to engage lopsided and truncated conceptualizations of justice that are refusing to engage the issues objectively; (5) the role of theology is not to be weaponized for political ideologies that seek to drive a deeper racial wedge and pit Black Africans against White Africans and; (6) the lessons from Boesak that Christian scholarship needs to be vigorous and thorough when engaging serious and complex concepts, and not be relegated to pietism that fails to witness to God's concern for the world.

4.6 Summary

As said in the summary of § 3.5 and the introductory remark of § 4.1, this chapter aims to provide a critical theological dialogue of Boesak's notions of justice. First, it analysed how his conceptual framework of Black liberation theology links to his understanding and interpretation of justice (see § 4.2). Second, it explored the critical questions his notion of Black Consciousness philosophy raises about human dignity, identity, and power relations (see §

---

247. Sagovsky, 38.
248. Sagovsky, 38.
249. Sagovsky, 39.
250. Forster, "Politics of Forgiveness?", 78.

4.3). Third, it discussed Boesak's theology of reconciliation and its implication for justice dialogue (see § 4.4). Lastly, we examined Boesak's theology of justice and the role of restitution as the logical outplay of reconciliation and as a material entry point of healing memories and history of injustice (see § 4.5). The conclusions regarding these issues are mainly that: (a) Boesak raises essential issues and indicators which need to be considered in the discourse of justice; (b) the Namibian context needs to be seriously investigated theologically to create dialogues that will genuinely challenge the present status quo; (c) Boesak offers invaluable insights, but these cannot be transplanted without profound understanding to engage the Namibian issues and context; (d) we need to pursue justice but not be oblivious to the realities of living in a fallen world so that some of our efforts may never be realized; and (e) finally, inasmuch as justice is a social, political, cultural, and economic issue, it has a spiritual component. It is missional that we need to call people to be reconciled to God and one another, as the first entry point to seeing the transformation in which justice could extend to sharing life-enhancing goods. The next chapter will explore whether a contextualized conception of social justice could help construct a theology of justice for the Namibian post-apartheid context in conversation with Boesak's notions of justice.

CHAPTER 5

Towards a Contextualized Conceptualization of Social Justice for Post-Apartheid Namibia

5.1 Introduction

This chapter analyses the role theology can play in the post-apartheid Namibian public dialogues. It revisits some of the literature mentioned in chapter 2 and examines a cluster of concepts related to social justice (reconciliation, restitution, forgiveness, democracy, affirmative action, and justice) and conceptualises their meaning for the Namibian context. The chapter is a theological contribution to the dialogue on social justice in Namibia. Its critical dialogue partners are Allan Boesak, in conversation with Nicholas Sagovsky, and John De Gruchy, who provide theological insight regarding participation in public discourse in post-apartheid Namibia. It demonstrates the conceptual nature of the study and the influences of public theology. As theologians, Sagovsky and De Gruchy offer the theoretical, philosophical, and theological framework needed for conceptualization in a secular public arena.

The previous chapters have all attempted to discuss the relationship between conceptualization and social justice (see § 1.2.3). As we explore this relationship, we need to speak not only of notions of social justice but also of just actions or practices of justice. In Boesak's view, contextualization is a prophetic search "to make critical use of those traditions from the past which can play a humanizing and revolutionizing role in contemporary society. It takes from the past what is good, thereby offering a critique of the present and opening perspectives for the future."[1] In relation to social justice, contextualization is an active search to participate in "the active rationality of God" to cultivate life enhancing virtues in the world. It goes beyond merely dealing with concepts to how concepts can be embodied to facilitate meaningful socioeconomic changes.[2]

As noted in chapter 2, discussions regarding social justice have not reached sufficiently nuanced levels of consolidation and organization to construct a full-fledged Namibian discourse. Boesak applies Black Liberation Theology as a contextual theology, even in the post-apartheid period, to a wide array of contemporary social justice conversations. What we intend to do is to interrogate, revise, and/or reject claims and practices which appeared to be self-evident, with the backdrop of today's socioeconomic realities.

We have not found evidence that a contextualized conceptualization necessarily leads to social justice; however, it is a good discussion starter for any society. There is also no adequate evidence that conceptualization spreads a far-reaching effect for a just culture; however, it creates a cultural template for people to think through their context and reflect upon what they think would constitute social justice for them. As Andrew Bradstock argues, conceptualization in the search for the common good "dares us to come together to find ways in which we can forge a fairer and more equal society, one in which all can enjoy fulfilment in the economic, political and cultural life of that society."[3]

---

1. Boesak, *Farewell to Innocence* (1977), 22.

2. Contextualization is a search for relevance, reflecting upon one's situation and context. The discussion of social justice in post-apartheid Namibia carries diverse perspectives affecting social, economic, political, and cultural aspects. Boesak's work is part of the ongoing theological, academic, and political discussions in South Africa; what can we learn from his work to address the Namibian context? Boesak's theological concepts and ideas are hybrids of Latin and North American liberation theologies which he seeks to contextualize for South Africa. He uses a Black Liberation theological framework, which he believes is the best response to the Black condition and is a theological position that "takes seriously the processes of the struggle for humanity and justice." Boesak, 21.

3. Bradstock, "Unexamined Society," 45. Boesak's work reflects part of the cultural consciousness of discussing apartheid and social justice issues. To what extent this contextualization reflects a collective social imaginary for the South African public is difficult to determine. *Pharaohs on Both Sides of the Blood-Red Waters* and *Children of the Waters of Meribah*, as theological works, also critique cultural imaginations in matters of social justice.

Dion Forster points out cultural, theological, and political paradigms that inform various understandings of how to address the context of injustice. In this diversity of perspectives, themes such as social justice, reconciliation, and forgiveness are understood differently. His focus on the epistemological nature of forgiveness in post-apartheid South Africa is enlightening for our study of social justice in Namibia.[4] Forster writes that

> interpersonal socio-political factors, such as the nature of the historical offences of apartheid, whether reparation has been made (or attempted) for these offences, the political identities of the parties involved, expectations and conditions for the self and for the other, also play a role in understandings of for-giveness. One significant problem that has been identified . . . un-reconciled persons . . . seldom have contact with each other because of the legacy of the apartheid system which separated persons racially, according to economic class, and geographi-cally . . . In at least this sense forgiveness remains improbable, even impossible . . . Not only is it impossible for persons to forgive one another since they have no proximate or authentic social engagement, forgiveness is also a theological impossibility because of deeply held and entrenched faith convictions about the nature and processes of forgiveness, which are frequently in conflict with one another.[5]

---

4. Boesak, *Tenderness of Conscience*, 21; Forster, "Nature of Public Theology," 17; DeYoung and Gilbert, *What Is the Mission?*, 17. South Africa has overshadowed the Namibian public discussions of politics, theology, and public policies. The mention of apartheid in research work mostly speaks of South Africa, and very few mention Namibia (and if they do, it is often only as an appendix). As Boesak notes, we need to address "the profound lack of theological debate throughout the process of political reconciliation, . . . and the poor quality of theological participation by Christians in the process itself." We are to do this to provoke a theological analysis that seeks to find robust scholarly engagements that cannot settle with generalities that do not speak to the reality of the Namibian context. We need to become better at articulating a careful and responsible theological discourse that can, according to Forster, engage the public or "facilitate meaningful engagement with all aspects of life." This is part of DeYoung and Gilbert's argument on being "able to pursue obedience to Christ in a way that is more realistic, freeing, and, in the long run, fruitful."

5. Forster, "Translation and Politics of Forgiveness?"

Jürgen Moltmann urges us to understand that theology "is imagination for the kingdom of God in the world, and for the world in God's kingdom,"[6] which by default makes it a public exercise of proclaiming God and not searching for an ideological presence in the public sphere. So, academic theology becomes missional as it seeks to reach out to affect the thinking and ethics that influence public policies regarding social justice. Such engagement is part of doing what Nicholas Sagovsky calls articulating the truth of Christ in a public that is constitutionally committed to secular philosophies: such a task would not take a simple theological application; instead, it would require "strenuous, self-critical, intellectual and political engagement in the public sphere in the service of the gospel."[7]

In Namibia, socioeconomic inequality expresses continued violence inherited from the apartheid system, protected today by various laws and policies or the lack thereof. This level of injustice calls for a reimagining that would challenge the intellectual and political public's status quo and intentionally seek workable solutions to the socioeconomic problems. With human dignity and freedom being trumped by structures that fail to intervene, we need to explore options of distributing goods and opportunities and the best measures to coordinate conflicting post-apartheid imaginaries and rationalities.[8] Contextualized conceptualization opposes vague ideas of social justice and argues that affected communities do have notions of justice, freedom, or a good life. The state should then facilitate the necessary processes to ensure the meeting of needs; for example, programmes of education, healthcare, decent and affordable housing, connection and access to electricity, clean water and washing facilities. It should facilitate a conducive environment for investors towards decent employment creation, and general socioeconomic conditions for equality of opportunity. In this chapter, we discuss both notions and practices of justice.

We begin this conversation with the role of the church as God's agent (see § 5.2.), the understanding of reconciliation in relation to social justice (see § 5.3.), the state's role in the promotion of social justice and the kind of social

---

6. Moltmann, *Coming of God*, xiv.

7. Sagovsky, "Public Theology," 268.

8. Sagovsky, *Christian Tradition*, 161.

dialogues to be had (see § 5.4.), the concretising of social justice (see § 5.5.), and the public witness theology should engage in search of social justice.

5.2 The Church and Social Injustice in a Post-Apartheid Context

In the thirty years after independence from the apartheid government, Namibia has settled for a vague arrangement regarding socioeconomic issues. Questions of social justice continue to receive casual responses and plans. Besides policy and national planning failure and lack of clear vision, incompetence and rampant corruption undermine the public institutions[9] from effecting better social safety nets. Alongside the political lethargy that has abandoned the "goal of socioeconomic transformation aimed at the reducing of inherited imbalances in the distribution of wealth"[10] is the lack of a theological voice in the public arena.

Christo Botha narrates the church's active participation (which served as a collective theological voice) during the liberation struggle but suspects that this might have been out of political expediency rather than out of principle.[11] He also alludes to how this politicized participation contributed to the silence of the church towards the corruption and mismanagement of resources by the SWAPO-led government when he writes:

> The church's failure to address this matter casts further doubt on the perception that it served as the "voice of the voiceless." Although it may be argued that the earlier fight against foreign oppression and racial discrimination represented a much more morally unambiguous position, it is difficult to defend widespread corruption and the appropriation of state resources as representing a lesser evil. Widely publicised cases of fraud did not seem to have been dealt with the severity that was required.[12]

---

9. Job Amupanda gives an outline of the level of corruption in Namibia and calls for civil society to make its duty to actively resist it and find better ways to hold state-operated institutions in particular to higher accountability levels. Amupanda, "Fight against Corruption."

10. Melber, "Introduction," xiv.

11. Botha, "Church in Namibia," 31.

12. Botha, 31.

He further points out how, church leaders, due to the political relationship, no longer command substantial public attention, except for "occasional expressions of concern with issues such as racial hostility, poverty, the gap between rich and poor and gender-based violence, are more directed at perceived deficiencies in society than at government policy as such."[13] In his conclusion, he reduces the church to nothing more than a human or social institution that should rearrange itself to find its proper place of usefulness to serve society's good.[14]

Botha's analysis makes the church just another civil society organization that should restructure itself to serve social, psychological, and political needs – leaving God out of the equation. He believes that a secularized version of the church is needed for Namibia if the church is to reorder itself to serve the nation's interest. Botha's revisionist historical analysis of the Namibian church is buried in conceptual misappropriations that do not consider the starting premises that inform the church's theology and philosophy – both locally and universally. While theology must work within the human context of meanings and actions, it cannot be theology without the supernatural, and the same applies to the church in Namibia. Boesak in *The Tenderness of Conscience* raises similar concerns in the South African public of academics and politicians who would like to appropriate the reconciliation and liberation processes as purely secular achievements.[15] Botha's secular religiosity seeks to divorce the role of the church during apartheid from its faith in God, highlighting ideals of democracy, liberty, freedom, or rights.[16]

Botha's admission that his reflection on the Namibian church uses what he calls a Western conceptual framework misappropriates his analysis and forces a Namibian conception of religion and faith into a secular framework with which it does not identify.[17] His narration of the church's history and participation in the liberation struggle provides valuable data for our analysis. However, he does not apply the same mindfulness regarding the task of religion, especially Christianity in Namibia, when he extracts it from its

---

13. Botha, 32.

14. Botha, 34.

15. Boesak, *Tenderness of Conscience*, 58–59.

16. Boesak, *Tenderness of Conscience*; Kameeta, *Towards Liberation*; Mujoro and Mujoro, "Namibian Liberation Theology."

17. Botha, "Church in Namibia," 8.

roots of faith in God. The church's participation in social activities is motivated by this faith; abandoning belief in God would alter the church's whole
purpose. For example, he chooses Reinhart Kößler and Henning Melber's
article *Political Culture and Civil Society: On the State of the Namibian State*[18]
to denounce the church as not "capable of contributing towards finding solutions for problems such as corruption, violence and poverty."[19] Neither
author embraces Christian views, and their paper is written with the secular
democratic-socialist state in mind. Botha's analysis appears lopsided because
the subsequent chapter titled *Detainee Issue and Unresolved Test Case for
SWAPO, the Church and Civil Society* is written by Christo Lombard, who
argues for the continued relevance of the church in post-apartheid Namibia.[20]

Botha deliberately ignores Lombard's arguments and only focuses on his
critique of how some church leaders failed to handle the issue of the Lubango
detainees. At best, this selective reading does not engage various conceptions
around the subject. Botha would like to make the secularized version of
religion the representative view for the Namibian public. Finally, the secularization of the Namibian narrative of reconciliation and nation-building did
not begin with Kößsler and Melber. Before and after independence as demonstrated in his work, *Searching for Justice – the Pursuit of a Liberal Tradition
in Colonial Namibia*, and Chris Tapscott's in *National Reconciliation, Social
Equity and Class Formation in Independent Namibia*, the role of religion or
the church is not mentioned at all.[21] Although it is borrowed, Namibian
Liberation Theology has always been because of faith in God and belief that
they were engaging in a transformative divine mandate or *missio Dei*. As
Paul Isaak puts it:

> It must be emphasised that the Open Letter forced the South
> African Government to recognise Church leaders as one of the
> major players in Namibian politics. Most importantly, the let-
> ter was the political conscientisation of the black population in
> general. The letter sought to reconcile spiritual commitment
> with political involvement. In short, the content of the letter

---

18. Kößler and Melber, "Political Culture."
19. Botha, "Church in Namibia," 31.
20. Lombard, "Detainee Issue."
21. Tapscott, "National Reconciliation, Social Equity."

signified that God was not to be diminished, that faith was not to be diminished, and that praxis was not to be avoided.[22]

De Gruchy contends for the crucial role of the church in Namibia, which for much of the liberation struggle against apartheid was the most significant public source of resistance within the country (while SWAPO was waging a guerrilla war in Angola against South African military forces). He dedicates a few lines to the Namibian church in his book, *Christianity and Democracy*, recalling its essential role. He notes how the church was the only institution that provided concrete structures for resisting the apartheid rule (inside the country). He provides us with the example of how we can engage in critical solidarity and avoid falling into the errors of political opportunism and acts that violate others' rights and dignity. This negligence of critically engaging in the struggle for social justice has sadly resulted in a post-apartheid theological engagement, in the case of the CCN, that became a casualty of the liberation struggle.[23]

We note Botha's critique that the church's absence warrants the state and corrupt political players to further social injustice in an already fragile environment. Regardless of his secularist reading of the church, his critique of the church's absence is hard to deny. The church is part of society's body politic – inescapably. It holds both a missional and cultural mandate. This cultural mandate derives from our understanding of God's active self-revelation through Jesus Christ. The church then is not a church unto itself but unto God by being present in the world. Smith points out that its purpose is "not in order to save it or conquer it or even transform it, but to serve it by showing what redeemed human community and culture look like."[24] This calls for participatory theology, which Boesak describes as a

> critical reflection on historical praxis; in other words, it is the active involvement of the church in the world. At the same time theology is faith manifested – the action of love within history. But it is a critical reflection in the light of the Word of God,

---

22. Isaak, *Evangelical Lutheran Church*, 32.

23. De Gruchy, *Christianity and Democracy*, 177.

24. Smith, *Desiring the Kingdom*, 204.

which means that all action and all reflection is finally judged by the liberating gospel of Jesus Christ.[25]

In this regard, the rest of this chapter examines how theological input can assist the Namibian post-apartheid community to conceptualize its notions of social justice. Theologians are intricately part of society's social structure and proportionately bearers of both the positives and negatives that affect it. Boesak's theological notion of justice is part of this struggle between the theologian as the servant of God and the community he or she serves. Niitenge affirms that engaging or assuming claims of faith in Jesus comes with social responsibilities and implications, and the role of calling people to faith is inseparable from participation in the social, political, and economic issues affecting the people.[26]

This realization of a divine mandate is the motivation to explore theological notions of social justice to address the socioeconomically fragmented public. The Namibian history of resistance is profoundly linked with the church and theology.[27] For example, *The Open Letter* to B. J. Vorster is one early open declaration of the public role of theology in social justice matters. Unfortunately, this nature of resisting injustice has not had a continued public presence in addressing the post-apartheid context,[28] except for a few.[29] Such a continued presence of resisting injustice needs more than impersonal rights; justice for Christians is a virtue that comes at a cost. Sagovsky argues against this impersonal approach to justice that "there can be no justice without the costly commitment of human beings to the identification and implementation of action for justice."[30]

Botha argues that this absence from the public sphere can be traced back to the church's pre-independence acquiescence regarding SWAPO's actions.[31]

---

25. Boesak, *Farewell to Innocence* (1977), 19.

26. Niitenge, "Evangelical Lutheran Church," 45.

27. Botha, "Church in Namibia"; Katjavivi, *History of Resistance*; Frostin, "Theological Debate on Liberation"; Niitenge, "Evangelical Lutheran Church."

28. Botha, "Searching for Justice"; Botha, "Church in Namibia."

29. This does not imply that there are no theologians or Christians participating in issues of social justice. Surely, there are countless Christian activities which involve working among the poor and destitute and providing financial, social, and moral support to women, children, and men.

30. Sagovsky, *Christian Tradition*, xvi.

31. Botha, "Church in Namibia," 30.

Thus, the public role of theology demonstrated during the liberation struggle against racism was reduced to private activities. These activities carry little significance to affect the government's policies, programmes, and structures. The unanimous verdict of Namibian academics is that the public presence of theology to address the lingering effects of social justice has diminished,[32] rendering the church in general of no use in the present social struggle. Botha argues that this absence from the public is because the church has failed to speak up against SWAPO.[33] Some church leaders became politicians, making the church a political handmaid of the majority Black government. Nevertheless, he concludes that this role could be reversed if the church and FBOs restructured themselves based on secular principles to become a force for social justice.

The above critique indicates that inconsistency coupled with conflict of interest by church leaders is the primary reason for theology's absence from the public arena in matters of social justice. Second, since its uncritical af-filiation with the liberation movement, theology has not created a culture of public presence and failed to question the movement's violations of human rights during exile and after apartheid. Third, the absence of consolidated, nuanced, and robust theological engagement, evidenced by the conspicuous withdrawal of academic discourse from challenging the secularized concep-tions of social justice, confined theological discussions on public issues to dominantly Christian and church-affiliated organizations.[34]

We do not dispute the critique mounted against the church; however, we need to be cognisant that "churches are constantly confronted by the chal-lenge of action for justice in the public. In some situations, the demands of justice are only too clear . . . In other situations it is not all clear what actions the church should take for justice."[35] This difficulty is also not an excuse for doing nothing. Sagovsky further suggests that when we are faced with the dilemma of action for justice, "actions can be defended as actions for justice if they enhance freedom, if they are in accord with the law [assuming that the

---

32. Botha, 31–33; Groop, "Church, State," 69–70; Horn, "Churches and Political Reconciliation"; Niitenge, "Evangelical Lutheran Church," 10, 21; Tötemeyer, *Church and State*.

33. Botha, 32–34.

34. Boesak, *Tenderness of Conscience*, 21.

35. Sagovsky, *Christian Tradition*, xvii.

law is just], and if they promote the meeting of need."[36] Such an understanding would have us raise questions regarding the socioeconomic measures in place and whether they carry any meaning in redressing the effects of injustice. Reconciliation will be explored in this light as a major public theme in Namibian political and social dialogues.

5.3 Conceptualising Reconciliation and Social Justice

5.3.1 Reconciliation, Honesty, and Making Amends

The need to conceptualize must consider how coming to grasp the various clusters of concepts could help construct social justice notions that can engage public policy discussions and Christian participation. Conceptualising social justice cannot happen in a vacuum; it is interconnected with many other issues to be considered. Without considering these other concepts, the discussion may be disproportionate, ignorant, and ineffective to suggest solutions. Below we will interrogate concepts of forgiveness, reconciliation, and social justice which are fundamental issues in the discourse of social justice for post-conflict societies.

Namibia is a young democracy riddled with many challenges that it needs to confront to address its problems effectively. The post-apartheid context is profoundly complex and politicized, and the theological participation must meander through these tensions. A large part of this search for a way forward is to address the unresolved social tensions. Especially the subject of "reconciliation," which has been given such poor treatment. Kim Groop gives some background of this conflict that

> it can hardly be denied that Namibia, in many ways, is still in the process of defining itself. It has not yet come to terms with its past. One of the reasons for that is that the past has never been openly and thoroughly discussed. Without such a discourse, I believe, it will be difficult for Namibia as a nation to achieve a comprehensive, unified (if ever possible) Namibian, and thus representative, view of its history.[37]

---

36. Sagovsky, xvii.
37. Groop, "Church, State," 67–68.

Groop's critique of Namibian politics includes the role of the church and by extension that of theology in public discourse. In particular, he thinks that the refusal to face the past has an enormous impact on how we address the present search of social justice, which is to a considerable extent the consequence of the past. Because of political fallouts between the church and political players, the voice of theology in the public has been equally silenced. Thus, the voice of theology has been side-lined in discussing the nature of social justice. Not only has the church been sidelined, but it has also resigned from the public discourse, due to having lost credibility. Added to this history, is a general absence of far-reaching conceptual frameworks that can generate authentic and far-reaching notions of forgiveness and reconciliation coupled with social justice.

Theological dialogue on political issues is an exceptionally challenging task because "the political climate in Namibia has not favoured the participation of church leaders in political matters."[38] However, a theological discourse seeking a contextualized conceptualization of social justice, does not have to engage partisan politics. Such participation, as Forster says, is an attempt "to understand a God who is lovingly at work with all God creates in all spheres of life."[39] Thus, engaging the discourse of social justice, even at a political level, matters for the sake of God's image-bearers who suffer the consequences and poor systems that do not speak to the context and lived experiences of the affected communities.

Many researchers on social justice in post-conflict societies agree that reconciliation and forgiveness are necessary ingredients to ensure a way forward for post-conflict societies and to create a sense of community.[40] Both concepts have received little attention in the Namibian context to start an honest (as difficult as it may be) public discourse regarding the past. For example, the Namibian constitution mentions reconciliation in a desultory fashion only in its preamble. There is no national policy around the subject, even though

---

38. Groop, 69.

39. Forster, "Nature of Public Theology," 16.

40. Forster, "Politics of Forgiveness?"; Girelli, *Understanding Transitional Justice*; De Gruchy, *Reconciliation: Restoring Justice*; Shore and Kline, "Ambiguous Role of Religion"; Tutu, *No Future Without Forgiveness*; Villa-Vicencio and Doxtader, *Pieces of the Puzzle*.

the official government position speaks of a national reconciliation policy.[41] Following the route of South Africa for a truth commission has been resisted from the early years after independence.[42] By the government's own admission, although in vague terms, "Namibia did not choose to deal with the past injustice in the form of a Truth Commission, the government has supported and adopted policies aimed at reconciliation."[43]

GRN's closest attempt to address the past was when it appointed the International Committee of the Red Cross (ICRC) investigation. Their task was to investigate the cases of persons who went missing since the war in the neighbouring countries. This report was not accurate because the Namibian government did not cooperate with the investigations. Despite these discrepancies and refusal to obtain an open public inquiry about the past, "the same Government . . . declared that the policy of national reconciliation had been accomplished."[44]

Although the CCN has been one of the bodies in the initial talks about reconciliation, the concept has taken more of a political leaning than a theological one. This interpretation of reconciliation was bound up in three facets: *racial reconciliation, social reconciliation,* and *economic reconciliation.* In Groth's view, the latter category meant different things to different groups, given the ambiguities in the foundational processes of such discussions. This ambiguity has been "interpreted by the propertied class as legitimating the status quo, and by the propertyless as requiring a significant redistribution of wealth."[45] In the early years after independence, Christian Tapscott bemoaned similar loopholes in the reconciliation process, which he saw as "entrenching the status quo by protecting the pre-independence gains of the minority and by legitimising patterns of social differentiation that had existed in the colonial era."[46]

---

41. A policy on national reconciliation does not imply legislating morality. Instead, it is an intentional way of addressing the past and present and of forging a plan that would reflect the social values we seek to embrace as a nation.

42. Balch and Scholten, "Namibian Reconstruction," 89–91.

43. Government of the Republic of Namibia, *Namibia Vision 2030,* 201.

44. Groop, " Church, State," 71; Groth, "Silence in Context."

45. Groth, 373.

46. Tapscott, "National Reconciliation, Social Equity," 29.

In agreement with Tapscott's analysis of Namibia's reconciliation, John Friedman argues that this adoption of national reconciliation was for pragmatic reasons, primarily to safeguard the flight of capital and international partners. However, the process of reconciliation has not adequately addressed the deplorable socioeconomic conditions resulting from the effects of apartheid. As such the reconciliation "policy," more than ensuring the stay of capital, "entrench(es) the colonial status quo by protecting a set of economic interests that were accrued under the former apartheid regime."[47]

Thus, the Namibian discourse of reconciliation (and forgiveness by extension) holds multiple conceptions, meanings, and expectations, which have not received open and honest public dialogue. These multiple conceptions, presently stifled by those in political power, create complex and injurious layers of social tension. They also put into question the dominant and official government position of reconciliation and national unity. Yet, regardless of a sombre conceptual gap regarding the meaning of reconciliation, it has been assumed (without any public dialogue) as something present in the current public sphere. It is even assumed to be a process inclusive of economic restoration or compensation.[48]

This assumed economic restoration has become a point of confusion between Black and White communities. The latter groups believe that any economic restoration demand should be requited by SWAPO accounting for its violations of human rights that happened during the liberation war to some Namibians (from the minority ethnic groups) who joined the liberation.[49] Depending on which side of the racial and ideological spectrum, the concepts of forgiveness and reconciliation mean different things and carry different expectations.

The post-apartheid political situation, at present, refuses to confront our history and hinders meaningful discussions related to the effects of apartheid. Despite this, politicians use vague rhetoric of restoration and measures of social justice against former beneficiaries of the apartheid system. Groop reports how both politicians and church leaders had different opinions on

---

47. Friedman, *Imagining Post-Apartheid State*, 48.

48. Groop, "Church, State," 76.

49. Botha, "Church in Namibia"; Dobell, "Silence in Context"; Trewhela, "Swapo and Churches"; Lombard, "Detainee Issue"; Groop, "Church, State."

reconciliation,[50] and Horn affirms the theological contribution to the issue is far from being a reality because of internal theological and ecclesiological divisions.[51]

The TRC process did not Impress many Namibians. It resulted in adopting what Akawa and Silvester call "a blanket amnesty" which "was announced with the public being encouraged to forget about the past, not to open old wounds and to move forward as a new unified nation."[52] Thus, some in the political faction and the church understand that a public discourse that would require confessing to the past would only open old wounds.[53] In contrast, others[54] believe that this approach fails to provide space for accountability and hinders the nation from genuine healing.

The official (according to GRN) version of reconciliation refuses to deal truthfully with the past or to have open dialogue for more adequate and elaborate understandings in the post-apartheid context. Thus, while the government has managed to advocate for creating spaces for social peace that ended a twenty-three-year war, the present avoidance to address this history's effects does not inspire confidence. This narrative is based on a precarious understanding of peace. It neither allows dissident views that require answers nor an open public discourse of the meaning of reconciliation.[55]

With the rising of neosocialist and neonationalist radical views like the South West African National Union (SWANU), Affirmative Repositioning (AR),[56] and Landless People's Movements (LPM) among youth groups that believe that the government has failed to pursue effective and transformative

---

50. Groop, "Church, State."

51. Horn, "Churches and Political Reconciliation," 61.

52. Akawa and Silvester, "Waking the Dead," 125; Du Pisani, "State and Society," 78.

53. Groop, "Church, State," 74–75.

54. Dobell, "Silence in Context," 375; Horn, "Churches and Political Reconciliation," 58–60; Kornes, "Negotiating 'Silent Reconciliation,'" 4–5; Lombard, "Detainee Issue," 68–71; Du Pisani, "Discursive Limits."

55. Oiva Angula's book *SWAPO Captive: A Comrade's Experience of Betrayal and Torture*, is one of the most recent post-liberation biographies that seeks to address these issues which have been restricted by a "wall of silence." As with previous writers on the subject, Angula's work has been riticized by SWAPO's stalwarts and dismissed as factually incorrect.

56. Heike Becker does not go into the political ideologies of the AR movement but does provide the role of the movement as one set to protest for justice, especially land distribution for Black Namibians. See her brief analysis of the movement on: https://repository.uwc.ac.za/xmlui/bitstream/handle/10566/3185/Becker_Nambias-moment_2016_.pdf?sequence=1&isAllowed=y (Accessed on: 17 June 2020).

socioeconomic measures for the majority, the narrative of reconciliation and social justice requires serious attention.[57] The rejection of the South African TRC approach because of fear of dealing with its past and opting for blanket amnesty based on a national or "collective amnesia which obscured contestations about the past" as an alternative to truth, fails to create a culture of honest engagement with our history.[58] Thus, while political reconciliation is said to have been achieved, it lacks integrity upon which to make just demands on anyone, especially former perpetrators and beneficiaries of the apartheid system.[59]

How vital is truth-telling or admitting to it? Lessons from the South African TRC seem to indicate that, despite all its faults and shortcomings, it helped clear the social burdens that would have been grounds for continued social mutiny. The South African process appears to have been a guided process to reconciliation while Namibia's approach has been directed. While the route of constitutional transition adopted at independence is a remarkable success story, it has not affected the understanding that shapes the political and public notions and expectations of reconciliation. A general casualness assumes that intuitively the public would eventually forget the past – leading to ignoring crucial components that could allow the process to attain genuine healing.[60] This reconciliation concept is incapable of seeking "to deliver an inclusive or holistic notion of justice that stresses both accountability for past wrongs and the need for future peaceful co-existence."[61]

The process of reconciliation requires honesty and truth. Without honesty and truth, Villa-Vicencio and Doxtader argue, it would be impossible to "chart the course forward turning the wounds of the past into the basis for

---

57. The ideological basis of both groups is that justice must precede reconciliation, particularly economic justice. Without a significant restructuring of the lopsided economic advantage of those who are beneficiaries of the then apartheid system, reconciliation carries no meaning and use for poor, marginalized, and landless people.

58. Höhn, "International Justice and Reconciliation"; Horn, "Churches and Political Reconciliation."

59. Boesak and DeYoung, *Radical Reconciliation*; Lephakga, "Radical Reconciliation."

60. Two nongovernmental organizations – the Namibian Society for Human Rights (NSHR) and Breaking the Wall of Silence (BWS) – have both been at the forefront of lobbying for open and honest talks about what happened during the liberation struggle, and campaigned for just measures regarding the wrongs of apartheid. BWS advocates for the missing detainees and NSHR for both the detainee issue and apartheid violations.

61. Villa-Vicencio and Doxtader, *Pieces of the Puzzle*, viii.

learning to live together within the rule of law and in pursuit of a culture of human rights,"[62] justice and dignity. It also places an inescapable demand on theologians to become intentional and active participants in promoting holistic notions of reconciliation.

It is crucial, not as an excuse, to be aware of complexities in the processes that have led to the outcome of this kind of reconciliation. Kornes raises these issues so that we do not think that the SWAPO-led government's decision simply happened in a vacuum. He wants us to keep in mind that post-conflict societies face a myriad of challenges in the "task of negotiating a disarray of antagonistic demands" ranging from, but not limited to, "facilitating social cohesion and reconciliation, achieving economic stability and international recognition."[63] With this complex compilation of issues, the reconciliation process, which nevertheless should be undertaken, is multiperspectival.

With a constitutionally guaranteed smooth transition, we need to ask whether the early and formative years of independence missed an opportunity that might have helped settle many past issues. It could have been much easier to implement some restitutive and restorative policies and programmes, meant to be interpreted as social justice (see § 2.2.1). Instead, a vague concept of reconciliation only increased "reluctance among the white population to embrace reconciliation and unification" due to the affirmative action and NEEEF policies "which are seen as apartheid in reverse."[64] Using SWAPO's policy of silence as an excuse to be absolved from the demands of social justice, only reflects the underlying resistance to do justice. It should not be assumed that reconciliation does not imply that apartheid beneficiaries should be absolved from the demands of social justice (particularly socioeconomic); instead, it should be seen as a vital component towards a reconciled society.

The challenge to overcome deep-seated structural issues remains in sight, but this requires honesty in dealing with the nation's history. The structural issues resulting from the apartheid system cannot be addressed effectively without an open, systematic, and intentional plan. This should be done to clear the understandings that underlie the meanings of national reconciliation, unity, and nation building and what it entails, especially as far as social

---

62. Villa-Vicencio and Doxtader, viii.

63. Kornes, "Negotiating 'Silent Reconciliation'", 5.

64. Groop, "Church, State," 75.

justice is concerned. With some end of society continuously bearing the brunt of the past as far as the appropriation of life-enhancing goods is concerned, the concept of national reconciliation cannot be said to have been attained. As a component linked to the formulation of our social ordering, reconciliation needs to be explored and reconceptualized. False notions of reconciliation are unsustainable as they only delay the inevitable social unrest it seeks to avoid. This is an ethical task which should not be left to politicians alone. Doing so would deny theology's participation and contribution in the very struggle of the nation's history of resisting the apartheid system.

5.3.2 Reconciliation and Socioeconomic Restoration

The search for social justice must be pursued in a context where other essential themes are considered and applied. Reconciliation needs to advocate something distinctive in the discourse of mending a post-conflict society and be salvaged from politics and ideologies that serve and protect special interest groups. While the concept may carry controversies, it is a central sociopolitical and theological concept in post-apartheid Namibia and cannot be ignored. Boesak believes that the decision to opt for "reconciliation was seen, not as a clever trick to allay the fears of Whites, or a tactic so as not to alarm conservative blacks, but as an indispensable end of the struggle."[65] He holds that arriving at the notion of reconciliation was intrinsically influenced by biblical or Christian conviction. He argues that "nothing in the legacy of Marxist-Leninist ideology could ever have prepared our people for the call for reconciliation, which for the Christian is rooted in God's reconciling work in Jesus Christ, who 'emptied himself,' and 'taking the form of a slave, humbled himself, and became obedient to the point of death' (Phil 2:7–8)."[66]

This conviction of reconciliation is expressed in *Radical Reconciliation*, confronting the public view, which has been overly romanticized without any bearing on social justice. The romanticized version of reconciliation needs to confront its conceptual vagueness if that is to be a realistic alternative "and a vital means of building a society on the rule of law and social reconstruction."[67]

---

65. Boesak, *Tenderness of Conscience*, 123.

66. Boesak, 124.

67. Villa-Vicencio and Doxtader, *Pieces of the Puzzle*, 3.

Boesak warns against "cheap reconciliation,"[68] which emanates from the process that entirely fails to consider the nature of the harm caused. Political reconciliation needs to take up a social justice component. Without this, it is unrealistic to expect victims and survivors of apartheid settle for social reconciliation.[69]

On the other hand, theological intervention and understanding of reconciliation serve both a vertical and horizontal purpose. If reconciliation will hold any theological and social value, it needs to embrace both the spiritual and political realities. Thus, structural systems that result in inequalities cannot be ignored under the banner of reconciliation; reconciliation needs framing with the history and effects of the apartheid system in mind.

The refusal to follow the South African TRC appears not to have been met by a worthy alternative other than suppressing public memory. Although well-intentioned, fostering reconciliation using half or decontextualized memory shades the ability to deal with problems.[70] Although well-intended as a way of not opening old wounds, there has been a lack of courageously pointing out that such an approach was not enough. Settling for a blanket amnesty without facing the truth did not allow room to construct notions of public or civic trust and realistic and measurable socioeconomic transformation. Programmes like BEE and NEEEF (see § 2.2.1.1) were not designed upon principles of a holistic approach to justice but became a means for acts of corruption, graft, and economic mismanagement in the new government's hands.[71]

The reconciliation concept was never coupled with integrity, which Boesak raises in his critique of the TRC process.[72] Lombard raises the same question of integrity and points out that the failure to deal with one issue with the required openness and integrity would affect many future social justice dialogues.[73] In general, theologians have been both complacent and silent in the face of poor governance and corruption – a silence that began before

---

68. Boesak and DeYoung, *Radical Reconciliation*, 54.

69. Villa-Vicencio and Doxtader, *Pieces of the Puzzle*, 3–4.

70. Villa-Vicencio and Doxtader, 55.

71. Institute for Public Policy Research, "Comment on National Equitable."

72. Boesak and DeYoung, *Radical Reconciliation*, 57.

73. Lombard, "Detainee Issue," 62–63.

independence.[74] No robust theological engagement seeks to challenge this complacency of the concept of reconciliation that refuses to embrace justice.

We have previously addressed the issue of SWAPO detainees in chapter 2. Although the quest for truth regarding those who went to exile is essential, it should not be confused with the effects of the apartheid system. Injustice suffered by exiles should seek its own form of reconciliation and not be the basis upon which the wrongs of the apartheid system should be evaded. Lombard thinks that the exile detainee subject "may become the acid test determining the nation's future."[75] SWAPO's avoidance of dealing with human rights violations and choosing silence over truth is a dangerous precedent.

However, the unresolved detainee issue does not carry the same effect as the unresolved gross human violations under the watchful eye of the South West Africa Territorial Force's (SWATF) counter-insurgency death squad, *Koevoet* (Afrikaans term for a crowbar), and the Afrikaner Nationalist Party.[76] Unresolved socioeconomic miscarriages are also looming today – especially over the subject of land. Justin Hunter notes these apartheid injustices, particularly the land question, as an "area of potential social conflicts . . . to create or even deepen racial mistrust or hatred."[77]

The grievous socioeconomic inequalities created under apartheid need redressing under the banner of reconciliation. These two aspects of Namibian history need to be dealt with separately so that the effects of apartheid are not given a cover under the guise of detainee issues. Part of the public witness of theology is to challenge this culture of silence that gives a false sense of peace amidst deteriorating human relations and socioeconomic conditions. We need to confront what Katongole and Rice refer to as "'reconciliation without memory,' that ignores the wounds of the world and proclaims peace where there is no peace."[78]

Political reconciliation alone cannot restore broken relationships manifested in racial mistrust and hatred.[79] Theology might have missed its op-

74. Botha, "Church in Namibia," 30.

75. Lombard, "Detainee Issue," 63.

76. Balch and Scholten, "Namibian Reconstruction," 87–88.

77. Hunter, "Who Should Own Land?," 1.

78. Katongole and Rice, *Reconciling All Things*, 33.

79. Boesak, "And Zaccheus Remained"; Boesak and DeYoung, *Radical Reconciliation*, 58, 137.

portunity here, by withdrawing too soon from the public discourse about reconciliation. Merely speaking of national reconciliation would not lead to reconciliation between Black and White Namibians. Reconciliation is only the basic entry-level of addressing broken trust due to the apartheid policies. It is impossible to work toward a process of reconciliation when there is no accountability and incentive to redress past wrongdoings and human rights violations. This process lacks integrity and cannot recommend real solutions to the existing conflicts resulting from historical happenings. If challenging the South African government in the 1970s expressed prophetic resistance towards a tyrannical government, challenging the official government position on reconciliation would continue that role.[80]

A theology of a holistic approach to reconciliation is crucial, not to convert the public to Christianity but as a means of participating in processes that affect the nation's progress. Such theology should understand the intricate sociopolitical issues and speak with integrity and courage. Reconciliation needs to happen within a context of honest historical memory and calling for appropriate accountability to ensure equitable measures concerning injustice's lingering effects. Boesak argues that

> reconciliation means uncovering the sin, showing remorse, making restitution, and restoring relationships with deeds of compassionate justice, then, and only then, is reconciliation complete, right, sustainable, and radical, because it becomes transformational. Then reconciliation has integrity, because it restores human integrity. That is its salvific power. Political reconciliation's concern is that we must come to a point where we do not kill each other. And indeed we do well if we do not kill one another, if we tolerate each other as political adversaries, no longer treating each other as deadly enemies who have to be eliminated. That is no small thing. But biblical, radical reconciliation wants to bring us to the point where we learn to live, not just *with* the other – because we have no choice – but *for* the other – because that is our choice – where the peace among

---

80. Lombard, "Detainee Issue," 66–68.

us is not just the absence of violence but the active presence of justice[81] (Italics in original).

Katongole and Rice hold that vague notions of reconciliation "offer little concrete hope that fundamental change is possible."[82] They do not faithfully embrace "God's desire and vision" and divorce reconciliation from God's story, making it but another version of reconciliation that fails to confront the prevailing injustice.[83] They cannot guarantee the careful design of justice measures, as they lack transparency. Various post-apartheid reconciliation and forgiveness theologians[84] also hold that these concepts cannot be discussed apart from justice and would only entrench the effects of apartheid.

The poorly developed political theology that has sided with the official government position of reconciliation is one more motivation why a far-reaching theology of justice is vital for the Namibian experiences. The current context, as demonstrated from Horn's analysis of the church's role in the process of reconciliation,[85] "requires theologies that are capable of holding to the historical theological convictions of the Christian faith in tension with social, political, ecological and economic realities."[86] Therefore, although the New Testament and Pauline concepts of reconciliation may serve as frameworks for developing our understanding, based on believers' relationship to God through Jesus Christ, the concept as we use it in post-apartheid Namibia encompasses dealing with complex sociopolitical, sociohistorical, and socioeconomic issues which the Bible does not directly address. While the meanings and applications of reconciliation will always be contested, it is agreed that there must be an open discourse upon the way forward. Simply saying, "Let us move on," is inadequate, cruel, dishonest, and condescending. Post-apartheid discussion of reconciliation needs to discuss the removal of present injustice.

---

81. Boesak and DeYoung, *Radical Reconciliation*, 58.

82. Katongole and Rice, *Reconciling All Things*, 29.

83. Katongole and Rice, 30.

84. Forster, "Translation and Politics of Forgiveness?"; Niitenge, "Evangelical Lutheran Church"; Villa-Vicencio and Doxtader, *Pieces of the Puzzle*; De Gruchy, *Reconciliation: Restoring Justice*.

85. Horn, "Churches and Political Reconciliation," 58–61.

86. Forster, "Politics of Forgiveness?", 79.

Seeking justice in a society that may not embrace the Christian ethos means searching for a language that makes sense to both Christian and non-Christian listeners, allows us to own up to our histories, and offers the chance to develop prospects to (re)construct a just society. In this regard, Boesak's view expressed in *Radical Reconciliation* becomes profoundly interconnected to the idea of justice. Apartheid violated Black people's human rights and tainted the humanity of the perpetrators. It violated the nature of God's created order by severing communion between people based on pretentious social categorization. With these violations came measures that disadvantaged Black persons while creating insurmountable socioeconomic benefits for White persons and their posterity. Without an honest confrontation of this history, the cherished official government policy of reconciliation needs reevaluation.

To bear God's witness in such a fragmented context not only seeks to bind the wounds inflicted by injustice but to also address factors that shield injustice and consider clear procedures on how to address the violations. Reconciliation cannot be left solely in the hands of government institutions; this is part of the Christian ministry in the world (1 Cor:15–20, 6: 2; Eph 2:14–16). Boesak argues that the post-colonial reading of these texts implies "that reconciliation is real, that is, experiential; reconciliation is radical, that is, focused on social justice; reconciliation is revolutionary, that is, oriented to structural change."[87] Not only are we to advocate for reconciliation as an event, but it should lead to perpetual recurring events of meaningful, equitable outcomes. Villa-Vicencio and Doxtader think that this process cannot be rushed: "at the very least, it is a generation's work, and [an] effort that must proceed within local, communal and national contexts."[88] This extended process is part of being objective about the reality of the nature of apartheid and how it came about.

Giada Girelli wants us to understand the pervasive nature of apartheid and its structures when she argues that the apartheid system took place over an extended period. Its effects require careful long-term mitigations to redress them. In the same way, the oppressive system was crafted using policies and programmes, Girelli argues, we need similar responses to reverse

---

87. Boesak and DeYoung, *Radical Reconciliation*, 8.
88. Villa-Vicencio and Doxtader, *Pieces of the Puzzle*, 32.

its effects.[89] The extent of damages resulting from these policies cannot be ignored or rushed as such only reinforce a new context of continued victimhood. Therefore, because we are concerned for God's image-bearers, theology needs to come in the public realm, interacting with the ideas that inform the concept of post-apartheid reconciliation. In this public conceptualization of what is needed in post-apartheid Namibia, theology becomes a tool of proclaiming God's kingdom, through which we affirm "God's public claim on the world and the lives of God's people in the world."[90] In this public participation of pursuing reconciliation, we embrace the nature of God fully when there seem to be firm demands for justice. Thus, theological participation in the public realm demands witness to the truth against impersonal reconciliation standards that fail to hold anyone to the highest accountability measures. Nico Koopman, speaking about the South African TRC experience, says truth is crucial for constructing a new nation, which implies that the absence of truth impedes nation-building and creates artificial social peace.[91]

Reconciliation is a process, but it requires radical action to affect prevailing injustice. Otherwise, we are only busy with what Katongole and Rice call a buffet notion of reconciliation "from which anyone from power brokers to minority groups can pick and choose whatever they might want."[92] According to them, such an understanding would only "result [in] . . . a fuzziness concerning reconciliation and with it the danger that reconciliation's popularity may result in it meaning nothing. In an attempt to appeal to as (sic) wide a constituency as possible, we leave reconciliation to stand on its own, without reference to an explicit vision of life and society toward which it should lead."[93] Boesak in *Radical Reconciliation* critiques empty reconciliation regarding the TRC's outcomes and advocates for reconciliation that takes justice seriously, particularly the restoration of human dignity by starting with the material aspect of reconciliation.

This means conceptualising reconciliation and truth for Namibia not as philosophical or theological abstractions but as social constructs employed

---

89. Girelli, *Understanding Transitional Justice*.

90. Boesak, *Tenderness of Conscience*, 3.

91. Koopman, "Towards Reconciliation," 97.

92. Katongole and Rice, *Reconciling All Things*, 31.

93. Katongole and Rice, 31.

with honesty about the history of apartheid and its effects, admission of socio-economic inequality, and commitment to make amends. This should apply to individuals and the community to create a more equitable new dispensation and hold the beneficiaries and perpetrators to account. But the conditions of reconciliation should not create a new form of alienation. Groop hints at this alienation using affirmative action policies to cut White Namibians from state programmes and benefits simply based on their skin colour.[94] Whatever the understanding of reconciliation, it must seek to protect the human dignity of all groups, which is Horn's concern and his reason for calling for a robust theological engagement with the subject.[95]

Engaging theology continues to be hampered as theology is entangled in partisan politics, intra- and interdenominational feuds, apartheid tendencies, and a general absence of engagement in "societal transformation endeavours."[96] These challenges underlying theology's presence indict the lost public witness and theology's relevance to challenging society's structural inequities. Without an intentional engagement in reconciliation, theology would be of no relevance to the public as it has withdrawn itself from the life of society or been domesticated to political ideologies. Theological public engagement is so stuck in its historical contribution that it has refused to present relevant answers to a post-apartheid context. Therefore, we need to ask whether theology has been sidelined because it is religion at work or has ceased to participate in society's emancipation?

As narrated by both Horn[97] and Botha,[98] the absence of public theology that would engage reconciliation only fuels a reductionist political narrative incapable of creating sustainable social peace. The voices that challenged the SWAPO paradigm that cordoned off talking about the past have often been sidelined or publicly humiliated or ostracized. Granting blanket amnesty without exploring the historical circumstances was termed reconciliation

---

94. Groop, "Church, State."

95. Horn, "Churches and Political Reconciliation," 61; Villa-Vicencio and Doxtader, *Pieces of the Puzzle*, 32.

96. Horn, 61.

97. Horn.

98. Botha, "Church in Namibia."

and putting the past behind.[99] Although well-intended, this declaration compromized justice for many victims of apartheid. South Africa followed a similar prescriptive reconciliation process that did not emphasize justice. The complexity and fluidity of the Namibian debate leaves everyone to assume whatever reconciliation means in their context. For the White Namibians, of whom the majority are beneficiaries of the apartheid system, this may simply mean we have stopped killing each other, and everyone can now go on living their lives.

To find its concept of social justice, Namibia needs to engage its history with integrity. The public memory needs to face the truth for any meaningful intervention towards being a more just society. Such silencing, and the absence of public discourse on our history, is no reconciliation at all and undermines why we should pursue justice at all. An honest reconciliation process is necessary for sustainable peace and justice. Otherwise, in an unjust form of peace, we are expecting that those most affected by history should simply accept living on with the effects.[100] Therefore, an open and honest public discourse is needed that speaks of reconciliation in the context of the socioeconomic realities and how to address extreme privation. This is part of reclaiming our human dignity and ensuring that the perpetual cycle of dehumanising conditions is addressed with measures that lead to agreeable outcomes of justice.

Although Namibia has had a remarkable transition from a White minority rule to an inclusive democracy, reconciliation remains incomplete and artificial without an honest confrontation of the past and engagement in justice measures.[101] A discerning theological engagement that can challenge this

---

99. Christo Lombard took an issue with this understanding of reconciliation in his *Open Letter to the President [Samuel Nujoma]*, in which he says, "I see that you have offered those 'caught in the cross-fire of war' the hand of friendship and reconciliation. You ask them: 'Let us all concentrate on the burning issues of the day, namely, ignorance, disease and poverty,' and to work together as a united people. I agree with you that we can be victorious as a nation, but I urge you to take the real process of reconciliation seriously: admitting first of all where things went wrong, confessing those mistakes in humility, restoring the honour of those affected and making good as far as possible. The proposed conference of the CCN may offer a golden opportunity to have these ingredients of reconciliation meet the other, equally important ingredients such as forgiveness, grace, restoration of dignity and integrity, harmony and acceptance, renewed humanity."

100. Botha, "Reconciliation as Narrative," 655–57.

101. Botha, "Church in Namibia"; Groop, "Church, State"; Horn, "Churches and Political Reconciliation"; Lombard, "Detainee Issue."

artificial public notion of justice is crucial which seeks to engage society with the common understanding that all citizens are collaborators in the quest for meaningful reconciliation. This dream would not be realized without an intentional collective soul-searching and creation of spaces for truth-telling. The present notion of reconciliation in Namibia requires embodying truth and justice. The discourse of reconciliation "requires theological explanation, and a theological concept seeking human and social embodiment."[102] Theological reflection is an ongoing process to establish a community who are willing to grapple with their issues openly until they are genuinely reconciled to work towards all persons' upliftment. This is a search for a better society than the one we have inherited from apartheid, and which is now exasperated by corruption, maladministration, and inadequate public policies.

5.3.3 Reconciliation and Contextual Awareness

Reconciliation carries with it deep political and theological notions. Boesak's work, especially *Kairos, Crisis and Global Apartheid*, asks how Christians can extend their faith to this public dialogue in search of a life-altering meaning of reconciliation.[103] We are to participate in peacemaking between persons of different social classes divided by the ideologies of colonialism and apartheid. We should also advocate for justice measures to restore the dignity of those still experiencing the effects of apartheid. This cannot be enforced by borrowing from other contexts, but it is also perplexing to claim, as Boesak,[104] De Gruchy,[105] and Tutu[106] do, that our theological basis for reconciliation should be derived from the Pauline interpretation. Political reconciliation, as interpreted post-apartheid, is not "shaped by the vicarious suffering of Christ, the one who takes the place of the 'other.'"[107] Reconciliation theologians who read the Pauline text of reconciliation to apply post-apartheid ignore the various theological perspectives and may undermine what is meant by reconciliation in the post-apartheid context. While we could derive principles based on how God has treated a sinful human race through the work of Christ, the

---

102. De Gruchy, *Reconciliation: Restoring Justice*, 26.

103. Boesak, *Pharaohs on Both Sides*.

104. Boesak and DeYoung, *Radical Reconciliation*.

105. De Gruchy, *Reconciliation: Restoring Justice*.

106. Tutu, *No Future Without Forgiveness*.

107. De Gruchy, *Reconciliation: Restoring Justice*, 168.

direct application of those reconciliatory expectations is placed upon those who have found such reconciliation by faith.

Katongole and Rice emphasize this spiritual reality when they say "an emphasis on right relationship with God is crucial to a Christian vision of reconciliation. Faithful obedience to God is an invitation into a whole new way of life, a journey where our desires are increasingly transformed towards God's desires."[108] This does not imply that our proclamation of reconciliation should ignore social realities. Such an approach is a false understanding of the gospel and, Boesak and DeYoung argue, we become "complicit in deceitful reconciliation. We deny the demands of the gospel and refuse solidarity with the powerless and oppressed. This we call 'Christian quietism.' Therefore, reconciliation must be radical."[109]

The language of reconciliation cannot be translated without careful consideration of the affected communities. How do we apply reconciliation to contexts other than that of Christians? This language of biblical reconciliation should neither betray the biblical text nor dilute the political context that seeks socioeconomic transformation. It could be a helpful framework for bringing together Black and White Namibian communities to pursue reconciliation, discard unhelpful social categories, and take up newer understandings. To redress these deep-seated identity issues would take more than political and social analysis. It requires people with an alternative vision – the church, inspired by Scripture but combined with the needed social, historical, and political analysis skills to pursue the meaning of reconciliation in meaningful ways from the local church to society. Boesak's far-reaching understanding of reconciliation is innately linked to the concept of *shalom*. According to Brueggemann, "*shalom* is the substance of the biblical vision of one community embracing all creation. It refers to all those resources and factors which make communal harmony joyous and effective."[110]

If reconciliation is a signature of being at peace, then it must extend measures of justice. Otherwise, it only becomes a term of securing the powerful elite's interest. Boesak argues that accepting a notion of reconciliation that does not inquire on justice matters for the victims is contrary to God's *shalom*

108. Katongole and Rice, *Reconciling All Things*, 32.

109. Boesak and DeYoung, *Radical Reconciliation*, 1.

110. Brueggemann, *Living Towards a Vision*, 16.

notion. He says, "this is not the shalom that Yahweh desires ... This is the murderous peace of violent pacification . . . It is for this that Yahweh laments and wails."[111] Such a theological understanding of reconciliation only shields the powerful perpetrators and beneficiaries who continue to "live well off the profits of their faithless complicity."[112]

However, this also implies that Christian participation in reconciliation needs to be grounded in the gospel imperative. Reconciliation theologians link the gospel and our social activities. The power of the powerful dictates the socioeconomic conditions. Confronting such power imbalances gives voice to the marginalized (excluded from participating) and oppressed (hierarchically held down). The biblical message firmly holds to God's rule for God's image-bearers, which we seek to inform and shape our social and political institutions and conduct. Such reconciliation would advocate universal human rights in the laws and constitutions of countries. Ensuring protection and implementation of rights becomes a critical agenda for action.

Boesak presents Christian understanding and experience of the effect of the gospel as the reason for participation in the search for authentic reconciliation.[113] Thus, the theology of reconciliation needs to be found in the gospel analysis of God's reconciling work through Christ, not by urging social uniformity but by encouraging these different communities to work together towards a more just society. It is a search for the recognition of the humanity of everyone and building an interdependent community. Thus, the responsibility to influence public opinion on reconciliation and justice needs to be demonstrated in the Christian community's intentional search for reconciliation.[114] Within this reconciliation dimension lies the gospel's true expression, which seeks to restore men and women divided by erroneous theological and philosophical concepts.

It presents a new perspective within the existing paradigms of reconciliation, presenting the gospel's radical nature, which restores relationships. It also precipitates new social imaginations that extend to how we think about justice using a relational approach. The narrative of Pauline reconciliation

---

111. Boesak, *Kairos, Crisis and Global*, 126.

112. Boesak, 126.

113. Boesak and DeYoung, *Radical Reconciliation*, 52, 54.

114. Bowers du Toit and Nkomo, "Ongoing Challenge."

addresses a unique public within a broader public, with the hope that their transformation would have a wider effect exemplified by Christian love as people transformed by the gospel affect society at large. If De Gruchy and Boesak's interpretations of reconciliation are to be improved upon, they need to be analysed within the context of various atonement narratives, which frame the search for reconciliation primarily as a gospel issue that seeks to reconcile people to God. Reconciliation through political measures alone, however, cannot be fully enacted without understanding that the actual union of life can only be actualized through hearts reconciled to God.

Principles derived to address the political understanding of reconciliation in a post-conflict society should avoid forcing a Christian narrative into a non-Christian space. Thus, the theological search for dialogue needs to allow genuine grappling with the realities of the harsh environment in which reconciliation is being discussed. This awareness, coupled with careful listening, provides authenticity for theology to regain public trust, which has been marred by either siding with the apartheid government or being complacent with injustice by SWAPO. Within this search, the is a need to grapple with our theological conception of reconciliation when we conceptualize the meaning of reconciliation as the entry point to the discourse.

Botha's critique of the church's absence from meaningful socioeconomic discourse, is by extension, a critique of the absence of theological participation, not in order to impose Christian beliefs but to provide the moral guidance needed to achieve reconciliation outcomes – especially social justice.[115] A theological motivation of reconciliation for the post-apartheid context requires sensitivity and firmness to advocate for the execution of justice. Thus, it should strive for reconciliation but not shy away from asking questions of "discomfort, struggle, and suffering," giving answers but at the same time raising new questions in places where pursuing truth is not commonplace.[116] As part of public participation, theology seeks to ask how the Namibian society provides a theoretical framework from which it can derive praxis of justice and how the sociopolitical system is being used towards ensuring this vision for a more equitable society. De Gruchy's book, *Christianity and Democracy*, helps us understand that theology has an essential task in ensuring that we

---

115. Botha, "Church in Namibia," 79–80.
116. Barth, *God Here and Now*, 20.

embrace the common good that binds a society. When we accept that we are God's image-bearers, we can then set up agreements to hold each other accountable towards creating a just social order. With a political aspect to consider, and whatever theological position one holds, the vision of God is required in the creation of a reconciled and just society.[117] This vision of God would motivate us to challenge possessive individualism, corruption, and ungodly silence in the face of ongoing injustice. This leads us to our next section in the discourse of conceptualising social justice in search of a more just post-apartheid Namibian context.

5.4 Conceptualising Social Justice for Namibia

This section discusses the meaning and the need for the conceptualization of justice, using De Gruchy's argument for a vision of democracy as an example of articulating Christian beliefs in the public sphere and contextualization. In chapter 2, we saw that apartheid had various dimensions: (1) to establish a cultural hegemony by obliterating Black culture; (2) to use political tools to gain legitimization through policies that enforced it, and (3) to channel economic resources alongside racial lines, using political and legal measures. These dimensions could increase White citizens' utility level only by decreasing that of Black citizens. The assumption that each would develop along their cultural line also meant setting up structures that ensured White dominance through systematic but brutal measures. They controlled the culture, religion, language, metaphor, politics, legal system, economy, and education. Such side effects have abrogated Black communities' social vitality, evidenced by rampant socioeconomic inequities that have continued after abolishing apartheid. Even though significant steps have been taken to ensure political equity, much still needs to be done to create more equitable socioeconomic standards. Therefore, justice talks, visions, plans, policies, and programmes must be far reaching and demand more than material restoration.

This dialogue of justice is multidimensional. In this section, we interact with some issues which could be essential in the conceptualization of justice for post-apartheid Namibia. For Namibia, where the need for self-articulation

---

117. Boesak, "Religions and Search"; De Gruchy, *Reconciliation: Restoring Justice*; Niitenge, "Evangelical Lutheran Church"; Palmer, *Healing the Heart*; Sagovsky, *Christian Tradition*.

is still in its developmental stages, Boesak's work may help to spark the theological contribution. Black Liberation Theology and Black post-apartheid contextual theology, while rich in facts and articulately presented, need to generate sound academic analysis to engage the broader social issues affecting society today.

5.4.1 Vision of Democracy: A Conducive Political Environment

The search for a contextualized conceptualization requires theology that can ask relevant questions and broaden its participation in addressing social issues. This means helping society define its social injustice context and honestly address and actively seek to rebalance historical imbalances. Chapter 4 noted in part (especially in § 4.1 and § 4.3) how Boesak argues for political participation and action. *The Tenderness of Conscience* advocates for this political role of the Christian faith to inject spirituality into the politics that could create just structures. De Gruchy in *Christianity and Democracy* systematically analyses theology's role in critiquing the status quo. Therefore, the absence of theology that engages these conceptions that can affect public policy, allows spaces for theology that accommodates infrastructure that enhances injustice. This section dialogues with notions discussed in these works as part of the search for theologies of justice conversant with the sociopolitical concepts needed to advocate for social justice.

Boesak's concept of democracy is linked to his understanding of the lordship of Christ over all human systems. As he puts it, "the Lordship of Jesus Christ is over every single inch of life, and its conviction that Christian witness against [injustice] ought to enter the real world and challenge it, shape it, subvert it, revolutionize it until it conforms to the norms of the kingdom of God – justice, mercy, equity, compassion, peace, inclusion, and humanness."[118] With a messianic vision that is inextricably allied to justice, we cannot imagine a vision of democracy without justice in mind. He says that "if the poorest of the poor have not arrived, if they cannot sit 'each under his own vine and his own fig tree,' the vision of justice from which the church lives has not been fulfilled."[119] He warns against allying with those in politics, and calls

---

118. Boesak, *Kairos, Crisis and Global*, 204.
119. Boesak, 157.

for vigilance, so that the church will continue to be a moral voice. Critical solidarity is needed so that the voice of the poor is not silenced in our proximity to political power.

Boesak's position towards the Christian relationship with politics seems to have been affected after his prison experience. Disappointed and betrayed by his political allies, he found himself in a political wilderness. His attempts to join COPE did not wield much political produce, if not adding to his despondence. *Running with Horses* narrates his political journey, successes, and failures. But it is *Pharaohs on Both Sides of the Blood-Red River* that exemplifies a much more objective analysis of the political situation in South Africa. He stands a bit far removed from the immediate context and observes the situation in South Africa. With this realization, he points out how those with proximity to political power regardless of gender, religion, nationality, and racial social classification are all capable of being perpetrators of injustice. It is a global phenomenon. Faced with the "politics of appeasing"[120] and a way of engaging infected by cowardice, he calls out for a "renewed struggle for justice"[121] (even against a system of politics he previously embraced). He does this not out of bitterness or malice because of betrayal by ANC comrades, but out of a renewed struggle for justice against the mindless and ineffective mantras of political cries for justice. He writes that

> it is more the expression of a desire for things yet to come, a longing for a God-given right yet to be recognized and realized. It is also the acknowledgment that, despite the centuries of pain and suffering and determined struggle, this struggle for justice is far from over and – one should hope – the acknowledgment of the incontrovertible truth that without struggle and pain, sacrifice and hopeful endurance, systemic transformation and redeemed politics, justice will not become reality.[122]

While he supports democracy, democratic structures, and systems, even those we may be subscribing to, we should not support them unquestioningly.

---

120. Boesak, *Pharaohs on Both Sides*, 35.

121. Boesak, 36.

122. Boesak, 36.

The role of prophetic proclamation is to call these structures to be human and strive towards justice.

De Gruchy embarks on a painstaking task, for which he should be commended, of providing systematic analysis of theological engagement with democratic systems and structures for a context affected by apartheid. From a philosophical perspective, the struggle for social justice is part of the search for Greek *eudaimonia*, which in the Hebrew conception has been referred to as *shalom*. De Gruchy argues that democratic systems, if well managed, can be used to achieve fulfilling democratic visions in which society can experience real and life-enhancing freedom, equality, and justice. He argues that this vision, at least for South Africa, reflects God's work of liberating Israel from Egypt. Because it is only within that vision, as opposed to the Greek conception of justice, that persons of all social groupings would receive justice as bearers of God's image endowed with infinite dignity.[123]

He seeks a human-centred democratic system that would then be considerate of human needs. Without a functional democracy, it would be impossible to have a democratic vision that cares for the vulnerable people in society. De Gruchy attempts to provide a framework in which people would act justly and the political system needed to serve that end. He is careful as he warns against the folly of assuming a utopian inauguration of "a new democratic order of world justice and peace."[124] Thus, the need for authentic and engaging theological participation in democratic transitions in the post-apartheid context is of utmost importance if we are to engage the actual issues instead of clouding them with elusive utopian visions. De Gruchy believes that although there appear to be serious challenges facing human societies, we are still in environments with considerable potential to realize justice. He argues that we appeal to our common good, enabling us to embrace mutual accountability, a long-term process. This implies the negation of selfish individualism upon which the apartheid society has been founded, to pursue a vision of a more just society (as a whole). He seeks to balance excessive liberal democratic capitalism and social collectivism in creating a political vision of distributing life-enhancing goods.[125]

---

123. De Gruchy, *Christianity and Democracy*, 8–11.

124. De Gruchy, 5.

125. De Gruchy, 22–23.

Like Boesak, De Gruchy holds that there is significant tension between those with power and those without it, which requires a thorough democratic vision to address it. For Boesak, the concept of democracy is deeply linked to its practical implications on ordinary persons, which can only be meaningful in terms of "genuine empowerment of people."[126] However, theology's role is essential in ensuring that those with power are held to high levels of accountability to use their power to benefit society. He believes "that democracy cannot survive without the spiritual basis which gives meaning to life."[127] Thus, he encourages a theology for a just democratic world order, grounded in Yahweh's self-revelation rather than in Plato and Aristotle's conception of the *polis*. This prophetic tradition, which he traces from the Hebrew Old Testament narratives, now finds its expression in Jesus Christ and his church. He believes the church or *ekklesia* is a community of persons who treat each other as equals, that is, manifesting what it means to be just among its members. In his suggestion, thoughtful and engaging theology is essential in establishing a stable democracy that can pursue a democratic vision for a just society.

De Gruchy does not offer us a theology of justice but a general framework conducive to rethinking a just society. He provides us with an example of what type of theological engagement Namibia may require for public discourse. It is also a work that would have us rethink Christian engagement in the world beyond socialism and liberation and how to engage the public with a robust prophetic vision. While he suggests a political framework, it is the type that has its foundations in God's self-revelation rather than in Athens.[128] Thus, he is suggesting theological participation that understands the language and functioning of the secular – without abandoning the hope of the role Christians can play in the transformation of society. While this democratic vision may sound to be a form of neo-Christendom or neo-Constantinian, he argues that, of the available options, this one is better and capable of creating an orderly society where sustainable peace and human flourishing can be realised. Well established systems of democracy become conduits to execute justice and fairness, or to the church can, according to Boesak, live

---

126. Boesak, *Tenderness of Conscience*, 59.

127. Boesak, 247.

128. De Gruchy, *Christianity and Democracy*, 7, 43.

the dream of God – that dream that envisions the inverted order of life: where the last shall be first, the poor filled with good things and the rich sent away emptyhanded; where the bow of the mighty is broken and the feeble gird on strength; where the powerful are scattered in the confused thoughts of their hearts, but the poor are raised from the dust of the earth – many write off the church as unrealistic and "otherworldly." But they are wrong. The church sees this dream, not in the clouds, or the cards, or the market, but in the promises of God as these are reflected in the faces of the poor, the courage of the weak, the hope of the downtrodden and the joy of the oppressed.[129]

The theological and critical aspect of De Gruchy's suggestion stands out because he does not call for blind solidarity with democratic governments and movements. Instead, he calls for "critical solidarity" to avoid being abused for political expedience and being complicit in unjust acts and policies.[130] These extremes have been witnessed in the apartheid support of the DRCSA and the liberation churches during and after apartheid. Both positions came with detrimental effects for the church's witness.[131] In this case, solidarity implies deliberating alongside and supporting systems that can provide *eudaimonia*, which he calls God's *shalom* to serve as an ethical and political principle. What is central in an authentic democracy? De Gruchy believes that only within a context in which human rights are genuinely allowed to thrive can a democracy result in justice. Attaining justice would then imply creating functional systems that ensure socioeconomic security for all citizens. Such a system should curb hyper-individualism and capitalism that encourage gross and degrading differences between the rich and poor.[132]

In De Gruchy's view, justice cannot happen without an intentional reflection and creation of a system to administer just measures. Christians have a role to play by participating in the public dialogues that decide and forge these policies and programmes. Democracy as a vision is external to the system itself. It requires tremendous work to be an integral component. A system

---

129. Boesak, *Tenderness of Conscience*, 157–58.
130. De Gruchy, *Christianity and Democracy*, 204.
131. De Gruchy, 177; Horn, "Churches and Political Reconciliation," 58–61.
132. Boesak, *Tenderness of Conscience*, 69, 92.

sworn to regard the majority as "the people" requires robust and intentional reforms to translate this vision into reality. While Namibia has opted for constitutional democracy, there have been inadequate efforts to ensure that democratic practice and values inform the public discourse on justice matters. Instead, neoliberalism permeates the socioeconomic structures, serving as the source for continued disparities in wealth, income, and resource access and distribution. Without a transparent political system and socioeconomic vision, the effects of apartheid will not go away in the foreseeable future until we start to generate notions of justice that inculcate a vision for human progress.

While this research does not say we should embrace De Gruchy's incorporation of vision into a system of democracy, he demonstrates the need for conceptualization. While he suggests this to be a framework for the global context of changing politics (in the context of world history and the 1989 collapse of the Berlin Wall) as far as democracy is concerned, he leaves room for every society to apply the vision of democracy according to their needs. While he accepts the wisdom from Athens, he advocates for a Christian engagement in the secular *polis*. This vision would allow moving beyond constitutional instruments, in his analysis, ensuring that the system is well-ordered and promoting human flourishing. This may sound utopian but is theological and reflective of the biblical kingdom language and vision. However, he is not naive regarding human nature, although he avoids touching on aspects of sin and confession and instead grounds his entire approach in an optimistic theology, as expressed in his book's last chapter.

De Gruchy holds that this vision of democracy incorporates life in the community as opposed to individualism. He argues that such collectivism can only be realised based on understanding the Trinitarian relationship in which all persons are equal without losing their individuality. It also encompasses the understanding of *imago Dei* which cannot find any fuller expression than in Jesus Christ, who is God's visible self-disclosure.[133] The God concept in this social imaginary is not merely for practical reasons of keeping society intact as assumed by Immanuel Kant; instead, "it has far-reaching consequences for understanding and renewing personal identity as well as human society."[134] This sort of conception, in its reach, looks at persons for who they are and

---

133. De Gruchy, *Christianity and Democracy*, 239–40.

134. De Gruchy, 240.

not based on their phenotypes. We have pointed out how the phenotypical approach is backward-looking in addressing the actual issue of systematic injustice. With this outlook in search of a new and reconciled community, De Gruchy argues that only by learning from the nature of God can we achieve it or at least experience significant glimpses. In his view, the Trinity provides the needed conception of a community in which all persons can and are treated equally. He argues that "God is not a homogeneous collectivity in which each person's uniqueness is subsumed within the whole, but a community within which the distinctness of each person is affirmed and therefore within which the other remains a significant other."[135] This God is ever-present and involved in human activities, which makes theology a calling of public engagement, speaking to the issues with which humans are struggling.

Theology in post-apartheid Namibia carries insignificant, or even no currency in the public discourse of social justice issues. Judging from De Gruchy's analysis, we can deduce that those at the forefront of theology need to engage more with society's language and issues. Even if they may be concerned with social injustice's continued presence, this needs to be enhanced by a more profound, nuanced, and engaging understanding of the language. Although De Gruchy writes within a global context, his argument for a democratic system and vision is specifically geared towards South African issues. Although he writes as a theologian/philosopher, it is indisputable how he also borrows from mostly Western conceptual frameworks to articulate his views. As such, his is a developing idea.

De Gruchy engages the history of democracy and how theological discussions and contributions have been central to the development of democracy in the West. He is concerned that if God's image-bearers are to experience a life of dignity, we need to be serious about the kinds of political systems that we engage to make this a reality. Theologians seeking to engage these public issues of law and justice need to acquire a thorough understanding rooted in God and the language of secular systems. De Gruchy holds to a utopian vision of democracy. He believes that the biblical expressions of God's kingdom and reign are deeply rooted in utopian terms that we cannot escape but must embrace in our advocacy for justice.

---

135. De Gruchy, 240–41.

This section was not meant to critique De Gruchy but to simply demonstrate the need for conceptualising a framework for a society to understand and address its context. The following section builds on this understanding of theological participation in a secular state and how Namibia's theology can be instrumental in social justice dialogue.

5.4.2 A Conducive Social Environment to Enable Social Justice

The liberation struggle was a compilation of various ideologies – among them were feminism,[136] socialism,[137] and nationalism mixed with Marxist ideas.[138] However, Saunders argues that, as far as socialism is concerned, it was only used as a framework when it was convenient and that those who participated in the liberation struggle were technically nationalists.[139] He points to Samuel Nujoma and says that he might have used the socialist themes, but there is no evidence that he had the discernment to identify socialist ideas if they were presented to him. These systems were imposed without giving adequate thought to the difference in context. Added to the mix of political and economic debates were identity politics in the form of nationalism. As Namibia was moving towards independence, the SWAPO party, a sworn Socialist-Marxist movement, adopted democracy as the form of government for the independent state. Progress has been made, which has put Namibia among the best democracies on the African continent. However, what does this mean in creating socioeconomic conditions to address the effects of injustice perpetrated upon the Namibian population by colonialism and apartheid?

A democratic system, even a constitutional democracy alone, poses challenges if it does not translate into the creation of a more just and equitable society. Boesak holds that this process requires a "rediscovery of a spirituality of politics in order to create true human democratic systems; or without spirituality our politics is vain . . . we shall not succeed, and without [this] our country and the world are doomed."[140] This spirituality humanises demo-

---

136. Akawa, *Gender Politics*; Namhila, *Mukwahepo*.

137. South West Africa National Union, *Basic Documents of SWANU*.

138. Katjavivi, *History of Resistance*.

139. Saunders, "Liberation and Democracy," 96–97.

140. Boesak, *Tenderness of Conscience*, 2–3.

cratic systems to take into consideration every society's unique "history and political tradition"[141] to create functional systems that can redress the gross violations against specific communities and posterity.

Thus, this consideration of traditions is not to be constituted for its end; instead, it should be embarked on to deliver "as far as possible . . . a true account of justice and practical rationality."[142] Given the history of how apartheid systematically and intentionally created structures that ensured people's disempowerment based on their social categorization, speaking of justice, especially social justice, needs to be geared at how it can intentionally affect and undo these structures. Without a counterpart that can affect the established structures, the existing system of democracy would only maintain the status quo.

As evidenced by the above summary discussion with De Gruchy, the outcome of our enquiry regarding the need for conceptualization is inescapable. This means for society to pursue justice, it needs a well-articulated vision of justice with a high view of human life. Within such an intentional approach towards history, context, and human value, can there be a creation of a new culture or tradition which embody particular social relationships born of justice. Namibia is a *polis* (broadly speaking) with its history, cultures, justice, and challenges. To adequately address its social conditions and ensure sustainable peace, there is a need to have a vision of justice. This must happen not only among those who have experienced injustice but inclusive of communities that perpetrated and benefited from the history of injustice. Thus, to conceptualize the meaning of justice for the Namibian context requires considering society's diversity even though its various members may hold different and competing visions of justice. That is,

> we need to encourage and embrace the public reasoning and envisioning . . . if we wish to forge an alternative to our current politics, in which sections of society, divided by competing interests, press their desperate concerns on a state which has no core of shared values to draw upon in order to adjudicate on these disputes. But how, concretely, might we develop a public

---

141. De Gruchy, *Christianity and Democracy*, 188.

142. MacIntyre, *Whose Justice?*, 389.

conversation about the "good life" in a society characterized by ideological, religious and moral plurality?[143]

As we have noted in the previous chapters, social justice differs from retribution because it aims to ensure that all persons' rights are protected and not violated in the name of undoing the harms of history. In this case, social justice integrated both a distributive and corrective element to result in the "good life" suited for society.[144] Wolterstorff's *Justice: Rights and Wrongs* provides us with insights into rights, not as political quests but as something rooted in God. These rights are to be accorded to everyone by being a human being. He claims that rights should be understood as "normative social relationships"[145] upon which sociality is to be constructed – thus, where they enhance an environment where each person can make claims against another, particularly that it enhances dignity or well-being. While the perpetrators and beneficiaries of apartheid should be drawn into the discussions and forging of a national vision of justice, the focus should remain on the wronged rather than the wrongdoers. Boesak is of the opinion that this entails the nature of *ubuntu* and

> without reciprocal sacrificial acts on the part of the beneficiaries justice will never be done, restitution will not become a reality, dignity will not be restored and human contentment will not be secured. As it is, the sacrifice in our reconciliation process was, and remains, decidedly one-sided, coming from those who, even while embracing and honoring *ubuntu*, have already sacrificed too much.[146]

That is, those deprived of the life-enhancing goods have the prerogative to be granted access to these goods as a way of restoring the violent alteration to their moral condition by an unjust system. In this discussion of rights, previous wrongdoers and beneficiaries are drawn into active solidarity, that

---

143. Bradstock, "Unexamined Society," 42.

144. We borrow both the Aristotelian concept of justice as a social virtue expressed in a community or *koinonia* and the Old Testament concept of *shalom* as elements of social justice. Complementary but different, our emphasis is on the latter in which humans are seen as equals, regardless of their social categorizations. And only God's *shalom* can foster a true community of a just society.

145. Wolterstorff, *Justice: Rights and Wrongs*, 4.

146. Boesak, *Pharaohs on Both Sides*, 142.

is, not only talking of rights but ensuring right order.[147] In so doing, "justice requires that each of us should receive what we need to flourish as a human being; and we should in justice respect the obligation to see that others flourish similarly."[148]

The right-order theory of Wolterstorff and De Gruchy's vision of democracy is essential to consider within the narratives that give rise to them – Yahweh's self-revelation. This understanding implies that theology, even in the Namibian context, can be a relevant contributor to the understanding and shaping of the meaning of justice that would be aimed at relieving the suffering of many. According to Christian understanding, as informed by the Scriptures, justice aims to create an inclusive society. It seeks to level out the false social analysis provided by unjust structures of colonialism and apartheid systems. Ensuring society's right ordering must begin in a robust articulation of what is meant by justice, in line with society's sociohistorical, sociopolitical, and socioeconomic experiences. Vinay Samuel writes in this regard that,

> justice has a ubiquitous presence in the prophetic literature of the Old Testament with narratives of justice beginning with the experiences of God's people in Egypt. The power of the powerful dictates, creates and sustains social conditions of exclusion, marginalisation and oppression of poor peoples. The biblical message is that justice as the Rule of God and God's Law for humanity must shape social and political institutions and life. Ensuring universal human rights in the laws and constitutions of countries, ensuring protection and implementation of rights is a key agenda for action.[149]

"Boundary-markers"[150] need to be applied in context to create a "particular type of practice-based community."[151] Furthermore, De Gruchy warns that the attempts to prescribe Western solutions for African challenges both need "to

---

147. Wolterstorff, *Justice: Rights and Wrongs*, 36.
148. Sagovsky, *Christian Tradition*, 79.
149. Samuel and Sugden, "Good News to Poor."
150. Wolterstorff, *Justice: Rights and Wrongs*, 4.
151. MacIntyre, *Whose Justice?*, 389.

be considered seriously" and must "be treated with critical caution."[152] Such complex situations as those of post-apartheid, which have painful elements, not as historical discussions but as present experiential realities, require a critical integration of political thought, values, and procedures from the local context. Without such recognition, a democratic system with no contextual roots cannot provide sustainable solutions to the history of injustice. In this discussion, the role of theological discourse is not to import Judeo-Christian principles as the basis for society but as part of navigating from various social imaginaries regarding justice in a post-apartheid context from various angles.

Inasmuch as we have adopted a constitutional democracy and a legal system after the Dutch-Roman law, this is yet to translate in practical terms of undoing the effects of apartheid. While conceptualization is essential, it should be understood as an inclusive attempt to analyse social justice holistically. Injustice took away and affected people's economic aspects. At its social base was the aim to strip Black persons of their sense of being. This was expressed in the stripping them of their cultural roots and forced adaptation of the oppressor's language, religion, economics, religion, politics, metaphor, and culture. It also robbed them of participating in self-propagating activities. This makes social justice conceptualization seek to restore the humanity robbed by an inhumane system by allowing Namibians to deliberate and interpret justice within their social settings and bring those understandings into the public dialogue. De Gruchy raised these issues and the need to incorporate African traditional insights into political discourse and particularly in the pursuit of social justice. He cites the Kenyan church leaders' deliberations that recognised and argued that social harmony and addressing colonialism's effects would not be of any significance if approached using Western political systems while excluding African understandings. When Boesak advocates for Black Consciousness, the search has validity in this context, although we have critiqued its phenotypical emphasis. Nevertheless, his claim that *ubuntu* needs to be more robust in seeking justice rather than as a concept of a comfortable escape from accountability[153] is a worthwhile suggestion, as a way of integrating this African notion in the public discussion of justice.

152. De Gruchy, *Christianity and Democracy*, 188.
153. Boesak, *Tenderness of Conscience*, 189; Boesak, *Pharaohs on Both Sides*.

Both De Gruchy and Boesak remind us of the importance of the cultural context in which the discussion of justice is taking place. They also indicate to us to be wary of theological, philosophical, and political discourses that are far removed from the African public's understanding and experiences. Such distant and abstract concepts only create further alienation and postpone meaningful and productive notions, policies, and justice programmes. *Ubuntu* philosophy advocates for a specific but intricate form of society or community. This community's religious and political values are not separate entities but coexist within an integrated and complex whole. Technically, communities are in a covenant with one another as enshrined in the concept of "I am because we are." This relational humanism needs to be more elaborated for the modern post-apartheid context as an alternative to the wretched individualism of the apartheid and present neoliberal democratic systems.[154]

However, the integration of African values does not necessarily imply that this will result in justice. Therefore, a naive endorsement even of concepts, including *ubuntu,* would place us in danger of ignoring the human heart's realities. Boesak critiques the way *ubuntu* has been used in South Africa for political window dressing when he writes,

> nowhere is *ubuntu* employed to critique and challenge the reality that our society is arranged in such a way as to deliberately place some (the wealthy and privileged elite) at the top and others (the impoverished masses) at the bottom. Doing justice means that one not only recognizes that the other is human, but that the other is trampled upon, purposely put, and kept, at the bottom.[155]

Joseph Diescho critiques this naive embracing of *ubuntu* when he writes,

> ubuntu . . . collapses in the face of private property and the expansion of communities and even countries to encompass those with whom there are no blood relationships. Greed, avarice, selfishness, lack of a sense of social justice, heartlessness, cruelty and sheer indifference are the result.[156]

---

154. Boesak, *Pharaohs on Both Sides,* ch. 4.

155. Boesak, 143.

156. Diescho, "Concepts of Rights," 26.

The conceptualization of justice for post-apartheid Namibia aims to redress the wrongs of apartheid, and safeguard against post-independence injustices perpetrated by majority black leaders. Apartheid has its significant portion of blame for contributing to the oppression of many Namibians; but the demise of many would have ended had there been a human-centred vision of democracy and social justice in the post-independence structures. The post-apartheid context continues to suffer the effects of an unexamined society, making us a collective whole living the "unexamined" lives referred to by Socrates.[157]

Diescho, speaking of the general African condition and history of slavery, colonialism, and even apartheid, would have us believe that the conceptualization of justice is not just for the sake of the White Africans who perpetrated and benefited from the system. He argues that inasmuch as the former might have had most of the benefits, apartheid "would not have lasted to the extent it did without the acquiescence of millions of Black people who opportunistically chose to behave in particular ways to survive or gain materially from a system that was so horrendous towards their own members."[158] Working in such a system, if we are to achieve the common good, cannot be done without careful reflection on the systems and structures of democratic institutions.

Thus, what De Gruchy refers to as "critical solidarity" with democratic governments and movements also needs to be critical in its advocacy for social justice. Inasmuch as black Namibians have suffered injustice at the hands of White Namibians, the present injustice can only be effectively corrected by also recognising Black people's contribution to the deteriorating socio-economic conditions. The majority-Black government is invariably hurtful to post-apartheid citizens' progress with rampant corruption, maladministration, and power abuse. This is not an apology on behalf of the apartheid crimes against Black persons, but a plea that the justice system needs to be such that it protects people from the effects of apartheid and the doings of the post-independence government.

Namibia's challenge as a young democracy is to ground its systems to deliver practical and effective justice measures. The ideas informing its systems are deeply rooted in Western notions of democracy that exclude African value

---

157. Bradstock, "Unexamined Society," 41.
158. Diescho, "Concepts of Rights," 26.

systems. Diescho argues the problem is not in the systems of democracy, but insufficient culture for human concern, even *ubuntu*, has been used to purport atrocities against the governed.[159] The post-apartheid government's focus only on "White" offences ignores the fact that social injustice continues at this rate due to "their inability to empathise with the people they purport to govern, their levels of greed and avarice – to the extent that they fleece the resources of their poorer citizens, and their unfettered arrogance as regards power cannot be the bases upon which ubuntu can be sustained."[160] Without being self-critical, the conceptualization of justice may ignore gross injustice perpetrated by post-apartheid political players and the various socioeconomic structures they control and of which they are beneficiaries.

This implies that there are grave conflicts that require to be resolved to allow a smoother environment in which the system of democracy may serve as an instrument for delivering sustainable social justice. Without clearing these tensions and conceptual disengagement, the process of seeking justice would be tedious and exhausting, even unattainable. The people most affected by the effects of apartheid's injustice need a robust system and structure that articulates and leads to action: a system that would accord them the rights they deserve because they are human beings. This conceptualization of justice aspires to create a culture of reflection on how society is structured and how these structures that hinder human flourishing should be redressed.

Theological participation in conceptualization aims to affect human well-being – a notion that has its roots, not in human philosophy but the order of God's creation. God loves justice, but such justice is more than merely the abstract philosophical notion; instead, it is justice manifested in action. Wolterstorff writes that "God desires that each human being shall flourish, that each and every one shall experience what the Old Testament writers call shalom. Injustice is perforce the impairment of shalom. That is why God loves justice."[161] Theological participation in the public discourse of justice ensures that God's shalom is present in a society so acutely damaged by the history of injustice. It is not aimed at White Namibians because they are White; instead, it aims to address society's social realities. Theological intervention in public

---

159. Diescho, 26–27.

160. Diescho, 27.

161. Wolterstorff, *Justice: Rights and Wrongs*, 82.

discourse is an act of worship that needs to engage our minds with honesty and the needed analytical rigour in challenging policy and discourse that are not reflective of God's shalom.

Revolutionary ideas of aggression, as advocated by Marxist-socialist philosophy, which have also influenced most of the Liberation Theology, are inadequate to resolve the cycle of socioeconomic violence.[162] An ungodly order and system need an interjection that "opens up the future for justice, peace, and the restoration of the integrity of creation"[163] because "God desires the flourishing of each and every one of God's human creatures."[164] The reduced presence of theology in the Namibian public discourse deprives society, with its majority Christian faith, of hearing Christian input on vital issues of contemporary life.

We intend to achieve here an intentional dialogue of measures of justice rather than what justice is. In the search for effective measures to ensure life-enhancing goods, each society needs to understand its social structures. Social justice implies the search and application of "ideal justice on a social scale in a given society."[165] This means for a society to attain acceptable justice measures, it needs the space to understand and deliberate its structures and not merely replicate what is prescribed in and for another context. The creation of socially cohesive societies needs and requires social justice, that is, socioeconomic equity. Ideas of justice are universal, which means to affect just measures every nation borrows ideas from others. But the borrowing of concepts needs to be contextualized to affect the socioeconomic conditions of the local community.

Contextualization for the Namibian context needs to translate to more than adopting another system, method, or concept. This includes the political system and theological hermeneutics and praxis to adopt a unique and specific way to address the Namibian context. Part of this, especially from the theological perspective, is the need to find authentic theological language for addressing social injustice. First, while we should be concerned with injustice issues, the articulation should not alter theological themes

---

162. Bradley, *Liberating Black Theology*, 42–46.

163. De Gruchy, *Christianity and Democracy*, 232.

164. Wolterstorff, *Justice: Rights and Wrongs*, 82.

165. Diescho, "Concepts of Rights," 29.

and turn them into political ones for the sake of seeking public recognition or dialogue. For example, God liberates Israel from Egypt, which shows that God is a liberating God. However, taking that theme of liberation as a ground for socioeconomic liberation and participation in society makes theological contributions suspect and unauthentic.

Rather than scouting for populist themes, theology should become ready to give answers to painful, difficult situations and even desperate people who continue to be victims of injustice. Is there hope for these people? Is theology capable of participating at a level at which it can meet the challenges of socioeconomic injustice (lack of decent housing, access to quality healthcare and education, access to decent income and employment and corruption that hinders access to equal opportunity) resulting from the apartheid and post-apartheid structures? These issues cannot be responded to without a self-critical analysis of our theology, theological methods, and applications. How do we join in as Christians to articulate ourselves in the interest of the affected people, embracing a theological position inclusively aware of the issues contributing to socioeconomic inequality without decapitating the gospel simply to make a political contribution?

Contemporary Namibia requires theological undertakings that are self-critical and that do not resort to social doctrines for their own sake. There can be no easy answers to these issues, and we need to intentionally labour both in Scripture and our context. So, we may avoid what José Miguez-Bonino calls the "idealistic fallacy" that believes and argues that "since the gospel is the revelation of God's purpose for humankind, we can directly derive from the gospel a political ethics or, even worse, a political ideology and program."[166] Concern for social justice needs to be rooted in a profound evaluation of the various concepts that inform our society and careful application of theological themes and concepts. While others may seek conceptualization only for the sake of self-centred humanistic ideas, the theological reason for contextualising justice goes beyond mere "virtue or the good of society in themselves, but because" we are "concerned with the goodness of God."[167] Contextualization of social justice then requires we should address the systems that inform our society's concepts of justice. This means becoming active participants in the

---

166. Miguez-Bonino, *Toward Christian Political*, 31–32.
167. Sagovsky, *Christian Tradition*, 83.

creative undoing of unjust philosophies and structures as we engage in the public discourse of social justice.

Contextualization for the Namibian context requires more than adaption and adjustment of concepts of social justice. Instead, it needs theologians to exercise critical interrogation and questioning of their own beliefs and society in search of "the creative doing of justice by God."[168] Without advocating for a neo-Constantinian view, but in the belief that God is sovereign over all spheres of human life, a robust theological contribution regarding social justice in Namibia is required. Contextualization requires engaging in deliberations that can liberate human persons to be as God intended them. Thus, it should allow the manifestation of humans' dignity as "creatures made in the image of God, for whom freedom is constitutive of their God-given humanity."[169] This is the starting point of Christian participation in social justice that humans are in the covenant and analogically related to God. As such, injustice is a violation of God's covenantal relationship with and between humans.[170]

Such contextualization does not seek to perceive people through their phenotypes but as God's image-bearers who have gone astray from their covenantal requirements. Contextualization is about being authentic and present in seeking answers and addressing structures and practices of injustice. In public issues, theological participation is the participation of bearing witness, not to impose but to be part of the solution among various possibilities. Race-based analysis of social justice, for example, only creates further tension, suspicion, and hate among Black and White Namibians (see § 5.4), thus the need to participate in the public dialogue to ease these tensions as we "work to see that all people have their needs met."[171] Although the talk of justice implies political participation, it is political participation emanating from our understanding of God's covenant through Jesus Christ, and within that context advocate for the rights of each person[172] to "receive what we need to flourish as a human being."[173]

---

168. Sagovsky, 80.

169. Sagovsky, 80.

170. De Gruchy, *Christianity and Democracy*, 239.

171. Sagovsky, *Christian Tradition*, 79.

172. Barth, *God Here and Now*, 108; Wolterstorff, *Justice: Rights and Wrongs*.

173. Sagovsky, *Christian Tradition*, 79.

As discussed in the reconciliation section, contextualization has not taken deep roots in the Namibian public, especially from a theological perspective. Theological participation has not had a meaningful contribution or role in the shaping of national policies and discussions. Thus, it has not taken up the challenge of seeking to articulate justice and human dignity in the post-apartheid context to a level of provoking public dialogue. However, to do this, we must address the issues that impede this participation; (1) The church's historical relationship with politics has compromized the role of theology which now needs to gain public trust. This trust must and needs to emanate from a place of honesty in thought and purpose to avoid naive politicization of Christian participation; (2) More academic rigour is needed to engage the conceptions that influence and determine public dialogue and policies on socioeconomic issues, and (3) The absence of meaningful Christian action that can be drawn into providing a vision of democracy to redress structures and systems that sustain the continuation of social injustice.

The task of theology during the liberation struggle might have been instrumentally relevant for the time; however, we can no longer dwell on that, for the present requires present answers. No theological notions of social justice simply collected, dusted off and remodelled from the archives of history can serve as solutions to post-apartheid problems. While on one end, we are battling with the horrible history of the church in Namibia, which has led to the total withdrawal from the public scene, on the other, we are required to be present witnesses of God both in word and deed. Complete withdrawal cannot be the option, but the church, as in Botha's view, needs to rediscover itself in a contextually relevant manner to offer the proper direction(s) needed to address the socioeconomic inequality and injustice plaguing our society.

This contextual discourse is yet to happen for the Namibian context to affect public conceptions of justice. What this would mean must emanate from the various conceptions that are thoughtful, engaging, and relevant to the Namibian context. Such discourse would provide arguments for classifying the needs of society and making deliberate efforts to address them. As a starting point for redressing social injustice, the most basic ones like food, shelter, healthcare, and education and decent employment should be brought into public discourse. When many speak of social injustice and apartheid, the whole blame is placed on White citizens; what should this discussion look like? How do we bring justice into discourse in ways that are appropriate for the Namibian context?

As mentioned before, the apartheid system did not only alter the political and economic landscape; it also affected the psyche of communities. The system stripped communities of their rightful social statuses and degraded them to subhuman levels within the superstructure of White supremacy. It was a violation of people's natural rights. The search for justice is part of handing society the power for self-determination and reclaiming their violated humanity. We have spoken of social justice, but the focus has so far been on socioeconomic issues. This type of narrow understanding fails to understand how much the apartheid system disempowered people.

Moreover, by focusing on socioeconomic issues, communities do not tap into their capabilities to shape their progress through their locally found social arrangements and context. Whatever are the measures engaged to advocate for justice, for example, De Gruchy's argument for a democratic vision or Boesak's restitution or any other argument, needs to be from informed self-reflection. Thus, the discussions and measures of justice need to represent the people's will and not just the state's dictates.

To redress the complex effects of apartheid, clear and robust efforts are needed to create functional and effective systems. In chapter 2, we outlined the challenges facing Namibia in determining measures of justice. We began by asking whether universal notions of justice can hinder the effective addressing of injustice. While conceptualization and contextualization are essential, it is impossible to imagine a society that does not learn from other societies. What is missing is not the lack of theories but robust applications of these policies and programmes. This shortcoming can be linked to the contextual divorce of such policies and programmes. The apartheid system's effects are ever-present, but these effects will continue to be without functional and well-ordered systems. Added to well-orderedness is an ethical demand, as Boesak puts it, "what is needed is *moral courage* to set the right priorities and make the right choices."[174]

Although it requires functional political systems, the quest for a more just society needs a moral vision. The liberation struggle has brought the desired independence from a racial system and ushered in a democratic system. This

---

174. Boesak, *Tenderness of Conscience*, 62.

state of independence, however, requires a collective input to create more just structures and systems. Theological participation in the formation of this post-conflict society is crucial. The shortage of theological participation as a way of engaging God's world deprives us of being conduits of God's *shalom*. Subjecting the Christian faith only to private aspects of life renders the whole exercise of no use for everyday life. To witness is to be present in every area of life that matters the most and help in whatever way possible to ensure that life-enhancing goods are accessible to all people.

Theological participation is not merely for discussion purposes but also for advocating for justice that the most disadvantaged society members are not receiving due to failed structural settings. The search for justice is not merely a political entity; we have established, so far, that God requires the doing of justice. The absence of justice implies the absence of right human relationships with creation. As Christopher Sugden alludes to this when he says that "if justice is not done, all the foundations of the earth are shaken."[175] Theological commitment to justice, therefore, demands beyond mere talks of social reconciliation. Do the current arrangements represent God's justice? Do the current arrangements of social justice represent the needs of most people? Do the current arrangements provide robust measures of doing justice to ensure the dignity of God's image-bearers? These questions should be at the heart of a contextualized conceptualization of justice – God, who is righteous, demands that we are candid and incisive in this quest.

5.5 Social Justice as Praxis

Considering the relative nature of social justice and to genuinely reflect the values we seek to embrace in the post-apartheid social context, there must be some outward action that can bear witness to this social order. Isaak, alludes to this that

> the status of religion and society in relation to God demands concreteness, since God's dealing with humanity is concrete . . . by implication, such concreteness maintains that faith and socio-political-economic action are bound together. *Ora et labora*, that

---

175. Sugden, "Identity and Transformation," 138.

is religious reflection (prayer) corresponds to effective societal engagement and liberational activism.[176]

Isaak speaks of religion (vaguely). We are particularly concerned with Christian participation in society as an expression of God's kingdom and witness to God's will and social order. The incarnation not only carries concreteness but provides us with a theoretical framework. Central to the mission of Christ's coming was to take away the sins of the world. Since social injustice is an effect of sin, social justice (in forms of meeting certain needs) cannot produce the best imaginable social harmony, but it provides "the best possible harmony within the conditions created by [the] sin [of apartheid]."[177] Thus, simply giving a theoretical affirmation of human dignity is not adequate. We need certain practical reforms – "material or social goods, conditions, opportunities and roles"[178] whereby human dignity is affirmed.

Boesak does not present us with a clear conception of justice. He uses various approaches as the situation demands. Chapter 4 presents an exploration of Boesak's public participation using Black Liberation Theology and reconciliation paradigms to advocate for social justice. While he presents us with several practical issues that need to be done, holding on to such an open view of social justice carries some benefits. First, it indicates sensitivity to a fragile context. Second, it opens a wider notion of social justice than limiting ourselves to limited definitions. Third, the fact that we are addressing a specific context should have us engage social justice in response to the various human experiences.

Commitment to "the good" and "the right" somehow requires a wide-ranging conceptual commitment that would allow us to be responsive to various manifestations of injustice. We see this conceptual commitment in Boesak's broad-based participation to redress injustice. This does not negate precision of thought; it may help in providing more accurate responses to the teleological questions and strengthen and authenticate the notion of Christian praxis.

The fact that we do not live in a social vacuum, requires some well-defined notions of what is the highest good to which we can orientate the right. Such

---

176. Isaak, *Religion and Society*, 1.

177. Lebacqz, *Six Theories of Justice*, 86.

178. Sher, *Desert*, 21.

development of notions provides the necessary material to address human needs in more meaningful ways to allow authentic human flourishing. For the Namibian context, creating systems of democracy, enabling social environments, opening to the past, forgiveness, and reconciliation are helpful aspects for creating a thriving social order; however, they do not address the question, "what does a human being need to experience life in its fullness?"

A fuller understanding of social justice must require addressing the external or visible needs that are manifestations of injustice. To be truly engaged in reflective theological praxis is to be engaged in "a never-ending spiral of action and reflection."[179] Contextualized conceptualization of social justice is not just mere intellectual reflection but a commitment to responsible action; action that would satisfy some standard of what is deemed a decent life in Namibia.

What kinds of needs would provide the best possible harmony and social conditions to live lives of dignity? The meeting of need should focus on the major issues mentioned in § 1.3.2 as key issues of public dialogue. While distributive measures might be thought complex in nature, they provide better alternatives to see a tangible presence of social justice. This might be interpreted as welfarism but if welfare could be an important entry level to self-ownership, then this becomes a welcome starting point. It would provide equal access to primary goods for communities that will never be able to achieve such goods without some strategic intervention. When access to basic goods is levelled, then can there be structures and systems that allow for equality of opportunity. Such would be a more adequate embodiment of social justice because it involves notions and practices of comparative allotment.

This allotment is not to replace long-term and bigger issues which require legislative processes. Their delay should not delay the basic life-enhancing goods needed to experience dignified living conditions. The list of goods, among others, should include decent housing, employment, economically viable skill development, and access to quality healthcare and education. Advocating for these needs which we believe provide the basis for decent and full humanity, "is indeed to affirm a Christian priority, for which Christian theological reasons can be given from the very depth of the tradition."[180]

---

179. Bevans, *Essays in Contextual Theology*, 18.
180. Sagovsky, *Christian Tradition*, 183.

Addressing these issues still leaves us with profound political questions of methods, strategies, and means by which these needs are to be met.

Sagovsky tells us that the task and process of how needs are to be met creates both among Christians and non-Christians "animated disagreement."[181] What we suggest with the meetings of these needs is the creation of systems and structures that would allow the poor to function; or to put as Sagovsky says, meeting "those needs which enable a person to be a fully participating member of society."[182] The anthropological assumption of specifying these life-enhancing goods or needs stems from the fact that humans are created with dignity. Meeting these needs is part of reaffirming God's created order and makes this a theological discourse with sociopolitical undertones.

The meeting of needs must be considered as the entry level to experience liberty and fullness of life. It is the tangible expression of God's *shalom* in the human society. Isaiah Berlin argues that true liberty is expressed in having the basic needs required to function. He writes that,

> it is important to discriminate between liberty and the conditions of its exercise. If a man is too poor or too ignorant or too feeble to make use of his legal rights, the liberty that these rights confer upon him is nothing to him, but it is not thereby annihilated. The obligation to promote education, health, justice, to raise standards of living, to provide opportunity for the growth of the arts and the sciences, to prevent reactionary political or social or legal policies or arbitrary inequalities, is not made less stringent because it is not necessarily directed to the promotion of liberty itself, but to conditions in which alone its possession is of value. . . .[183]

The concept and policy of affirmative action (assuming it is well thought-out, planned, contextualized, and executed), with all its challenges, may become a starting point to work towards tangible social justice. A complex social and political dialogue is necessary, and choices (even difficult ones) must be made to counter the socioeconomic structures and systems that

---

181. Sagovsky, 183.
182. Sagovsky, 184.
183. Berlin, *Liberty*, 45.

protect historically acquired privilege. This would provide an entry "to create conditions in which those who lack them will be provided with opportunity to exercise"[184] their full liberty. By starting, for example, with basic needs and the ability to choose what to eat, where to live and where to school, this would then open doors for full expression and participation in society. At present, even though persons from disadvantaged communities have freedoms which they can use, "they are not identical with the conditions indispensable for their utility."[185]

While we commend the various programmes of the state, these need to become intentional towards fulfilling human needs. Simply creating social and political spaces which emphasize human rights and human dignity without creating social and economic conditions that would enhance living is of no value to the affected. True liberty is expanded or enhanced in the availing of material needs – for it is the noticeable form of answering the question – "what does it mean to be human in post-apartheid Namibia?" Being human implies being able to enjoy access to food, water, home, education, health, and decent employment. It is a cruel choice to provide social conditions without actual conditions of freedom; the lived experiences dictate for the presence of the latter conditions.

A redistributive course of action, considered among other choices, embraces the concept of *shalom* in its holistic sense. The idea of critical political participation and commitment becomes central to theological dialogue in the public sphere. Witnessing to the reality of the risen Christ in the context of inhumane conditions of injustice implies, according to Sagovsky,[186] creating space for political action in view of God's "eschatological action."[187]

While meeting needs should be central to the dialogue of social justice, we must admit that this is no simple task. Like Berlin, we admit that "the right

---

184. Berlin, 46.

185. Berlin, 46.

186. Sagovsky, *Christian Tradition*, 193.

187. The eschatological action points to how God will heal the troubles of those who have suffered immensely because of their faith in Christ, and John writes that "they will hunger no more, and thirst no more; the sun will not strike them, nor any scorching heat; for the Lamb at the center of the throne will be their shepherd, and he will guide them to springs of the water of life, and God will wipe away every tear from their eyes" (Rev 7: 16–17). This future hope of healing becomes the transcendent hope through which we engage Christian theology to witness to the values of Scripture and the gospel.

policy cannot be arrived at in a mechanical or deductive fashion: there are no hard-and-fast rules to guide us; conditions are often unclear, and principles incapable of being fully analysed or articulated."[188] A contextualized dialogue, in this case, takes these complexities into consideration without avoiding the pressing socioeconomic issues. A contextualized conceptualization of social justice ought to be open to thicker descriptions of lived experiences; it should be aware of the social, political and economic complexities but without the pretence to provide "an all-embracing coherent vision."[189] Instead, it advocates for the rallying of various and alternative visions and notions of justice to resolve the different needs.

This project is not an exercise in casuistry wrapped in theological arguments or imaginations. Berlin points to the futility in such thinking when he says,

> the notion that there must exist final objective answers to normative questions, truths that can be demonstrated or directly intuited, that it is in principle possible to discover a harmonious pattern in which all values are reconciled, and that it is towards this unique goal that we must make; that we can uncover some single central principle that shapes this vision, a principle which, once found, will govern our lives – this ancient and almost universal belief, on which so much traditional thought and action and philosophical doctrine rests, seems to me invalid, and at times to have led (and still to lead) to absurdities in theory and barbarous consequences in practice.[190]

Advocating for praxis is a way of putting the symbolic language of reconciliation and justice into concrete forms. Advocating for conceptual frameworks that can capture the Namibian context, may provide the platform of critical participation in the public sphere. What are the symbols used in the Namibian context that represent a just order? Reconciliation continues to be one key concept. In it is the notion of community, fellowship, and coexistence. However, this needs to be concretized by means of mutual sharing

188. Berlin, *Liberty*, 47.

189. Berlin, 47.

190. Berlin, 47–48.

of burdens. Sagovsky uses the concept of *koinonia* to advocate for the kind of life expected within the church community.[191] We would like to think that this idea is deeply rooted in the creation covenant. That is, being created in the image of God expresses a covenantal reality about humans in which they are not only expected to co-exist but are also expected to participate in ways that embody and reflect the dignity bestowed upon each human being.

To speak of reconciliation and nation building without concrete measures of adding dignity to the living conditions of those affected by injustice, enhances a life of injustice. Such government policies and programmes cannot be said to have the interests of the affected at heart for they trample on the virtue of justice which holds communities together. The need to embrace symbols associated with social justice is a task of theology that seeks authentic faith in the world.[192] These symbols are not merely to communicate abstracts but to seek their concrete expression in the human society.

For example, the biblical anthropology we employed, especially of humans as God's image-bearers, embraces a concrete manifestation of God's order. God created humans and entered in a covenant relationship with them, and in return they were to be in covenant with one another. God's provision for human basic needs expresses an eternal principle. Apartheid violated this eternal principle and God's covenant by creating structures and systems which placed millions of men and women in positions where they could not have access to the goods God had provided. This included access to the goods created by humans as they employ God's intellectual and manufacturing gifts to bring about life-enhancing goods.

A truly free society is the kind in which the poor, weak, and vulnerable are not sacrificed to the arbitrary forces of the market, but where there is a deliberate and just distribution of goods. Thus, freedom "must always be 'relegated' to justice, community and equality."[193] To love God and neighbour requires supporting and promoting practices that enable political and economic resemblances of Christian love. Ensuring structures and practices that will allow for my neighbour to *eat* (as a metaphor for access to life enhancing goods) is the best approximation to express God's love and community. Social

---

191. Sagovsky, *Christian Tradition*, 10.

192. Migliore, *Faith Seeking Understanding*, 26.

193. Lebacqz, *Six Theories of Justice*, 87.

justice in which needs are not only imagined but met, in response to sinful dehumanising conditions, is the best rational goal. Lebacqz further argues that "the rule of equality includes both concerns for process (e.g., impartiality in the calculation of needs) and also for equality as a substantive goal (e.g., equal civil rights)."[194]

Boesak's social conflict because of disproportional access to socioeconomic power implies that such conflict cannot be addressed if barriers to access life-enhancing goods remains. The role of the state is to use measures that would intervene to ease the disproportionality inflicted upon the citizens through a violent history. How this intervention should be remains an area of conflict. Coercing former perpetrators and beneficiaries has been discouraged and dismissed. Could there be rational justifications, supposing we live in a rational society, for the state to use coercion "in the service of a rationally acceptable social end, and condemn its use when it is in the service of momentary passions"?[195]

Creating structures and systems that would allow equitable access to life-enhancing goods is a way of addressing the social conflict resulting from apartheid. If the social conflict will not go away by means of dialogue, then perhaps a justifiable measure of coercion may be needed. In this case then, to use Niebuhr's argument, "a social conflict which aims at greater equality has a moral justification which must be denied to efforts which aim at the perpetuation of [dehumanising] privilege."[196] The state as God's vicegerent would act out of moral justification. For whatever other ideals and virtues we seek to promote, for example, peace, community, and liberty, cannot be attained in an unequal, unjust, and dehumanising environment.

The kind of political power needed to redress social injustice because of apartheid must advocate for equality of access to life-enhancing goods. This is the symbol of true peace and reconciliation. Even though equality cannot be fully attained, it will go a long way to eliminate the levels of inequalities of power and privilege. While Christians should seek peaceful ways to resolve conflict, we cannot assume that all forms of coercion by the state represent oppression and injustice. If Christians are called to be peacemakers, then

---

194. Lebacqz, 87.

195. Niebuhr, *Moral Man*, 234.

196. Niebuhr, 234.

the meeting of human needs, currently hindered by unjust protection of class and privilege, must be addressed as a matter of urgency. And rational measures of coercion may be an option among others. Niebuhr continues to argue this view that,

> the rational use of coercion is a possible achievement which may save society. It is of course dangerous to accept the principle, that the end justifies the means which are used in its attainment. The danger arises from the ease with which any social group, engaged in social conflict, may justify itself by professing to be fighting for freedom and equality. Society has no absolutely impartial tribunal which could judge such claims. Nevertheless it is the business of reason, though always involved in prejudice and subject to partial perspectives, to aspire to the impartiality by which such claims and pretensions could be analysed and assessed. Though it will fail in instances where disputes are involved and complex, it is not impossible to discover at least the most obvious cases of social disinheritance. Wherever a social group is obviously defrauded of its rights, it is natural to give the assertion of its rights a special measure of moral approbation. Indeed this is what is invariably and instinctively done by any portion of the human community which has achieved a degree of impartiality.[197]

Boesak uses similar arguments in the land debate, and this is also the general stance of many Namibians who are engaged in the land question.[198] However, that is the long-term issue of creating equal access to land, its use, and restoring the cultural and social values that come with owning land. The fortunes of many Black Namibians have not changed and this creates an unstable and dangerous social environment. What may seem reconciliation at present may simply be "deferred revenge"; especially amidst deteriorating social-economic circumstances escalated by the current global pandemic of the COVID-19 disease.

---

197. Niebuhr, 235.
198. Hunter, *Who Should Own Land?*

Dialogue is good and important to penetrate false social biases and barriers, but to forge a true community of equals would require more than just dialogue. Social justice requires concrete action. Sagovsky argues that to form a true community or *koinonia* requires more than dialogue and that there cannot be a community in its truest sense without "common sharing" which is the symbol to concretize community, fellowship, society, and nationhood.[199] This common sharing is emancipatory participation in what would be an experience of life in its fullness. It is the kind of common sharing that requires "authentic human action" which is "at the deepest level, the free exercise of a free will, and the freeing of the human will to act in accord with the will of the Creator is perhaps the deepest meaning of liberation which participation in the Eucharist sacramentally enacts."[200] Sagovsky's conclusion links this reality of a Christian search for functional ways of justice and participation to God's miraculous working in the human community. He writes that

> freedom of the will, properly exercised in action for justice cannot be understood without a rich account of the activity of the Holy Spirit. It is in the power of the Spirit that the believer and the Church exercises that responsible judgment which transcends wooden adherence to the letter of the law. It is the Spirit that guides the exercise of this liberty in creative action for justice, which is to say in accord with the mind of Christ . . . Action for justice by Christians in the public domain is nothing other than the public enactment of the prayer which sums up this whole dynamic of the Eucharist: "Thy Kingdom come."[201]

Embracing a vision of human dignity, liberty, and justice creates a new but dynamic way of relooking at society for humanized forms of participation. Theological participation then becomes a concrete form of witnessing to the reality of God's kingdom on earth. The post-apartheid context can then be engaged to pursue the values of liberty, reconciliation, and peace when we adequately address the obstacles that hinder the full expression of being human. It is a vision which seeks to attain a common membership to

---

199. Sagovsky, *Christian Tradition*, 10.

200. Sagovsky, 214.

201. Sagovsky, 214–15.

participate in the values we hold dear as a society. At a theological level, we need the kind of astuteness in which our theological convictions are not just words to the church but a bearing of public witness.

5.6 Theology As Public Witness

The theological quest for justice should be indiscriminate. It must demand it from all persons (Black and White) with social, economic, and political power who create and impose injustice. The pharaohs are on both sides and to this Boesak calls Christians to reclaim a new zeal of reengaging the present structure. He argues that,

> reclaiming the prophetic tradition of the church would mean discerning the *kairos* moment, repenting of our silence, our complicity, and our cowardice; turning anew to the God of our liberation, embracing once again the hopes of our people in our preaching and in our public witness. We must repent of our sentimentalized politics and recognize that a black face in high office is no automatic guarantee of justice for the poor and oppressed. We must understand much better than we do the seductive power of power and that it is not so much a question of *who* is in power but what they do with their power when in power. Suspending, even better, *abandoning* the credulous politics so harmful to the people and our witness, we must examine whose interests they serve while in power[202] (italics in original).

Boesak approaches injustice with God's impartiality because the continued socioeconomic injustice is an affront to God and the rights of God's image-bearer. This theological participation in the public is a gospel demand and reflective of "God's eschatological justice."[203] Boesak uses this eschatological approach in his work *Comfort and Protest,* in which theological reflection refuses to allow injustice to continue because silence in the face of such injustice denies our witness and God's lordship over creation. Robust, organized, and engaging theology of justice is reflective of being part of God's kingdom.

---

202. Boesak, *Pharaohs on Both Sides*, 59–60.
203. Sagovsky, *Christian Tradition*, 67.

Therefore, to borrow Sugden's development language, we seek to understand "where in the world the Kingdom is working and link our involvement to what God has said he is already doing."[204]

Such a search implies embracing an understanding of justice in which needs are met as an entry-level to restoring people to what God has intended them to be. These needs involve every aspect of their rights, which were taken away from them by violence. For example, the land question needs to be discussed within this context, not as an economic entity but as a restoration of their rights and social identity.[205] Thus, theological participation in the public discourse of social justice needs to defend people's rights and call to account the perpetrators and beneficiaries. Realising that a grave evil has been perpetrated against communities in Namibia should result in more than social reconciliation; it requires tangible measures of justice in which needs are met. Without the authentic confrontation of the absence of life-enhancing goods, there can be no genuine *shalom*. Sagovsky reminds us that,

> it is in accord with the justice of God that Christians should work to see that all people have their needs met; justice requires that each of us should receive what we need to flourish as a human being; and we should in justice respect the obligation to see that others flourish similarly.[206]

Other than advocating for the meeting of needs is theological participation towards functional systems of law. In this system, rights can be protected, as Wolterstorff suggests in *Justice: Rights and Wrongs*, but the system requires a democratic vision to ensure these rights are accorded to all people. A functional and effective law system is required, and Christians should consider democratic systems as God's blessing and stand with them in critical solidarity. This requires theological undertakings that are aware of the system of governance's political framework and advocate that it upholds some fundamental principles that need to be upheld to create an environment in which justice can be served. The problem of continued injustice is not only due to the apartheid system; working within a legal framework is essential

---

204. Sugden, "Identity and Transformation," 138.

205. Boesak and DeYoung, *Radical Reconciliation*, 66–68; Hunter, "Who Should Own Land?," 4; Ntsebeza and Hall, "Introduction," 8.

206. Sagovsky, *Christian Tradition*, 79.

to be "able to hold accountable those who infringe the standards of conduct laid down"[207] in the system of democracy.

Thus, theology needs allies in critical solidarity with civil society to hold these systems accountable for delivering justice. Forster calls on theologians to be equipped to engage the public,[208] citing De Gruchy as an example of informed Christian scholarship that challenges public conceptions.[209] In *The Nature of Public Theology*, Forster emphasises the need to know how to engage the public's various aspects besides the church and faith-based organizations.[210] As mentioned in previous sections, the need to dialogue and create a meaningful theology would require understanding and speaking the language required for engaging the public. Forster argues that if "we claim to believe that God is active in all of life, in all spheres of society . . . we need to talk about theological truths with people in nonchurch contexts . . . In other words, we need to find ways of 'translating' God's presence and putting it into public language, that is language used by . . . politicians."[211] In a sense, this is an activist role in addressing systems and structures that abuse less advantaged groups and does not ensure the delivery of justice to redress the effects of apartheid.

Christian scholarship that can engage public conceptions is to be understood as an exercise of our gifts in God's honour and our duty as citizens. Here the theological engagement required for addressing issues of injustice is an extension of grace and hope. It is not necessarily participation driven by political ideology, but because God uses our gifts and participation to change societies. Seeking and participating in a meaningful discourse of justice is an expression of an inward experience of God's grace imparted by the Holy Spirit as we become instruments of transformation in return.[212] As Forster notes, it is essential that we develop our theological gifts in the exercise of "linking faith and life, of having meaningful exchanges between theology and other academic disciplines, and of being aware of the need for critical reflection

---

207. MacIntyre, *Whose Justice?*, 241.
208. Forster, "Social Identity, Social Media."
209. Forster, "Politics of Forgiveness?"
210. Forster, "Nature of Public Theology."
211. Forster, 17.
212. Sugden, "Identity and Transformation," 140.

on the historical and contextual factors"[213] that affect the public playing out on matters of social justice for post-apartheid Namibia.

The critique of the church for being dormant in the post-apartheid context suggests withdrawal and a failure to be part of the needed societal transformation. Theology is not only for addressing the theological questions and challenges that arise in the seminary or academy. From what we have noticed from various theologians, theology can influence public thinking and decisions that affect people's lives.[214] This approach does not impose ideas and programmes but seeks to understand and represent local understanding and to respect their self-definition. Theological participation in the present ongoing struggle against the effects of apartheid and those by the post-apartheid systems needs models of sound theological practise for engaging public issues.[215]

Sound models of theological practice engage the "broad social, political, economic and historical concerns"[216] without losing their essence as theology. They continue to speak to these various publics as Christian witnesses. This is a witness carried out to advocate for contextually relevant systems and policies to redress the effects of injustice – not because we seek to make Christianity the preferred public religion "but to witness to values that we believe are important for the common good."[217] Part of that witnessing ought to advocate for a reconciled and just community. Theological participation should be at the forefront as part of Christian ministry and should participate in the expression of God's kingdom and *shalom* in the Namibian public sphere.

There is no easy way out of the situation, and it is not going to change by itself without wilful and intentional theological engagement. The gospel is shaped and takes place in social contexts; only by participating in these social contexts can we help correct the visions of social justice that shape the Namibian society. Failure to participate in these acts of transformation may be denoting denial of injustice and the absence of functional and effective measures of addressing it. The level of social concern is not in question. In that area, many theologians are participating in their various groups. It is the

---

213. Forster, "Politics of Forgiveness?," 19.

214. Forster, "Nature of Public Theology"; De Gruchy, *Christianity and Democracy*; Smit, "Does It Matter?"

215. De Gruchy, "Public Theology as Christian Witness," 28.

216. Forster, "Nature of Public Theology," 19.

217. De Gruchy, "Public Theology as Christian Witness," 31.

absence of public social concern that can affect the public dialogue, where theology and the church at large are failing to be the moral guide of the direction taken in matters of social justice. The concept of humans being God's image-bearers implies working towards a universal manifestation of God's glory by participating in activities that manifest God's sabbath through the creation of a more just society.[218]

The labour for spiritual salvation should not be reduced to the afterlife only, for such understanding of theology "loses its power to renew life and change the world, and its flame is quenched; it dies away into no more than a gnostic yearning for redemption from this world's vale of tears."[219] Theological participation in addressing human spiritual needs is not divorced from striving to provide care in the natural order and ensuring the attainment of goods required to live a life of dignity. Suppose our hope, as Moltmann argues, is for the kingdom of God; In that case, the task of theology in the Namibian public sphere needs to live up to that hope by searching and contributing to the public conceptualization and praxis of social justice. The eschatological vision of this kingdom is not only for the future but affects the present life in which humans experience injustice wrought upon them by the sinfulness of others, inadequate political systems, and impaired social vision for justice. In this regard, *Comfort and Protest* by Boesak offers a new reading of eschatological texts in the face of present human suffering.

Finally, demanding justice and a just system are not additional tasks to theology but part of its foundations.[220] This is the theology that should confront false if not precarious notions of national reconciliation and peace, determined to ensure that the talks regarding these concepts render justice with tangible outcomes.[221] As Alex Boraine argues, serious "moral, psychological and political arguments"[222] need to be addressed, as the past cannot entirely be erased by "let bygones be bygones" when its effects are ever-present and actual.

---

218. Moltmann, *Coming of God*, xi.

219. Moltmann, xv.

220. Boesak, *Farewell to Innocence* (1976), 9–14.

221. Boesak and DeYoung, *Radical Reconciliation*; De Gruchy, *Reconciliation: Restoring Justice*.

222. Boraine, "Retributive Justice," 39.

5.7 Summary

This chapter explored the context of post-apartheid Namibia regarding the public conception of social justice. It explored the existing public conceptions and indicates there are no well-defined systems and directives regarding the course for social justice. The concept is used in various contexts; and it is challenging to locate the ideas that inform these conceptions. In many cases, the meaning of justice is left for interpretation to those with political power. The post-apartheid context has not adequately addressed justice, while robust and intentional discourse is being avoided for political and social peace (see § 5.2). The concept of reconciliation is being used to cover serious talks about justice, yet there are BEE programmes in place that disadvantage White communities. The reconciliation concept is assumed as an official government position, but there is no evidence of this at the policy level (see § 5.3.1). Theological input in the discussion of justice has long left the public scene. Many secular researchers criticize the church for being dormant in the face of post-apartheid structures that enhance injustice. Yet there is also hope that the church and theological participation in the public could positively impact society's socioeconomic conditions. In this chapter, we have used Boesak, De Gruchy, and Sagovsky's works to demonstrate how theology could participate in the public discourse of justice. This requires advocating and providing for critical solidarity with government systems that can create the platforms and structures to administer justice (see § 5.4.1 and § 5.5). Theological dialogue about justice is part of fulfilling God's eschatological justice. Being engaged in the construction of the meanings and notions of justice serves towards ensuring the restoration of the dignity of those affected by injustice. This chapter concluded that theology must demand justice; what this justice should look like must first address the goods required to live a life of dignity. Added to this is bringing the affected into the dialogue, acknowledging them as thinking beings, and recognising their voices in the conceptualization and contextualization of justice. Beyond the economic outcomes, people have capabilities that need to be recognized and affirmed. Justice requires allowing the affected to participate in the creation of memory and positive social imaginaries through which future generations may conceive their roles in a more fully human society. Surely, this is what God would require of us.

CHAPTER 6

Towards Some Tentative Conclusions

6.1 Introduction

The research explored the need for a contextualized conceptualization of social justice in dialogue with Allan Boesak. This last chapter summarises this dialogue and gives recommendations for future Namibian theological dialogue and engagement. It is an important chapter because it summarises the entire research and what the researcher contributes to the body of theological knowledge.

6.2 Research Summary

The first chapter established that this study would explore, from a theological perspective (see § 1.1), the need for a contextualized conceptualization of the concept of justice in post-apartheid Namibia (§ 1.1.1), in conversation with Allan Boesak. We engaged a contextual theological critical engagement as our research method (§ 1.10). With this method, we examined the effects of social injustice from the apartheid era, combined with the post-independence government corruption. The conversation with Boesak seeks for an authentic Namibian theological participation (which is presently inadequate); participation that engages the prevailing public notions of justice (§ 1.7), because injustice is an affront to the person of God and God's image-bearers. Such participation seeks to find a robust, organized, and engaging theology that can articulate itself as God's witness in public matters that affect the quality of life and living standards (§ 2.4). We have assumed in this opening chapter the inadequacy of such theological participation and that the prevailing public tools for critique are still scattered and hindered by administrative ineffectiveness. This inadequate theological participation is further weakened by a history of uncritical solidarity, either with the apartheid system or in support of the liberation movement. To address present notions of social justice, we proposed this as our primary question:

6.2.1 What Can a Contextualized Engagement with Allan Boesak's Theologies of Justice Provide for a Theology of Justice in the Post-Apartheid Namibian Context?

We set out to explore the concept of social justice (both secular and theological) in the Namibian public sphere. God's nature (righteous, see § 3.2.4), we argued, motivates theological grounds for participation in the conceptualization of justice because all these decisions have existential effects on people's lives. We also said God's self-revelation in human affairs invariably shows God's concern for the created order (emphasis on humans as God's image-bearers, see § 5.4.1. and § 5.4.2). In that regard, Christians ought to show distress for the effects of apartheid upon communities that were victims under such a brutal system. We engaged Allan Boesak as an example of a Black theologian who has been actively involved in the fight against apartheid. Dialoguing with him, we seek to learn valuable lessons in the Namibian search for public participation in the conceptualization of justice. If God through Christ has manifested sharing in human affairs as part of redeeming creation, theological participation becomes part of God's redemptive work and Christian witness. This participation is to be understood as a continuation of God's kingdom and a trajectory to reconcile all creation in Christ through human participants as bringers of God's *shalom*. We contended throughout the research that for a society to attain justice, a contextualized conceptualization of concepts of justice is required. This question is explored in conjunction with the following secondary questions:

6.2.2 How Just or Unjust is the Namibian Society in Its Current Post-Apartheid State?

This question explored how the post-apartheid Namibian society is just or unjust and examines the local understandings and expressions of justice (see § 2.2). It gave a brief mapping of the concept of justice and how Greek conceptions have influenced many modern renditions – including the apartheid system's idea of justice (§ 1.1). It outlined the understanding of (re) distribution, restoration, and affirmative action in the public sphere of what we should do to reverse the rampant effects of socioeconomic inequality (§ 2.2.1). Theological notions were also examined to test the contribution and participation of theology during and after apartheid (§ 2.3). Evaluating the various Namibian dialogues on the subject locates the gap, especially theology's role and place in the public discussion. It also examined the current policies and programmes the post-independence government has adopted to effect social justice and create a fairer society (§ 2.2.2). The interrogation of the sources available showed a gap in the conceptual processes, policies, and programmes that seek to effect social justice (§ 2.4).

6.2.3 How Does Allan Boesak Engage Notions of Justice in His Theological Work?

Here we engaged Boesak's theological notions and examples of calling for participation in the public matters of justice. It outlined selected key works of Boesak (§ 3.1) and how he sees his faith – as a public faith that should engage every sphere of life – especially in matters of justice. He approaches justice from the understanding that God is a liberating God,[1] so that liberation is the central theme of Scripture. We also outlined the philosophical framework that has influenced his ideas – Black Consciousness. Boesak insists that his theology provides reason for his participating in public life that involved politics.[2] He believes Christ's lordship over creation connotes God's sovereignty over all human affairs, including history.[3] Therefore, he does not distinguish a divide in history but sees it all as one – redemptive history.[4] This perspective forms his basis for Christian activism in society, to stand up, speak up, and resist all forms of oppression and injustice.[5] Boesak also addresses identity and self-discovery as the basis for breaking loose from oppression.[6] Thus, he

---

1. Boesak, *Farewell to Innocence* (1976), 20–22.
2. Boesak, *Running with Horses*.
3. Boesak, *Kairos, Crisis and Global*, 20–21, 61, 67.
4. Boesak, 22–23.
5. Boesak, *Comfort and Protest*, 10–19; Boesak, *Kairos, Crisis and Global*, 13–36.
6. Boesak, *Black and Reformed*, 1–21; Boesak, *Kairos, Crisis and Global*, 103, 112, 173.

places emphasis on Black Consciousness,[7] which he believes is the doing of God, even though it came through the Marxist ideology of Steve Biko. These conceptions of Boesak, however, do not provide a systematic study of justice. Instead, he uses the concept of reconciliation as the basis for justice,[8] arguing that true reconciliation is that which demands justice,[9] famously used in his interpretation of Zacchaeus's conversion.[10] He understands justice as restitution[11] and that we must similarly demand material restitution from the perpetrators and beneficiaries of the apartheid system.[12] To achieve this, Boesak believes theology has a role in public action.[13] It can advocate for fair distribution of these life-enhancing goods and opportunities to allow people to live out their full humanness. Boesak insists that faithful Christian participation and advocacy should demand justice and not settle for "cheap" reconciliation that is unwilling to ensure restitutive measures.[14]

6.2.4 What Are the Notions of Justice Being Employed to Address the Namibian Context? In What Ways Are They Helpful, and in What Ways Are They Inadequate?

This third question analysed Boesak's theology towards deriving helpful insight into the Namibian context. It examined the understanding and application of Black Theology of Liberation (see § 4.2), Black Power, and Black Consciousness (see § 4.3), reconciliation (see § 4.4), and restitution (see § 4.5) in constructing a framework for dialogue and discussing issues of justice. It acknowledged that Boesak provides us with helpful notions of understanding the background and framework of the effects of injustice. While Boesak's work provides huge motivation for active participation, prophetic witness, and faithful presence, some of his suggestions (reconciliation, restitution, consciousness, and power) need to find an authentic Namibian understanding. Critical to these dialogues, we drew upon the theology of Nicholas Sagovsky,

---

7. Boesak, *Tenderness of Conscience*, 8–16.
8. Boesak, *Farewell to Innocence* (1976), 74–75.
9. Boesak and DeYoung, *Radical Reconciliation*, 47–51.
10. Boesak, "And Zaccheus Remained," 643–49.
11. Boesak, *Tenderness of Conscience*, 177, 187, 197.
12. Boesak and DeYoung, *Radical Reconciliation*, 51–59.
13. Boesak, *Tenderness of Conscience*; Boesak, *Kairos, Crisis and Global*.
14. Boesak, "Religions and Search," 49.

John De Gruchy, and Anthony Bradley to supplement as models for Christian participation in the public issues of justice. From Sagovsky, we drew upon his theology of justice in *Christian Tradition and the Practice of Justice*; From De Gruchy, we drew upon his work *Christians and Democracy*, in which he offers theological arguments for being in critical solidarity; and Bradley offers in *Liberating Black Theology* a theological reevaluation of Black Theology of Liberation and examines how it can reconstitute itself to be relevant not only to the Black church in particular but to the universal church in general. He focuses particularly on systems and movements that could be more conducive to provide platforms for justice.

We acknowledge that Boesak raises essential questions of power, culture, identity, systems, structures, and justice, and why it is crucial for Christians to be part of the public dialogue and not shy away. But we need to keep in mind that he is not writing for the Namibian context, and his own experiences inform his understanding and approach. His work and voice remain relevant for theological dialogue; whether one agrees or disagrees with him, his ideas are relevant for analysis as he raises issues of concern, even for Namibia.

6.2.5 In What Ways Could Allan Boesak's Theologies of Justice Be Built Upon to Serve Theologies of Justice More Effectively for the Namibian Context?

We linked the second part of the above aim to the previous question. It discussed the ongoing dialogues and efforts towards social justice (see § 5.2) and how acts of corruption and maladministration affect the realization of justice (see § 5.2.2). It explored the critical concepts of reconciliation and social justice, and theological participation in the Namibian public discourse (§ 5.3). We also indicated that the Namibian conception of justice lacks the integrity and openness of addressing its history (see § 5.3.2.). This insufficiency of integrity hinders how the nation can construct meaningful social justice measures.[15] It also showed the need for theology to take a critical role in these public discussions (see § 5.3 and § 5.4.2) and undo the criticism of the church (and, by extension, theology) as absent and withdrawn from the public issues (§ 5.2.2). We indicated that part of this withdrawal is the

---

15. Boesak, "And Zaccheus Remained," 643–49; Horn, "Churches and Political Reconciliation"; Lombard, "Detainee Issue."

history of negative interactions between politics and the church. However, this could also be due to inadequate training and not knowing how to engage the secular platform and be God's witnesses in such public issues. Moreover, we indicated a shortage of constructive public participation models, both in the secular and theological communities engaging in understanding justice (see § 5.4). The subject is politicized, and many are using it to advance their political careers.

We argued that a contextualized conceptualization does not necessarily translate into justice (see § 5.2). Nevertheless, we argued that it may provide the necessary platform for rethinking what are the best possible measures of justice for the post-apartheid society. It also requires multiple dimensions, for example, (1) a vision for justice combined with a system for justice (see § 5.4.1 and § 5.4.2); (2) the construction a vision of reconciliation that seeks to restore humans as relational beings (see § 5.3); (3) integrating contemporary democratic and African values (see § 5.4.2); (4) moving away from concepts of social justice that entrench inaccurate sociocultural epistemologies (see § 5.4); and, (5) the role of theology in the public discourse as a voice of conscience, and helping to reimagine humanness in the post-independence context (see § 5.4.2 and § 5.5).

Although Namibians are politically reconciled, they are yet to experience a genuine reconciliation in which Black and White persons perceive each other as people of the same community. Boesak and other liberation theologians seem adamant about what should be the necessary steps. We leave this discussion open – that there needs to be much profound dialogue(s) on understanding social justice in the context of reconciliation. This dialogue(s) must happen in a context of mutual respect, calling for mutually beneficial and constructive ways rather than forcing, especially the former victims, to consent to the current inequities. It is a fragile context in which all stakeholders need to contribute, and this is where we believe theology can play a role towards reconciliation and justice.

6.3 Theology and Participation in the Public Sphere

6.3.1 A Vision for Justice

At the centre of this research is a concern for humans to be recognized, and to be able to act, as God's image-bearers endowed with dignity – that is, "to be a human being is to have worth."[16] Unfortunately, many of these image-bearers are not enabled to live this out because of injustice and continued structural inequities. God's image-bearers, not as socially constructed entities, humans as end in themselves, are the motivating factor behind Boesak's theology of justice. When communities of victims of injustice are not part of the discourse on fostering justice measures, it only continues the vicious cycle of disempowerment. There can be no proper measures of justice until affected communities regain their sense of humanity. This must happen in a community where there are adequate opportunities to flourish. Therefore, to plead for theological participation in a community and society's reimagining is to advocate for the creation structures in which communities experience God's *shalom*.

Shalom demands a vision for a just world.[17] The kind that extends beyond political ideologies but requires society members to acquire positive duties.[18] Theological participation for justice is a practical way of putting our faith in the public dialogue to craft laws needed in making a functional society. This demand is not to impose Christian beliefs, but we need a system(s) of social justice designed with the context of the Namibian experiences in mind if we are to move towards a fairer society. Namibians, as God's image-bearers, are endowed with the ability to design their approach to justice. A society's genuine autonomy is much dependent on the creation of a system and structure of justice (Boesak suggests this through reconciliation (§ 3.5.2) and De Gruchy suggests supporting democratic systems (§ 5.4.1)). When God's prophets demanded justice, they referred to God's laws and Israel's self-constructed sociopolitical structures. They operated within the provided legal, political, and social structures (sometimes in rebellion towards these structures if they did not serve God's purposes for humanity) – driven by their understanding of *shalom*. Furthermore, with this motivation, Namibian theology needs a public presence that participates in the conceptualization and contextualization of social justice.

---

16. Boesak, *Kairos, Crisis and Global*, 109; Wolterstorff, *Justice: Rights and Wrongs*, 131.

17. Boesak, *Kairos, Crisis and Global*, 22, 126; De Gruchy, *Christianity and Democracy* 7, 12, 44; Wolterstorff, *Justice: Rights and Wrongs*, 82, 117.

18. Sagovsky, *Christian Tradition*; Villa-Vicencio and Doxtader, *Pieces of the Puzzle*; Wolterstorff, *Justice: Rights and Wrongs*.

The dialogue around justice is complicated. Nonetheless, without a vision for justice, the socioeconomic effects of apartheid will continue to weigh down all other discussions and plans of economic and social progress.[19] A community that has been affected by injustice can turn out more positive and transformed if it applies itself to a meaningful search and application of social justice. However, no matter how complex the conception of justice is, it encompasses a sense of belief that certain duties need to be carried out towards those affected by the unjust system of apartheid. Boesak, in *Radical Reconciliation*, constructs the concept of the expectation of justice with respect to White Africans who perpetrated or benefited from the apartheid system. He believes the Bible mandates such expectations and being human incorporates a sense of normalising such expectations.

Thus, besides God commanding that justice must be done to victims, being human (God's image-bearer) requires fostering peace through restitution and creating a new social life.[20] This implies the post-apartheid society requires an intentional vision of how it would reconstruct itself. It must do so by taking deliberate measures to buttress its reconciliation policy to assure justice for the affected communities. Such a reconciliation system invalidates itself because it is incomplete if it does not advocate for justice to allow those on society's margins and in lowly positions to live in dignity.[21]

Boesak's arguments make a moral appeal to society and the kinds of systems that govern its operations. Using a liberation framework, he holds that political liberation has failed to achieve material liberation, making the process incomplete without the latter. Justice, according to Boesak, is essential to understanding what it takes to live in a post-apartheid context. Without it (justice), as Rawls says (although from a different perspective), everything else bears no meaning or power to uphold society.[22] Thus, the concept of justice in his view is not arbitrary and would not make sense without the just measures he proposes.

However, Boesak's subject of restitution needs to be examined to speak to the contemporary Namibian context. He provides us with a rich platform

---

19. Boesak, "And Zaccheus Remained"; Boesak and DeYoung, *Radical Reconciliation*; Lephakga, "Radical Reconciliation."

20. Boesak, "And Zaccheus Remained"; Boesak, *Kairos, Crisis and Global*, 31.

21. Boesak and DeYoung, *Radical Reconciliation*, 4.

22. Rawls, *Theory of Justice*, 3.

for engaging social justice issues. To do justice to the critical questions he is raising must be done through careful contextualization. This would require a careful and intentional process to combine theological skills with the needed historical, social, and political information to advocate for social justice. Boesak also calls for praxis rather than solely dwelling on abstractions; he focuses on undoing the persisting socioeconomic conditions caused by the then apartheid system. He believes wholesale social transformation will only happen when justice becomes part of political reconciliation's central discussion. This would require a vision for justice as none of the systems and structures will go away voluntarily. Social justice requires planning to intentionally transform violent systems and structures to pave the way for a new order. Thus, even suggestions such as restitution, no matter how plausible, would need to be evaluated within a context of a sustainable vision of justice. This vision needs to be formulated in cognisance of the experiences, context, and language where this vision would be enacted.

6.3.2 Conceptualization and Public Participation

While this research focuses on conceptualising the meaning of justice, it is not a mere mental exercise. It aims at provoking active theological participation in the public discourse of the Namibian context. Boesak encourages putting ideas into action and interrogating reconciliation and justice concepts that do not reach the root issues. He challenges us not to settle for empty political notions that do not address the unjust social, economic, and political structures, systems, policies, and programmes. In Boesak's view, the post-apartheid societies need to ask perplexing questions and not settle for vague interpretations of justice.[23] He also calls for the rejection of theological notions that "accept the existing unjust order as God-ordained."[24] Participation in the cause of justice is an act of participating in the things of the earth, and dialogue with Boesak provides much needed insight into theological socioeconomic issues and ethics for the Namibian context.

From this analysis, the Namibian context and theology's role to participate in this public issue of justice cannot be presented in any other way but as urgent. First, there is an urgent need for a theological conceptualization

---

23. Boesak, *Kairos, Crisis and Global*, 23–24.
24. Boesak, 26.

of justice as informed by Scripture. Second, there is need for contextualized hermeneutics of justice that would speak to actual issues being experienced. Third, it (theology) needs to engage beyond the boundaries of Christian dialogues and be present where life-altering decisions are being made. Fourth, theology should advocate for a meaningful understanding of reconciliation coupled with demands for justice. Fifth, there is a need for a theological vision to hold the government accountable. This accountability extends to calling the government to attend to the current inequitable distribution of goods and opportunities that continue to affect previously disadvantaged communities. Thus, the need for policies and programmes that would translate into measurable outcomes.

6.3.3 A Moral Voice

Theological discourse in the Namibian public sphere needs a decisiveness that will distinguish it as a moral voice in the face of ravaging social injustice, as defined by poverty and socioeconomic inequality.[25] Such a resolution is one rooted in robust biblical foundations and conversation with the ideas informing and shaping social justice conceptions. The Namibian theological tradition with roots in Black Theology of Liberation has neither shown a critical public culture nor critical solidarity towards the government.[26] While there has been an active presence during the apartheid times, it presented itself as pro-SWAPO.[27] This association has comprimized the effectiveness of theology in the post-independence context. On the other end of this dilemma were dominantly White churches that decided to either take the route of silence or supported the apartheid government. This latter group is more silent in public matters, as it has invalidated its presence and relevance, especially with most Black citizens. There continues to be a divide among churches and theology. Additionally, they lack a shared prophetic vision to rethink their presence and participation in reshaping the public conception of justice.

This diminished presence and participation in the post-independence public imply a diminishing moral and prophetic voice. The struggle of the

---

25. Boesak, *Dare We Speak?*, 139.

26. Botha, "Church in Namibia," 31–34; Groop, "Church, State," 74–75; Horn, "Churches and Political Reconciliation," 16.

27. De Gruchy, *Christianity and Democracy*, 177.

Namibian post-independence church to inspire the ecumenical and theological social thinking needed to address social injustice's continued presence only deepens this dilemma. Critical social thinking, dialogue, and participation are not simple tasks. It requires creative dialoguing regarding the pressing socioeconomic issues and how the church can mitigate social injustice. The challenges to the church that are mentioned in § 5.3 do not only indicate a lack of clear thinking and articulation but mainly that the church's prophetic voice and faithful witness have diminished. Along with that, the moral voice that the church ought to be cannot be heard clearly to call people to God's standards, as Christ's representative.

6.3.4 Public Witness

The call for theological participation does not mean that a uniform understanding of justice should be reached, but those theological notions should contribute to the reshaping of our unstructured and inarticulate public perceptions of fairness. Various theological notions should speak to secular justice systems, creating a dialectic but interactive relationship (see § 3.4). Based on the understanding that theology is God's tool of working in human communities, we seek mutual transformation by engaging the various means available in our contexts. Injustice implies a breakdown in the social relationships of the community. The Christian understanding of humans as God's image-bearers can serve as a helpful starting point to mend this relationship (see § 5.4.2) – through critical participation in the political community that affects certain forms of justice and policies. Questioning the role of theology in public dialogue should result in positive participation rather than the pietism Boesak is criticising (see § 4.2).

If we suppose critical theological participation in the public originates in God's creation account, this carries profound implications. Thus, if we believe Jerusalem to be the earthly emblem of God's earthly self-revelation,[28] then this is a crucial call for witnessing (see § 5.6.). First, we engage the concepts of justice because injustice affects God's image-bearers. Second, by questioning specific ideas, policies, and programmes, we engage in the manifestation of God's *shalom* in being part of those advocating for better living conditions. Third, engaging in the search for contextually relevant meanings and justice

---

28. De Gruchy, 40–41.

measures cements our witnessing (in actual human society and not in the abstracts) (see § 5.5).

This witnessing has a political implication (see § 3.2.3). In chapters 3 and 4, we saw how Boesak, Sagovsky, and De Gruchy use this concept of *shalom* as the basis for examining concepts, systems, and practices of what is righteous; not to establish Christian rule but as public participation of redeeming creation from both spiritual and socioeconomic conditions. Theologians are co-participants with the rest of human society to ensure God's *shalom* in forms of reconciliation, justice, and restitution (see § 4.4 and § 4.5). This participation comes with an intensive conceptual and practical break from the precarious social arrangements that protect injustice, both historical and post-independence. Thus, theological involvement in the conceptualization of justice not only seeks to ensure social functioning but that such social processes ought to manifest themselves in virtuous acts. The inhumane and unjust Land Acts combined with forceful removals and economic exploitation cemented a society of privilege. It is a privilege that results in immense resource, economic, and social inequality, which cannot be left unaddressed. The present social and political window-dressing of justice presented in various policy documents only deepens and widens social inequality (see § 5.2).

6.3.5 Collective Social Imaginary

We propose that justice should emanate from a collective social imaginary (see § 4.4 Application). This imagination should begin in the moral order and must be accompanied by certain expectations and benefits. Chief among these benefits should be *security.* That is, within a safe environment, there should be life-enhancing goods. This should include, but is not limited to, access to quality healthcare, quality education, decent employment, the opportunity for life-enhancing skills, decent housing, and food security in the Namibian context. This security is socioeconomic, but the state is responsible for making these goods available for its citizens by a rearranged, and enduring social contract. The state's role in ensuring that it sets up functional structures that are well managed to channel the resources to those who need it the most cannot be ignored. Among these goods should be social goods that would restore the lost culture, metaphor, spirituality, language, self-acceptance, and restoration of the dignity of the Namibian people (see § 5.2). However, without a clear conceptualization and vision of justice, these life-enhancing goods cannot be channelled to those who need them the most.

The reconciliation process was a good entry point to create this social imaginary and nation-building; however, partisan politics undermines it. For reconciliation to take its full meaning and application, unlike Boesak's argument that it should deal with justice, we believe it should stand on its own merits. Therefore, we find Boesak's mixing of reconciliation and justice wanting and not helpful. However, we accept that reconciled persons need and must also think about justice and the common good. Social justice from those who have perpetrated and benefitted from the apartheid system can only be based on a restored relationship and an appeal to conscience. Affirmative action policies, for example, would be, and have proven to be, a futile process. They have been weaponized to enforce programmes that only benefit a minority of politically well-connected individuals and not communities. Not that these programmes, of necessity, cannot work, but that they are placed within structures that offer inadequate accountability. These policies, unfortunately, have become a means for relentless looting of state resources at the expense of the most affected persons and communities.

The idea of the social imaginary we are proposing is part of creating social norms that would create a culture and society of mutual sociopolitical life. It is a moral call to rethink society, not as something established just by the state and political systems but as the co-existence of humans with various visions of justice and needs. Part of this moral call is finding a valuable understanding of what it means to be human and co-exist. Liberation Theology, particularly Black Liberation Theology, needs to come to grasp the realities of society's dynamics, not as Black and White, oppressor and oppressed, or perpetrator and victim. Theological discussion and participation should aim at confronting the myth of social analysis that is not of value to the realities of the post-apartheid context. Not that theology is the guardian of political thought but of seeking and promoting a moral order. A voice to form a humane social imaginary would create an environment in which life-enhancing goods are attainable.

6.3.6 Restitution and Restoration

We pointed out that Namibia's post-apartheid context focuses on restitution. This restitution has not been realisable because of the inadequacy of structures and lack of clarity of the process. Added to that are the political corruption and lack of a contextualized conceptualization that can help structure social justice measures. We do not dismiss restitution as a measure of justice. We question its effectiveness and ability to serve those other than already well-off individuals. Boesak and many Namibians argue that restitution needs to be demanded from former perpetrators, beneficiaries, and their posterity. While this is an agreeable demand, it is complicated and challenging to carry out without causing considerable unrest. Who should be the beneficiaries? What goods warrant restitution?

The researcher argues that restitution should address the material aspect and existential realities beyond economics – restoration of identity. For example, the land question should be addressed not only for its economic value but also for its cultural value for communities dispossessed of their land. However, where commercial land is needed, there should be adequate provision of skills to function within a modern agricultural setting. There are already processes in place that are addressing land distribution, however slow. These government initiatives can be profitable economic turnover if those who are receiving farmlands can use them effectively.

It must be noted that restitution does not provide adequate evidence that it would enhance the living standards of many, except for a selected few. These few could benefit but with no assurance that their benefits would trickle down to profit society at large. Moreover, so much time has passed, and that restitution may only result in destruction, as it happened in Zimbabwe. The "willing-buyer, willing-seller"[29] policy could be enhanced to deal with the land issue. This process may only happen in the context of a functional system, free (to a more considerable extent) of corruption and mismanagement. Nevertheless, this is a community call; affected communities must be part of the discussion processes, and the policies and programmes must be need-oriented.

The land question for most Namibians in urban areas is for domestic, not for commercial purposes. Market prices are unfairly high so that the average Black Namibian cannot afford housing land. Many of them have no surety

---

29. The national policy that was adopted after independence by the government paved the way for the land-buying programme from private farmers and distribution to previously disadvantaged individuals. The land is sectioned to accommodate several households. Some land is communal and others for commercial farming.

to provide when seeking to purchase properties, so they often lose out on acquiring assets (in the form of land and housing). This practice continues the cycle of disempowerment as many previously disadvantaged people have no bargaining power with financial institutions to acquire properties. Financial institutions continue to cater only for a select category of the country – an economic and political elite who buy up and hoard land. Boesak raises this issue of financial institutions and corporations that need to come on board to be part of the solution to socioeconomic inequality – a call many are refusing to heed.

Boesak insists that the biblical understanding of justice speaks of restitution (Exod 21:33–22: 1–15);[30] even then, this should not be seen as an indiscriminate universal prescription. Every group of people needs to find their approach to restitution based on their context (see § 5.4.2). The research concurs that restitution carries the potential to redress the socioeconomic inequality affecting and preventing many Namibians from leading dignified lives. To be effective, it needs suitable structures and institutions that would allow just measures in the case of injustice. Thus, social justice, especially in matters of restitution, requires just, transparent, functional, and effective institutions, as Rawls argues, "the primary subject of justice is the basic structure of society, or more exactly, the way in which the major social institutions distribute fundamental rights and duties and determine the division of advantages from social cooperation."[31]

This is an interchange towards a common good, which, according to Andrew Bradstock,

> impels us to move beyond the . . . political agenda to consider the kind of society we wish to live in. Placing both human dignity and human community at the centre of the political and economic decision-making, the common good challenges us to consider the extent to which we live in solidarity with each other, recognise our interdependence, and seek the wellbeing of all.[32]

---

30. Boesak, "Doing of Little Righteousness," 37; Boesak and DeYoung, *Radical Reconciliation*; Lephakga, "Radical Reconciliation."

31. Rawls, *Theory of Justice*, 6.

32. Bradstock, "Unexamined Society," 46.

Without reliable social institutions to provide social structures (policies and programmes), pursuing social justice could be futile. Restitution needs these structures, not only in discussing restitution but how to set up functional social safety nets. These structures need a contextualized framework that would discuss the principles, and they can be used to provide the needed conceptual links to redress the effects of apartheid. The idea of restitution should, however, be holistic. It should address land issues (historical damages) and how it can mitigate missed opportunities (survivor justice). It is restitution that seeks to deal with human insecurities (past, present, and future) and necessary for consolidating the kind of democracy we envision. There is no easy way to this; that if we intend to create a different kind of society, we cannot escape the question of socioeconomic justice.[33] Far from the romanticized version of neosocialist groups, we need a public dialogue that acknowledges the moral demands. It should do so without diluting the social momentum with vain abstractions that only remain at the policy level.

The need for creative dialogue to hold the necessary tension in the balance undermines the creation of constructive political compromise regarding socioeconomic justice. This compromise implies using different measures where appropriate. As Villa-Vicencio and Doxtader argue, this requires "a level of inspired moral leadership."[34] Whatever form of justice we embark on, as in restoration, should reaffirm selfhood, dignity, and humanity – that is, making justice about the community and not the individual. It is a collective rather than individualized future in which communities are restored to live in dignity and to be fully functional.

6.4 Recommendations

In chapters 1, 2 and 5, I outlined the challenges facing theology in post-independence structures, especially its abridged prophetic voice and witness regarding social justice. Since independence, the church and theology have withdrawn from the public and became confined to local churches and

---

33. Villa-Vicencio and Doxtader, *Pieces of the Puzzle*, 8.
34. Villa-Vicencio and Doxtader, 35.

faith-based organizations.[35] The withdrawal is attributed to the shortage of local models of how to engage the public with alternative ideas. While this project challenges such narrow conceptualization, it also presents the role of theology as a public witness to promote God's *shalom* in the post-apartheid context.[36] It is not my intention to provide a theory or definition of justice but to highlight that we need to ask what the current concepts mean, in the light of God's self-revelation and the social context of Namibia. We have clearly offered some characteristics and understandings of contributions to the field because of this research.

So, what must be done to create this theological engagement that can speak to the policies, programmes, and structures? We keep in mind that our task is theological, but that we also need to speak to socioeconomic and sociopolitical decisions and contexts.[37] However, it is an engagement based on seeking God's kingdom and where it is manifesting in the world.[38] Thus, we are to ask, what is God doing? And how can we be part of what God is doing? This research seeks that we interrogate the participation in exploring notions of social justice and the support for institutions, systems, and practices that promote justice for all persons as part of Christian witness in the public sphere.[39] Theological participation in this public space needs to be done with a *critical solidarity* which De Gruchy explains as,

> giving support to those initiatives which may lead to the establishment not only of a new, but also a just, social order. It means that the Church remains prophetic in its stance towards a new democratically elected government, that it must continue to stand for the truth, but now on the basis of a shared commitment to the realisation of national reconstruction. Being in critical solidarity means continued resistance to what is unjust and false, and continued protest on behalf of what is just and true.[40]

---

35. Botha, "Church in Namibia"; Horn, "Churches and Political Reconciliation"; Kameeta, *Towards Liberation*.

36. De Gruchy, *Christianity and Democracy*, 7, 12, 44; Wolterstorff, *Justice: Rights and Wrongs*, 82.

37. Forster, "Nature of Public Theology," 20–23.

38. Boesak, *Kairos, Crisis and Global*, 91.

39. Boesak and DeYoung, *Radical Reconciliation*, 123–24.

40. De Gruchy, *Christianity and Democracy*, 222.

This requires that theology familiarises itself with issues and language that permeate the public dialogue without which it will be difficult to provide an informed view.[41] Hence, the need for a critical engagement that can provide a robust challenge to the concept and practice of justice is crucial and urgent. Meaningful public discourse can be adversely affected in the absence of a well thought, organized, and engaging theology of justice. This work seeks to create such a platform of engagement for Christian academics who can use their gifts and skills to witness to God's moral order. It includes understanding the political environment and the role we are to play today.[42]

It also implies moving away from the stagnant rhetoric that refuses to abandon the distortions of a narrow socialist-Marxist historical analysis.[43] It distorts socioeconomic and sociopolitical realities in post-independent Namibia. This is particularly so for Black Liberation Theology which remains tied up in the "prophetic critique" of the apartheid era. This implies embracing new theological critique and practice that resonates with the sociopolitical context, yet remains deeply rooted in biblical motivations to stand out as Christian witnesses in the struggle for social justice. As Forster says, this is an act of "linking faith and life, of having meaningful exchanges between theology and other academic disciplines, and of being aware of the need for critical reflection on the historical and contextual factors that affect our thinking" and society.[44] It also may imply that theology will not have meaningful impact on the public notions of social justice without understanding the roots of the notions and systems applied today. Therefore, theologians need to acquaint themselves with the subjects needed to understand the dominant ideas and practices of social justice. The gospel demand to be light and salt should not only consist of spiritual realities but also of knowledge with which we can engage the world. Finding ourselves in a context that has no intentional culture about justice besides the political rhetoric, theology could play an essential role in providing direction. However, ill-equipped theology cannot support public institutions, systems, and political practices that need to

---

41. Forster, "Nature of Public Theology," 20–21.

42. Boesak, *Kairos, Crisis and Global*, 30–32.

43. Bradley, *Liberating Black Theology*, 42–47.

44. Forster, "Nature of Public Theology," 19.

ensure the realization of social justice or equitable society. Thus, it needs to have the knowledge, robustness, and courage to articulate critical solidarity.

The Namibian context continues to experience socioeconomic racism, and the division of much of the national wealth is along these social lines.[45] Thus, the talk of socioeconomic justice carries profound racial language. The prevailing narrative (discussed in chapters 2 and 5) is that we are to demand justice from White Namibians because they either perpetrated or benefitted from the then apartheid system. The political environment remains tense on this issue, and there are inadequate platforms to express these frustrations. What does this mean for theology? We propose critical solidarity with human suffering and support structures and systems that genuinely seek to address this socioeconomic injustice. Theologians need to look much deeper into this historical and social analysis and expose the false epistemologies. First, the belief that White people (indiscriminately) are perpetual oppressors and Black people (indiscriminately) are perpetual victims needs redressing. If the latter see themselves as always being victims, they remain in self-imposed social imprisonment. Using past oppression to brand Black identity without accounting for the post-apartheid (majority Black) contribution to present injustice, would only "foster an unfocused resentment" and even false alienation.[46] While it is true that it was a history that favoured White persons, today, we now need to hold both the past and present accountable. The pharaohs are on both sides of the river.[47] We need to confront both old and new forms of incessant socioeconomic violence manifesting in forms of "exploitation and the perpetuation of impoverishment set against the extreme, but undeserved wealth of a few."[48] The church has a moral duty to confront this socioeconomic evil and resist the lures of being caught up in structures that have no respect for God's image-bearers. As such, the church should stand with all who advocate for the creation of systems and structures that will ensure equitable access to life-enhancing goods. Failure to see through this narrow interpretation of history fosters the growing corruption and mismanagement due to lack of appropriate accountability structures. In

---

45. Melber, "Limits of Liberation," 9–10.

46. Bradley, *Liberating Black Theology*, 43.

47. Boesak, *Pharaohs on Both Sides*, 46; Melber, "Limits of Liberation," 9.

48. Boesak, 46.

our anticipation of the kingdom of God, we are to be the voice of truth amid false narratives that delay and pervert the course of justice.

Second, injustice needs to be reconsidered as not only something that is exclusive to specific social communities. Instead, injustice should be confronted in all its forms regardless of race, gender, religion, political affiliation, and sex.[49] This approach would also serve as the route for theology to redeem itself from the absence and the political handmaiden it has become since independence, and become an authentic voice of conscience in society.[50] Third, theology must foster a sense of community by avoiding the divisive language of racial categorization. This approach must be made both within the community of faith and the public at large.[51] It is a community based on principles of restoring the humanity and dignity of all, which is inclusive of reconciliation demonstrated by tangible measures of justice, for community must exercise and uphold justice.[52] This call should not be misconstrued as a blind calling to community that ignores justice. A community that refuses to demand justice to be done to the living is a cruel and ungodly one. Fourth, theologians need to intentionally organize themselves, to become a participating community in the sociopolitical and socioeconomic dialogues of the country. Discussing issues of justice have political consequences both for individuals and systems.[53] One of the contributing factors to the public absence is the lack of a platform for theological ideas and discussions on public matters. Whether this requires new institutions and structures, or the restructuring of already existing ones, needs careful planning; efforts of individual theologians alone will not suffice. Therefore, the possible best way is to consider an ecumenical yet independent arrangement that focuses on public issues and represents the voice of theology.[54] Fifth, there is a need to equip individual Christians in their various capacities to become active participants and witnesses. In a country of eighty to ninety percent Christians, many Namibians are church-going. The churches (given that they are well equipped)

---

49. Boesak, 32–45.

50. Botha, "Church in Namibia"; Lombard, "Detainee Issue"; Niitenge, "Evangelical Lutheran Church."

51. Horn, "Churches and Political Reconciliation."

52. Boesak, *Pharaohs on Both Sides*, 135–36.

53. Boesak, 136.

54. Boesak, *Kairos, Crisis and Global*, 19–25.

can conscientize members to live out their faith in the various public spheres. The *ekklesia* is a community called out to serve God by bearing witness to God's work through Jesus Christ and demonstrate what redeemed humanity looks like.[55] The kingdom of God is a political concept, and its citizens are called upon to practice righteousness (justice). As far as justice is concerned, it cannot be exercised in private when its effects are public. The public presence of the gospel requires participating in the public life of society as an act of worship and public display of Christian civic commitment (see § 5.4.2).

The future of theology and its relevance in public matters is highly dependent on becoming involved – in a much more intense and meaningful way. The post-apartheid context requires a theological stand to confront the effects of apartheid and post-independence social injustice. While apartheid is gone, demanding for justice must be a continuous activity as long as there remains systematic and structurally enforced injustice. This participation includes not only calling for reforms but also facing the truth of our nation's history. Although political players thwarted a national process of reconciliation, it does not imply that theology should not engage in a continuous quest for truth and justice. Part of this engagement requires defining and constructing a socially just society. For justice, God's justice, should demand nothing less than a system that assures decent living standards for the less advantaged.

The state needs to provide for universal social insurance – to lessen the socioeconomic burden imposed upon communities and their posterity. Such social insurance should address poverty, healthcare, access to quality education, decent employment, housing, and advocate for better systems of governance that would ensure equitable access to these goods. This intervention does not imply that perpetrators and beneficiaries of the apartheid system are under no obligation. While the state should be held accountable to ensure functional systems and structures, perpetrators and beneficiaries of apartheid should play their role of rebuilding by committing themselves to social justice. Thus, collective participation is essential to *construct* a conducive social environment for equitable and more just nation-building; nevertheless, this must be accompanied by appropriate measures of justice to restore the living conditions of those who are affected. Everyone must play their role to

---

55. Smith, *Desiring the Kingdom*, 204.

intentionally construct genuine reconciliation and tolerance and eventually a lasting community of equals.

However, this calling of society at large to become a truly reconciled and just one would require theology and the Namibian church at large to admit its guilt. First, it is the failure of the church that it did not stand up to injustice wrought by post-independence structures (see § 5.3.1). Second, the church has failed to stand up courageously against continued corruption and mis-governance (see § 5.3.2). Third, the church did not embrace the democratic structure and system to model itself as an agent of social justice (see § 5.4.1). Therefore, in its repentance, theology in Namibia must develop a robust social reference that it will provide as a model for society to follow. Courage requires both confronting unjust systems and providing alternatives that can be used as models for transformation.

For public theology to serve as a credible witness of the truth of Jesus Christ in matters of social justice, it requires an integrated approach that is robust, self-critical, intellectually credible, and politically informed. Namibian theology needs such a reordering to engage in the public dialogues of social justice in service of the gospel. It is an earthy and spiritual struggle in which our worldview and convictions may conflict with the popular versions of social justice. Yet, we need to unashamedly allow our faith to speak in the public and not engage in dialogues of social justice to the detriment of our public witness. Although this research aims at the academic public, the critical task of the theologian is not merely intellectual. We work within the confine-ment of our calling – doing theology. However, we embrace the ambiguous nature of this task of creating a public presence and witness to God's truth without seeking to usurp the roles of political philosophers, economists, and social theorists. Instead, we want to examine justice within the realities of the Namibian public and encourage all sectors concerned with justice to develop their reason. This task is complicated, given the multidimensional nature of living in a young democracy that is still seeking to find its own identity as a sovereign state. However, it is precisely this complexity that theology must capitalize on to call for public dialogue, not confined to political players but to public reasoning regarding the kind of justice we need to become a more just society.

6.5 Limitations of the Research

This research aims at examining social justice in the post-apartheid Namibian context in dialogue with Allan Boesak's theological notions of justice. Since this project is highly focused, it has some understandable and necessary limitations: first, it only engages selected texts of Allan Boesak, which were argued to hold qualitative theological value for the intentions and aims of this study. Of course, one could approach this issue from Boesak's work in several ways. This study chose a set of texts since they were found to best address the research questions and research objectives. Second, other theologians might choose to engage with different theologians to engage the Namibian notion of justice. Of course, such work is both important and necessary and could constitute valuable further research for either this researcher or other researchers in the years to come. Third, this research developed a particular theological understanding of Namibian social and political life. Again, these were considered choices related to the specific research questions and objectives that needed consideration in this study. Researchers from other fields of study (economics, political science, and social sciences), may come to a different understanding of this context and identify additional aspects for consideration. Fourth, I chose a particular methodological approach – a contextual theological critical engagement with some of Allan Boesak's theological works on justice – some other researchers might choose a different theological methodological approach, for example, critical theology, historiography, biblical theology, or a feminist reading. Fifth, the research is limited to the field of systematic theology and ethics. As such, it does make pastoral suggestions and missiological claims, and offers ways of understanding theological concepts concerning the contemporary context. Making such recommendations will require a different research project(s) to test and implement the proposals from this research in the church and society. Finally, while I do engage some biblical scholarship, I am particularly engaging Boesak's use of Scripture (not my own interpretations of texts). Thus, I am not making any evaluation of the texts that Boesak uses, how he interprets them, and what he emphasises as essential. Instead, I am merely representing how he uses these texts and how he brings his interpretations into the conversation with issues of justice for purposes of theological reflection and constructive theological development.

6.6 Suggestions for Future Research

The research focused on the need for a contextualized conceptualization of social justice. It was limited to learning from Allan Boesak and how Namibian theologians can engage with public dialogue on issues of justice. We have also engaged various South African theologians whose context is related to that of Namibia to rethink the construction of appropriate theologies of justice for this context. Having dealt with conceptualization, we have become aware that this project only covers one angle and future research may need to focus on some areas such as:[56]

- *A feminist conceptualization of justice in post-apartheid Namibia.* Women were particularly discriminated against by the apartheid system; this created various layers of disadvantage for women. While there are feminist explorations, there is inadequate theological work that explores social justice from a post-apartheid feminist Namibian perspective.

- *An African conceptualization of justice from a cultural perspective.* We have mentioned part of this in chapter 5; however, the subject needs further but focused exploration, using a theological method.

- *The conceptualization of justice in northern, central, and southern Namibia as both apartheid and colonialism affected these regions differently.* For example, forced labourers were mostly from the northern regions, and northern lands were not expropriated. While central and southern regions had few forced labourers, all their land was confiscated, and they were forced into settlements.

---

56. Added to the above remain questions that need to be explored as part of theological participation in the Namibian public and dialogue of justice. Among these should be: (1) How are we to respond to the past human rights violations to correct their effects in the post-apartheid context? (2) How do we intend to hold to account those who have participated in the violations of their people? (3) How do we intend to address the marginalization caused alongside gender categories? (4) How should we participate in actively ensuring that perpetrators in the current system are held accountable for their actions that contribute to the widening of social injustice? (5) What sort of institutional reforms need to happen that will provide effective structures to ensure justice? (6) What type of justice do we need that best meets the demands of our society? What kinds of goods need to be met at an entry-level to meet this long-term goal? Each of these could become a study of its own. It is hoped that this researcher, and some others, will be able to undertake some of this research alongside others in the years to come.

- *The conceptualization of justice within different theological traditions in Namibia, for example, Roman Catholic, Pentecostal/ charismatic, Lutheran, Anglican, Methodist, African Initiated Churches and Reformed and how they can be enhanced to engage public issues.* If theology needs an ecumenical approach, then these traditions need to be engaged, so that they are represented in the public theological dialogues.
- *The effects of apartheid on rural and urban citizens are also different and need to be explored as a research area.*
- *The various social groups also carry different conceptions and visions of justice and need to be explored as to what justice is for Black and White Namibians.* The theology of racial divide has barely been explored and could be part of the healing process as we address racial biases and false epistemologies.

The issues mentioned above are hinted at in various sections of this study but have not been adequately addressed. These themes cannot be addressed in one project; therefore, they may need research projects going forward. Theologians seeking to address post-apartheid injustice in Namibia need to engage the public conceptions before they can offer alternative solutions. Furthermore, intentionally developing theologies of justice appropriate to the Namibian contexts will contribute immensely to the public presence, credibility, and participation of theology.

6.7 Conclusion

The role of Black Liberation Theology in mobilising people to resist the apartheid system will always remain as a remarkable time in the history of theological and Christian participation against injustice. Theological works of several Namibians,[57] especially those written during the height of apartheid policies, laws and state brutality, testify to the vital role that Christians and theologians played in the anti-apartheid struggle. Namibia's independence from the apartheid government could have been delayed in profound ways, had it not been for the role of the church. This study has argued that contextual

---

57. Kameeta, *Why, O Lord?*; Katjavivi, "Role of the Church"; Mujoro and Mujoro, "Namibian Liberation Theology"; Nambala, "From Colonialism to Nationalism."

theology is crucial for Namibian theologians to construct theologies of justice which can dialogue with the post-apartheid context. The researcher has considered the Namibian context (chapters 2 and 5) and found that these early engagements are important but need to be updated to address contemporary contextual challenges adequately.

To address the problem of the lack of contextualized conceptualization of social justice, I engaged with Allan Boesak's work which challenged me to think about:

1. The important and relevant questions Liberation Theology poses regarding the continued nature of systemic injustice.
2. How the concept of reconciliation needs to be used in the context of justice, otherwise it does not carry any deep meaning for the victims.
3. The role of theology to dialogue with the political structures and find democratic structures as its ally without necessarily succumbing to everything in politics (to be engaged with, but not embedded in, political structures).
4. The need for a more integrated theology that can converse with the post-apartheid context.

This challenge is valuable because it helps theologians in the Namibian context to reconsider:

1. The lost prophetic role of the church and theology that can boldly confront both old and new structures and forms of social injustice.
2. The social context in which they engage, and how to seek an appropriate language for dialogue.
3. To find a theological language that genuinely addresses the concerns of the Namibian narrative, that is, identifying how they can join in God's holistic redemptive work in Namibia; and,
4. To construct a meaningful theology of presence and witnessing to God's truth regarding the present dehumanising socioeconomic conditions.

The concern of this study has been that both theology and social systems have adopted notions and practices that have enhanced the continued presence of injustice in the Namibian society. While Namibia has developed many social policies, some of them are broad and do not seek to put right the effects of apartheid. Theology has also taken a relative backseat in the public sphere and recent dialogues. It seems to have resigned itself to private and church-based activities – what the Kairos document would call a "church theology." The voice of the church remains a somewhat compromised voice which has lost much of its moral authority to rebuke the post-apartheid structures. In terms of preparedness to engage the public discourse of social justice, many Namibian theologies lack the needed integration that can dialogue at the level that would earn it the respect to be listened to. The absence of a con-textualized theology and lack of participation in the public sphere not only represent a sad withdrawal from God's world, but they also perpetuate missed opportunities to take part in God's work in the world. Continuing to use the historical analysis given by a theology that can no longer address the present context undermines our call to be God's disciples in the place and time in which God has placed us. What if a contextualized conceptualization of social justice were to emerge unashamedly in the language of theology (living and present), was true to Scripture, and was deeply conversant with other fields of knowledge? It could pave the way for a new opportunity to redress post-apartheid social injustice. It is my hope that this thesis will serve as a tentative contribution to this important task of engaging the intricacies of justice in post-apartheid Namibia. I do so as one among the many voices in southern Africa and the Global South who long to see an unapologetic theological presence and participation in the various public dialogues as evidence of the Christian witness of participating in God's redemptive activity in the world.

Bibliography

Akawa, Martha. *The Gender Politics of the Namibian Liberation Struggle*. Basel Namibia Studies Series 13. Basel: Basler Afrika Bibliographien, 2014.

Akawa, Martha, and Jeremy Silvester. "Waking the Dead: Civilian Casualties in the Namibian Liberation Struggle." *Journal for Studies in Humanities and Social Sciences* 1, no. 1 (2012): 117–28.

Aldama, Arturo J., and Naomi H. Quiñonez. "Introduction: ¡Peligro! Subversive Subjects: Chicano and Chicano Cultural Studies in the 21st Century." In *Decolonial Voices: Chacana and Chicano Cultural Studies in the 21st Century*, edited by Arturo J. Aldama and Naomi H. Quiñonez, 1–10. Bloomington: Indiana University Press, 2002.

Althaus-Reid, Marcella. *Indecent Theology: Theological Perversion in Sex, Gender and Politics*. London: Routledge, 2000.

Amathila, Libertina I. *Making a Difference (Namibia)*. Windhoek: University of Namibia Press, 2012.

Amukugo, Elizabeth. "Liberal Democracy, Education and Social Justice in Africa." *Journal for Studies in Humanities and Social Sciences* 2, no. 1 (2013): 144–57.

Amupanda, Job Shipululo. "The Fight against Corruption in Namibia : An Appraisal of Institutional Environment and a Consideration of a Model for Civil Society Participation." *Namibia Law Journal* 11, no. 1 (2019): 187–203.

Aristotle. *The Complete Works of Aristotle*. Edited by Jonathan Barnes. Vol. 1&2. Bollingen Series LXXI. Princeton: Princeton University Press, 1984. Electronic version.

Balch, Jeffrey, and Jan Nico Scholten. "Namibian Reconstruction and National Reconciliation : Putting the Horse Before the Cart." *Review of African Political Economy*, no. 49 (1990): 82–93.

Barth, Karl. *God Here and Now*. Translated by Paul M. Van Buren. London: Routledge, 2003.

Berlin, Isaiah. *Liberty*. Edited by Henry Hardy. Oxford: Oxford University Press, 1969.

Bevans, Stephen B. *Essays in Contextual Theology*. Boston: Brill, 2018.

Biko, Steve. *I Write What I Like. African Writers Series*. London: Bowerdean Press, 1987. Electronic version.

Bobek, Vito, Jellenz Moritz, and Tatjana Horvat. "Namibia's Triple Challenge and Its Economic Development." In *Perspectives on Economic Development – Public Policy, Culture, and Economic Development*, 1–21. IntechOpen, 2019. https://doi.org/10.5772/intechopen.88638.

Boesak, Allan A. "And Zaccheus Remained in the Tree: Reconciliation and Justice and the Truth and Reconciliation Commission." *Verbum et Ecclesia* 29, no. 3 (2008): 636–54.

———. Black and Reformed: Apartheid, Liberation and the Calvinist Tradition. Braamfontein: Skotaville Publishers, 1984.

———. Children of the Waters of Meribah: Black Liberation Theology, the Miriamic Tradition, and the Challenges of Twenty-First-Century Empire. Eugene: Wipf & Stock Publishers, 2019. Kindle.

———. Comfort and Protest: The Apocalypse from a South African Perspective. 1st ed. Philadelphia: The Westminster Press, 1987.

———. Coming in Out of the Wilderness: A Comparative Interpretation of the Ethics of Martin Luther King, Jr. and Malcolm X. Kok: Kampen, 1976.

———. Dare We Speak of Hope? Searching for a Language of Life and Faith in Politics. Kindle. Grand Rapids: Eerdmans Publishing, 2014.

———. Die Vlug van Gods Verbeelding: Bybelverhale van Die Onderkant. Stellenbosch: SUN Press, 2005. Electronic version.

———. Farewell to Innocence: A Social-Ethical Study of Black Theology and Black Power. Johannesburg: Ravan Press, 1976.

———. Farewell to Innocence: A Social-Ethical Study of Black Theology and Black Power. Maryknoll: Orbis Books, 1977.

———. "'A Hope Unprepared to Accept Things as They Are': Engaging John de Gruchy's Challenges for 'Theology at the Edge.'" *Stellenbosch Theological Journal* 55, no. 1 (2014): 1055–74.

———. *If This Is Treason, I Am Guilty*. Grand Rapids: Eerdmans Publishing, 1987.

———. *Kairos, Crisis and Global Apartheid: The Challenge to Prophetic Resistance*. New York: Palgrave Macmillan, 2015. Electronic version.

———. *Pharaohs on Both Sides of the Blood-Red Waters: Prophetic Critique of Empire: Resistance, Justice, and the Power of the Hopeful Sizwe, a Transatlantic Conversation*. Eugene: Cascade Books, 2017. Kindle.

———. "A Restless Presence: Church Activism and 'Post-Apartheid,' 'Post-Racial' Challenges." In *Contesting Post-Racialism: Conflicted Churches in the United States and South Africa*, edited by Drew R. Smith, William Ackah, Anthony G. Reddie, and Rothney S. Tshaka, 14–36. Jackson: University of Mississippi, 2015.

———. "Religions, Pluralism, the Common Good and Poverty." *Supplementum 2* (2012): 1193–204.

———. *Running with Horses: Reflections of an Accidental Politician*. Cape Town: Joho Publishers, 2009.

———. "The Doing of the Little Righteousness – The On-Going Search for Justice After the TRC." *Dutch Reformed Theological Journal/Nederduitse Gereformeerde Teologiese Tydskrif* 54, Supplement 5 (2013): 37–49. https://doi.org/10.5952/54-0-341.

———. *The Tenderness of Conscience: African Renaissance and the Spirituality of Politics*. 1st ed. Stellenbosch: SUN Press, 2005. Electronic version.

———. "Theological Reflections on Empire." *HTS Teologiese Studies/Theological Studies* 65, no. 1 (2009): 645–51. https://doi.org/10.4102/hts.v65i1.291.

———. *Walking on Thorns: The Call to Christian Obedience*. Geneva: World Council of Churches, 1984.

———. *When Prayer Makes News*. Edited by Allan A. Boesak and Charles Villa-Vicencio. Philadelphia: Westminster Press, 1986.

Boesak, Allan A., and C. P. DeYoung. *Radical Reconciliation: Beyond Political Pietism and Christian Quietism*. Maryknoll: Orbis Books, 2012. Kindle.

Bond, Patrick. *Elite Transition: From Apartheid to Neoliberalim in South Africa*. London: Pluto Press, 2000.

Bonhoeffer, Dietrich. *Letters and Papers from Prison*. New York: Touchstone Books, 1997. Electronic version.

———. *Life Together*. Translated by John W. Doberstein. 1954: SCM Press, 1954.

Boraine, Alex. "Retributive Justice and Restorative Justice: Contradictory or Complimentary?" In *Genocide and Accountability*, edited by Nanci Adler, 39–52. Amsterdam: Vossiuspers Uva, 2004.

Botha, Christo. "Searching for Justice – the Pursuit of a Liberal Tradition in Colonial Namibia." *Journal of Namibian Studies* 14 (2013): 7–45.

———. "The Church in Namibia: Political Handmaiden or a Force for Justice and Unity?" *Journal of Namibian Studies* 20 (2016): 7–36.

Botha, N. "Reconciliation as Narrative: Witnessing Against a Too Easy and a Too Difficult Reconciliation." *Verbum et Ecclesia* 29, no. 3 (2008): 655–80.

Bowers du Toit, F. Nadine, and Grace Nkomo. "The Ongoing Challenge of Restorative Justice in South Africa: How and Why Wealthy Suburban Congregations Are Responding to Poverty and Inequality." *HTS Teologiese Studies/Theological Studies* 70, no. 2 (2014): 1–8. https://doi.org/10.4102/hts.v70i2.2022.

Bradley, Anthony B. Liberating Black Theology: The Bible and Black Experience in America. Perlego eP. Wheaton: Crossway Books, 2010.

———. The Political Economy of Liberation: Thomas Sowell and James Cone on the Black Experience. New York: Peter Lang, 2012.

Bradstock, Andrew. "The Unexamined Society: Public Reasoning, Social Justice and the Common Good." In *Together for the Common Good: Towards National Conversation*, edited by Peter McGrailand and Nicholas Sagovsky. London: SCM Press, 2015. Electronic version.

Brueggemann, Walter. *Living Towards a Vision: Biblical Reflection on Shalom*. New York: United Church Press, 1982.

———. *The Prophetic Imagination*. 40th Anniv. Minneapolis: Fortress Press, 2018.

Burke, T. *The Concept of Justice: Is Social Justice Just?* London: Continuum International Publishing Group, 2011.

Buys, G. L., and S. V. V. Nambala. *History of the Church in Namibia 1805–1990: An Introduction*. Windhoek: Gamsberg Macmillan Publishers, 2003.

Cabral, Amilcar. *Return to the Source: Selected Speeches of Amilcar Cabral*. Edited by Africa Information Service. New York: Modern Reader, 1975.

Clark, Nancy L., and William H. Worger. *South Africa: The Rise and Fall of Apartheid*. *Seminar Studies in History*. 2nd ed. London: Routledge, 2013.

Cone, James H. *A Black Theology of Liberation*. 20th ed. Maryknoll: Orbis Books, 1990.

———. *Black Theology and Black Power*. Maryknoll: Orbis Books, 1997.

Copeland, Shawn M. "Black Political Theologies." In *The Blackwell Companion to Political Theology*, edited by Peter Scott and William T. Cavanaugh, 271–87. Oxford: Blackwell Publishing, 2004.

Dalferth, Ingolf U. "Philosophical Theology." In *Modern Theologians: An Introduction to Christian Thoelogy Since 1918*, edited by David Ford and Rachel Muers, 303–21. 3rd ed. Oxford: Blackwell Publishing, 2005.

Deneulin, Severine, Mathias Nebel, and Nicholas Sagovsky, eds. *Transforming Unjust Structures: The Capability Approach*. Dordrecht: Springer, 2006.

Deneulin, Séverine, Mathias Nebel, and Nicholas Sagovsky. "Introduction." In *Transforming Unjust Structures: The Capability Approach*, edited by Séverine Deneulin, Mathias Nebel, and Nicholas Sagovsky, 1–10. Dordrecht: Springer, 2006.

DeYoung, Kevin, and Greg Gilbert. What Is the Mission of the Church?: Making Sense of Social Justice, Shalom and the Great Commission. Apple Book. Wheaton: Crossway, 2011.

Dibeela, Prince, Puleng Lenka-Bula, and Vuyani Vellem, eds. *Prophet from the South: Essays in Honour of Allan Aubrey Boesak*. Revised Ed. Stellenbosch: SUN MeDIA, 2014.

Dickey, Walter J. "Forgiveness and Crime: The Possibilities of Restorative Justice." In *Exploring Forgiveness*, edited by Robert D. Enright and Joanna North, 106–20. London: University of Wisconsin Press, 1998.

Diescho, Joseph. "The Concepts of Rights and Constitutionalism in Africa." In *Constitutional Democracy in Namibia*, edited by Anton Bösl, Nico Horn, and André Du Pisani, 17–34. Windhoek: Macmillan Education Namibia, 2010.

Dobell, Lauren. "Silence in Context: Truth and/or Reconciliation in Namibia." *Journal of Southern African Studies* 23, no. 2 (1997): 371–82. https://doi.org/10.1080/03057079708708544.

Dommisse, John. "Apartheid as a Public Mental Health Issue." *International Journal of Health Services* 15, no. 3 (1985): 501–10. https://doi.org/10.2190/xrwq-r9ma-06wr-09a5.

Duddy, Jo-Marra. "Corruption Bigger Than Crime, Fraud." *The Namibian*. Windhoek, 6 December 2011. https://www.namibian.com.na/index.php?id=89037&page=archive-read.

Eckstein, Susan Eva, and Timothy P. Wickham-Crowley, eds. *What Justice? Whose Justice?: Fighting for Fairness in Latin America*. Berkeley: University of California Press, 2003.

Enquist, J. Roy. *Namibia: Land of Tears, Land of Promise*. Cranbury: Associated University Presses, 1990.

Fanon, Frantz. *The Wretched of the Earth*. Translated. New York: Grove Press, 2004.

Fay, Derick, and Deborah James. "Restoring What Was Ours: An Introduction." In *The Rights and Wrongs of Land Restitution: Restoring What Was Ours*, edited by Derick Fay and Deborah James, 1–24. Oxon: Routledge-Cavendish, 2008.

Ferm, Dean W. *Profiles in Liberation: 36 Portraits of Third World Theologians*. Eugene: Wipf & Stock Publishers, 2004.

Fitch, David E. *Faithful Presence: Seven Disciplines That Shape the Church for Mission*. Apple Book. Downers Grove: IVP Books, 2016.

Flaendorp, C. D., N. C. Philander, and M. A. Plaatjies-Van Huffel, eds. *Festschrift in Honour of Allan Boesak: A Life in Black Liberation Theology*. 1st ed. Stellenbosch: Rapid Access Publishers, 2016.

Fleischacker, Samuel. *A Short History of Distributive Justice*. Harvard University Press, 2004.

Forster, Dion A. "A Politics of Forgiveness? Engaging the Ontological and the Structural in the Dialogical Theology of John de Gruchy." *Stellenbosch Theological Journal* 5, no. 3 (2019): 77–97.

———. "A Social Imagination of Forgiveness." *Journal of Empirical Theology* 32 (2019): 70–88.

———. "Social Identity, Social Media, and Society: A Call for Public Theological Engagement." In *Theologische Medienethik im digitalen Zeitalter*, edited by Gotlind Ulshöfer, pp. 85–106. Stuttgart: Kolhammer,2019.

———. "The Nature of Public Theology." In *African Public Theology*, edited by Sunday B. Agang, H. Jurgens Hendriks, and Dion A. Forster, 15–26. Carlisle: HippoBooks, 2020.

———. "Translation and a Politics of Forgiveness in South Africa? What Black Christians Believe, and White Christians Do Not Seem to Understand." *Stellenbosch Theological Journal* 4, no. 2 (2018): 77–93. https://doi. org/10.17570/stj.2018.v4n2.a04.

———. "What Hope Is There for South Africa? A Public Theological Reflection on the Role of the Church as a Bearer of Hope for the Future." *HTS Teologiese Studies/Theological Studies* 71, no. 3 (2015): 1–13. https://doi.org/10.4102/hts. v71i3.2814.

Fortein, Eugene A. "Allan Boesak, Black Theology and Apartheid: A Theological-Historical Approach." *STJ | Stellenbosch Theological Journal* 4, no. 2 (2018): 505–19. https://doi.org/10.17570/stj.2018.v4n2.a23.

———. "Allan Boesak En Die Nederduitse Gereformeerde Sendingkerk: 'n Teologies-Historiese Ondersoek." PhD Thesis: Stellenbosch University, 2016.

Freire, Paulo. *Pedagogy of the Oppressed*. 30th ed. New York: Continuum, 2005.

Friedman, John T. Imagining the Post-Apartheid State: An Ethnographic Account of Namibia. New York: Berghahn Books, 2011.

Frostin, Per. "The Theological Debate on Liberation." In *Church and Liberation in Namibia*, edited by Peter Katjavivi, Per Frostin, and Kaire Mbuende, 51–92. London: Pluto Press, 1989.

Fuller, Ben. "A Namibian Path for Land Reform." In *Who Should Own the Land? Analysis and Views on Land Reform and the Land Question in Namibia and South Africa*, edited by Justine Hunter, 83–86. Windhoek: Konrad-Adenauer-Stiftung and Namibia Institute for Democracy, 2004.

Gadner, E. *Justice and Christian Ethics*. Cambridge: Cambridge University Press, 2009.

Gerhart, Gail M. *Black Power in South Africa: The Evolution of an Ideology*. Berkeley: University of California Press, 1978.

Gerth, H. Hans, and C. Wright Mills. *From Max Weber: Essays in Sociology*. New York: Oxford University Press, 1946.

Girelli, Giada. *Understanding Transitional Justice: A Struggle for Peace, Reconciliation, and Rebuilding*. Philosophy, Public Policy, and Transnational Law. London: Palgrave Macmillan, 2017.

Goulet, Denis. Development Ethics at Work: Explorations – 1960–2002. Oxon: Routledge, 2006.

Government of the Republic of Namibia. "Affirmative Action (Employment) Act of 1998" (1998).

———. "Harambee Prosperity Plan 2016/17–2019/20: Namibian Government's Action Plan towards Prosperity for All" (2016).

———. *Namibia Vision 2030: Policy Framework for Long-Term National Development*. Windhoek, 2004.

———. "The New Equitable Economic Empowerment Framework (NEEEF)" (2016).

Gready, Paul. *The Era of Transitional Justice: The Aftermath of the Truth and Reconciliation Commission in South Africa*. London: Routledge, 2011.

Groop, Kim Stefan. "The Church, the State and the Issue of National Reconciliation in Namibia." *Journal of Namibian Studies: History Politics Culture* 11 (2012): 63–82.

Groth, Siegfried. "Silence in Context: Truth and/or Reconciliation in Namibia Reviewed." *Journal of Southern African Studies* 23, no. 2 (1997): 371–82.

Gruchy, John W. De. *Christianity and Democracy: A Theology for a Just World Order*. Cambridge Studies in Ideology and Religion. Cambridge: Cambridge University Press, 1995.

———. "Public Theology as Christian Witness: Exploring the Genre." *International Journal of Public Theology* 1, no. 1 (2007): 26–41. https://doi.org/10.1163/156973207x194466.

———. *Reconciliation: Restoring Justice*. London: SMC Press, 2002.

———. *The Struggle in South Africa*. 2nd ed. Grand Rapids: Eerdmans Publishing, 1979.

Gruchy, John W. De. "Constructing a South African Theological Mind." In *Shaping a Global Theological Mind*, edited by Darren C. Marks, 35–40. Hampshire: Ashgate, 2008.

———. "Kairos Moments and Prophetic Witness: Towards a Prophetic Ecclesiology." *HTS Teologiese Studies/Theological Studies* 72, no. 4 (2016): 1–7.

Grugel, Jean, Jewellord N. Singh, Lorenza B. Fontana, and Anders Uhlin. *Demanding Justice in the Global South: Claiming Rights*. Cham: Palgrave Macmillan, 2017.

Gutiérrez, Gustavo. *A Theology of Liberation: History, Politics, and Salvation*. 20th Anniv. ed. Maryknoll: Orbis Books, 1986.

Hanlon, Joseph, Armando Barrientos, and David Hulme. *Just Give Money to the Poor: The Development Resolution from the Global South*. Sterling: Kumarian Press, 2010.

Hauerwas, Stanley M. *Wilderness Wanderings: Probing Twentieth-Century Theology and Philosophy*. Edited by Stanley M. Hauerwas and Peter Ochs. Radical Traditions: Theology in a Postcritical Key. Boulder: Westview Press, 1997.

Hauerwas, Stanley, and Samuel Wells. "The Gift of the Church and the Gifts God Gives It." In *The Blackwell Companion to Christian Ethics*, edited by Stanley Hauerwas and Samuel Wells, 13–27. 2nd ed. Oxford: Wiley-Blackwell, 2011.

Hegel, Georg W. F. *The Philosophy of History*. Kitchener: Batoche Books, 1991.

Herbstein, Denis, and John Evenson. *The Devils Are Among Us: The War for Namibia*. London: Zed Books, 1989.

Hishoono, Naita, Graham Hopwood, Justine Hunter, Frederico Links, and Masoma Sherazi. *The Constitution in the 21st Century.* Windhoek: Namibia Institute for Democracy and Institute for Public Policy Research, 2011.

Höhn, Sabine. "International Justice and Reconciliation in Namibia: The ICC Submission and Public Memory." *African Affairs* 109, no. 436 (2010): 471–88.

Horn, Nico. "Churches and Political Reconciliation in Post-Apartheid Namibia." *The Review of Faith & International Affairs* 8, no. 1 (2010): 55–62. https://doi.org/10.1080/15570271003707952.

Houston, Walter J. Contending for Justice: Ideologies and Theologies of Social Justice in the Old Testament. London: T&T Clark, 2006.

Hull, George. "Black Consciousness as Overcoming Hermeneutical Injustice." *Journal of Applied Philosophy* 34, no. 4 (August 2017): 573–92.

Hunter, Justine. "Who Should Own the Land?: An Introduction." In *Who Should Own the Land? Analysis and Views on Land Reform and the Land Question in Namibia and South Africa*, edited by Justine Hunter, 1–7. Windhoek: Konrad-Adenauer-Stiftung and Namibia Institute for Democracy, 2004.

———, ed. Who Should Own the Land? Analysis and Views on Land Reform and the Land Question in Namibia and South Africa. Windhoek: Konrad-Adenauer-Stiftung and Namibia Institute for Democracy, 2004.

Iikela, Sakeus. "144 Apartheid Laws to Be Repealed." *The Namibian.* 3 December 2018.

Immanuel, Shinovene, and Sakeus Iikela. "Harambee Fails Economy." *The Namibian.* 23 April 2019.

Institute for Public Policy Research. "Comment on the National Equitable Economic Empowerment (NEEEF) Bill." Windhoek, 2016.

Isaac, Eugene Nicholas. "A Critical-Theoretical Study of the South African Truth and Reconciliation Commission: With Reference to the Work of Jürgen Haberman." PhD Thesis: University of Leeds, 2006.

Isaak, Paul. *Religion and Society: A Namibian Perspective.* Windhoek: Out of Africa Publishers, 1997.

Isaak, Paul John. *The Evangelical Lutheran Church in the Republic of Namibia in the 21st Century.* Edited by Paul John Isaak. Windhoek: Gamsberg Macmillan Publishers, 2000.

Johnston, David. *A Brief History of Justice.* West Sussex: Wiley-Blackwell, 2011.

Johnstone, Gerry, and Daniel W. Van Ness. *Handbook of Restorative Justice.* Devon: Willan Publishing, 2007.

Kaapama, Phanuel. "Commercial Land Reforms in Postcolonial Namibia: What Happened to Liberation Struggle Rhetoric?" In *Transitions in Namibia: Which Changes for Whom?*, edited by Henning Melber, 29–49. Upsala: Nordiska Afrikainstitutet, 2007.

Kameeta, Zephania. *Towards Liberation: Crossing Boundaries Between Church and Politics*. Windhoek: Gamsberg Macmillan Publishers, 2006.

———. Why, O Lord?: Psalms and Sermons from Namibia. Geneva: WCC Publications, 1984.

Kasera, Basilius Mbanze. "The Biblical and Theological Examination of Prosperity Theology and Its Impact Among the Poor in Namibia." MTh Thesis: South African Theological Seminary, 2012.

Katjavivi, H. Peter. *A History of Resistance in Namibia*. Trenton: Africa World Press, 1988.

Katjavivi, Peter. "The Role of the Church in the Struggle for Independence." In *Church and Liberation in Namibia*, edited by Peter Katjavivi, Per Frostin, and Kaire Mbuende, 3–26, London: Pluto Press, 1989.

Katjavivi, Peter, Per Frostin, and Kaire Mbuende. *Church and Liberation in Namibia*. London: Pluto Press, 1989.

Katongole, Emmanuel. A Future for Africa: Critial Essays in Christian Social Imagination. Eugene: Wipf & Stock Publishers, 2017.

———. *Born from Lament*. Grand Rapids: Eerdmans Publishing, 2017.

———. The Sacrifice of Africa: A Political Theology for Africa. Grand Rapids: Eerdmans Publishing, 2011.

Katongole, Emmanuel, and Chris Rice. *Reconciling All Things: A Christian Vision for Justice, Peace and Healing*. Apple Book. Downers Grove: IVP Books, 2008.

Keulder, Christiaan. *State, Society and Democracy: A Reader in Namibian Politics*. Edited by C. Keulder. Namibia: Macmillan Education Namibia, 2010.

Keulder, Theunis, and Naita Hishoono. "Guide to Civil Society in Namibia." Windhoek: Namibia Institute for Democracy, 2009.

Kgatla, Selaelo T., and Jinho Park. "Healing in Herero Culture and Namibian African Independent Churches." *HTS Teologiese Studies/Theological Studies* 71, no. 3 (2015): 15–17.

Kidwell, Jeremy, and Sean Doherty. "Theology and Economics: A Christian Vision of the Common Good." In *Theology and Economics: A Christian Vision of the Common Good*, edited by Jeremy Kidwell and Sean Doherty, 1–7. Hampshire: Palgrave Macmillan, 2015.

Kobe, Sandiswa Lerato. "Black Theology of Liberation (Is It the) Thing of the Past? A Theological Reflection on Black Students' Experiences." *Missionalia* 46, no. 2 (2019): 288–303. https://doi.org/10.7832/46-2-316.

Koopman, Nico. "Towards Reconciliation and Justice in South Africa: Can Church Unity Make a Difference?" In *Peace and Reconciliation*, edited by Sebastian C. H. Kim, Pauline Kollontai, and Greg Hoyland, 95–108. Hampshire: Ashgate, 2008.

Kornes, Godwin. "Negotiating 'Silent Reconciliation': The Long Struggle for Transitional Justice in Namibia." Institut für Ethnologie und Afrikastudien, 2013.

Kößler, Reinhart. "Public Memory, Reconciliation and the Aftermath of War: A Preliminary Framework with Special Reference to Namibia." In *Re-Examining Liberation in Namibia: Political Culture Since Independence*, edited by Henning Melber, 99–112. Stockholm: Nordiska Afrikainstitutet, 2003.

Kößler, Reinhart, and Henning Melber. "Political Culture and Civil Society: On the State of the Namibian State." In *Contemporary Namibia: The First Landmarks of a Post-Apartheid Society*, edited by Ingolf Diener and Olivier Graefe, 147–60. Windhoek: Gamsberg Macmillan Publishers, 2001.

Kothari, N. *Research Methodology: Methods and Techniques*. 2nd ed. New Delhi: New Age Publishers, 2004.

Lebacqz, Karen. Six Theories of Justice: Perspectives from Philosophical and Theological Ethics. Minneapolis: Augsburg Publishing House, 1986.

Leonard, Garry D. S. *The Moment of Truth: The Kairos Document*. Edited by Garry D. S. Leonard. Kwazulu-Natal: Ujama Centre for Biblical and Theological Community Development and Research, University of KwaZulu-Natal, 2010.

Lephakga, Tshepo. "Radical Reconciliation: The TRC Should Have Allowed Zacchaeus to Testify?" *HTS Teologiese Studies/Theological Studies* 72, no. 1 (2016): 1–10.

Leynseele, Yves Van, and Paul Hebinck. "Through the Prism: Local Reworking of Land Restitution Settlements in South Africa." In *The Rights and Wrongs of Land Restitution: Restoring What Was Ours*, edited by Derick Fay and Deborah James, 163–84. Oxon: Routledge-Cavendish, 2008. https://doi.org/10.4324/9780203895498.

Lombard, Christo. "The Detainee Issue: An Unresolved Test Case for SWAPO, the Churches and Civil Society." In *Contemporary Namibia: The First Landmarks of a Post-Apartheid Society*, edited by Ingolf Diener and Olivier Graefe, 161–84. Windhoek: Gamsberg Macmillan Publishers, 2001.

MacIntyre, Alasdair. *Whose Justice? Which Rationality?* Notre Dame: University of Notre Dame, 1988.

Macintyre, Alasdair, Eric A. Havelock, Alasdair Macintyre, and Eric A. Havelock. *The Greek Concept of Justice. From Its Shadow in Homer to Its Substance in Plato*. Cambridge: Harvard University Press, 1978.

Makheta, Lesekele Victor. "Doing Liberation Theology in the Context of the Post-Apartheid South Africa." PhD Thesis: University of South Africa, 2014.

Maluleke, T. S. "Boyhood Lost Too Soon: A Bio-Theological Appraisal of the Contributions of Allan Boesak." In *Festschrift in Honour of Allan Boesak*, edited by C. D. Flaendorp, N. C. Philander, and M. A. Plaatjies van Huffel, 3–16. Stellenbosch: Rapid Access Publishers, 2016.

———. "Justice in Post-Apartheid South Africa: Towards a Theology of Restitution." *Verbum et Ecclesia* 29, no. 3 (2008): 681–96.

———. "The Making of Allan Aubrey Boesak: Theologian and Political Activist." *Missionalia* 45, no. 1 (2017): 61–76.

Mbembe, Achille. *Critique of Black Reason*. Translated by Laurent Dubois. Durham: Duke University Press, 2017.

Mbembé, Achille. *On the Postcolony*. Berkeley: University of California Press, 2001.

Melber, Henning. "Colonialism, Land, Ethnicity, and Class: Namibia after the Second National Land Conference." *Africa Spectrum* 54, no. 1 (2019): 73–86.

———. "From Controlled Change to Changed Control: The Case of Namibia." In *Limits to Liberation in Southern Africa: The Unfinished Business of Democratic Consolidation*, edited by Henning Melber, 134–54. Cape Town: HSRC Press, 2003.

———. "Introduction." In *Limits to Liberation in Southern Africa: The Unfinished Business of Democratic Consolidation*, edited by Henning Melber, xiii–xxiii. Windhoek: Konrad-Adenauer-Stiftung and Namibia Institute for Democracy, 2003.

———. "Limits of Liberation." In *Re-Examining Liberation in Namibia: Political Culture Since Independence*, edited by Henning Melber, 9–24. Stockholm: Nordiska Afrikainstitutet, 2003.

———. "Namibia: A Trust Betrayed – Again?" *Review of African Political Economy* 38, no. 127 (2011): 103–11.

———. *Re-Examining Liberation in Namibia: Political Culture since Independence*. Edited by Henning Melber. Stockholm: Nordiska Afrikainstitutet, 2003.

———. "Transition in Namibia – Namibia in Transition: An Introductory Overview." In *Transitions in Namibia: Which Changes for Whom?*, edited by Henning Melber, Sweden, 7–12. Upsala: Nordiska Afrikainstitutet, 2007.

———. Understanding Namibia: The Trial of Independence. New York: Oxford University Press, 2014.

Migliore, Daniel L. *Faith Seeking Understanding: An Introduction to Christian Theology*. Apple Book. Grand Rapids: Eerdmans Publishing, 1991.

Miguez-Bonino, José. *Toward a Christian Political Ethics*. Apple Book. Minneapolis: Fortress Press, 1983.

Miller, Jamie. An African Volk: The Apartheid Regime and Its Search for Survival. Oxford: Oxford University Press, 2016.

Ministry of Poverty Eradication and Social Welfare. "Blue Print on Wealth Redistribution and Poverty Eradication," May 2016, 1–60.

Moltmann, Jürgen. *The Coming of God: Christian Eschatology*. London: SCM Press, 1996.

Mosala, Itumeleng J. *Biblical Hermeneutics and Black Theology in South Africa*. Grand Rapids: Eerdmans Publishing, 1989. https://doi.org/10.1017/CBO9781107415324.004.

Mujoro, Zedekiah, and Emma Mujoro. "Namibian Liberation Theology and the Future." In *Church and Liberation in Namibia*, edited by Peter Katjavivi, Per Frostin, and Kaire Mbuende, 93–108. London: Pluto Press, 1989.

Murray, Douglas. *The Madness of Crowds: Gender, Race and Identity*. London: Bloomsbury Continuum, 2019. Electronic version.

Nakale, Albertina. "40% of Namibians Live in Shacks," *New Era* (Windhoek, 4 October 2018), https://neweralive.na/posts/40-of-namibians-live-in-shacks [Accessed on 31 March 2019].

Nambala, Shekutaamba. "From Colonialism to Nationalism in Namibia." *Lutheran Quarterly*, no. 2 (1988): 391–581.

Namhila, Ellen Ndeshi. *Mukwahepo: Woman, Soldier, Mother*. Windhoek: University of Namibia Press, 2013.

National Planning Commission. "Status of the Namibian Economy." Windhoek, 2018. Accessed on 31 March 2019. https://www.npc.gov.na/?wpfb_dl=315.

Ndekwila, Samson. *The Agony of Truth*. Windhoek: Namibia Scientific Society, 2014.

Niebuhr, Reinhold. *Moral Man And Immoral Society: A Study in Ethics and Politics*. New York: Charles Scribner's Sons, 1932.

Niitenge, Gideon. "The Evangelical Lutheran Church in Namibia (ELCIN) and Poverty, with Specific Reference to Semi-Urban Communities in Northern Namibia – A Practical Theological Evaluation." PhD Thesis: Stellenbosch University, 2013.

Nkrumah, Kwame. *Consciencism: Philosophy and Ideology of De-Colonization*. New York: Monthly Review Press, 1970.

Noble, Alan. *Disruptive Witness: Speaking Truth in a Distracted Age*. Apple Book. Downers Grove: IVP Books, 2018.

Ntsebeza, L., and Ruth Hall. "Introduction." In *The Land Question in South Africa*, edited by L. Ntsebeza and R. Hall, 1–26. Cape Town: HSRC Press, 2007.

Ntsebeza, Lungisile, and Ruth Hall, eds. The Land Question in South Africa: The Challenge of Transformation and Redistribution. Cape Town: HRSC Press, 2007.

Nussbaum, Martha. "Capabilities and Social Justice." *International Studies Review* 4, no. 2 (2002): 123–35.

Ogunmokun, Ademidun O. "An Analytical Exposition on the Influence and Relevance of the Liberal Feminist Theory in Namibian Legal Framework." *Namibia Law Journal* 5, no. 1 (2013): 3–46.

Olivier, M. P. "The Withdrawal of a Passport: An Own or General Affair or a Residual Category?: Boesak v. the Minister of Home Affairs." *1 SA Publiekreg/ SA Public Law* (1986): 115–20.

Olusoga, David, and Casper W. Erichsen. The Kaiser's Holocaust: Germany's Forgotten Genocide and the Colonial Roots of Nazism. London: Faber and Faber, 2010. Kindle.

Palmer, Parker J. Healing the Heart of Democracy: The Courage to Create a Politics Worthy of the Human Spirit. Ebook. San Francisco: Jossey-Bass, 2011.

Parratt, John. "Introduction." In *An Introduction to Third World Theologies*, edited by John Parratt, 1–15. Cambridge: Cambridge University Press, 2004.

Paul II, John. The Catechism of the Catholic Church. Revised in accordance with the Official Latin Text. 2nd ed. Vatica: Libreria Editrice Vaticana, 1994.

Pears, A. *Doing Contextual Theology*. London: Routledge, 2009.

Pereira, Gustavo. *Elements of Critical Theory of Justice*. New York: Palgrave Macmillan, 2013.

Pesch, Lisa, and Gudrun Murray. *Omaruru (Namibia): Once Upon a Time*. n.a.: Unknown, 2004.

Petrella, Ivan. The Future of Liberation Theology: An Argument and Manifesto. Perlego Version. London: Routledge, 2016.

Phelps, Teresa G. "Narrative Capability: Telling Stories in the Search for Justice." In *Transformating Unjust Structures: The Capability Approach*, edited by Séverine Deneulin, Mathias Nebel, and Nicholas Sagovsky, 105–20. Dordrecht: Springer, 2006.

Phiri, Isabel Apawo. "African Women's Theologies in the New Millenium." *Agenda: Empowering Women for Gender Equity*, no. 61 (2004): 16–24.

Pisani, André Du. "The Discursive Limits of SWAPO's Dominant Discourses on Anti-Colonial Nationalism in Postcolonial Namibia – A First Exploration." In *The Long Aftermath of War – Reconciliation and Transition in Namibia*, edited by André Du Pisani, Reinhart Kössler, and William A. Lindeke, 1–40. Freiburg: Arnold-Bergstraesser-Institut, 2010.

Pisani, André Du. "State and Society under South African Rule." In *State, Society and Democracy – A Reader in Namibian Politics*, edited by Christiaan Keulder, 49–76. Windhoek: Macmillan Education Namibia, 2010.

Plato. *The Republic of Plato*. Edited by Allan Bloom. 2nd ed. USA: BasicBooks, 1968.

Price, Taylor, and Hannah Britton. "'If Good Food Is Cooked in One Country, We Will All Eat from It': Women and Civil Society in Africa." In *The Handbook of Civil Society in Africa*, edited by Ebenezer Obadare, 293–309. New York: Springer, 2014.

Rawls, John. *A Theory of Justice*. Rev. ed. Cambridge: Harvard University Press, 1999.

Rooyen, J. W. F. Van. *Implementing Affirmative Action in Namibia*. 3rd ed. Windhoek: Namibia Institute for Democracy, 2000.

Rowland, Christopher. *The Cambridge Companion to Liberation Theology*. Edited by Christopher Rowland. 2nd ed. Cambridge University Press, 2007. https://doi.org/10.1017/CCOL0521868831.

Sabbagh, C., and M. Schmitt. "Past, Present, and Future Social Justice Theory and Research." In *Handbook of Social Justice Theory and Research*, edited by C. Sabbagh and M. Schmitt, 1–15. New York: Springer, 2016.

Sagovsky, Nicholas. *Christian Tradition and the Practice of Justice*. London: Society for Promoting Christian Knowledge, 2008.

———. "Public Theology, the Public Sphere and the Struggle for Social Justice." In *A Companion to Public Theology*, edited by Sebastian Kim and Katie Day, 251–70. Leiden: Brill, 2017.

Samuel, Vinay, and Chris Sugden. "Good News to the Poor." In *Grove Booklet on Ethics*. Cambridge: Grove Books, 2021.

Sandel, Michael J. *Justice: What's the Right Thing To Do?* 1st ed. New York: Farrar, Straus and Giroux, 2009.

Saunders, Christopher. "Liberation and Democracy: A Critical Reading of Sam Nujoma's 'Autobiography.'" In *Re-Examining Liberation in Namibia: Political Culture since Independence*, edited by Henning Melber, 87–98. Stockholm: Nordiska Afrikainstitutet, 2003.

Schneider, Geoffrey E. "Neoliberalism and Economic Justice in South Africa: Revising the Debate on Economic Apartheid." *Review of Social Economy* 61, no. 1 (2003): 23–50.

Schoeman, Marelize. "The African Concept of Ubuntu and Restorative Justice." In *Reconstructing Restorative Justice Philosophy*, edited by Theo Gavrielides and Vasso Artinopoulou, 291–310. Surrey: Ashgate, 2013.

Sen, Amartya. *Identity and Violence: The Illusion of Destiny*. Apple Book. London: Penguin Books, 2006.

———. *The Idea of Justice*. Cambridge: The Belknap Press, 2009.

Sharifian, F. *Cultural Conceptualisations and Language: Theoretical Framework and Applications*. Amsterdam: John Benjamins Publishing, 2011.

Sher, George. *Desert: Studies in Moral, Political, and Legal Philosophy*. Edited by Marshall Cohen. Princeton: Princeton University Press, 1987.

Shore, Megan, and Scott Kline. "The Ambiguous Role of Religion in the South African Truth and Reconciliation Commission." *Peace & Change* 31, no. 3 (2006): 309–32. https://doi.org/10.1111/j.1468-0130.2006.00377.x.

Silvester, Jeremy, and Jan-Bart Gewald. *Words Cannot Be Found: German Colonial Rule in Namibia. Sources for African History*. An Annotated Volume 1. Leiden: Brill, 2003. https://doi.org/10.1017/CBO9781107415324.004.

Simcock, Julian. "Unfinished Business: Reconciling the Apartheid Reparation Litigation with South Africa's Truth and Reconciliation Commission." *Stanford Journal of International Law* 47, no. 239 (2011): 239–63.

Sister Namibia. *Sister Namibia* 1, no. 1 (July 1989): 1–10.

———. *Sister Namibia* 2, no. 2 (1990): 1–15.

———. *Sister Namibia* 31, no. 1 (July 2019): 1–29.

Smit, Dirk. "Does It Matter? On Whether There Is Method in the Madness." In *A Companion to Public Theology*, edited by Sebastian Kim and Katie Day, 67–92. Leiden: Brill, 2017.

———. Essays in Public Theology: Collected Essays 1. Edited by Ernst M. Conradie. Study Guides in Religion and Theology 12. 1st ed. Stellenbosch: SUN Press, 2007.

———. "On Belonging: Doing Theology Together." In *Shaping a Global Theological Mind*, edited by Darren C. Marks, 153–62. Ebook. Hampshire: Ashgate, 2008.

———. "Resisting 'Lordless Powers'?: Boesak on Power." In *Prophet from the South: Essays in Honour of Allan Aubrey Boesak*, edited by Prince Dibeela, Puleng Lenka-Bula, and Vuyani Vellem, 11–35. Stellenbosch: SUN MeDIA, 2012.

Smith, James K. A. *Desiring the Kingdom: Worship, Worldview, and Cultural Formation.* Apple Book. Grand Rapids: Baker Academic, 2019.

Smith, Paul. Moral and Political Philosophy: Key Issues, Concepts and Theories. Hampshire: Palgrave MacMillan, 2008.

Sonneborn, L. *The End of Apartheid in South Africa.* New York: Chelsea House Publishers, 2010.

Sousa Santos, Boaventura De. *Epistemologies of the South: Justice against Epistemicide.* London: Routledge, 2014. Electronic version.

South West Africa National Union. *Basic Documents of SWANU: Constitution* (1985).

Storrar, William. "The Naming of Parts: Doing Public Theology in a Global Era." *International Journal of Public Theology* 5, no. 1 (2011): 23–43. https://doi.org/10.1163/156973211X543724.

Sugden, Chris. "Identity and Transformation: The Oxford Lectures of Vinay Samuel 1998–2006." *Transformation* 24, no. 3 (2007): 133–50.

Tapscott, Chris. "Class Formation and Civil Society in Namibia." In *Contemporary Namibia: The First Landmarks of a Post-Apartheid Society*, edited by Ingolf Diener and Olivier Graefe, 307–25. Windhoek: Gamsberg Macmillan Publishers, 2001.

———. "National Reconciliation, Social Equity and Class Formation in Independent Namibia." *Journal of Southern African Studies* 19, no. 1 (1993): 29–39.

Taylor, Charles. *Modern Social Imaginaries*. Durham: Duke University Press, 2004.

Tenai, Noah Kiptoo. "The Poor and the Public: An Exploration of Synergies between Black Theology and Public Theologies." PhD Thesis: Stellenbosch University, 2010.

The Third Lausanne Congress on World Evangelization. "The Cape Town Commitment: A Confession of Faith and a Call to Action." *KAIROS – Evangelical Journal of Theology* 1 (2011): 165–224.

Tötemeyer, Gerhard. *Church and State in Namibia: Politics of Reconciliation*. Freiburger Beiträge Zu Entwicklung Und Politik. Germany: Arnold Bergstraesser Institut, 2010.

Trewhela, Paul. *Inside Quatro: Uncovering the Exile History of the ANC and SWAPO*. Sunnyside: Jacana Media, 2009.

———. "SWAPO and the Churches : An International Scandal." *Searchlight South Africa* 2, no. 3 (1990): 65–88.

Tshaka, R. S. "African, You Are on Your Own! The Need for African Reformed Christians to Seriously Engage Their Africanity in Their Reformed Theological Reflections." *Scriptura* 96, no. 1 (2016): 533–48. https://doi.org/10.7833/96-0-1173.

———. "On Being African and Reformed? Towards an African Reformed Theology Enthused by an Interlocution of Those on the Margins of Society." *HTS Teologiese Studies/Theological Studies* 70, no. 1 (2014): 1–7. https://doi.org/10.4102/hts.v70i1.2070.

Tshaka, R. S., and M. K. Makofane. "The Continued Relevance of Black Liberation Theology for Democratic South Africa Today." *Scriptura* 105 (2010): 532–46.

Tutu, Desmond. *No Future Without Forgiveness*. Apple Book. New York: Doubleday, 1999.

Ukpong, Justin S. "Developments in Biblical Interpretation in Africa: Historical and Hermeneutical Directions." In *Voices from the Margin: Interpreting the Bible in the World*, edited by R. S. Sugirtharajah. Apple Book. Maryknoll: Orbis Books, 2006.

United States Agency for International Development, Conflict and Humanitarian Assistance Bureau for Democracy, and Human Rights and Governance Center of Excellence on Democracy. "2019 Civil Society Organization Sustainability Index for Sub-Saharan Africa: Namibia," 2020.

Verdoolaege, Annelies. *Reconciliation Discourse: The Case of the Truth and Reconciliation Commission. Discourse Approaches to Politics, Society and Culture.* Amsterdam: John Benjamins Publishing, 2008.

Villa-Vicencio, C., and Erik Doxtader, eds. *Pieces of the Puzzle: Keywords on Reconciliation and Transitional Justice.* Cape Town: Institute for Justice and Reconciliation, 2004.

Villa-Vicencio, Charles. *A Theology of Reconstruction: Nation-Building and Human Rights*. Cambridge: Cambridge University Press, 1992.

Vries, Keith. "SWAPO Pays Lip Service to Socialism." *Windhoek Observer*. Windhoek, 15 March 2013. https://www.observer.com.na/index.php/national/item/1116-swapo-pays-lip-service-to-socialism.

Wallerstein, Immanuel Maurice, and Aquino De Bragança. *The African Liberation Reader: The National Liberation Movements, Vol. 2*. London: Zed Press, 1982.

Wielder, Alan. *Praise for Ruth First and Joe Slovo in the War against Apartheid*. New York: Monthly Review Press, 2013.

Wiredu, K. "Introduction: African Philosophy in Our Time." In *A Companion to African Philosophy*, edited by K. Wiredu, 1–28. Oxford: Blackwell Publishing, 2004.

Wolterstorff, Nicholas. *Journey towards Justice: Personal Encounters in the Global South*. Grand Rapids: Baker Academic, 2013. Ebook.

———. *Justice: Rights and Wrongs*. Princeton: Princeton University Press, 2008.

Ya-Otto, John, Ole Gjerstad, and Michael Mercer. *Battlefront Namibia*. Westport: Lawrence Hill, 1981.

Ziegler, G. Philip. "Christ's Lordship and Politics: Visser 't Hooft and Bonhoeffer." In *Bonhoeffer, Religion and Politics*, edited by Christiane Tietz and Jens Zimmermann, 55–80. Frankfurt am Main: Peter Lang, 2015.

🐑 Langham PARTNERSHIP

Langham Literature, with its publishing work, is a ministry of Langham Partnership.

Langham Partnership is a global fellowship working in pursuit of the vision God entrusted to its founder John Stott –

> *to facilitate the growth of the church in maturity and Christ-likeness through raising the standards of biblical preaching and teaching.*

Our vision is to see churches in the Majority World equipped for mission and growing to maturity in Christ through the ministry of pastors and leaders who believe, teach and live by the word of God.

Our mission is to strengthen the ministry of the word of God through:
• nurturing national movements for biblical preaching
• fostering the creation and distribution of evangelical literature
• enhancing evangelical theological education
especially in countries where churches are under-resourced.

Our ministry

Langham Preaching partners with national leaders to nurture indigenous biblical preaching movements for pastors and lay preachers all around the world. With the support of a team of trainers from many countries, a multi-level programme of seminars provides practical training, and is followed by a programme for training local facilitators. Local preachers' groups and national and regional networks ensure continuity and ongoing development, seeking to build vigorous movements committed to Bible exposition.

Langham Literature provides Majority World preachers, scholars and seminary libraries with evangelical books and electronic resources through publishing and distribution, grants and discounts. The programme also fosters the creation of indigenous evangelical books in many languages, through writer's grants, strengthening local evangelical publishing houses, and investment in major regional literature projects, such as one volume Bible commentaries like the *Africa Bible Commentary* and the *South Asia Bible Commentary*.

Langham Scholars provides financial support for evangelical doctoral students from the Majority World so that, when they return home, they may train pastors and other Christian leaders with sound, biblical and theological teaching. This programme equips those who equip others. Langham Scholars also works in partnership with Majority World seminaries in strengthening evangelical theological education. A growing number of Langham Scholars study in high quality doctoral programmes in the Majority World itself. As well as teaching the next generation of pastors, graduated Langham Scholars exercise significant influence through their writing and leadership.

To learn more about Langham Partnership and the work we do visit **langham.org**

Milton Keynes UK
Ingram Content Group UK Ltd.
UKHW020025040624
443552UK00014B/560

9 781839 738791